$\dfrac{y\,76}{X_2}$

CAMBRIDGE IBERIAN AND
LATIN AMERICAN STUDIES

GENERAL EDITOR

PROFESSOR P. E. RUSSELL, FBA

EMERITUS PROFESSOR OF SPANISH STUDIES
THE UNIVERSITY OF OXFORD

Muslims, Christians, and Jews
in the
crusader kingdom of Valencia

already published

STEVEN BOLDY, *The novels of Julio Cortázar*

JOHN EDWARDS, *Christian Córdoba: the city and its region in the late middle ages*

MAURICE HEMINGWAY, *Emilia Pardo Bazán: the making of a novelist*

JUAN LÓPEZ-MORILLAS, *The Krausist movement and ideological change in Spain, 1854–1874*

LINDA MARTZ, *Poverty and welfare in Habsburg Spain: the example of Toledo*

JOHN LYON, *The theatre of Valle-Inclán*

JULIÁN OLIVARES, *The love poetry of Francisco de Quevedo: an aesthetic and existential study*

ANTHONY PAGDEN, *The fall of natural man: the American Indian and the growth of historical relativism*

EVELYN S. PROCTER, *Curia and cortes in León and Castile, 1072–1295*

A. C. DE C. M. SAUNDERS, *A social history of black slaves and freedmen in Portugal, 1441–1555*

HENRY W. SULLIVAN, *Calderón in the German lands and the Low Countries: his reception and influence, 1654–1980*

DIANE UREY, *Galdós and the irony of language*

DAVID E. VASSBERG, *Land and society in Golden Age Castile*

future titles will include

HEATH DILLARD, *Medieval women in Castilian town society, 1100–1300*

FRANCISCO RICO, *The picaresque novel and the point of view*

Thirteenth-century Spanish Muslims and Christians clash in battle.
(Alfonso X, the Learned, *Cantigas de Santa María, cant.* 63)

Muslims, Christians, and Jews
in the
crusader kingdom of Valencia

Societies in symbiosis

ROBERT I. BURNS, SJ

UNIVERSITY OF CALIFORNIA AT LOS ANGELES

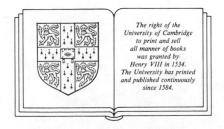

The right of the
University of Cambridge
to print and sell
all manner of books
was granted by
Henry VIII in 1534.
The University has printed
and published continuously
since 1584.

CAMBRIDGE UNIVERSITY PRESS

CAMBRIDGE

LONDON   NEW YORK   NEW ROCHELLE

MELBOURNE   SYDNEY

Published by the Press Syndicate of the University of Cambridge
The Pitt Building, Trumpington Street, Cambridge CB2 1RP
32 East 57th Street, New York, NY 10022, USA
296 Beaconsfield Parade, Middle Park, Melbourne 3206, Australia

© Cambridge University Press 1984

First published 1984

Printed in Great Britain at
the University Press, Cambridge

Library of Congress catalogue card number: 83–2007

British Library Cataloguing in Publication Data
Burns, Robert I.
Muslims, Christians, and Jews in the Crusader
kingdom of Valencia.—(Cambridge Iberian and
Latin American studies)
1. Spain—Valencia (Region)—711–1516—Social
conditions
I. Title
946'.02'08 DP96
ISBN 0 521 24374 2

WV

My heart has adopted every shape. It has become a pasture for gazelles
      and a convent for Christian monks;
And a temple for idols, and a pilgrim's Ka'ba,
      the tables of a Torah, and the pages of a Koran.
I follow the religion of love; wherever love's camels turn,
      there love is my religion and my faith.

Ibn al-'Arabī, of Murcia (d. 1240)
tr. Monroe, *Poetry*

Contents

Illustrations

Maps

Abbreviations

1. ARCHIVES AND MANUSCRIPT COLLECTIONS

ACA   Arxiu de la Corona d'Aragó, Barcelona
ACV   Arxiu Capitular de la Catedral, Valencia
AHN   Archivo Histórico Nacional, Madrid
ARV   Arxiu General del Regne de València, Valencia
ASV   Archivio Segreto Vaticano, Rome
BUV   Biblioteca de la Universitat, Valencia

2. PUBLISHED MATERIAL

AEM   *Anuario de estudios medievales*
AHR   *American historical review*
BRABLB   *Boletín de la real academia de buenas letras de Barcelona*
BSCC   *Boletín de la sociedad castellonense de cultura*
CHR   *Catholic historical review*
Col. dip.   Huici ed., *Colección diplomática de Jaime I*
Congrés   *Congrés d'història de la corona d'Aragó*
Documentos   Huici and Cabanes eds., *Documentos de Jaime I*
EEMCA   *Estudios de la edad media de la corona de Aragón*
EI²   *Encyclopaedia of Islam*, 2nd edn
Fori   *Fori antiqui Valentiae*, Dualde edn (Latin text)
GEC   *Gran enciclopèdia catalana*
GERV   *Gran enciclopedia de la región valenciana*
Itinerari   Miret i Sans ed., *Itinerari de Jaume I 'el Conqueridor'*
Llibre dels feyts   Jaume I, *Llibre dels feyts del rei En Jaume*, Soldevila edn
MCV   *Mélanges de la casa de Velázquez*
MW   *Muslim World*
Partidas   Alfonso X, *Las siete partidas*

ABBREVIATIONS

REJ	*Revue des études juives*
Repartiment[1]	Ferrando i Francés ed., *Llibre del repartiment de València*
Repartiment[2]	Cabanes and Ferrer eds., *Libre del repartiment del regne de València*
RHCM	*Revue d'histoire et de civilisation du Maghreb*

Preface

While preparing the laborious volumes of my *Diplomatarium regni Valentiae* now in press, and postponing a previously announced work in progress on Muslim–Christian relations in Valencia, I have had occasion over the past five years to approach that crusader kingdom from novel angles and with varied methodologies. The resultant studies, published and especially unpublished, provide a different opening on this fascinating, pluri-ethnic crossroads kingdom. This book is not a series of random articles around a lifetime theme, therefore, like my recently issued *Collected studies*. It comprises rather an interrelated set of explorations; an alternative subtitle might well have been 'Explorations and adventures.'

These ten studies have six characteristics in common. (1) All focus on the same Mediterranean kingdom, immemorially Islamic, whose landforms and human ecology are among the most diversified in Spain or indeed in Europe. (2) All concern the same time span, roughly 1245 to 1285, stressing the last quarter-century in the reign of Jaume the Conqueror but ranging forward or backward to afford a wider perspective, particularly during the decade's reign of Jaume's son and successor Pere the Great. (3) All deal with the same theme, colonial coping and the symbiosis of cultures in the restructuring kingdom. (4) All are drawn particularly from the marvelous and varied registers of King Jaume and King Pere. These codices represent the first monumental use of paper for governmental records in the West, a phenomenon made possible by Jaume's acquisition of Valencia's celebrated Islamic paper industry at Játiva. The registers are lodged at the royal archives, in a sixteenth-century annex to the rambling palace complex in Barcelona. This Arxiu de la Corona d'Aragó is cited here throughout as ACA, meaning the *cancelleria reial* section and Jaume's reign, except where indications have been added. Five other manuscript

xv

depositories have been laid under tribute. (5) Each of the studies approaches the crusader society from a different and unusual vantage point: the Mediterranean context and Mudejar methodology; the Mudejar constitutional framework *in situ*; the milleniary urgency and peculiar character of the new conversion movement; the naval Reconquest, with piracy as a common enthusiasm of Muslims and Christians; the promise and problems in reconstructing the neglected Jewish communities of the kingdom, as well as an introduction to specific Jews in their respective social contexts; the hotly debated theme of language, with its cultural and acculturative implications; battles over interior boundaries, which shook the new kingdom, and the recourse to local Muslims for their resolution; the hitherto hidden history of how the Valencian crusade really ended – a secret concealed in the only bilingual treaty to have survived King Jaume's campaigns; and finally the Islamic component in Jaume's memoirs, affecting our view of the Valencian data there. (6) With one exception, all the studies have emerged within a brief period, so each bears some echo of the others, and as a group they share naturally an underlying structure. Methodology, whether context to provide wider circles of meaning, or the resolution of sterile polarities, or an archeology of the representative singular, supplies a supporting pattern. Law dominates two chapters and surfaces in others. Prosopography is an explicit concern in at least three chapters. Acculturation provides a constant theme. Violence and religion echo recurrently. The basic categories are universal, and only artificially separable: war, language, religion, law, literature, administration, real estate, and 'race' relations.

The final chapter, while resuming major themes in its central episode, sites them in King Jaume's international context. From unnoticed papal documents it reveals Jaume's military adventure of 1245 in southern France, its fatal impact on his whole Valencian enterprise, its personal effect in stylistically destructuring his very memoirs, his reactive project for crusading to Byzantium, and the implications for this Guelph champion's drift into enmeshment with the imperial Hohenstaufens.

As in my other books, toponyms are Castilian rather than Catalan, since they invariably appear so in maps and finding-aids. Names of persons I tend to Catalanize, since the Valencian kingdom seems to me a rather Catalan and urban–mercantile world from the start; in deference to the double Arago-Catalan character of the settlement, and to the emphases of some Aragonese historians, however, I have not infrequently given either two forms of a name or even a Castilianized or an Aragonese version alone, sometimes only at the name's first appearance. Like Christian names, which appear in distorted or ambiguous Latin forms often enough, Arabic names require translation or reconstruction from the Latin garble of various scribes; since this can be risky, the scribal version is supplied except in the case of identified historical figures. The complexities of Jewish names are discussed in chapter 5. Royal names offer a particular challenge. 'Don Jayme' was king in upland Aragon proper; as 'En Jacme' and 'En Jaume' he was sovereign count in Catalonia; as king of bilingual Valencia he has both spellings. Choice of either name is unsatisfactory and can offend local patriotisms. I use his Catalan form, as also for his son Pere, since he affected a persona more Catalan than Aragonese; his son Alfonso, thoroughly identified with Aragon, has his name in Aragonese. I acknowledge in chapter 7 the regional sensibilities which designate the crusader kingdom's evolving language 'Valencian' or 'Romance' rather than Catalan; but I resist being drawn further into this problem of expression and linguistics.

The incarnational calendar, most common for the Valencian documents cited, began its year with Christ's presumed conception on 25 March, nine months before Christmas. Valencians used the forward or Florentine system, however, as against the more logical recoil of Pisa to the previous 25 March. From 1 January through 24 March, consequently, the old year continued into the new. In practice, these nearly three months need to add one year to the manuscript's date to arrive at the year corresponding to our own calendar. In the notes, such double dates appear with the manuscript's own 'false' year in parentheses or brackets, and the preferred or adjusted year in the clear. For transcription sigla in the notes and appendices, see the introduction to appendix 2. Other minutiae, such as local money or measures or geography, are explained in my *Crusader kingdom*, *Islam*, and *Colonialism*.

My use of the terms 'crusade' and 'colonialism' still meets some resistance, but I think unwarranted and now fading. The Valencian conquest was a formal crusade, preached and indulgenced by the popes, supported by international funds and volunteers, with Islam the foe on sea and land, and with cross and piety prominent. Antonio Ubieto's current compromise, to concede 'crusade' only for the

Catalan contingents but to cling to a secular 'Reconquest' for those from Aragon, cannot survive close scrutiny. Terms like colonialism require more caution, but are employed commonly for medieval situations less suitable than Valencia's. It is not a concept rising from a modern context and projected backward, but one stage of an evolving genre of relationship, an analogue which helps clarify later or other colonialisms. The analogy of the colonial experience itself with those of the sixteenth and later centuries is clear: the seizure and control by a dominant alien minority, supported from the homeland, growing by steady immigration, disdainful and wary of the native population. In Valencia the overgrid of settlers and administrators left the conquered majority to its own culture, religion, language, and internal administration – a majority consciously dismissed as inferior, progressively more restricted and ruralized, intimidated by the superpower's imported patterns of public building, technologies, and attitudes, until that majority shifted its own self-image.

A more serious problem is Pierre Guichard's misconception that my books posit an Islamic feudalism in pre-crusade Valencia, down to military feudal lords and tenants living under European-style landlords. This relates to his wider belief that I follow the Nationalist school of 'continuity' between the Islamic and Christian Spains, and of 'optimism' consequently, in refusing to see the damage done by the colonialist crusaders to the essential structure of Islamic society. Such positions are anathema to me, and indeed would shame a neophyte in this field. In chapter 1 at length, and more briefly elsewhere, I address these misconceptions in their several elements, as well as the puzzle as to how they arose.

Much of this material was presented in part in a preliminary form as public addresses. Occasions included: the Congress of the History of the Crown of Aragon (Zaragoza, 1976); the Conference of Mediterranean Studies (Malta, 1977; Barcelona, 1978); the Medieval Academy of America's convention (Toronto, 1977); the American Historical Association's conventions (Dallas, 1977; New York, 1979; Los Angeles, 1981); the Ancient World Lecture Series (University of California at Berkeley, 1977); the Conference of Medieval and Renaissance Studies (Ohio State University, 1978); the Southeastern Medieval Association's plenary session (University of Kentucky, 1978); lectures sponsored by the University of San Francisco, and by the Arxiu de la Corona d'Aragó (1979); position-papers in the International Congress of Historical Sciences

(Bucharest, 1980); and the Medieval Workshop (University of British Columbia, 1982). A final study belonging to this set, delivered partly as a public address for the history faculty at the University of Mainz in Germany and partly as my presidential address before the American Historical Association's Pacific Coast Branch, both in 1980, concerning Islamic paper technology in crusader Valencia, will appear more appropriately as part of the introductory volume in my forthcoming *Diplomatarium*. I have recast and revised whatever materials have appeared in print; in any case their preliminary versions are often difficult to come by, especially for congresses abroad.

To save publishing costs and the reader's purse, I have reduced footnotes drastically. I have then grouped the essential citations at intervals, inviting the reader to relate a given component in such a group to the pertinent point in that section of text by clues such as date or name. Author with short-title can convey much of the merely bibliographical information, while author and short-title with pages can serve for all the usual citations. Since there is no initial full reference in either case, the reader must consult the bibliography, which comprises all and only published works cited, with subtitles or extensions occasionally omitted. In this consultation the reader should take particular note of the abbreviations on pp. xi–xii. The bibliography thus becomes an essential component and tool of the reading process; bibliographies more organic can be found in my previous books. Of special note is the discussion of Islamic sources in chapter 10.

Finally I must express my gratitude to the National Endowment for the Humanities, under whose yearly series of grants for the *Diplomatarium* the above explorations were also undertaken, to the Institute of Medieval Mediterranean Spain for its support, and to the University of California faculty senate for its series of research grants. For typing and incidental assistance, usually onerous, I wish to thank John Moniz, SJ, Agnes Stephens, Erika Garcia, and my graduate student assistants at UCLA Leila Berner, Paul Padilla, Larry Simon, and Jane Wilman. Míkel de Epalza offered valuable suggestions on the first chapter. My debt to Paul Chevedden, with additional help from James Monroe, will be made explicit in chapter 10 and appendix 4. Thanks are also due Professor Emilio Sáez, now of the University of Madrid and of the Consejo Superior de Investigaciones Científicas, for his many kindnesses. A very special debt is owed to Dr Federico Udina Martorell and his unfailingly helpful staff at the Arxiu de la Corona d'Aragó. And I must acknowledge the encouragement given to my researches this year when the Serra d'Or awarded me its Premi de la Crítica in history, and the Institut d'Estudis Catalans its Premi Catalònia.

University of California at Los Angeles 1983

I

Muslim–Christian conflict and contact:
Mudejar methodology

Nineteenth-century historiography, the child of Romanticism and Nationalism, sang the medieval glories of contemporary industrial–political giants like England, Germany, and France; Italy intruded where she could not be ignored and France was imagined as having always extended south to the Mediterranean. This narcissistic framework prevailed deep into our own century, falling progressively into ruins as its parent states declined from world control; its elements and emphases still echo hollowly in textbooks on the Middle Ages. This northern historiography tended to dismiss medieval Spain as a quirky appendage to Christendom, a fusion of barely reconcilable Islamic and Christian values, useful as a bridge over which valuables traveled to be domesticated in more self-aware lands. A continuum of eight centuries of Reconquest defined this Quixotic and bloody semi-Africa, culminating in the Inquisition.

A quarter-century of abundant scholarship has changed much of that, creating a new landscape for medieval studies and especially for Spain. Lack of syntheses and translations rather masked the improvement from English-speaking medievalists; but the 1970s finally closed the textbook gap; displacing Roger Merriman's half-century-old volume on medieval Spain with surveys short and surveys magisterial in English from sound scholars like Hillgarth, Jackson, MacKay, and O'Callaghan. Dufourcq and Gautier-Dalché have capped their sweeping bibliographies of the 1970s with a fine social–economic synthesis.[1] All of this parallels two more general phenomena: the remarkable growth of organized medieval studies over the past two decades, and the rediscovery of the Mediterranean littoral lands as the dynamic heartland of medieval civilization. The new history, which involves also new methodologies including the Braudelian 'total history,' has made it possible to approach from novel angles perennially fascinating themes like Muslim–Christian relations in the Iberian peninsula.

APPROACHES AND CONCENTRIC CIRCLES

On a topic so broad and recalcitrant as contact–conflict of Spanish Moors and Christians, one can too easily babble his way into the bibliographical undergrowth, never again to emerge. (Morisco studies alone have multiplied and even cloned until they now form a separate field of historical endeavor.) Conversely, a specialist today is tempted to retreat within his own *alcázar*, conducting restricted tours of its premises, where no man can with impunity lift a fist. The current situation demands more of us: a pause in the shelving of monographs and bibliographies in order to orient ourselves with general scenarios.

This cannot be done after the fashion of Américo Castro or Claudio Sánchez-Albornoz. Their all-too-familiar debate, still carried on with undiminished zeal by aging disciples, assumes that some magic key exists. Sánchez-Albornoz proposed an almost genetic Spanishness which defied Islamic or Semitic acculturation, as well as single-minded Reconquest during eight centuries of linear, spontaneous action. Castro saw instead an amalgam of Christian, Muslim, and Jew which distorted the host culture into something alien from the rest of Christendom. For Sánchez-Albornoz the Muslims badly deformed the natural development of *homo hispanus*; for Castro they constituted with the Jews the creative addition which yielded a *homo novus*. The Muslims of Sánchez-Albornoz are not really Muslims; the Christians of Castro are not really European. The first thesis misses the lessons of structural anthropology; the second is cut off by an essentially literary and maneristic approach from the hard discoveries of the current school of historians, and it never grasps the creative power of adaptive cultures to transmute and remain (in a new manifestation) somehow integral. Of the two, Castro did the greater service and forced a confrontation with the more essential questions. A student of Spanish literature and national character, rather than an historian, he stands like a giant in modern historiography, a kind of St Augustine with a City of Spain vision. The polemic took on new life among English-speaking medievalists in the 1970s when Castro's last reworking of his major book appeared in English as *The Spaniards*, followed posthumously by his collected essays, while the major statement of Sánchez-Albornoz, *Spain: a historical enigma*, finally appeared in (bad) translation. The dispute is liveliest in literary circles and displays all the unforgiving vituperativeness and tearful loyalties of any literary feud.

It is time to approach the problem of Muslim–Jew–Christian interaction by posing new questions. Restatements have been attempted from within the assumptions of the older disputants. Like the work of Castro and Sánchez-Albornoz, for example, the recent thesis of Vicente Contarino assumes a dichotomy between Europe and Spain, a national character qualitatively different from the common denominators of the rest of Europe; however, 'it was not Islam, but what orthodox medieval Christianity, of monastic and ascetic cast, made of the intellectual values of Islam, that engendered the peculiarities which characterize Spaniards and separate Spain from Europe.' Reyna Pastor de Togneri has taken a bolder step to 'replant' the problematic by analyzing the 'empirical' case history of conquered Toledo. Dismissing the 'liberal bourgeois historiography' of Castro and Sánchez-Albornoz, she focuses instead on the 'destructuring' of the Muslims' economic system and mode of production, followed by 'structural recomposition' by the aggressors' very different economic system with its social implications. A book so slight and a case history so short (seventy pages) is made to bear its own heavy burden of theory, preoccupied in an almost nineteenth-century fashion with the greed of elites and the priority of economic structures.

More impressive than such replacing of one set of philosophic manifestos by another is the recent study of Thomas Glick on the Muslim–Christian interface in Spain. The new questions he asks, and the new vantages from which he observes, promise to help us move beyond the stalled polemic. Glick stresses that covert and continual acculturation in the three ill-documented centuries before the year 1000 was more significant than the direct contact and borrowing of the central Middle Ages. Changes in social structure precede and control cultural recrystallization; they underlie them as a pathology underlies symptoms, or a rooted tree its leaves, or a value system its legal expression. Cultural diffusion is modified by the receiving society's current structure; and any element, either received or formally resisted, affects the entire organic system of the receiver. Glick is at his best in charting the passage of technologies

3

and techniques between the two cultures, and in translating into functional concepts opposed poles of passage – the monastery as early counterpart of the Spanish–Islamic city, for example, the culture's communication center and point of secondary diffusion.

His analyses of the innovations in either society just before the millennial year particularly deserve attention. While settlement and quest for pasturage in northern Spain filled the buffer zones with Christian families from the over-populated mountains (a classic development), in the Islamic south a logarithmic curve of conversions suddenly and tardily culminated to make the body of native population into Muslims. (Glick here borrows Richard Bulliet's much-controverted theory on the rhythm of mass conversion elsewhere in Islam; however moot as a proven proposition, this provides a frame which persuasively organizes the otherwise intractable Spanish data.) The result would have been massive assimilation to Islam within al-Andalus, waning of bilingualism, and so radical a reapportionment of governmental power away from the Arab elite to the regional Berber–native principalities as to seem the 'fall' of the caliphate, an illusion analogous to the myth of Rome's fall. The consequent cycling of tributary gold from these prosperous principalities fueled the growth of Christian cities, cultural life, and more settlement, while the gold returned in that very process to the Islamic south – a powerful complex of contacts in itself. This also increased contact to the north; in Richard Fletcher's recent expression: 'What Mexico was to the Europeans of the sixteenth century, [Christian] Spain was to their ancestors of the eleventh and early twelfth': a beckoning land of gold.

For the Valencian region, which will occupy us in most of this book, Míkel de Epalza firmly dismisses the thesis of late conversion. He counters that Bulliet's model does not fit the non-personal conversion structure of Islam. Equally important, it does not fit new findings about the superficial, spotty Christianity that Islam displaced in eastern Spain. Christians entered the Koranic protected status in an Islamic polity basically as communities around their bishops; when not properly organized under a bishop, they forfeited the privileges which made life tolerable. The absence of episcopal lines in the conquered Visigothic littoral here, and the prevalence of rural paganism, favored swift conversion of the populace. So complete was this shift, Epalza argues, that a native Mozarabism did not survive; Valencian Mozarabs were Christians immigrant or tran-

4

sient, not properly a protected element enclaved but a motley of people officially strangers. This boded ill for them in times of crises, and may explain their harassment and flight under the Almohads. This thesis allows to Valencian-resident Christians under Islam only the Romance they had imported, not a surviving bilingualism; in its own way this aspect of Epalza's thesis supports conclusions reached below in chapter 7 on other grounds, about bilingualism and the absence of Mozarabic communities on the eve of Valencia's conquest by the crusaders. In Epalza's framework, the collapse of the caliphate and the rise of independent region-states in its wake were merely a 'manifestation of the regional government, typically Islamic,' which characterized 'the whole Islamic period' here rather than only those more noticeable times when 'a vacuum of central power' prevailed. Thus Valencia's Islamic history began with a sharp break from the past and ended with another sharp break at the crusade.

The second break was not so total as some 'discontinuists' make it, however, a topic given special attention below; retention of language, religion, and many lesser elements transformed into the Mudejar subculture should induce caution in that regard. The Epalza theses do not embrace that school of radical discontinuity under the crusaders. Indeed he sees as 'evident' that the process of 'total Islamization,' begun here so early and reinforced by later religio-political episodes, had become 'perfectly realized at the moment of the Christian conquest in the thirteenth century, and allowed the Valencian Mudejars and Moriscos to persevere in their Islamic faith down to the general expulsion of the seventeenth century.' Dolors Bramon has taken that wider trajectory of Mudejar—Morisco persistence in an Arabo-Islamic culture as the theme for her recent brilliant book on that Valencian triumph and tragedy. James Monroe has developed the rich interweaving of rivalries and interests, especially the 'counter-Arabic' urban dynamics, which were at work on the Mediterranean coast as elsewhere in al-Andalus, and which seethed below the surface of political and religious evolution. More such contributors will make their appearance below in the course of these explorations.[2]

Other approaches have been developing in the search for new frameworks in which to study Spain's mix of cultures. Scholars like Archibald Lewis and Pierre Bonnassie have been reinterpreting the Occitan—Catalan flanks of Spain, the curve of the Mediterranean from the Rhone to the Ebro. (The trajectory recalls the claim of Jaume the Conqueror at mid-thirteenth century to rule 'from the Rhone to Valencia.') Some prefer to see a unity larger than the linguistic, and extend the arc for immemorial general relationships from the Ebro to the Tiber.[3] In the Occitan or southern French curve the eleventh-century Gregorian Reform, with its programmatic Peace of God, supplied fanatic dynamism and the broadly based militarism of a society evolving toward crusade. 'Cursed be he who does not dip his sword in blood' to restore justice: already the Holy War elements of Christendom had fused, which (as Emmanuel Sivan has shown) were to radicalize Islam into a Holy War reaction of its own. This violent readjustment of Christian society, at its moment of urbanization and expansion, marks the beginnings of whatever 'Reconquest' Spain underwent. Indeed the very term 'Reconquest' has outlived much of its usefulness, except as the medieval canonists' synonym and justification for crusade against Islam in the East as in the West. After the millennial year, Spain's congeries of border raids, mixed alliances, and opportunistic settlements and seizures gradually gave way to something more ominous: a Christian and an Islamic society each thoroughly restructured, with a new and more violent perception of self.

Perhaps the most exciting work being done on medieval Spain today concerns the Mediterranean coast, Christian and Islamic.[4] This is no accident, since the structural dynamics there of both societies from the twelfth century on were those of mercantile civilizations, locked on to international trade routes, with a vivid city life in some ways common to all the port cities of the western Mediterranean. Islamic Valencia by then was reputed a paradise of advanced civilization and luxury by Muslims, a byword still echoing today; Barcelona and its sister ports in southern 'France' were upwardly mobile international centers, taking advantage of every stage in the trade wars between Italian city-state giants. It is very difficult to convey to the traditionalist Spanish historian that Christian Spain's center lay here in the thirteenth century, for example, and not in the more parochial dynamics of upland or (in commonly used shorthand) meseta Spain.

The difference between Mediterranean Spain and meseta Spain was not merely that they spoke different languages, had different authority structures (the count or even count-cum-king was not like the Castilian suzerain), had evolved differing social forms, or lived

6

on very different landscapes dominated by different economies; it was rather that the Mediterranean littoral formed a continuum with its sister ports, was turned outward by the linking sea as much as by the mountain masses and unnavigable rivers at its back, so that the great movements of Mediterranean Europe centered here as much as in Italy or Languedoc–Provence. Spanish unity was not a destiny but an accident, just as the unity of Frankland and the Occitan south into one 'France' evolved by circumstance from the thirteenth century on. The patriarch–king on the Castilian meseta enjoyed a personal power and direct personal or crown resources superior to those of the sea-count; he could single-handedly deploy these to orient and elevate his country's cultural life or to wage impressive cavalry war. Paradoxically the Mediterranean count's personal power and resources were far weaker, so that he half ruled his cities and half deferred to them; but his potential power diffused over these semi-autonomous centers was immeasurably greater, when by charisma he could rally them to a single purpose. This perception of coast versus upland is important to the study of Muslim–Christian interaction, since it defines the nature of the Christian terms interacting. The comital units of the Mediterranean, with their public institutions dominating any feudal traces, and with a mercantile mentality engaging every class from aristocrat to shopkeeper, entered a different kind of dialogue with Islamic neighbors. The Catalan 'knight,' or even Dante or Assisi, riding in armor to his local wars, had more psychologically in common with the Muslim *fāris* or consciously gallant horseman, despite very differently structured societies, than he had with the English or the Frankish knight.

Here the framework must be widened further. Not only was the Spanish Christian center (the coast) very different from the Spanish Christian hinterland (the meseta), but the Christian–Muslim interaction worked in synchrony with wider circles of non-Spanish action. Part of Spain's seemingly peculiar character, insofar as it does not stem from the viewer's over-concentration on Castile and insofar as it does not merely state the normal cultural autonomy of regions or nations (admittedly with reference here to Islamic influence), comes from ignoring this dependence upon and relation to the rest of Mediterranean Christendom.

To borrow an example from Archibald Lewis, the period 950–1050 marked an 'age of transition' away from Islamic naval–commercial hegemony in the Mediterranean, with the next fifty years ushering in 'the triumph of the West.'[5] Thus the Fatimid caliphs, removing from Tunis to Cairo in 969, had confronted the victorious reconquest forces of Byzantium, resulting in truce and division of power in 999. The neglected central Mediterranean regions of Tunis, Tripoli, the Algerian areas, and Islamic Sicily suffered decline. Spanish–Islamic sea-power faded away with the caliphate except for two decades of Denia's 'pirate' fleets. Byzantine attempts at naval–military support for Italy proved sporadic and in the early 1000s abortive; Genoa, Pisa, Venice, and Amalfi aggressively filled the vacuum of sea-power, and from the Tiber to the Ebro a defensive stance turned offensive. The last fifty years of the eleventh century saw disasters shake the older powers: the Turks moving into Byzantium's heartland, Asia Minor, by the great battle of Manzikert, nomads ravaging North Africa, civil war and anarchy upsetting Syria and Egypt, and the eastern Maghrib breaking into independent units. Genoa and Pisa at the urging of Pope Leo IX ousted the Muslims from Sardinia in 1050, and with papal and Amalfitan troops invaded Tunisia in 1087; Norman south Italy at papal invitation absorbed Islamic Sicily and Malta between 1061 and 1090. For Western Christendom, livid with the reformist turmoils of the Gregorian movement and burgeoning with surplus population, Reconquest and proto-crusade were everywhere in the air.

Thus the Castilian surge southward, marked by Toledo's conquest in 1085, and the Catalan stirring, marked by attacks on Tortosa and in 1089 by an abortive restoration of their western metropolitanate at Tarragona (where the themes of pilgrimage, indulgences, and war first fused in Europe), not to mention the Cid's carving of a Valencian principality briefly in the later 1090s, formed part and parcel of a general Mediterranean situation, one issue of which was the culminating call for the First Crusade in 1095, a movement soon divided officially into a Holy Land pilgrimage or crusade and the equivalent Spanish pilgrimage (*iter hispanicum*). To discuss conflict and contact on the Spanish frontier without reference to these concentric circles of meaning is folly. In this selected sample, the fall of Toledo had a Spanish–Islamic context, a Spanish–Christian context, a western Mediterranean context both Islamic and Christian, a demographic context, and a shift in power relationships and siting both for the larger Islamic and for the larger Byzantium–Rome contexts.

Within that essential framework of power relationships, ideological furies swirled: the Almoravid and Gregorian fanaticisms, Spanish–Islamic neo-convert sensibility, Italian–Norman and Seljuk puritanisms, commercial greed in an era of new possibilities, ecclesiastical and political antagonisms which were building toward the East–West split of 1054 (not yet definitive but symbolic of deep tensions), the fading shadow of Byzantine domination in the West after its last military campaign to seize Islamic Sicily in 1040, the rising star of Venice with its Golden Bull in 1082, and the pretensions of a Germanic revived 'Roman Empire' as savior of Christendom against the Muslims in Italy. And this is merely the framework, without the subtler movements, the local variants, or the individuals who rode or deflected these winds of change. This episode alone, merely as a setting for subsequent discussion of Spain's Muslim–Christian interface during this turbulent century of the Cid, cries out for a Fernand Braudel or even for two Braudels.

Since we are dealing with history rather than with literature or philosophy, and treating of a region of striking diversity and kaleidoscopic changes over a half-millennium, transcendental abstractions cannot serve. An invitation to variety is needed, and a summons to look away from narcissistic preoccupation with a unique and isolated 'Spain.' Most of the new textbook syntheses serve us badly here. Having used them for general orientation, however, we can discard them like a highway map and strike out on foot to explore any given local situation. Each juncture of time and place in Spanish medieval history was so unique that its measure of contact and conflict was qualitatively different from that of conditions a generation before or a province away. This individuality affects place, time, associative setting, and behavioral context.

THE WORLDS OF CRUSADER VALENCIA

If the historian must approach conflict and contact between Spanish Muslims and Christians in a defined context of space and time, the conquest and colonial pacification of the Almohad waliate of Valencia in the thirteenth century offers a suitable area for experiment. A short essay can only sketch the outlines. Christian advance in Spain was mainly accomplished in two surges: by the generation which took Toledo (and briefly Valencia) in the late eleventh century, moving the frontier halfway down the peninsula in a bulging crescent, and more strikingly by the generation which swept over the south in the second quarter of the thirteenth century, from Cordova–Seville to the Balearics–Valencia–Murcia, leaving only the rump enclave of Granada as a pathetic survival for two more centuries. The confrontation between the variegated realms centered on Aragon–Catalonia and the Muslims of Valencia, in battle from about 1230 and in reconstruction from 1245 to 1285 – a total of fifty-five years – covers the reigns of Jaume the Conqueror and from 1276 of his son Pere the Great. During the reconstruction or colonial period the conquered kingdom (roughly the size and shape of the crusader kingdom of the Holy Land at the opposite side of the Mediterranean, during its prosperous days) enjoyed as much stability as any generation in troubled times, due regard being had for the evolutions and rebellions of frontier life.

Settlers gathered from diverse parts of Jaume's realms to forge a new society, customs, and balance of institutions, creating their own complex history without explicit reference to the Muslim majority. The conquered Muslims (Mudejars) remained largely in place, though with severe structural dislocation and a loss of elites by emigration, going their daily round as a stable generation deserving to be studied in and of itself, its balance of distorted survivals with adaptive and reactive acculturation endlessly fascinating. Here one should apply the factors of geographic and generational difference. Islamic Spain of the Mediterranean coast had its regional differences from other areas of al-Andalus in physical, human, and historical contexts. At the moment of its fall, its internal political situation was so passionately confused as to defy brief explanation, and the crusade had begun as a Christian alliance intruding into an Islamic civil war on behalf of the beleaguered *walī*, the last great prince of the Almohads left in Spain, against nativist factions. In the event, the Almohad converted to Christianity, the Muslim allies were suitably rewarded with lands by the victorious crusaders, and conquered Muslim leaders were sometimes left in place as vassals (until rebellions thinned their number and eventually extinguished them). The religious animosities among Muslim factions here, the anti-Berber sentiment, and the crushing blows to communal self-confidence as Mongol forces promised to extinguish Islamic power in the wider Islamic cosmos, constituted a negative experience for that generation, such as neither predecessors nor successors had to suffer.

Islamic Valencia would be mourned in Islam as a paradise lost, for the prosperity and beauty of its physical and human ecologies.

Jaume's conquest was a radical and destructive departure from the previous succession of different existences (caliphal frontier, *taifa* or independent principalities, Almoravid, and Almohad), each of which had related in its own way to Christian neighbors. Even as a Mudejar society, dissident majority status here made Valencian Muslims very different in lifestyle and attitudes from their colleagues in Aragon or Catalonia, and as small farmers different from their large-estate colleagues in Castilian Andalusia. Whether examined vertically in time or horizontally in geographical space, these differences stand out in demography, economy, and social psychology.

The other term of contact—conflict, the realms of 'Aragon,' not only differed from meseta Spain as already noted, but constituted an amalgamation united mostly by the accident of a common dynasty. The relatively dominant element in Valencian reconstruction seems to have been the Catalan—Occitan bloc – in a collection of coastal cities where commerce was paramount among all classes including 'nobles' and churchmen, in a literate troubadour—urban society already versed in the new-model finance and evolving under the impact of the new-model Roman Law, proud of its great university at Montpellier, and producing in this century a range of notable European figures such as Ramon de Penyafort in law, Arnau de Vilanova in medicine, and Ramon Lull in literature and philosophy. A seesaw of trade agreements and hostilities joined this complex with the Islamic principalities replacing the Almohads in North Africa, and especially with Hafsid Tunis. Before the century was out, Pere the Great would seize Sicily and invade Italy as successor to the Hohenstaufen claims. All the current movements of the Mediterranean lands had their strong echo here, from the obsession with technology to the mendicant enthusiasm for converting the Muslim, and from city militia or public baths and hospitals to Roman Law barratry and manneristic chivalry for merchants' sons.

During the Valencian crusade and reconstruction, Mediterranean Christendom reached a peak of prosperity and expansion, with a generation of growth ahead before the dynamism slackened and the Black Death generation took new directions at 'the closing of the medieval frontier' – all those external and internal frontiers which had characterized the expansive central centuries of medieval Europe, and of which the Spanish frontier constituted only a segment. Thus Valencia's Mudejars and Christians had confronted each other at the lowest point of morale in Islam's long history and at the height of Mediterranean Christendom's dynamism and sense of expectations, factors which were bound to affect the direction and impact of acculturation. The relatively bloodless strategy of the nearly fifteen years of military conquest, by which walled towns and castles were maneuvered progressively into surrendering on conditions, with treaty-constitutions guaranteeing autonomous communities analogous to the Muslims' own *dhimma* model for protected unbelievers, also facilitated peaceful interaction. Though this framework is expressed as a static model, it too evolved and changed even as Jaume's own attitude toward his Muslim subjects hardened from friendly openness to suspicion and resentment. But the main point stands clear: the dynamics of each society at this precise time and place were unique, each in its own category, so that the mutual influences and interaction between these two evolving terms constituted in turn a unique dynamics of conflict and contact.

Neither society documented this interaction, and almost nothing of any kind survives from Valencia's Muslims after the conquest, so the researcher must glean his basic data by indirection, sifting the abundant Christian records for random information, assumptions, clues, and the universally revealing singular. The few documents touching the theme of interaction tend to stress legal disabilities, tax collections, administrative interventions, religious tension, the *chronique scandaleuse* of the police blotter, and clashes at arms. Patient archeological probing, analyzing, and reflectively interrelating the indirect data, across the gamut of possible categories and against the complicated background just sketched, can consume an historian's lifetime for one region and/or period alone.

After grasping how Christian–Muslim interaction, formal and informal, occurred in successively different contexts both general and local, in space and in time, and having sketched such a situation for mid-thirteenth-century Valencia, with the added caution that every few years of time meant change in the framework, we have one final piece to fit in the frame. The interaction of the two societies was mutual and continuous, by creative diffusion, manneristic borrowing, informal infiltration, and reactive or rejective adaptation. The results can be arranged and listed, but they are symptoms rather than the deeper reality of contact. More important was the context or associative setting: effective points of transmission and confrontation. The elites come first, with overt contact at the academic, nobiliary, merchandising, and administrative levels. Then come basic needs common to both: irrigation and farming techniques (but *not* those favorite fantasies, Islamic Valencia's 'communal' water-courts and 'mechanized' paper mills), mingling at markets or by domestic service or at entertainment (including also prostitution, taverns, and gambling halls), the slavery prominent in both societies, military service to which both were subject, and language or costume crossovers. Another category is hostility: restrictive legislation, the anti-Muslim riots from 1275, recurrent rebellions by the Muslims, conversion–apostasy, mutual contempt, and the overreaction by either side in stressing characteristics which excluded the other or intensified the boundary-maintaining mechanisms of one's own culture. Not to lengthen the list, a final category could be innocent displacement and environmental change as the newcomers repeated the behavioral and economic patterns of the home regions, while equally innocent patterns of the Muslims inertly redefined these intrusions by their own very persistence.

To carry such categories into specifics for Valencia, and to relate those specifics into patterns meaningful in the total context, would require a book apart. Here we can only select for passing notice some of the ways in which the two peoples impinged on each other. The settlers came into a land encumbered by Arabic names and customary divisions; they retained much of that ambience, consulting elderly Muslims commonly in cases of boundary imprecision or agricultural custom. Outside a few cities the parish churches remained converted mosques, while real mosques far outnumbered those few colonial churches and continued to bustle with Islamic community life. Surrender treaties guaranteed services there, the sitting of Koranic courts, and religious schooling. At regular intervals the keening call of the muezzin rose over every Valencian locality, and in time came to seem to Christians a notable grievance. Though a popular polemic obscures the fact today, few Muslims in the new kingdom knew any Romance; their academic Arabic and their local dialect closed them into a solidarity as strong as their religious and demographic unity. Moors formed the mass of farmers and a large part of the artisan work force; they dominated some industries like ceramics and paper. They were present as household servants, slaves, merchants, tenants, entertainers, shopkeepers, and sailors.

For the Christians this was more than contact: they were awash on a sea of Muslims. Their reaction was a classic response of colonials. Accepting a measure of external fashion, alien custom, and linguistic infiltration, without reflection or real choice, they busily erected barriers against deeper influence. To 'reform' the heathen environment, they threw up a number of imposing Gothic churches, insisted on reckoning public finances in a new money stamped with Christian symbolism, held to their own calendar, imported their round of feasts and ceremonies, avoided Moorish or Mudejar art forms, did not welcome the stratum of converts from Islam with their foreign ways, and hardly adverted to the ubiquitous Muslims in their general documentation. The Christian response, despite a measure of unavoidable acculturation to surface patterns, was a reactive concentration on self-conscious identity.

The Muslims, for their part, despite interior community life at the local level – the official political body or *aljama* – had become strangers in their own land. The conquerors held the central part of large cities, imposed their presence by an immediate network of parishes (sometimes with no parishioners), visibly ruled through a bureaucracy of officials and taxmen, assumed control of commerce, garrisoned a network of strongholds, dictated unseemly restrictions to erode the surrender concessions, and formed a direct landlord class. As the Muslim elites drifted south to Granada and North Africa, and as those who stayed behind banded closer together and began to lose their urban makeweight, Islamic society threatened to ruralize and condense into an infinitely replicating village pattern. The realities of the new political situation – the way in which the new rulers viewed and treated their Muslim subjects, as vassals, jurats, and tax-sources, for example – affected the self-perception of the Muslims, so that in their daily behavioral patterns toward the landlords and rulers they responded in the expected and less in their inherited Islamic fashion. Though they kept their language, many learned a sufficiency of Catalan; soon European name-forms would gain scattered acceptance; the autonomy of Koranic courts, already somewhat limited, eroded. In these ways the Muslims too felt beset, by a Christian dominance psychological and ubiquitous, and they too responded with necessary adaptation and reactive recoil.

More formal encounters heightened that general contact. A new phenomenon, schools of Arabic dedicated to philosophical conversion of elite Muslims, were set up by Barcelona-based Dominicans, with major centers in the recent conquests of Murcia and Valencia. Muslims hired to teach there, and those drawn by curiosity and dialogue, were influenced directly; the Muslim community at large, also harassed by Franciscan sermons imposed by public authority, must have been acutely disturbed by these intrusive institutions. There was a measure of conversion both from and to Islam at this time; the Dominicans characterized their Valencian conversions as 'considerable enough.'

Military action, quite apart from Muslim—Christian hostilities, provided a friendly contact. Not only did Valencian landowners employ contingents of Muslim warriors, but the *aljamas* of Valencia had to send large drafts of crossbowmen to help King Pere roll back the French invasion. Military mixing worked both ways. Ordinary knights from Catalan lands not infrequently sought hospitality and adventure among Muslim aristocrats in North Africa or Islamic Spain; the intelligence preceding the Valencian crusade relied on such a returning knight. And contingents of troops from the realms of Aragon were stationed in North African emirates or even rented out. In fact the overseas movements of merchants, pilgrims, soldiers, diplomats, emigrants, immigrants, and travelers were constant and considerable. Valencia city's fonduk, or caravanserai-warehouse for foreign Muslim merchants, brought great profit to the crown, as did Catalan merchant quarters in cities like Tunis.

Among the upper classes an osmosis of manners is obvious. King Jaume was proud of his esoteric knowledge of Muslims' susceptibilities and prejudices, and he described the almost liturgical ceremonies he used to woo their favor. In the Cid's expression, he also acted as their chief $q\bar{a}d\bar{\imath}$, heard contending Muslim parties sworn on the Koran, consulted Islamic jurists, and could render judgement expressly as successor to Abū Zayd and Zayyān. Because of the mercantile and small-farmer character of Valencian Christians, the two peoples assimilated somewhat in economic practices – irrigated farming, dry farming, herding, crafts, fisheries, and merchandising. Perhaps piracy should be added, since that was merely another face of commerce and could operate with mixed crews. The many land charters of the Valencian settlers reveal how the plots of either people could mix; and because townsmen commonly held an extramural farm, even artisans and merchants had contact with Muslim farmers.

Sections of town held by the Muslim community (wherever indeed Muslims did not outnumber Christians and simply mingled, as was more usual) were not ghettos during this period; some Christians lived in them, Muslims could live outside, and each shopped and circulated throughout the town. Each paid taxes not dissimilar, frequented the same mills, and (on separate days) enjoyed the same baths. Valencian hospitals received Christians and Muslims alike, while physicians of both faiths practiced. (Valencia would publicly license physicians from all groups.) To probe the interaction more subtly, one might study intensively the evolution of a specific element such as international merchants, or a single institution like the *aljama*'s tax-gathering *amīn*; or some literate figures like King Jaume (in his autobiography), the Valencian settler Arnau de Vilanova in whom Arabic and European medicine converged, or Ramon Lull in the contemporary and analogous conquest of Majorca who enthusiastically engaged his Islamic milieu in both Latin and Arabic writings.

John Boswell, in his comparative study on a decade of Mudejar life in the separate provinces of the fourteenth-century realms of Aragon, found that northern Mudejar groups had strikingly assimilated to the Christian majority, and lived in Christian dress, language, and 'cooperation and cultural absorption.' By comparison the very different system among Valencia's Muslim majority hardly seemed to deserve the description *convivencia*, but rather mere 'physical proximity' and 'absence of conflict' in a 'tense stalemate.'[6] To some extent this impression arises from the crises through which both societies were then passing; and partly it may reflect impatience with Castroite interweaving of the two peoples. But there is also a problem of interpretation. Many models exist for cultural mixing or general influence, ranging from the extreme of assimilation to the extreme of rigid mutual hostility. Even within a given model (Jews of thirteenth-century Barcelona, or American Indians of mid-nineteenth-century Montana) various strata or inner groups can conform to altogether different models. Assuming even a 'pure' model, however, cultural flow inevitably is constant and mutual. There is no effective distancing or reduction to mere physical proximity. As Ibn Khaldūn saw in the case of independent Granada in the fourteenth century as well as of the subject Mudejars, profound structural and psychological changes occur in the recessive people. Eventually Bishop Figueroa of Segorbe in a memorial to the crown assessed the Valencian Moriscos as 'not knowing how to be Muslims or Christians' but clinging to community identity under each local *faqīh*.

That the victors had an equivalently intense experience can be seen in their reactive expressions, in their technological adaptation, in literary, musical, and occupational trends. Valencian Christians would soon become a distinct type, visibly different in character from other Catalans, forming a kind of Mediterranean 'Andalusia' remarked upon by neighbors and travelers in its many strange expressions. The interchange is visible from the first generation, and affected both sides. Because Valencia remained demographically an Islamic land and in its dominant life a proto-colonialist Christian land, the general dynamic later became confrontation rather than overt mixing. But the Muslim infrastructure was always the base on which rested the disparate Catalan and Aragonese settler groups, the city and the countryside, the seignorial and the royal and the burgher. Interpenetration of Muslim and Christian remained mutual and forceful.

HISTORIANS' BATTLEFIELDS: THE 'CONTINUIST' PARANOIA

Ancient quarrels lurk just below the surface of Valencian historiography. Like the Castro and Sánchez-Albornoz debates which reflect them on a larger stage, they politicize history, forming orthodoxies and inhibiting new frameworks in which to view the data. The unwary outsider, tripped up by someone's clue word or by citing someone's despised adversary, finds himself pitched on to an alien battlefield, dodging irrelevant missiles and fending off strangers. Rejecting both sides means being perceived by each camp as adhering to the other. Conceding merit to an aspect of either becomes proof of complicity. This can become disconcertingly grotesque, as my own case illustrates. Some currently perceive me as in the nationalist–continuist school, while others contrariwise make me a champion against that school. Joan Fuster has publicly hailed me this past year as a long-time leader against the nationalist–continuist 'ideology,' indeed as persecuted and 'silenced among us' by continuist historians like Antonio Ubieto; conversely Pierre Guichard in a series of articles attacks me as framing all my data within that very ideology, following leaders like (again) Ubieto![7] Mere citation of Menéndez Pidal's name, precisely to refute his continuist position on Islamic cities in Spain, caused an otherwise laudatory reviewer to rebuke my supposed support. A topic such as Muslim–Christian interaction, or Mudejar evolution, particularly evokes such polemical stances.

17

The problem in connection with these polarities is not so much to make one's own position clear (though that must be done, over and again), but rather to dismiss the entire war as a set of false problems impeding historiographical progress. It is better to have come at Spanish and at Andalusī Valencian problems initially from outside these schools. My own first approach, while taking a doctorate under R. Rahmann of the Anthropos Institut (which had temporarily moved from Nazi Germany to Fribourg University in Switzerland), went not through Spain but through colonialist interaction with Indians of the United States northwest. Later, after a very different doctoral experience in medieval history at Johns Hopkins, my Mudejar books profited from the acculturative themes explored in that parallel field. Current arenas of the Valencian conflict include: 'continuity' of cultural structures versus discontinuity, 'optimism' in assessing the Mudejar's situation and the 'tolerance' accorded him versus 'pessimism,' and acceptable terminology. More specific Valencian reflections of the conflict currrently include a concern with feudalism, castles and castle lords, and the farmer. Each will be considered in turn.

Of all six themes the underlying dispute centers on continuity–discontinuity. Combatants can be moderate, stressing the elements apparently carried over from an Islamic society into the Mudejar condition, or conversely dwelling by preference on the factors of loss, displacement, and mutilation consequent upon destructuralizing the conquered society. Historians endowed with a deeper rage can be radical, insisting that nothing remained after the holocaust beyond sorting out the bones and charting stages of the disaster, or conversely repeating blandly that the underlying structures simply persisted as in Menéndez Pidal's 'eternal' flow of a uniquely Spanish history. The very word 'continuity' agitates the discontinuist, even when applied to mere antecedents in Roman times or to physical survivals in Mudejarism, or when its gross polemic meaning is not at issue. Whatever its context or explication, 'continuity' contains for the discontinuist one linear and univocal meaning. Continuists stubbornly respond by citing the multiplicity of Islamic survivals.

Neither side in this dialogue of the deaf is likely to shed light on the transitions Mudejarism involved. A third position is necessary, away from the noise of the contending parties. It is obvious that numerous elements and even component substructures, from language to religion to irrigation communities, carried over into the conquest generation. These destructured survivals are interesting not so much for themselves as for their function in the acculturative process, and for their place in the Mudejar culture. The key here is that the very survivals or continuities in *themselves* constituted discontinuity, and the more so the longer they survived. Islamic religious life 'continued,' for example, with its mosques, schools of Koranic instruction, religious courts, Friday worship, *ramaḍān*, alms, and the like. Yet this continued element became different immediately upon being sited within a Christian environment and domination, in its whole as in its parts. The perverting changes ranged from an intolerable split between religion and the controlling society, to the appointment of religious functionaries, and to entanglements with the Christian courts.

It is upon this basic distortion of structure, with consequent tragedy, that the very drama of my own books rests. Book titles were devised precisely to evoke this destructively transforming embrace by a conquering and immigrating alien culture – an *Islam under* the crusaders, a medieval *Colonialism*, and the present *Societies in symbiosis*. My basic monograph on this theme was similarly subtitled 'Acculturative survival and its price.' Something more positive has been equally a pervasive theme: the concomitant formation of a brave subculture, the survival and mutation of myriad elements into a new life, the courage and dignity and tenacity of those who made a new world out of the old. Despite the pain inherent, the human story here is the Mudejar society itself in as many aspects and people as can be unearthed in new manuscripts. It was in this sense that I compiled my study on 'Socioeconomic structure and continuity in the tax records'; and in this sense that I described how 'the component elements of the old Islamic polity perdured' at lower levels, despite the fact that 'this infrastructure was affected by many colonialist factors.' Continuity here is the transformed substratum, the stage for change, not integral structural continuity. A factor which can mislead the rapid reader in such a treatment is my perception that the first or conquest generation retained more of the visible elements, so that much of daily routine and views could seem on the surface not to have changed.

It is ironic that those survivals most analogous to elements in the conquerors' alien system, which might seem to bridge the gap between wholly different structures, were the most vulnerable to very active distortion, viewed and manipulated by the receiving society in a highly transformative manner. The Valencian conquerors did not alter worship in the mosque, but did cheerfully create Mudejar 'feudal' lords and address the *aljama* councilors as corporate jurats. This did not convert the Muslim into a knight or the *aljama* into a commune with communal privileges; it merely distorted both into bastard forms of their previous selves. A final caution is needed. In the appalling sparseness of Arabic records, the ample Mudejar manuscripts now coming to light may offer many echoes of late Almohad Valencia. Each such element has to be carefully disentangled from its Mudejar survivalist context and coloring, however, and restored to its presumed previous context by analogy with Islamic elements elsewhere, if something is to be reconstructed of that previous society. Mistakes will afflict this minute task, and many minds must bend to it; but it lies open as a pioneer field of Arabist study.

In the Mudejar records being recovered, the human drama is what fascinates, more than the process of devolution into a subculture which colored even the physically unchanged elements. To miss this, in favor of continuing the sterile battle over continuity–discontinuity, is to miss not only the realities of Mudejar Valencia but the very problematic by which an historian can approach them. Mudejar society was a survival society, an adaptive society, its members living as Muslims as best they could. They were allowed to do so because there was a level of Islamic structure below which Muslims refused to live, a level the crusader masters had to tolerate if they hoped for a prosperous Valencia, and a level outside which no medieval government could control or administer its Muslims. They largely 'remained in the kingdom, their society and institutions wounded and withdrawn but still omnipresent,' in fact 'a sea on whose sullen surface Christian immigrants at first had to cluster like infrequent atolls.'[8]

MORE FALSE POLARITIES: 'OPTIMISTS' CONFRONT 'PESSIMISTS'

A distinct field of battle, for which many of the same troops muster, is the squabble between 'optimists' and 'pessimists,' involving one's views on tolerance and intolerance in treatment of the Mudejars, the worth of whatever structures survived or resulted, and the presumed reaction or feelings of the Mudejars themselves. The optimist can complacently focus on the survivals or the 'continuities,' on the sense of identity and well-being he discerns in his documents, or on every evidence that Mudejarism was a viable society, protected by law and privilege, given freedom to worship and to function as separate communities. The pessimist is unmoved by these appearances. He is impressed by what seems absolute loss of Islamic frame and structure, numerous abuses and brutalities, the insecurity necessarily resulting from popular and clerical hostility, the instability of his community subject to the ruler's whim and to cancellation or erosion of privileges, and the anguish of living lives scorned and rejected by the ambient Christians.

The judicious try to strike a balance, and to distinguish between regions and time-periods. Even for a period and place as restricted as those in my books, Valencia from about 1245 to 1285, the opponents square off. Cagigas and Menéndez Pidal see the surrender agreements of King Jaume as vindictive intolerance and 'spoliation'; a more popular view sums crown policy by both Jaume and Pere as cynical expediency; a variant by Michavila y Vila argues that Jaume treated his Muslims badly but that Pere after the great rebellion was able to be more humane. My own impression after reading every Mudejar document in the registers of Kings Jaume, Pere, and Alfonso was that basic policy owed more to inherited tradition as modified by the unique circumstances of Valencia, that it did not change in basics for better or worse under Pere, and that many personal attitudes or reactions must be taken into account, as influencing its accidentals and application, from greed to common sense to fear to chivalric self-image.

Choosing sides or striking balances reflects more than the historiographical stances just discussed. Insights from the social sciences, fresh data from the archives, and our contemporary disillusions, moralisms, and sensitivity to the plight of minorities can all enter into one's judgement. An overall assessment contains much that is subjective, as the cultural and personal background of the historian comes powerfully to bear. A Marxist historian, for example, can be most sensitive to dislocation of the economic order, unimpressed that taxes are not all that different, and outraged at the victims' loss of control over their own economic life with all the social and psychological impiications. Conversely he may hardly notice or care that religion and ritual are salvaged, with a life-framing legal system profoundly religious. Within the economic sphere he can even throw emphasis upon worker and farmer, the forgotten men of history, to the point of seeing the classes involved in administrative, cultural, and spiritual leadership as a separate transient phenomenon little connected with that worker.

An Islamic observer, on the other hand, might concentrate on the retention of religion with its rituals and feasts, mosques, schools, courts, and financial support (the *waqf* foundations). He might note the persistence of diet, communal baths, intra-*aljama* administration, the right to exclude Jews from one's quarter, and Boswell's elite of well-off and wealthy Mudejars even late in the next century. He would certainly remark above all on the persistence of language, even when as dialect and even as later corrupted; Louis Cardaillac assesses this as the central custodian of Mudejar and Morisco culture in Valencia, the shield and sword of Islam. All of this and the religious elements incarnate in it might strike that Islamic observer as essential salvage, an Islamic central structure outweighing losses more visible to us. Though their communities were fragmented one from the other (the 'acephalous' predicament stressed by Bramon), Valencia's conquered Mudejars retained a sense of commonalty. They united to choose al-Azraq their leader for the post-conquest rebellion; they held a general assembly each year in the kingdom of Valencia in the fourteenth century, according to the crown instruction of 1356 which feared its discussion of 'matters injurious to the kingdom' and sought 'means whereby this sort of assembly may be done away with.' And they identified themselves later, when Moriscos, as the 'nation' or people of Valencian Moors.[9]

A main problem for interpretation is that medieval minority-communities, within Islam or Christendom, were not modern minorities striving to assimilate in all but a single element such as color, residual ethnicity, or compartmentalized or privatized religion. Each in his community shrank from the other, despised the inseparable religio-cultural package the other represented, and actively resisted assimilation. Tolerance, had he thought in terms of tolerance, might well have meant to the Mudejar the retention of the exclusionary factors we most deplore: Arabic uni-language, community walls, dietary obligations, separate schools and courts, and everything that turned him from the general Christian context and so by our standards oppressed him. He was an accomplice in his own exclusion, to a point, and wary of compromise. In any case our post-Enlightenment concept of tolerance must have seemed to Muslim and Christian alike unacceptable.

As with the continuist polarities, the balancing schools as well as the optimist–pessimist schools may pose the wrong problematic, so that debate might proceed for ever as to whether Valencian Mudejars were officially oppressed, reasonably well off, living a nightmare, or (in Roca Traver's phrase) 'at no time the object of intolerance or misunderstanding.' In real life the good and the bad were rather mixed than balanced, the one being a function of the other for a Mudejar society surviving in the infidel world. Knowing that, one can present as many 'optimist' elements as possible, with no danger of presenting an 'optimist' viewpoint. They are celebrations of how the Valencian Mudejar achieved his integral society, rich in texture and proud in identity, religion, degree of local autonomy, comforting customs and routine, prosperity, and endurance, but simultaneously his world of pain.

Because my books gather a harvest of such 'optimist' findings, it is important to see in and through them my equally 'pessimist' conclusions. In an address at the first international congress on Mudejarism at Teruel, I called attention to 'the disintegrative acculturation of Islamic Valencian institutions, [which] can be observed already in the first years, [and] which altered the Mudejar social forms'; to 'the essential and disorienting distortion which the conquest produced in the society's equilibrium in Valencia and in the Muslims' concept of themselves'; and to the riots or anti-Moor pogroms I had discovered as widespread throughout the Valencian kingdom as late as 1275, which 'reflect a basic antagonism of cultures in classic conflict.' My *Colonialism* found 'inevitable disorientation and change' immediately in the defeated society, with the conquerors 'a deliberately transformative society' which eroded the Muslim's essential identity and 'worked larger mischief.' The Muslims 'became mere guests in their own home as these new owners moved in'; those who did not emigrate had to choose between uncreative cultural intransigence or an adaptation which 'lost their sense of self,' while their society's multiple surviving elements 'suffered a profound dislocation.' Just as 'every strain of his environment betrayed the infidel's pollution,' so the Mudejar's own 'Disneyland replica of his father's world stood as an affront,' its 'cultural ecology askew.'

My address at the Von Grunebaum invitational in 1975 bore the significant title 'Spanish Islam in transition: acculturative survival and its price.' My theme was the 'destructive or alienating acculturation' in post-conquest Valencia, whose effect was neither assimilation nor integration 'but a certain divergence of the subjected group into the alien perspective,' as well as adoption of 'novel behavioral patterns or institutions.' All this was 'strongly at work from the first generation'; the expanding Christian settlement and fourteenth-century oppression 'accelerated the process but did not dominate, much less initiate it.' Though I discovered that Mudejar taxes were 'not onerously exploitative' and bore comparison with the Christians' burden (an assessment Boswell later found true even for mid-fourteenth century), 'this benign conclusion does not exculpate the crusaders, whose colonial system incorporated grosser, psychologically more wearing forms of oppression.'[10]

Such conclusions were not meant to 'balance' my findings that a form of Islamic society did survive and did retain a surprising degree of autonomy, identity, religious freedom, and wealth in these first generations, as well as a comforting ambience of physical appearances. Balancing may be a useful preliminary or pedagogical tool, but Mudejars did not live a balanced life of discrete elements. The distinct or distinctly observed was not separate; each element defined and colored all the others. And the bottom line for Mudejars was that they inhabited a colonialist, survivalist subculture. My final assessment is that of Ibn Khaldūn, fourteenth-century Islam's 'founder of sociology,' himself from a refugee Sevillian family: conquered societies lose hope, the dynamism generated by hope, and the commercial and civilizing results of that dynamism, promoting the society's disintegration. The resultant subculture, always enduring though always eroding, Islamic to the core, remained (as a complaint of 1525 put it), 'more Moorish than ever before.'[11]

PHANTOMS OF 'FEUDALISM': ISLAMIC BUT ALSO CRUSADER

If 'continuity,' 'optimism,' and 'tolerance' represent false problems, nervousness about Islamic 'feudalism' comes close to absurdity. There are two reasons for this. First, Islamic society had no place in its structures for feudalism, so that the fussiness of the discontinuist over the historians' occasional and metaphorical borrowing of certain of its terms, after due explanation, seems unwarranted. And secondly, Valencian Christian society itself was not feudal except in a very qualified and partial sense, so that the continuist would actually frustrate his own cause by making Islamic Valencia feudal!

The substantive issue is the phenomenon of *de facto* principalities, semi-autonomous breakaway districts large or very small, during the political chaos and counterclaims of the disintegrating Almohad empire, and during the decade and a half of crusader intrusion and piecemeal conquest which progressively isolated sections of Valencia. The very different business of 'landlord' and tenant will be considered in its separate context below.

Before considering the evidence for a stratum (not a class) of Mudejar lords, and the propriety of such terminology as 'lords,' I must briefly state my past and present position on the general question of a Valencian Islamic or a Valencian crusader feudalism. Guichard in a series of otherwise excellent articles assumes that I believe in both and 'dangerously' see in them a linking ideological 'continuity.' I do not recall that any other of my innumerable reviewers, including the eminent Arabists here and abroad who gave my *Islam* a careful reading in manuscript, took away this impression. (Chalmeta, cited as sharing this disquiet, was bothered by a different problem, considered below in the section on farmers.) Terminology, as a battlefield of its own as we shall see below, may have encouraged this bizarre impression; if it misleads even one scholar, it must be reexamined.

In first presenting my Mudejar 'feudal' lords, at an address in 1970 at Western Michigan University, I put their Islamic non-feudal status clearly as men 'whose aristocratic manner of life and military or warrior gloss assimilated them in a complex of externals to the corresponding knightly strata in Christian Valencia'; any number of those identified with castles 'remained in place, exercising military–political control over some small area still Islamic to all appearance.' The correspondence between Muslim and Christian did not go deep: 'the Islamic society was far more undifferentiated, its unstructured forms held from the top by the ruler and linked or netted crosswise by a combination of familial and group solidarities, intermeshed particularly by an interpenetrating, coordinating elite.' Here the overriding qualification came: 'there is no question here of Islamic "feudalism" or deep social analogies.' Moreover, 'in the Islamic principality which became the crusader kingdom of Valencia, Muslim lords as castle holders did not constitute the essential [local] strength; somehow they had first to participate in the more diffused but nuclear power of the towns.' And 'what seems "feudal" in the life of such [Islamic] lords proves upon closer examination a

gloss, a makeshift, or at best one element in a complex construction.'
In ruling power 'the weightiest counterbalance was the ubiquitous
town, considered as at once a political alliance of families and a
territorial unit.' It ought to be possible to 'isolate castle-
management as one facet rewarding examination,' because 'superficial resemblances to Western [European] structures did allow the
Muslim [castellan] to cope with his new overlord, and tempted that
Christian overlord [King Jaume] to perceive these aliens from his
own deceptive angle.'

My sequel article in the *Annales* in 1973, while citing the found-
ational Michigan study in its first footnote, may have muddied the
waters for a French audience by translating terms like English 'lords'
and 'castellans' into the more feudalized 'seigneurs' and 'châtelains.'
That article must not only be read in the context of the Valencian
Christian 'feudal order' of the previous study (or of *Islam*) but its
reference to feudal Mudejar lords and castellans must be carefully
distinguished from references to the antecedent Islamic castellans
and lords thrown into independence by the collapse of central power.
Throughout my *Islam*, a *qāʾid* surrendering his castle normally does
so in consultation and association with the *aljama* sheiks, even in the
case of a ruler so independent by then as Ibn ʿĪsā of Játiva. The book
extensively disassociated the *fāris* from the European meaning of
knight, and the *iqṭāʿ* from the European fief, stressing that the
acceptance of the nobiliary Muslim by the Christians as a 'knight'
amounted to 'the natural affinity' and manneristic acceptance–
assimilation of aristocratic strata in societies differently structured.[12]

Those who would see some feudalism in Islamic Valencia, and
those who deny it altogether, are both engaged in a dispute
irrelevant to the problematic and to understanding the acculturative
transition there. *Islam* took pains to argue, against the general consensus, that Christian Valencia itself was not a feudal society. The
crusaders set up an urban–mercantile society, under a Roman Law
monarch who took the lion's share of power and almost all the cities,
a society held together by the first generally applicable code of
Roman Law promulgated in Europe. This situation makes nonsense
of any attempt to posit an Islamic feudalism to mesh that society
with that of the conquerors. My own argument has been precisely
the opposite: the active, dominant elements of Islamic Valencia had
less difficulty in understanding and adjusting to an alien system
which had a strong monarchy, a city orientation, and a universally

26

commercial ethos than it would have had with a feudal regime. There were of course some feudal mechanisms in the Christian structure, especially where non-regalian Aragonese lords took root; but such elements were so qualified by the larger structure, and so flattened down from the hierarchical and oriented toward the monarch, with Christian ordinary landlords and Christian nobiliary lords tending to assimilate into one alodial class, each group frequently involved both in investment-commerce and in manneristic chivalry, that ideally the term 'feudal' ought always to be predicated of Valencia's Christian society in quotation marks. I acquiesce in the term, however, after painful delimitation of its meaning, as being simpler than constant paraphrase, and often dispense with the intrusive marks.

COLLAPSE OF CENTRAL POWER: ISLAM'S 'LORDS'

Why posit such castle holders in pre-crusade and crusade Valencia? The reason is not that attributed to me by the same critic: belief in 'a social category of Muslim *alcaits*, which he assimilates to the military class of western feudal society.'[13] Such an absurdity violates the interpenetrating nature of the aristocratic strata in al-Andalus, which had no military class but at best a function one easily took up and left. The men I call 'the patriot lords' of Islamic Valencia had nothing to do with feudalism. They were not patriots in our modern secular and nationalist sense, of course, but exercised a religio-cultural participatory leadership in arms in order to defend their religious community. The more prominent among them would have been drawn from among respected and influential families of the local town. Ibn Khaldūn notes that 'as a rule, such leadership goes to members of great and noble houses who are eligible for the positions of elders and leaders of a city' of the Maghrib. Speaking of Zayyān, Ibn Hūd, and Granada's Ibn al-Aḥmar at our period, Ibn Khaldūn describes them as belonging to 'descendants of Arab houses who had to some degree kept away from urban civilization and the cities, and were firmly rooted in military life.' In neither case is there question of a 'military' class. What is at issue here is something very different: the tendency of the crusaders to accept the Islamic military function and ideals as though they could be domesticated into a kind of European equivalence. Jaume's repeated admiration of the Muslims 'of good lineage' so frequently encountered in Valencia has no

27

reference to a landed baronage or hereditary property, but rather to 'the nobility and prestige' described by Ibn Khaldūn as deriving from 'noble and famous men among his forebears,' which along with wealth and other factors 'give him great standing among his fellows,' even when the family line is illusory.[14] On the Mudejar side, wherever units surrendered with a castle and its *qāʾid*, they doubtless saw themselves as a tributary fragment. As Muntaner reports this situation, each *qāʾid* took responsibility for collecting public revenues, for the castle itself, and by implication for general overseeing of the *aljamas* in the district. Acceptance by the colonial power in definite feudal terminology, as will be seen in the case of al-Azraq below in chapter 10, falsified the Mudejars' different image of this transaction and by innocent insistence facilitated the conversion of Mudejar castle-district tributary into Mudejar 'baron' or 'castellan' (*alcait*). Since neither Islamic nor crusader Valencia was a castle society, much less feudal, this aspect of the region's transition is partial, by no means as important as acceptance of town and village Muslim officials. It did guarantee some leadership to an otherwise acephalous Mudejar people for brief decades, and thus it has significance in the total picture of transition.

Unlike feudalism, the phenomenon of breakaway districts as *de facto* mini-principalities was familiar enough to Islam. In the fourteenth century the historical-theorist Ibn Khaldūn studied the general process of such fragmentation in his *Muqaddimah*; among his examples are the *taifa* rulers during Spain's eleventh-century disintegration. He also cites the last years of twelfth-century Zirid Ifrīqiya as a pathetic case, 'when every castle was in the possession of an independent rebel.' He describes the emergence of factions at the outset of such crises, the widening gap between higher and lower classes, and how the notables were in rivalry for allies and clients until one emerged as leader. Henri Bresc and Aziz Ahmad both describe the same phenomenon for Sicily as the Kalbite emirate broke into five or more 'petty principalities' and anarchy in the decade before the eleventh-century Norman invasion. In 'a kind of Islamic feudalism,' Bresc found the big families dividing the island, each *qāʾid* having his stronghold or a castle which at times bore the family name; whether converted or faithful to Islam, numbers of these entered the Norman system as feudal lords. In eleventh-century Spain, Abū ʿUbayd Allāh al-Faqīr wrote, 'each emir had taken control of a district,' and 'everyone who held some stronghold

28

came to rule his city.' Ibn Sa'īd in the thirteenth century contrasted al-Andalus, in its liking for revolutionary heroes and its shifting of allegiance, to the politically more stable East. When the Valencian Ibn Jubayr in the late twelfth century saw petty rulers dividing an area, especially a ruler with four cities, it reminded him 'of the regions of al-Andalus.' There may well be, as we saw Epalza suggesting at the start of this chapter, a more normal dynamic of Andalusī localism at work, visible particularly when central power fell into crisis. Ibn Khaldūn says of Spain during the period of Almohad dissolution after the Las Navas defeat in 1212 to the time of Cordova's and Valencia's fall: 'every qā'id and man of influence, who could command a score of followers or possessed a castle to retire to in case of need, styled himself sultan and assumed the insignia of royalty,' so that al-Andalus 'afforded the very singular aspect of as many kings as there were castellated towns.' We shall see in a moment that Valencia was renowned for the abundance and quality of its fortified places. The chronicle of Alfonso the Learned reflects the continuing disintegration: 'after the death of Ibn Hūd [in 1238] the land split up among many small kings.'[15]

That Valencia would have been particularly affected can be conjectured from its frontier position, vulnerable to insistent Christian raids, and from the circumstance of its civil war, with Abū Zayd, Zayyān, and Ibn Hūd contending for popularity and power. Three other large blocs, important to Islamic chroniclers by reason of their marginal involvement in Ibn Hūd's attempts to form an extensive rule, are particularly visible: Alcira, Denia, and Játiva. Even before the fall of Valencia city, Zayyān seems to have lost control of those regions, while Ibn Hūd could do no more than declare a Játiva incumbent as ally to be his governor. Supporters and allies must have gravitated toward, even fluctuated between, the six larger blocs, a situation which would have encouraged degrees of local independence. Though we know only the most important rebel or breakaway or semi-autonomous leaders, Cristóbal Torres Delgado and others 'suspect [they] were numerous.' As the crusade ground on for some fifteen years, various regions became isolated and defended by men who from all appearances had similarly emerged — either as left-over garrison leaders, state fiscal—administrative functionaries, or more plausibly as thrown up by the dynamics of town aristocratic families and factions to captain the local defenses.

Where civil leaders of important aljamas made their separate peace treaties with Jaume, Barceló Torres reasonably assumes that a military leader there had retreated or fled. In many cases, such a person handled the surrender and then remained. Our most valuable witness here is the Valencian Ramon Muntaner, later a trusted crown agent and man-of-affairs, a junior contemporary of the Conqueror, who as a child had seen Jaume the Conqueror accept the hospitality of his father's house in Valencia. His memoirs record how the crusading King Jaume 'made treaties with many (*molts*) Saracen barons in the said kingdom' of Valencia. 'And all those with whom he made the said treaties answered to him for [each] year's revenues.' The chronicle of San Juan de la Peña or of Pere III in mid-fourteenth century recounts that 'many Saracens holding castles in that [kingdom] remained,' later rebelling. We know little more about these 'many,' but can conjecture that the civil war had caused the emergence of some, and the crusade itself others.[16]

When Jaume struck into Valencia from Teruel to start his crusade, and used his maritime resources to help take and hold coastal Burriana as a key, in effect he split northern from central Valencia and intensified the native chaos. Zayyān does not seem to have had effective rule during Jaume's maneuvers, though he rallied eastern al-Andalus including Murcia into an army of volunteers for one pitched battle of resistance, before he himself fell back into his capital. When Zayyān then offered to surrender to Jaume all castles north of the Guadalaviar River in return for tributary-ruler status at Valencia city, and was refused, his own situation was obviously desperate; by the time Valencia city subsequently fell, Zayyān had no broad support south of the river and would be offering next year to give his last bit of sovereignty, Denia city, in return for Majorca island as his Mudejar fief. The decisive defeat at the Puig in 1237, which allowed Jaume to begin his siege of Valencia city, and the assassination of Ibn Hūd in 1238, left no real center for the Muslims. Each locality had to look to itself. If Jaume's description of Alcira's *ra'īs* as collecting the state revenue and exercising 'rule' is not unexpected, his description of the *qā'id* of Bairén near Gandía leaves the impression of a leader now equally the soul of resistance for that district's abandoned castles and people.

Records about Valencian Mudejars are random, so there should be little hope of catching sight of one of Muntaner's 'many' Mudejar 'barons' who had surrendered. Happily a prototype is available, though absent from Islamic chronicles, or from King Jaume's extensive memoirs until the period of rebellion. This is al-Azraq, whose surrender agreement survives and who will appear at length in chapter 10. He collected his region's revenues, hired troops, and sent diplomatic embassies to both Aragon and Castile. His power and position are obvious. The 1276 countercrusade began under a figure even more unknown, the *qā'id* Ibrāhīm, who set up headquarters at Finestrat castle, from which he controlled other 'castles and places'; at the end of the war he surrendered in Garg castle on honorific conditions. Another unknown named Ibn Isḥāq (Emnebenezach) held Tárbena castle, 'with its villages, districts and all belonging to it and with all its rights.' After the 1258 revolt his nephew Bakrūn (Bocharon) received part of the district, and Ibn Isḥāq had to turn over half of all the region's revenues annually to the king, after deducting from the gross 'a suitable expenditure for the task of custody of the same castle.'

Biar, surrendered by the *qā'id* Mūsā al-Murābiṭ (Muça Almoravit) in 1245, turns up as a major focus of revolt thirty years later. Carmogente castle surfaces after the revolt as having been 'held by' the *qā'id* 'Abencablia,' a man still in the crown's good graces. A more ambiguous protectorate under Castile, only later in the century absorbed into Valencia, was the Crevillente district of the Banū Hudayr. Reading King Jaume's memoirs of the previous Majorca island conquest discloses similar leadership there in the wake of the central city's collapse. Three thousand Muslim fighters with fifteen thousand non-combatants remained in the mountains with castles under Ibn Shu'ayb (Xuaip), 'whom they had made their head and lord.' After he surrendered on very good terms, two-thirds of this force still held the mountain castles against Jaume's troops 'all winter,' succumbing only to starvation and surrendering under terms. The Majorcan case illustrates captains successively thrown up by the disappearance of central power during revolution or war.[17]

The significant aspect of all the Valencian notices from the period of Jaume and his son Pere is that they came to us quite by chance. If we did not have such passages as that of Muntaner, conveying a more general situation, they might be thought anomalies. They illustrate a range of contrasting situations, from rival claimants to rule over the former Almohad province, through major breakaway areas like Játiva, to districts exposed by the disappearance or virtual disappearance of central power such as the cases of al-Azraq and the *qā'id* of Bairén, to leaders for whom possibly the crusaders assigned castles at the time of surrender or who may have seized them during Mudejar revolts. This last situation must have been more common from the Guadalaviar (Turia) River south, where mountainous country and the threat of Castilian intrusion surely made the crusade leaders more generous. And it must have characterized particularly, as already noted, the periods after 1236 and 1238. Can we dismiss such fragmentation for the early north, however, especially the northeast mountainous inland, where Abū Zayd (perhaps already a secret convert to Christianity) was already raiding the Valencian border zone along with Christian barons, and when the three-sided civil war still raged?

Focusing upon the transition into Mudejar structures, I am less concerned with precisely when these men emerged: during the chaos of Almohad decline and the tripartite civil war in Valencia from 1228 onward, or only progressively during the stages of the fifteen-year Christian crusade. They would have had no importance in pre-conquest political geography except as implied elements in the general collapse, and would not have been mentioned by geographers or by chroniclers of larger episodes of that confusion. Following Ibn Khaldūn and especially Muntaner, and aware of the random character of our documentation which implies much parallel loss, I tend to maximize their number; others may incline to reduce their number or dismiss them as few. The actual number of such leaders identified with specific castles at the moment of surrender and transition is less important to the Mudejar situation than their mere existence, both as leadership symbols accepted at the highest level of the conquerors' society and as nuclei of the future string of revolts. In a non-feudal Christian society like Valencia's, they facilitated acceptance and respect by the Christian aristocratic elements during the painful first decades.

CASTLES IN VALENCIA: MORPHOLOGY AND MEANING

The castles involved in Valencia, both just before the crusade and under crusader administration, deserve notice here. Bazzana and Guichard are publishing as a team pioneer explorations in these structures, attempting a typology and collating field-work with post-conquest documentation. Nervous about any Islamic 'feudalism,' their articles stress that the Islamic fortifications were not residences of lords, did not usually collect rents or govern, were by common Islamic polity at most a state-garrisoned entity (only occasionally having a fiscal–administrative role), and in their more numerous rural manifestations a function of the villages themselves, without warder or garrison. The ubiquitous 'castle and town' of post-conquest records conceals various types of reconverted Islamic defenses, including the simple tower-cum-enclosure refuge. These findings carry forward from the syntheses of Lévi-Provençal and others, which describe how al-Andalus had early sprouted great numbers of fortifications for interior control, frontier defense, settlement protection from deep raids, and watchtower function. These ranged from walled city with citadel, to the garrisoned castle complex (qal'a, the Maghribian meaning here divergent from the Eastern), the ordinary castle (ḥiṣn) often on a walled rise or height, which were numerous and could withstand minor sieges, and the tower (burj) with enclosure outside, this last shading off into all manner of refuges. At conquest by Christians, Lévi-Provençal noted, these almost always underwent reorganization to express and contain European socio-political structures. The new investigations stress the conversion of the refuge or defensive work into the residential–jurisdictional purposes of the feudal conquerors. While these painstaking labors, still tentative, are going forward, two cautions need to be put forward, respectively concerning residence and the military significance of Valencian defensive works.[18]

The distinction between Islamic non-residential castle and European residence–castle is sound, especially in the context of excluding an Islamic feudalism. It is important to know, however, that Spain was very slow in following the familiar northern-European pattern by which a Christian lord lived in his castle during the eleventh and following centuries. Except for Catalonia, lords in Aragon and usually elsewhere in Spain lived in houses or farms, and hereditary castles in any case were few. Thus most castles built in the kingdom of Aragon proper in the thirteenth century, according to their recent historian, were 'strictly for defense,' and 'almost none had a residential character.' They were mere 'military constructions without any character of habitability,' into which garrisons were thrust 'in time of war,' though they could be simultaneously symbols of seignorial power. The shift to habitually lived-in castles, ranging 'from castle–palace to seignorial tower' and from luxurious to brutally rude, came essentially in the period 1283–1348.[19] Did Valencia reflect rather the

Catalan model, and to what extent? Or did Aragonese lords dominate castle-holding in the first forty years before the switch began on any scale, and did the Valencian situation alter their traditional ways? Perhaps archeology cannot date the moment of conversion from Islamic to either Catalan-residential or Aragonese non-residential models precisely enough, and documentation may have to be sought.

Sometimes one can see reluctance by Christian settlers to move from a comfortable countryside into the castle; after the 1276 war King Pere had to order his officials to see that 'those designated to reside in the bailey of Biar castle' were to 'transfer immediately and keep their domiciles in the bailey.' We also find King Pere in 1280 warning his officials at Corbera not 'to force Peret de Sobirats to construct a domicile or make residence within the castle of Corbera, since we allowed as a favor that he construct his house and make his residence just as others do outside the wall of the said castle.' In the following year, however, the defense-minded king ordered the settlers of Corbera to 'build houses in the bailey of the castle of Corbera' forthwith, and to 'destroy and tear down all the villages and homes in the vicinity.' The strategic castle of Bocairente either had no lord's residence or none adequate to the king's rare stops there, when in 1274 Jaume gave it 'in fief' to Ximèn Pere d'Orís with permission 'that he could do construction on the said castle, and make any buildings there he might wish for the purpose [for the improvement?] of his dwelling,' so as to afford hospitality to the king 'and his [retinue] whenever he came to the said place.'[20]

In any event, encastellated or ensconced in a house, the arrival of 'feudal'-type landlords and even the centrality given castles by the crusaders meant a traumatic change of socio-economic structures for the local population. A significant factor in assessing castle-management was that King Jaume had the larger number of Valencia's castles in the crown's keeping; he and Pere favored a life-assignment, which in fact as often turned out to be short-term, in naming castellans to these. More striking is that the half-century after the crusade saw an evolution here away from the life or even hereditary castellan-lord of a 'feudal' sort into a mere royal functionary, a short-term administration specialist.[21] Thus the terms of Mudejar transition, where castles come into play, may involve complexities.

A vital element in considering various Islamic fortifications, castles, towers, or refuges, whatever their objective appearance to the modern eye, was King Jaume's experience of them as strategic and tactical obstacles. This had little to do with their small size or ungarrisoned status in peacetime; the smallness of Christian Spanish castles, and their proliferation (thousands in Catalonia alone) can puzzle historians familiar with the northern model. The king's assessment relates rather to his own army's poor logistics, short-term turnout, smash-and-grab-raid mentality, primitive weaponry except where artillery was emplaced, and to the peninsula's adaptation to networks of defenses designed to slow and soften the invader, while major forces held back in reserve or locked themselves into walled towns.

A handful of farmers in a cave-refuge on Majorca island kept the crusading King Jaume at bay despite his raiding party having set twenty of the huts in there afire; the Muslims finally negotiated to surrender if no help came to them within eight days. After the island was effectively conquered, Jaume had to set about 'conquering the mountains and the castles they held'; these inconsiderable fortifications required 'a war lasting all winter into May,' the king's armies able to do 'no great harm' except by starving them into surrender. On the more complex Valencian scene, the knowledgeable Balasc d'Alagó (Blasco de Alagón) warned the king from personal observation that 'forty or fifty' castles there could each hold against 'all your power' so long as their provisions lasted. The contemporary chronicle written in 1243 by Rodrigo Jiménez de Rada, primate of Spain and crusader, tells us that Islamic Valencia surpassed other regions as 'pre-eminent by [its] many fortified places.' Bernat Desclot, contemporary and probably the crown functionary and Valencian office-holder Bernat Escrivà, included all the towers and minor refuges in summing Valencia as 'well-castellated with many strong castles,' specifically 'three hundred castles of stone.' Slyly, Jaume bypassed many defenses to hit Burriana; against all advice, with luck and open sea lanes, he took it by threat of starvation, isolating the inland castles for the same fate while he destroyed their wheat fields.

Three raids he describes prove particularly instructive. He took 130 horse, 700 foot, and 150 commando-type 'almugàvers' down to the Júcar River, the Muslims 'alerting' the farmers all along his route by fire signals disconcertingly 'from all the towers of Valencia' until he retired in disgust with little to show for his trouble. He wisely withdrew from a stronger raid against Cullera castle, since his food supplies could last only five days. Embarrassed, he determined at least to siege one of the main rural towers in the capital's countryside. Estimating eight days for the task, against his skeptical barons, he sent back for artillery, then swept over the outer stockades and pounded the refugees and cattle within the refuge–enclosure at the tower's skirt. Only the stench of the dead, and probably consideration of hygiene, forced the tower to capitulate. Jaume's impressive little army, even with artillery, thus took five days of siege to reduce an inconsequential rural refuge. The fewer than fifteen hundred non-combatants and fighters went into slavery, while the crusaders whooped off to tackle another pitiful tower. Valencia city itself, King Jaume realized, 'has to be conquered by hunger.' Near the end of his crusade, seven hundred Muslims held the small castle of Biar, by then totally isolated and with no hope of help or even a Muslim government in any direction, against Jaume's determined siege for nearly half a year. The military significance even of lesser fortifications must therefore be assessed not only by structural morphology but against the patterns of contemporary warfare.[22]

BORROWED WORDS: ANALOGY, SUBSTANCE, STYLE

One avoids the polarities of continuity and discontinuity, in the matter of feudalism, by focusing on acculturative transformation – from a non-feudal but fragmenting Islamic society into a Mudejar society, enclaved in a non-feudal Christian Valencian society displaying elements of military, estate, and manneristic feudalism. The problem of terminology, style versus substance, remains. The very words carefully explained away in their substance must be introduced again stylistically, if the unknown is to be conveyed to the reader without repeated paraphrase, a clumsy new vocabulary, or an armory of unfamiliar Arabic terms requiring elucidation. The dilemma is compounded when dealing with figures moving from one society into the other, or where analogous poles of transit recommend a single term employed at very different levels of meaning. It is further compounded by the varying precision or cultural baggage involved in addressing an international readership as well as one's own countrymen. Thus the word 'lord' serves admirably in English for the Islamic leader-identified-with-a-castle, because its primary meaning is 'a person having great power and authority' or 'a ruler.'

At the same time its residual or secondary meaning of feudal lord allows its application to the not-really-feudal Christian lords in Valencia and to the legally-'feudal'-but-actually-Mudejar castle holders. The adjectival 'seignorial' and noun 'seignory' for a semi-autonomous emirate, while more compromising, are hard to avoid as collaterals. Spanish Arabists commonly enough employ 'señors' and 'señoríos' in the same way. Purists object that this is necessarily misleading, smuggling historical meanings into a different culture.

Purists would ban the word 'castle,' for example, since European castles were morphologically and socio-culturally very different from the Islamic, a topic taken up just above. 'Castle' has become a generic term in English and some other languages, however, and the scholar would object more to an Islamic *ḥiṣn* being called a 'fort' (shades of the Wild West!), while 'fortification' at least in English fits rather the two extremes of elementary defenses or scientifically prepared elaborations; 'fortresses' is too overwhelming to designate the run of smaller castles in al-Andalus. Again, Arabists, including Spaniards, tend to employ 'castle' generically, distinguishing by a further typology. 'Castellan,' which says 'feudal' to some, is innocently in English the 'warden' or the 'governor' of a castle, neither excluding nor necessitating a feudal regime. In Valencia the figures associated with a castle, either as mini-ruler as at Játiva, state-appointee as in some *huerta* towers, or *de facto* leader of an embattled community by the fortunes of war as at Bairén or Alcalá, go by the title *qāʾid*, a term so generic that context must define it – suitably here as 'castellan.' Purists also shun 'Islamic Spain' and its cognates, their paranoia summoning visions of continuists who make the Muslims there a phenomenon outside the usual context of Islam; they would have us write always 'al-Andalus' and 'Andalusī Muslims.'

Certain words seem too useful to jettison altogether. After careful explanation of the difference between the state-assigned *iqṭāʿ*, and the flat statement that 'an *iqṭāʿ* was not a fief,' it is still difficult to avoid referring to 'the Islamic *iqṭāʿ*' or money-fief' held by a 'beneficiary' or 'fief holder.' The reader must be trusted to remember the context. While similarly explaining that Mudejars never lived in a 'ghetto,' the word still seems proper in another context to convey the general exclusion of Mudejars from the dominant society. More arguable perhaps is the use of 'feudal' itself to express disintegration of a central state into breakaway units. My *Islam* notes how 'in times of chaos central government gave place to both city and semiauton-omous or feudal units, combining or recombining,' and speaks of 'a species of feudal or local lord, responsible to the Valencian ruler only after a tenuous fashion,' as well as of 'feudal or fragmenting periods.' The term can also be used of Islamic parallels and analogies, as in comparing admittedly different elements such as chivalry in each society, but this can be misleading to a reader. Discussing Poliak's 'attempt to isolate general lineaments of an Islamic feudalism' in that direction, I concluded that he 'forces a quite different society into an alien conceptual frame' and that it would be better to confine comparison simply to 'a number of points at which the two societies displayed strong analogies.'

My instinct here is shared by any number of Arabists who trust the reader's common sense and the context supplied. Mohamed Talbi, in his recent brilliant analysis of Tunisian rural society of the ninth century, unabashedly discusses 'lords,' 'the great landlords,' their 'real fiefdoms' of property, and even of 'ranches'; he employs within quotes both "the great 'feudal lords' and 'serfs.'" Ira Lapidus describes the 'local landed aristocracy,' in the Middle East, and how 'landowners become local lords.' A. L. Udovitch talks of 'agricultu-ral fiefs' and the farmers' relation to 'fief holders,' Eliyahu Ashtor of 'feudal lords' and their land 'fiefs,' Bent Hansen of the Mamluk 'feudal system,' and both V. F. Nowshirvani and Nikki Keddie of 'feudalism.' All these authorities reject feudalism, but each stylistic use here seems appropriate in its context.

In his classic rebuttal of feudalism as applying to al-Andalus, Pedro Chalmeta is not bothered by such occasional stylistic recourse to its words, qualifying them with 'to use the feudal terminology' or 'so to call them' or 'quasi-feudalistic.' Jacinto Bosch Vilá similarly qualifies but uses 'the lordships and domains and benefices of land which some authors want to call fiefs (*feudos*).' If not carefully qualified and sparingly used, of course, stylistic borrowing can not only corrupt the substance under discussion but wrongly define the terms of comparison. There is a real difference between ignorantly framing data within a borrowed European feudalism or chivalry, however, and expressing Islamic realities by European words whose meaning is defined as analogical. If we need not eschew the literary relics of a feudal vocabulary, it may be well to restrict them, like a drug with possible side-effects on this or that reader. Such self-denial should extend both to the Islamic and to the Mudejar societies in

Valencia. Greater latitude, but not much, might be extended to descriptions of Valencian crusader society, so long as *its* basic non-feudalism is made painfully clear. Indeed the whole concept of feudalism as a tool for understanding Spain's Christian societies is questionable.[23]

MUDEJAR FARMERS: CONSTRUCTING 'MODELS'

A final confusion must be faced in the 'feudal' or more properly 'seignorial' category: the role of the farmer and the conditions of his landholding. Here again Guichard misunderstands me to predicate a European-type landlord, which he sees as contradicting the 'Asiatic model' of Islam by which free cultivators owned and controlled their own farms, paying taxes to the central state or to *iqtā* stipendiaries. I had early concluded to the prevalence of free farmers, in my *Islam*, from the manner in which crusader surrenders and documents allowed these men to sell, will, or otherwise alienate their farms, and freely to own or buy land anywhere in the kingdom. That this was normally individual and not communal ownership is suggested also by the disputes over the lands of converts; conversion in effect introduced a Christian family into the religio-social Mudejar community, setting up a conflict between individual land-ownership rights and the community's tropism toward exclusivity.

The farmers I found in their hamlet–villages (Catalan *alquerias*) were involved in 'specialization and intense cultivation in huertas and valleys' on 'multiple minifarms.'[24] John Boswell, in his book on the fourteenth-century Mudejars, catches my meaning well: 'as Burns points out, during the thirteenth century free Muslim farmers lived under conditions generally similar to those they had known,' except for the intrusion of a Christian overlord or ambiguously feudal lord; 'and the maintenance of a prosperous class of free farmers was still possible.' Under the strong fourteenth-century government, Boswell continues, 'the untidy remnants of the "free" Mudejar population were swept aside into one category or another of feudal servitude.' I had found this freedom remaining even under crusader landlords, despite the traumatic change of status which made them now tenants upon land owned by someone else; 'theoretically all land was held by Christian owners though served by Muslim tenants or sharecroppers (*exarici*); in practice Mudejars were masters of their own properties, their rents assuming the nature of taxes.'[25]

39

Within this framework two problems had to be faced. First, it tells nothing of the precise relationship between the immediately post-conquest Mudejar and the Christian who owned the land – as king, 'feudal' grantee, city, or individual (even a Muslim at times) in alod. Secondly, a simple population of free cultivators, whatever the Asiatic model desired in theory, was not characteristic of al-Andalus. The *sharīk* or sharecropper who contracted with a free proprietor, to work his land for an agreed number of years in return for a share of the harvest (on occasion as high as a half) after shared taxes, was also very common. Glick believes 'that sharecropping was the universal form of agrarian exploitation in Islamic Spain.' It seemed reasonable that an agricultural cornucopia like Valencia, with its cosmopolitan mercantile society, would have elicited over the centuries the speculative money such expanding commercial-farming regions attract, and that resultant sharecropping must have been prominent. How could I resolve the dilemma of my free-farmers norm in a region where I had expected widespread share-cropping? Perhaps the demands of irrigation-intense cultivation may have modified the conditions of sharecropping contracts here? The irrigated plains (*huertas*) of Valencia required denser concentrations of cultivators, permanently resident near the farms and special-ized in irrigation skills. A *sharīk* contract to meet such irrigation conditions was the *musāqāt*; some further evolution in its Valencian form might be presumed.[26]

The word *exaricus* in Latin records seems to define the basic model of land tenure in the many past conquests by Christians of Aragon and elsewhere. Could it not supply a clue? Here etymology can mislead. The Latin term covered both the free proprietor and the *sharīk* in Ramon Martí's thirteenth-century Arabic–Latin wordlist. Thus its universal presence may testify only that the *sharīk* system was the most prevalent; the virtual absence of that Latin term, in the sparse documentation for early Valencia pertinent to agriculture, may conversely hold no implication one way or the other. With no documentary resources to reveal the Valencian farmer or to advance us toward a solution, I suggested that the remarkable complexity of Valencia's water communities had elevated the *sharīk* there into holding permanent contract, a usufruct, designed to retain his skil-led and profitable presence. This would have made him in effect 'a free farmer capable of selling his property even though it was en-globed in the larger economic unit of his landlord and burdened with [annual share-]rents and taxes.' This 'landlord' was the normal free proprietor, such as commonly contracted with his *sharīk* elsewhere in al-Andalus; the 'overlord' would be the *de facto* government or its *iqṭāʿ* stipendiary. There was never any question of European-type landlords receiving either kind of rental-taxes a cultivator paid.

Further clues might come from the already established Mudejar *exarici* in pre-crusade Aragon. Exemplars ran the gamut from wealthy proprietors to humble tenants. This, and the double meaning of *exaricus*, led me to propose in my second book that: 'beyond its base meaning or common usage, [Mudejar] *exaricus* constituted a relative or analogous concept, embodying a proportional rather than a univocal meaning.' When not confined to its original prime analogue, it meant any Mudejar with rural properties, from grand lord to humble sharecropper. This situation seemed a plausible model, if one had to be invented in the near total lack of documentation. It seems plausible to others too. Glick sees the Valencian *exaricus* as holding 'the same status under the Christians as under Islamic rule: he was a contract tenant with real, but limited ownership rights'; with a perpetual set of taxes and shares, he was 'a free man and could alienate a parcel held under such a contract at will.'

As for the excessively obscure and atypical rural history of pre-Islamic Valencia, Miquel Tarradell finds only 'one incontrovertible fact' from archeological and other evidence: the mode of production was not latifundist but by small or medium farms or farm-centers, the cultivators or laborers being free rather than slave, with pre-Roman elements prominent. The Roman villa was rare enough, it is now thought. With the coming of Islam, cultural transformation would have substituted an entirely different set of human relations and structural organization on such farm units, while Berber and other immigrating populations further transformed and expanded the rural scene. The underlying antecedents and patterns, what Glick calls 'the classical inheritance' in his Islamic Valencian irrigation researches, must never be confused of course, with the 'continuity' bugbear of discontinuists.

My second book did not explore the mode-of-production situation much further, merely presenting the *exaricus* as a free farmer with residual obligations to his associate, or as a Mudejar to his landlord. Since this question is one of the least well documented for Islamic Spain, and since the book as a whole entered 'an untilled field' which might be expected to yield clues, a review article by Pedro Chalmeta regretted that this second book, 'awaited with impatience,' contributed nothing on that incidental or parenthetical score. "The question of a 'mode of production' is sidestepped, and it is not specified whether that Mudejar society is to be included within a 'seignorial,' an 'Asiatic,' or an 'Islamic' mode of production." In response it might be noted that tax revenues paid to the state under Islam, and to the king or 'feudal' lord as a Mudejar, are by their nature unlikely to clarify the inner or *sharīk* arrangements, and that our records are more abundantly regalian than seignorial. Still, I share Chalmeta's regret and hope that future research into ecclesiastical or other estates can clarify this issue. Chalmeta also remarked that the random tax information, though abundant for any given tax, did not form a coherent system, including totals. He concluded his generous review article, after the manner of the genre, with those reservations, confessing that they affected him with 'a certain disappointment.' Guichard has cited and generalized this expression, very differently meant, as though it supported his own misconception that my books and articles propose an Islamic Valencia run along the European fashion.[27]

My free-farmer model with *sharīk* obligations is a compromise. Perhaps it is still serviceable. After further reflection, however, I shall now propose an alternative and perhaps more satisfactory reconstruction. The Mudejar surrender constitutions for the kingdom, our basic evidence, may well have adverted in their landholding references to the free proprietor and to the free proprietor alone, whether large or small, rich or poor. In this interpretation the *sharīk* stratum, however numerous, fell into the category of internal affairs of the given *aljama*, along with all the multifarious private contracts forming part of *aljama* life. In a traditional *sharīk* situation, taxes came directly from the gross, and the harvest share-portions were then private income for both associate sharers. Things had been different from the start around Valencia city and in the Castellón region around Burriana. Radical surrender there, with mass expulsion of the city-dwellers, had wiped out in the countryside the kind of title to sell and alienate retained elsewhere. The capitulation at Valencia city therefore instructed the Mudejar cultivators of that district to 'make arrangements with the landlords (*componant cum dominis*) who shall hold the farms (*hereditates*).' These are formerly free proprietors, wholly dispossessed, entering upon a tenant relationship on the European model, doubtless classed with the masses of *exarici* in the crusaders' homelands. That is why the very different mode-of-production charter at Eslida lets the free farmer there keep title to his lands at Eslida and anywhere else in the whole kingdom *except* at Valencia city's district and Burriana's. It also helps explain why Muslim cultivators disappeared sooner from those two great *huertas* later on, and not at Játiva.

At Eslida, the more typical free-farmer arrangement with the crusaders included as well an intriguing provision: 'Saracens who want to contract (*contrahere*) outside their town can do so without fee or impediment by the (king's) castellan'; is this a glimpse of the *sharīk* mode, or simply laborers at hire, or generically both of these private modes? The new kingdom's *Furs* or law code makes general provision for a class of permanent as well as more transient contract tenants, present and future, by private arrangement: 'any person of the city or kingdom can install (*mittere*) Saracen cultivators (*laboratores*) to cultivate on his farms (*hereditates*) for a specified time or in perpetuity.' In the seignorial charter of Chivert's Mudejars in 1234, they were free of 'rent or tribute,' perhaps indicating that the Templars as landlords there would receive the classic agricultural taxes of Islam and no tenant or sharecrop rent besides.

In this more complex rural scene, the free farmers at Valencia city and Burriana had become mere tenants, while the surrender-on-terms majority in the kingdom continued as free farmers to pay no rent beyond their usual Islamic state taxes (the agricultural taxes going to king, lord, or landlord according to the nature of the king's respective grants). The *sharīk* tenant as well as the hired laborer functioned as before but privately. Would the true *sharīk*, not mentioned in the surrender constitutions, have been common or even dominant in numbers? The constitutions show that Mudejars of any one area owned land elsewhere in the kingdom, presumably farmed by sharers. The ubiquitous mosques in Valencia kept their supporting revenues (the *waqf*) routinely guaranteed; would they have given the farm properties out at fixed rent to concessionaires, who in turn then arranged *sharīk*-type contracts for actual cultivators, as Lévi-Provençal found at Cordova and elsewhere? Arié found that the Granadan state property, and the sultan's extensive private lands, were worked by the *sharīk* model. And surely the extensive lands received as dowry at Murviedo in 1297 by the bride Maryam bint 'Alī b. Madyān, in our only early such contract in Arabic for Valencia, did not expect her husband Yūsuf b. Yaḥyā to work all the

43

'farms, vineyards, fields, and olive groves' on both banks of the Palancia River which are described there. Boswell found wealthy commercial and aristocratic strata perduring in Valencian Mudejarism even late in the fourteenth century, with servants, slaves, estates left in wills, money invested, and properties owned and rented, as well as 'a prosperous middle class': surely such people, more numerous in pre-crusade and early Mudejar Valencia, would have amassed land as investment-proprietors. Indeed, Ibn Khaldūn notes that the Muslims of Spain 'of all civilized people are the ones most devoted to agriculture; it rarely happens among them that a man in authority or an ordinary person has no tract of land or field or does not do some farming.' Ibn Khaldūn, though speaking directly of Granada, is contrasting countries in a general way. Such universal farm-ownership suggests the *sharīk* as the only practical expedient for much of the cultivation.

The mix in Islamic Valencia on the eve of the crusade would seem to have been not a nearly universal 'Asian' model of free cultivators but a complexity of farmer proprietors, absentee free proprietors, fairly permanent *sharīk* populations, a less rooted *sharīk* population, some hired labor of a transient sort, and almost surely some slaves in agriculture, now that Boswell has corrected Verlinden on even Mudejars often owning slaves. The sharecropper phenomenon was probably widespread. And above this scene one assumes the ubiquitous *iqṭāʿ* pseudo-proprietor. As a Mudejar, the free proprietor would pay the usual state taxes to king or lord, but the pressure of Aragonese and Catalan homeland customs would inexorably treat him as a tenant paying rent, reducing him eventually everywhere to the servile status Boswell finds in the fourteenth century. The *sharīk* would have paid no rent except to his associate, and may have continued undocumented as he too assimilated to a class of tenant. The Valencian and Burriana districts would convert to tenant-operated status from the fall of their respective cities. Trauma and production 'discontinuity' would thus be more severe in the Valencia city and Burriana *huertas*, which should not be generalized.

In all this complexity, what happens to the 'Asiatic model' and its simpler free peasants, where large private farms are a marginal intrusion? That aprioristic construct is of little use here. Nikki Keddie puts it well, in discarding both the 'feudal' and the Asiatic models as tools for analyzing Islamic rural society: 'sweeping and unhelpful is the concept of the Asiatic mode of production, applicable from China to Egypt,' including 'the autarchy of the village community.' The Asian model assumes 'that there is more like than unlike between, say, China and the Middle East; but this assumption is usually based not on a study of presumed likeness, but rather on the fact that neither [area] developed capitalism, with Western Europe implicitly taken as a norm.' She notes: 'it is not any correspondence to a general model of oriental society that is [the] characteristic of the Middle East.' The concept and terminology of an 'Asiatic model' impedes clear analysis of our data and ought to be retired. It would be more helpful to seek analogies from al-Andalus and the Maghrib in general, selecting places and periods marked by an especially prosperous urban—commercial framework and by irrigation resources. Each such area had its own peculiar evolution, of course, but is more likely to suggest clues for understanding thirteenth-century Valencia.

Mohamed Talbi has analyzed the agricultural modes of Islamic Tunisia in the prosperous centuries of widespread commercial farming before the disasters of the eleventh century wrecked its irrigation system, emptied many of its farms, and precipitated an ailing agricultural—urban economy into a 'largely pastoral' economy with consequent social restructurization – its permanent structure from then on. He found in those earlier centuries no Asiatic model but a bewildering complexity: 'enormous diversity,' 'very heterogeneous,' a 'mosaic' of patterns and holdings. 'Particularly striking is the extreme inequality which characterizes' that agricultural scene, large and medium estates bordering wretched little parcels. Only the tiny subsistence farms had free cultivators, the medium and large farms depending largely on slaves and on the few indigent seasonal laborers. Slaves were abundant in the Maghrib then, and their agricultural role here in Ifrīqiya 'was of capital importance,' even 'modest farms' and single cultivators using them. Sharecropping was common, with half-shares the norm. Communally owned family estates were also in evidence, each apparently under the direction of a respected family leader, where the individual could alienate his share or parcel under condominium-like restrictions. All these persistent patterns dictated great diversity in the farmers' lifestyles: the more prosperous divided their time between town and countryside, often merely supervising by occasional visits to the farm or through stewards.

Disturbances in international trade, price rises, political upheav-

45

als, constant immigration, the Muslims' preference for putting into cultivation new lands unencumbered by claims, and all the market forces of an advanced society affected the evolution of such a scene, within its constant patterns. Udovitch has noted that 'one of the major unanswered questions' of Maghribian and Middle Eastern history is that of land tenure and rural society, with even such preliminary concepts as 'ownership' and the nature of control needed to define it coming under debate. Putting aside the aprioristic Asian model and pseudo-feudalism, anticipating the complexity found in comparable Islamic societies, trying not to outrun the exiguous Valencian data, and prepared to jettison any resultant model for a more satisfactory variant or substitute, we can make cautious progress toward some future consensus, or at least contribute small insights and data toward that end.[28]

Can there be other models? Two original hypotheses are currently being advanced, for the rural zones of Valencia and Majorca, proceeding from toponymy, particularly from the place-names in the respective *Repartiments*, with allied crown documentation. Guichard's structure includes both free farmers in their small communities and free proprietors of an estate or farm with hired farmers (*colons*). Place-names indicate that settlement in rural Valencia after the Islamic conquest was characterized by both Berber tribal and 'clan-like' families (*clanique*), gathered in the *qarya*-type village of independent farmers. At the margin of such a village with its lands, 'private landed domains' arose (*domaines fonciers privés*) with hired help and were probably walled, something like the *ḍayʿa so common* elsewhere in Islamic Spain. Such a farm–estate virtually always went under the designation *raḥl*. For Valencia his distinction is absolute: free-farmer community in a *qarya* versus private domain as a *raḥl*. He concludes that 'the larger part' of rural farming was done by that free-villager model, with the 'domains' both fewer and smaller. The *raḥl* was also common in town suburbs. Its propername titles suggest passage from owner to owner as the norm, rather than inheritances long held by a family lineage; the village thus contrasted strongly with the estate in respect to permanence of owners. To assess the size of the dominant *qarya*-type, he moves into the fourteenth century, whose ampler Mudejar data reveal a characteristic hamlet of only 'some tens of houses, and at times less than ten,' in association with a village area of cultivated and uncultivated land ranging from less than 250 acres to over 1,000; in the pre-conquest era he reckons they must have been even smaller and more numerous. (This leap to the fourteenth century is troubling, since Boswell has found that the Mudejar population fell drastically after the early part of that century, less as a function of general population decline, lack of prosperity, war damage, or the Black Death than from massive emigration.)

Though toponyms in themselves cannot reveal the evolution or nature of a contract-farmer stratum, Guichard does find in Ibn 'Idhārī a late-eleventh-century movement by which some villages lost their farms when the owners could not meet burdensome new taxes, so that the formerly free cultivators had to continue on the appropriated lands as hired farmers (*colons*) of state or proprietor. This process, by which a *qarya* takes on the nature of a *raḥl*, he is reluctant to generalize. Because the word *exaricus* is rarely found in Valencian early Mudejar documentation, he believes *sharīk*-contracts to have been relatively few. This may be a weak point in the thesis. As we have seen, Latin *exaricus* as ambiguously both free farmer and *sharīk* helps little in reconstructing rural Valencia, while Christian authorities may well have treated only with owners in the laws and public documentation, leaving the private contract of the Mudejar sharecropper to the inner life of variegated socio-economic contracts within each *aljama* and to the private arrangements of Christian landlords with their wholly-hired tenants.

This entire model rests upon continuance of the original settlement system adumbrated in Valencian place-names. Is it plausible that this perdured through all the Islamic centuries of evolution and expansion in this region? Guichard argues in the affirmative, by analogy with some Maghribian village models; he 'infers' survival of the clanic social organization by that analogy, down to the eve of the crusade, resistant to proprietorial expansion into direct ownership, resulting in a 'system' of rural villages more or less homogeneous in structure. Toponymy, as Ibn Khaldūn thought, may be a deceptive guide to continuance over the centuries; and Valencia was not a backland. Given our barren desert of data, however, this can make a consistent model. Final judgement depends on whether the context of the Valencian region's development allows the parallel, which seems more persuasive if focus is kept on toponymy and on the hamlet alone without the enveloping urban structures. Meanwhile Míkel de Epalza and J. M. Rubiera Mata are challenging Guichard's entire approach, with its Berber emphasis and its toponymic conclusions, as an 'anachronism'. In detailed toponymic analysis, Rubiera dismisses his 'false' Berber names and wide Berber presence as a 'simple' misunderstanding of philology.[29]

Angel Poveda Sánchez has been following the same line of toponymical researches for neighboring Majorca. Though the region is less complicated to study than Valencia, the existence of a crusader *Repartiment* or land-division book in Arabic as well as in Latin allows for deeper penetration of place-name data. Poveda's analysis concludes to a hamlet or *qarya* of free farmers as the dominant model of rural exploitation, with the larger *qarya* the basic unit. In some areas a powerful tribal group came into the *iqṭāʿ* tax concession, lending the farming units there a fiscal role for central administration. The other form of cultivation-organization, the *raḥl*, Poveda sees as a single non-village farm unit, averaging a little over half the size of the *qarya* and relatively rarer. The crusaders saw little difference between the two, and confusingly substituted either word in the Latin equivalent; they frequently used *aldea* (the *ḍayʿa*) as well, but the Arabic has it only once. Rural organization must have been by 'political' instead of 'private' family. The crusaders privatized this landholding by intruding European landlords with dominion over land and people, a traumatic evolution for the rural structure.

King Jaume himself has left us a description of his view over the villages of one of the kingdom's great zones of irrigation, at then-Islamic Játiva. 'I saw the most beautiful *horta* [irrigated countryside] that I ever saw at town or at castle: there were more than two hundred flat-roofed dwellings (*algorfes*) throughout the *horta*, the most beautiful a man could find, and villages (*alqueries*) about the *horta* numerous and close together (*moltes e espesses*), and I saw the castle as well, so noble and beautiful, and so beautiful a *horta*; and from this I had great joy and happiness in my heart.' Ibn al-Khaṭīb describes the 140 *qarya*-type villages around Granada as similarly crowded.[30]

An extraordinary penetration into Islamic and Mudejar Valencia's agriculture is Thomas Glick's extensive book on the region's irrigation techniques and the villages considered as a cooperative water community. Glick distinguishes the imported Syrian system for fairly distributing water as against its Yemenite rival, with implications as to early settlement where either is encountered. Though 'dry' and 'watered' land are common designations respectively for the dry-farming and irrigation-farming regions or zones in

Valencia, the terms take on special meaning within the irrigation-farming zones, whether spring or river fed. The 'watered' parts in this inner context meant, not a distinction of soil, but parcels with customary right to a share of the common water. Where the Syrian system prevailed, this was measured proportionally and inhered inalienably in each parcel. Where the Yemenite method prevailed, characteristically in oasis-like or spring *huertas*, the water was measured by time-units, and the right to a water-share could be sold or alienated separately from the land parcel. In both systems the Valencian farmer received mixed irrigated and dry-farming parcels, both within a basic 'watered' zone.

Glick also reveals the overarching bonds uniting the disparate villages to a discipline which, in its very small way, evokes the Egyptian Muslim's servitude to the Nile. The crusaders absorbed the techniques, administrative patterns, water-community union, some of the judicial arrangements, and the physical bounds or limits of each water-resource area in Valencia. This has nothing to do with the fantasy of 'continuity' in the ideological sense, but is nevertheless a massive example of cultural transmission. The tragedy of the Muslim in this rural context was only partly due to the intrusion of a European-model landlord. A more terrible fate was in store. Within a hundred years of the conquest, Christian settlement would have pushed the Muslims out of this paradise into the non-irrigated or dry-farming zones. From mid-fourteenth century, Glick can find no Muslims in Valencia city's celebrated *huerta*; only Gandía, Játiva, and Elche among important irrigated zones mustered 'significant numbers,' and the latter two places only in a few suburban settlements. For Castellón, virtually no Muslims kept their irrigated parcels except at marginal Canet. Some 'secondary centers' of watered land kept 'substantial numbers,' as at Benaguasil or Vall de Uxó, as did numerous 'relatively unimportant villages and hamlets.' Glick's findings tie in with my distinction between the mode of production set up by the crusaders at Valencia city and Burriana (Castellón) after radical surrender, and the normal mode elsewhere of free farmers paying taxes as rents to crown or grantee with actual cultivation a mixture of proprietor and *sharīk* models. Many Mudejars of the late fourteenth and fifteenth century must have envied their fathers of our post-conquest generation, before that great trek began into arid, dry-farming exile.[31]

All societies progress by acculturation and recrystallization. The process is not damaging except in extreme cases where loss of too many boundary-maintaining mechanisms spells assimilation from one culture into the other. Even then, as Boswell argues, assimilation to the conquering colonial society *can* be regarded as an ultimate good, a Darwinian variation. Generally a culture adapts each alien element, transmuting it to conform to some proper element of its own or giving it a transformative setting. Before 1000 the Spanish interchange flowed more strongly from Islam to underdeveloped Europe. In Valencia now, with Islam in recoil and distress, facing a society technologically advanced and psychologically aggressive, the process flowed the other way and with destructive results. That the interchange took place between two exclusivist societies of high culture, each an integral part of a larger world culture, kept the erosion from being overwhelming. The very mass of Muslims here contributed to the same effect. Pre-crusade Islamic structures collapsed, and the elements that remained were distorted and disconnected. The Muslims proved strong enough, in language, religion, and myriad lesser elements, however, to receive the impact without succumbing and yielding the community's innermost identity. They crystallized into a new society, the Mudejar, stronger in its first half-century than later, but stubbornly resilient even through the fourteenth-century woes, as Boswell's detailed researches reveal.

During the immediately post-crusade decades, much of daily life went on for Valencian Muslims after the crusade more or less as before, despite the disappearance of native governance, the intrusion of Western landlords, the progressive dismantling of Islamic structure, and the drastic diminution of elite groups. The local *faqīh* rose in importance as the larger figures emigrated, and the local schools achieved an excellence which attracted students from Catalan and Aragonese Mudejar families. Valencia's thirteenth-century Mudejars mounted well-conducted revolts, and they survived a period of pogrom. The very resistance of Christian Valencia to Mudejar art, and its embarrassment over the capital city's 'quasi Moorish' morphology, is a tribute to the strength of the Mudejars here and an index of Christian unease. The Mudejar condition was to grow much worse as the fourteenth century advanced. The roots of this worsening lay in the thirteenth-century Mudejar's condition as despised for his religion, hated by the mobs for his ethnic difference, feared for his potential for revolt, and marginalized in Christian eyes as inferior, irrelevant to public life, as an object of revenue-milking and grudging concessions at best, and of callous harassment and unpunished brutalities at worst.

Was there more conflict in the thirteenth century than mere contact? Each society nourished a posture of public hostility toward the other – expressed in its laws, religion, refusals, exclusive communities, attitudes, and sense of superiority. Still, much of this tropism was conventionalized, even impersonal, freeing individuals occasionally to act humanly across the social boundaries and to share significant psychological elements, values, and mentalities. This element of ritual must qualitatively have affected each side's perception of the other. Ritual expression consecrates societal hostility but also frees the participants from much of the burden of personal hostility. Time and again in the documents, various Muslims and Christians join, share, work, and interact in a reasonably non-conflictive ambience. This was not tolerance. Neither people would have conceded that our modern tolerance was a virtue; neither could have sympathized with our secular–humanistic principles. But it was a *modus vivendi*, an experience not without its human warmth and practical respect for irreconcilable difference. And it provided an effective ground for unremitting cultural interchange.

Surrender constitutions:
the Islamic communities of Eslida and Alfandech

In stubborn rhythm for more than a decade, Islam's Valencian centers had succumbed by the many dozens to the siege armies of crusaders. After the general peace, countercrusades regained some lost ground, only to end with rebels recapitulating the desperate scene of surrender. Isolated, outflanked, each detached center's final collapse makes poignant reading. As enveloping hosts poised uneasily on the plain, a scouting party would enter the enemy town or stronghold, now sullen in defeat, to run up the royal standard. In the jubilant hail which then rang out, King Jaume would dismount, ceremoniously face east where Jerusalem lay, and weeping kiss the ground. From that moment, at geometrically increasing pace, daily life for the local Muslim shifted from an immemorial reality of conflict to the predominant reality of contact. That primal episode of surrender, replicated as in a hall of mirrors, echoing with negotiated arrangements and salvaged autonomies, carried the seeds of all the contact to come.

In receiving the surrender of an Islamic district, the ruler of the realms of Aragon followed a traditional ritual, including concession of a constitution modeled loosely on the Christian settlement charter. Basic liberties and concessions remained the same in each constitution, so that a common or underlying model might today be devised. The charters varied in their negotiable details, however, gave more generous terms where siege circumstances dictated, spelled out items about which local Muslims were sensitive, and ranged in length from allusive summaries to minute lists. Sometimes a charter even identified by name the significant notables of its region.

Out of many dozens of such mini-treaties negotiated during the Valencian conquest from 1232 to 1245, and again during the revolts under both Jaume the Conqueror and his son Pere the Great, a

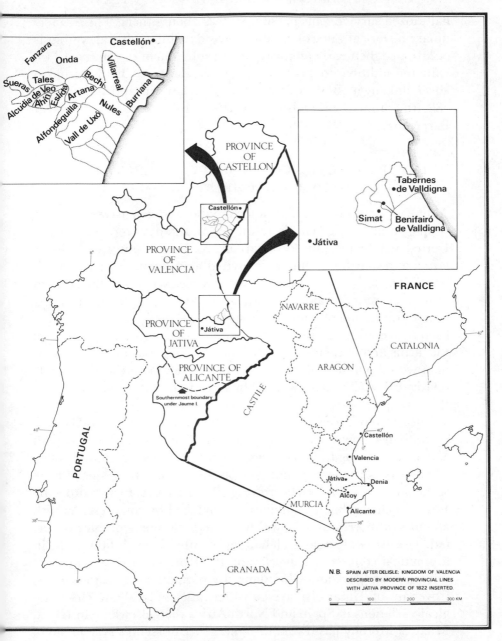

The kingdom of Valencia. Insets: Eslida and Alfandech

53

half-dozen survive, plus passing notices about others. The extraordinary historical value of these few records of intercultural symbiosis occasioned their early publication and subsequent reprintings. Two valuable additions to this corpus, however, languish unedited and in effect unknown. Both are transcribed below (in appendix 2, pp. 288–91), from their registered versions in the royal archives at Barcelona.

THE 'PROTECTED COMMUNITY': ALIENS WITHIN ISLAM AND CHRISTENDOM

Almohad Valencia had been a formidable and extensive region for Jaume to invade, given his resources and limited territorial base. Dotted with some fifty fortifications, and burgeoning with fertile farms and maritime centers, it invited a strategy of surrender-on-terms. The king's crusade, with two notable exceptions, thus turned into an exercise in raiding, feinting, bypassing, blocking, storming minor points, and offering generous terms. Jaume was concerned to keep the conquered Muslims (only much later called Mudejars) on the farms and in their crafts. Revenues of king, baron, and churchman would plummet if the local Muslims left in disaffection, while relatively few Christians were willing to take up the reconstruction of this strange frontier.

Custom reinforced necessity. For over a century Arago-Catalan rulers had followed the same tradition of surrender charters, with Valencia differing from past frontiers mostly in the magnitude of its Muslim population remaining in place. These arrangements have seemed to many simply a borrowing of the *dhimma* status accorded by Islam to alien religious populations englobed by conquest. As with all cultural borrowings, however, something more complex occurred. The *dhimma* system itself had represented an evolution, siting in a practical context and developing the Koran's brief statement of tolerance for Jews and Christians. Its normative expression in the Covenant of 'Umar displayed a wider range of local and chronological variations in Spain and North Africa than elsewhere in Islam. Michael Morony has traced the emergence of Islam's system out of pre-Islamic Iraq's policy toward such unassimilable groups as Nestorian Christians and Jews. From his angle of vision, the arrangement was learned by Islam and represents a revival of Sasanian policy. Taken in a wider view, both Sasanian and early Islamic institutions embody an impulse variously expressed elsewhere in the Mediterranean world.

The stratagem received pre-Islamic expression also in Byzantine provision for Jews, whose communities had a status apart. Joseph Schacht indeed argued that Islam's own *dhimma* application had derived from the Byzantine model. Precedents and parallels can be found also in the necessities of any ancient empire with subject or client groups. In Byzantium the law code of Justinian, destined to be so influential in the medieval West, had adapted the pagan Roman privileges for Jews, setting up a protected community but intimidating it with the severe restrictions to be expected from a religiously unitary host society, much like the later Mudejar status in Spain. The formative period of Spanish Mudejarism was to coincide with a particularly mild expression of this Byzantine condition, from 1000 to 1204, characterized by immigration of many Jews into the empire, multiplication and expansion of their communities, and prosperity as a group integrated yet alien.

King Jaume's friend Pope Innocent IV expressed the political theology underlying this institution, in the West as in Byzantium, when rebuking the 'reprehensible zeal or abominable cruelty' of those doing violence to Jews in the Rhone area: 'the gentleness of the Catholic religion admitted them into living together with us [and] decreed they must be tolerated in their own religious customs.' Scriptural validation came from chapter 11 of Paul to the Romans, in which the community of unconverted Jews remained 'very dear' to God, so that in his good time 'all Israel will be saved,' and was understood as the remnant still faithful to Judaism near the end of time. An Augustinian theology interpreted this tradition, by which God destined Jews for a communal role within medieval Christian society, at once a witness to the Old Testament as prefigurative and a cautionary example of grace refused. Though antisemitism and polemics glossed this ideology, it defined basic relations until either the period of crusader massacres or (as Jeremy Cohen so cogently argues now) until the mendicant friars radically displaced it by their campaigns to convert or destroy rabbinic Judaism from the thirteenth century on. Alongside that older or classic tradition an assimilative parallelism had emerged for Muslims, such as our late version of Alfonso the Learned's laws still reflected, an assimilation not resting upon any scriptural or religious validation as with the Jews.

55

In Western Europe the Mediterranean separatist mentality was reinforced by the long tenure of the barbarian nations as garrisons from the fourth century onward – with their own law, institutions, political structure, and heterodox Christianity which separated them, psychologically and by perception rather than physically, from the late Roman establishment. It was reinforced too by what Goitein calls the 'indifferent' government, where even the strongest Muslim or Christian state concerned itself mainly with supplying justice and security, leaving all its various kinds of communities otherwise to their own devices and initiative. In short, the *dhimma* policy was not uncongenial to the history and psychology of Mediterranean Christendom.

These reflections, which provide background for exploring the dynamic by which Spain borrowed Mudejarism, in no way diminish Islam's distinction in having developed the most comprehensive expression of this enclaving and extruding of an alien guest people: Jews and Christians, as people of the Book, should persist within Islam in their respective societies, aloof and excluded in essential ways, but interacting and to some degree sharing. The Islamic institution, besides being a more universal and intrinsic function of its total society, was more congruent with Islamic Spain's general governance. The political rule which Epalza calls 'eminential' or pre-eminent left its subordinate regions largely autonomous, even under a governor, while each region stayed a similarly 'eminential' distance from its own local components. In that context, Muslims could view even external Christian states of Spain as clumps of politically autonomous *dhimmī* requiring occasional disciplining; conversely, the same rulers could treat acephalous Christian masses as Epalza's 'juridical converts' to Islam who enjoyed their own version of benign neglect. Chapter 10 will touch upon a very different aspect of the problem: that the *dhimma* mechanism, whether in Islamic or Christian hands, and despite kindly intentions by its wielders, was intrinsically a tool of distortion, oppression, and ethnic tragedy.[1]

The ruralized western Mediterranean, which had succeeded vanished Rome, at first hardly needed such sophisticated socio-political devices. As the concept of a Christian Roman empire devolved there into the Christendom of Carolingian and subsequent centuries, assisted by the defining presence of a hostile Islam all across the opposing southern shores, the corollary of religious citizenship became ever more overtly the structured exclusion of Jewish communities. By the time Mudejars entered Spanish kingdoms in serious numbers, in the eleventh century, this experience had at least prepared the way for the ideological concept of Mudejarism. Urbanization of Mediterranean Europe at that precise period, and the traumatic formation of a new Europe in the fanaticism of the Gregorian Reform, made the incipient structuring of a formal Mudejarism urgent. Was the *dhimma* institution imported bodily at this stage? Possibly so, though one must avoid the fallacy of the single origin and the temptation to relate the institutions of separate, interacting cultures in terms of linear causality (as in imprudently deriving crusade from Islamic holy war, or military Orders simply from the Almoravid *ribāṭ*). Supportive causality was certainly at work: the influence of a neighboring model reinterpreted as an expression of one's own values and mechanisms, reinforcing and supplanting the analogous institution. Islamic *dhimma* models in Sicily and in Spain's al-Andalus doubtless influenced the emerging counterparts, first in Norman Sicily and then in Christian Spain, interacting with European perceptions and experiences, and arriving not as alien but as reasonable expressions of domestic attitudes.

The actual tactics, by which the strategy of Mudejarism was first applied on an institutional scale in the realms of Aragon, are a matter of conjecture. Ramón Menéndez Pidal and José Lacarra have argued that Alfonso the Battler, king of upland Aragon proper, finding himself the conqueror of a Muslim population larger than his Christian home-base, simply applied the policies he had observed the Cid using in Valencia, since Alfonso had adventured there briefly as a young man with the Cid in 1097. Antonio Ubieto has added that this contractual form of Christian-over-Muslim administration was peculiarly compatible with the experience of 'pactist' government in Aragon proper. Before these later developments, however, the generous conditions at the fall of Toledo in 1085 undoubtedly served as the prime paradigm (itself already fullblown), not only as the first serious occasion for such a charter but especially because that conquest was hailed with international publicity as a transcendent event. But this origin and spread is rather a matter of mechanics than of substance.

Whether brutally borrowed, or insinuated by progressive meshing with native elements, the *dhimma* model did not merely arrive intact in the realms of Aragon. After the fashion of such cultural interchange it suffered massive restructuring, especially by the instrumentality of Roman Law with its passion for explication, articulation, and universalizing. Roman Law traveled down Mediterranean Spain hand in hand with the Reconquest, culminating in a generalized surge during the thirteenth century. One example of the Law–Reconquest symbiosis, as it affected Mudejarism, was the surrender constitution. Strictly speaking, such a *carta puebla* is thought of as any collective agreement or concession by which political authority established or reorganized an agrarian or village community; it was frequently used from the eleventh century onward as an expedient for settling a frontier. But the concept resists definition, shading off into other categories of grant, exemption, privilege, or incipient code of local law. In his monumental study of the Catalan *cartas pueblas*, J. M. Font Rius grapples with its inherent ambiguities, eccentric evolution, and various models. Limitations of extant materials allow him to advert to the Mudejar *carta* only briefly, without coming to grips with its distinctive nature, though of course he supplies its structural context. Later he published and discussed an unknown Mudejar charter, for Ascó and its region of Catalonia on the Ebro, probably from 1153.

From the surrender of Valencia to the Cid (1094), and the subsequent surrenders of Tudela (1119), Zaragoza (1118), and Tortosa (1148), Mudejar *cartas pueblas* functioned as surrender constitutions, whose teleology was neither settlement nor consolidation of a community but rather the formal disposition of a social group as an extraneous but supportive element within the Christian order. Such a pact established the Moorish community or *aljama* within that larger political framework, settled its mode of administration and its juridical bases, spelled out its privileges and exemptions, and fixed the basic conditions of land tenure, residence, and norms for living. This Mudejar version of a settlement charter created at a stroke an objective law which incorporated the usual structures of Islam and related them formally to the Christian structures.

Humanistic legalism, creative in myriad other circumstances over Europe in this age of the renaissance of academic law, thus reshaped the *dhimma* model and its antecedent or corollary Christian analogues. The European institution was less stable in character and tenure than Islam's model, and thus less a guarantee of basic tolerance; the Christian model rested not upon revelation but merely on a human situation that would assume new contexts and would continue to evolve in unforeseeable directions. But the humanistic novelty this new model posed, as the product of a community's rational manipulation of experience rather than as application or acceptance of a religious structure, marks it off from its *dhimma* antecedents, as an advance in dealing with large minorities. It is important to realize that this structure for handling the infidel within would not remain static. Legal scholars, after the fashion of that adventurous breed, were forever tinkering with the component concepts, and particularly in the thirteenth and following centuries. The thirteenth was a turning point in this reshaping of attitudes, partly because the great research canonist and friend of King Jaume, Pope Innocent IV (1243–54), reoriented legal thinking about relations with non-Christian societies, and partly because the stunning success of Spain's crusades in that century drew Europe's attention to the Mudejar predicament. Canonists like Hostiensis and Oldratus de Ponte affirmed that Christians could not expel such communities without offending charity, and that these guest-communities had a right to administrative autonomy and freedom from conversion by force; on the other hand, the lawyers feared these bodies of aliens inside the gates and they contrived principles by which to erode their integrity. From the Muslims' side meanwhile, as Epalza notes, each component community was able to cohere in 'an original Islamic structure,' the local *aljama*, an institution remarkably tough and more than equal to the basic challenge of community survival over the coming centuries.[2]

In Mediterranean Spain the application of traditional Mudejar surrender constitutions reached its pre-eminent expression in the kingdom of Valencia, where the Mudejar model functioned on an unprecedented scale. An experience so quantified becomes different qualitatively; and the masses of conquered supply an inert resistance to acculturation. Both legal evolution and demographic weight thus made Valencia's Mudejarism unique. This situation also occasioned revolts in the late 1240s, 1250s, 1260s, and 1270s. Bitter fighting over several years eventually rewon the lost territory of the final great revolt of 1276; King Jaume had died on the war-torn Valencian frontier meanwhile, leaving his heir Pere to sustain the struggle. The two charters transcribed and examined on pp. 288–91 come from this final revolt. Together they increase our store of published Mudejar *cartas pueblas* for thirteenth-century Valencia by an additional forty percent.

Besides this valuable service, each charter offers its particular interest. The Eslida charter of 27 June 1276 is from the last frantic months of battle leading up to the aging crusader king's death. It marks a repetition of Eslida's original surrender to King Jaume thirty-five years earlier. Eslida is thus the only Valencian stronghold for which double surrender-documentation survives, lending the 1276 charter unique importance. The Alfandech document is something quite different. It comes to us in a roundabout way: through the archives of the conqueror's grandson, King Jaume II, at the very last years of the century. Our surviving version incorporates the contents of an earlier surrender conceded by King Pere during the 1276 revolt, just after the death of Jaume the Conqueror. The occasion for this renewal by Jaume II was pacific enough. Alfandech Valley was coming under monastic ownership, and tenants were prudently clarifying their privileges before the new broom could sweep any away. Like the Eslida document, Alfandech's charter follows the form and content of crusade surrenders. It provides important information about the district and its Islamic community in 1276. And it offers sidelights about chancery and archival proceedings in the thirteenth century. To increase the percentage of available surrender constitutions, and to afford comparisons, I have also transcribed (pp. 291–2) three new charters and added them to appendix 2. These too were drawn up by Pere, as repeating his crusader father's original concessions. They went respectively to Cuart de les Valles, Seta, and a group of twelve mountain districts which formed the heartland of that same revolt. The intervention of the Jew Samuel 'the alfaquim,' in drafting the most detailed of these three, suggests that the king's Arabic secretary was paraphrasing Jaume's Arabic original.

MUDEJAR ESLIDA IN WAR AND PEACE

Eslida, a hilltop castle protecting a clustered town, dominates a valley of the Sierra de Espadán in northern Valencia. Its previous surrender arrangements had involved other towns with their villages. For generations to come, the region would remain a military problem, a refuge for Muslim malcontents and brigands, as well as a potential focus for revolt; an ultimate Valencian revolt of 1526 centered here. Eslida's sparse soil supported a modest production of olives, grapes, and cereals. For a generation after the conquest no

Eslida with the ruins of its castle. The view evokes the rugged small-mountain country of the Sierra de Espadán; note terracing and cultivated fields. Compare with map (p. 53). (Cavanilles, *Observaciones sobre el reyno de Valencia*, 1795)

parish priest was needed, since 'none live there but Saracens, nor are there Christians except for the castellan and some saloon-keepers selling wine' (an occupation Muslims frequently relegated to such outsiders).

Eslida had first fallen to King Jaume in or probably before May 1242, some three years before the close of the crusade. Current contentions that it simply passed into the Christian camp as an ally seem to rest upon a double misapprehension. Some assume that the Eslidans had thrown in with the ex-sultan Abū Zayd as he fell back upon their Segorbe Valley region just before the crusade, and that they remained faithful even after Abū Zayd apostatized to Christianity. Another assumption buttresses the first: since Eslida's privileges were generous, it must have been friendly to the crusade. The record of a lawsuit between Eslida and neighboring Vall de Uxó rectifies the first error. On the vigil of the crusade Eslida had indeed 'revolted against' the Valencian usurper Zayyān (possibly in support of Abū Zayd, or possibly for the more general hero Ibn Hūd of Murcia), and as punishment had lost control of the Uxó irrigation system. But

Eslida soon made timely peace with Zayyān, regaining the water jurisdiction. Much later the conqueror Jaume had to resolve the resultant lawsuit between Eslida and Uxó; his summation carries no hint of (Eslidan) support for Abū Zayd or for the crusade, but expressly states that the district after its 'revolt' returned to Zayyān. Nor do the apparently generous concessions prove anything: they are the standard provisions of Mudejar charters. Even after Eslida's treason and major revolt in 1276 King Pere would restore such privileges to Eslida, Alfandech, and the rebels generally.[3]

Garrisoned by Jaume's crusaders, the Eslida Valley slipped quietly from the public record, with only a stray notice of an administrative or revenue sort. Its economic status was not commensurate with its military importance. An Islamic enclave in the mountain hinterland, it carried on its immemorial daily round. The crown assigned its taxes to pay crown debts to the Templars and to barons like Guillem d'Anglesola or Galcerà de Montcada; it soon removed custody of the castle from the series of appointees and creditors to the more permanent overlordship of Jaume's commoner wife Teresa Gil de Vidaure and their son Jaume de Jérica. Eslida perhaps held aloof from the revolt which agitated its area less than five years after the surrender, only to become embroiled in the final revolt against Jaume. On 27 June 1276 Prince Pere acting for his father granted Eslida a surrender charter replacing that of 1242.[4]

A problem of chronology intrudes here. The Conqueror died on 27 July 1276 at Valencia city, with Prince Pere in attendance. A month earlier Pere had been conducting the war from Játiva in the south, where as 'prince' he had issued our present agreement for Eslida in the kingdom's more northerly part. Yet as late as 29 December Pere, now 'king' and at Daroca in Aragon for a great rallying of military force to retake Valencia kingdom, was authorizing a Templar commander, Pere Peyronet, 'to negotiate and act toward concluding agreements and treaties with the Muslim castle-wardens (alcaydi) and sheiks (veteres) of the aljamas of the Saracens of Eslida and of other places of the Sierra de Eslida.' How could the crown be negotiating treaties signed solemnly a full half-year earlier according to our document? Worse yet, the itinerary compiled for Pere by Soldevila puts the king at 'the siege of Eslida' on 23 March 1277, still fighting almost a year after our surrender.

The vagaries of the incarnational and nativity calendars, normally the villain in such confusions, cannot be involved here. Pere was at

Játiva in 1276 on the date of our Eslida treaty, for example, but not at Játiva on that day in 1277 to sign a treaty late enough to account for the Templar's negotiations and Pere's siege of 1277; in any case, a summer date is not ambiguous in the incarnational calendar system. Nor does calendar confusion affect the document authorizing the Templar to make peace; even if it did, this would only increase the difficulty, advancing the negotiations to 1277, still longer after our treaty. The date lines in the king's register, tracking Pere at Artana and the siege of Eslida, do allow some ambiguity technically, but not for long; these '1276' dates in place of '1277' dates deal with Pere as king and necessarily refer to 1277.

Soldevila, the only historian to have adverted to this surrender to Pere, and indeed the only one to have studied seriously the 1276 revolt, did not take our document into consideration; he therefore assumed that the Templar's peace negotiations had succeeded in the weeks following his commission of 29 December 1276, that the Eslidans broke faith within a month or two, and that King Pere opened a siege in March 1277 to retaliate. The scenario, unlikely in itself, falls apart when confronted with our much earlier treaty of June 1276. What did happen? Probably Eslida (but not its Sierra de Espadán neighbors) carried negotiations wholly or nearly to conclusion in June 1276, but swung again into the hostile camp at the death of King Jaume a month later. This would have necessitated Pere's siege and second pacification. With the main war still ahead of him in southern Valencia, and the Eslida region a threat to his supply lines, King Pere would have been disposed to close the Eslida hostilities by simply confirming in March 1277 the terms and very contract negotiated the year before.[5]

King Pere's concessions in the 1276 surrender agreement granted amnesty from any imposition or charge which might be brought 'because you were in the war against us.' It guaranteed the houses, farms, possessions, and right of perpetual tenure to each Muslim owner. Absentees, presumably those who had fled or had joined enemy forces, could return without onus, recovering their properties with full rights. Those who preferred to emigrate were free to do so, and could sell their properties to other Eslida Moors (a restrictive clause protecting the *aljama* from Christian settlers intruding). Rents and taxes came basically to Islam's classic tenth on crops raised for sale, plus maintenance of the defensive walls and a yearly lump sum of 400 besants; the besants were to exchange at the rate of $3\frac{1}{2}$

63

Valencian sous, yielding a total of 1,400 sous. The tax tenth fell on cereals, oil, and produce, excluding vegetables and fruit consumed at home. Bathing establishments and public bakeries were to function according to local Islamic custom. Past taxes and rents, bound to have accumulated during the rebellion years, were waived. Even allowing for the further small fee a Muslim paid in his own *aljama*, and for the poll-tax besant (unless, as is probable, the lump sum included that), the tax schedule compares well with those of contemporary Christian charters in Mediterranean Spain.

The usual establishment of religion was programed. Eslida's Muslims kept their 'Law' intact. Specifically guaranteed were 'prayers in the mosque,' schooling 'your children in your Koran and your other books,' drafting 'your documents of marriage, sales, and all other contracts' through the *qāḍī* and *qāʾid*, and operating the *waqf* or accumulated funding which supported religion. Wills, a particularly complicated proceeding, fell expressly under Islamic Law. In their life style, business, and religion the Eslidans were put under the crown *guidaticum*, a form of insured protection functioning at that time with reasonable effectiveness. Political notes hardly intrude, except that Eslidans were to choose an *amīn* from among themselves. The *amīn* in the Valencian Mudejar context was the finance officer designated as go-between for Christian overlord and Muslims (in fact their *ṣāḥib al-sūq* or community economic–commercial inspector), a position pregnant with future influence in *aljama* councils; to allow control over his election was a significant concession. Finally, the towns and small districts of Ahín, Beat, Guairaga, and Lloret were to follow the Islamic customs of Eslida, as subordinate parts of its regional unity. Ahín, with its own little 'castle' or refuge, had figured in Eslida's first surrender, as had its neighbor (Alcudia de) Veo. Three other small 'castles' from that first treaty are unmentioned in the second: Pelmes, Sueras, and Xinquer or Jinquer. Eslidan Muslims seem to have been preoccupied then and later with preserving their regional jurisdiction over neighboring small towns. The Christian lordship over these places, as distinct from their unity in surrender privileges and *aljama* administration, was split; thus the Hungarian crusader Count Dionís received Ahín and Veo as a fief from Jaume in 1244, exchanging them for a larger fief in 1253.

When the original charter of 1242 is compared with this reorganization of thirty-five years later, what had Eslida lost by rebellion or gained during the negotiations designed to reconcile and restore the valuable kingdom? The primitive charter of 1242 had been longer, largely by reason of non-essential details in the tax and religion segments; thus the cemetery and the muezzin's call had been expressly guaranteed, while 'the other books' of the later charter appeared there specifically as 'all the books of the Hadith.' Another example may be the inclusion of military taxes and legal fines in the first version, and their omission in the second. Bees and livestock received special attention in this first charter; public utilities like mills and caravanserais were specified, not just ovens and baths; and six towns with castles or local strongholds had at first been given, constituting 'the whole *aljama*' of Eslida, of which three such castles disappear in the second treaty, replaced by village names. A section on irrigation usage appeared only in the first charter, doubtless because the intervening courtroom victory over Uxó had amply documented Eslida's customary water rights. The Mudejars certainly lost some ground in the later charter's demand for daily water and wood at the castle: the 1242 agreement had explicitly excluded these two services. Substantive also, though long without practical effect, was the loss of the early charter's guarantee against Christians intruding or even staying in the neighborhood without Muslim acquiescence in each case.

If the tax schedule in Eslida's new charter roughly equals that of Christian settlements, does the lump sum of 400 besants represent an onerous and therefore punitive tax, relative to this single *aljama*'s resources? A tax instruction for Eslida in 1258 suggests that it does not: the collector was expected to take in 2,916 Valencian sous annually, more than double the amount of the lump-sum substitute. The difference between the two tax totals may derive from factors like the collector's added ten percent, or the possibly separate poll tax of three and a half sous per adult, or more plausibly the basic tenth of produce which the lump sum does not reckon. Did Eslida's regional jurisdiction shrink – incidentally diminishing its tax base and thus solving the problem of a smaller tax yield in 1276? The charters themselves do not resolve the problem; the first enumerates five allied town-cum-stronghold districts, the second extends Eslida's customs to only two of these plus two fresh villages.

Two years after the second Eslida constitution, in late 1278, King Pere billed 'his faithful [subjects] of the *aljama* of Saracens of Eslida' a fee of 500 sous, 'by reason of the charters you had from our chancery'; he threatened seizure of persons and property unless payment was made. Though a similar bill went to nearly a hundred *aljamas*, it is noteworthy that Eslida's provided the form letter for all (the model registered in full), and that it demanded as well an unusually high payment. The privileges, charters, and records secured from the king's chancery by Eslida doubtless included the original Arabic and Latin parchments of the registered surrender constitution transcribed below.[6]

This was not the last reorganization of Eslida's privileges. Over eighty years later, in the entirely different context of 1355, Eslida's Moors again 'rebelled and rose' to join a Castilian invasion of Valencia. In restoring control, the crown responded to a list of grievances; the erstwhile rebels demanded in the first place 'that the lord king give them the charter made by the king Sir (*En*) Pere of happy memory to the Moors of Eslida.'[7] That charter was of course the document of 1276 transcribed below. The grievances make a lengthy, convoluted document, which Boswell has carefully summarized in twelve points. Besides amnesty, temporary tax relief to rebuild, and confirmation of their 1276 charter and all privileges, they asked for specific confirmation of the muezzin's call, freedom from church tithes, and an end to the service of provisioning the castle with water. The tithe and muezzin items may represent real or anticipated encroachments. In general the charter-privileges of Eslida had not deteriorated much, to judge by these demands, despite the worsening position of Mudejars in post-Black Death Spain. The most notable point about Eslida's situation is that it had lost its dominance over much of the surrounding Mudejar territory. Veo, Alcudia de Veo, Benitandús, Jinquer, Ahín, and the 'Sierra de Espadán' banded together to present their own similar grievances, particularly asking that they be independent of Eslida and not subject to its *qāḍī*, and that they have their own (Christian) castle instead of coming under the protection of Eslida's. The Eslida petition included no effort to retain these breakaways, except for a provision that Lloret's Mudejars be put under the Eslida *qāḍī*.

The region remained independent of spirit. Between 1363 and 1365 Eslida and its neighboring districts constituted twelve of the twenty-nine Valencian *aljamas* who 'abandoned or surrendered' to Castile in the war then raging: Ahín, Alfondeguilla, Artana, Azuébar, Bechí, Benitandús, Castro, Ennueyo, Eslida, Fanzara, and Jinquer. As before, they returned to the fold, regaining their privileges intact. Much later, in 1417 at the city of Valencia, the crown again confirmed the privileges and documents of the Sierra de Eslida Muslims. Seven years afterwards the same *aljama* sent representatives before the king, again at Valencia city and again bearing their documentation, and elicited a royal warning for all officials to respect Eslida's privileges. The general bailiff soon ordered neighboring Artana's officials to respect these exemptions and to return to Eslida certain sums collected. The full story of these fascinating mountain Moors, so central to Mudejar history, still lies buried in the crown and local archives. But the structural support which held their generations together for centuries is revealed in their surrender privileges.[8]

CASTLE PROVISIONING: *SOFRA* AS LINK AND RUPTURE

Before we leave Eslida, some comment is needed about the imposition of a service or provisioning of wood and water, which Eslida escaped in the first charter but fell under in the second. Because my views on that tax have occasioned debate, Eslida's new burden invites comment both substantive and methodological. I have explored elsewhere the nature and application of this *sukhra*, Catalan *sofra*, noting its triple expression. As public works or community repairs, it was a form of service to the community demanded from Islamic societies whether in Egypt or Spain; in Spain it stressed the repair of town fortifications so frequently that Torres Balbás, the standard authority on Hispano-Islamic cities, viewed it mostly in that context. In Valencia's early post-conquest records it meant provisioning the local castle with wood and water (in one case wood for a landlord's kitchen), or paying a landlord the equivalent commutation. In the next century, and during this one in older regions of Christian Spain, however, it could mean a day's labor for the landlord, including plowing. A gift of chickens frequently seems connected with the *sofra* in Valencian tax lists and sometimes merged with it, doubtless related to provisioning. Public works were an obligation at times in Mudejar Valencia, and a rare vineyard service occurs; but these were not designated *sofra*. Though a number of charters formally excluded *sofra*, many more owed it. It can be seen at Alfandech, Játiva, Peñíscola, Alcoy, Biar, Cocentaina, and a dozen other places for which records survive, and was routinely collected from communities south of the Júcar River. A small and easily commuted obligation, its interest lies mostly in its evolution by the fifteenth century into a complex of personal services or eventually fees for one's landlord.

The *sofra* had not been studied until I became intrigued by its elusive nature and presented preliminary archival findings to an invitational symposium at Princeton in 1974, belatedly published in 1981. Encouraged at the reception by Islamicists of every field there, I reworked this material soon afterward into my *Colonialism*, hoping to elicit further reflections from colleagues. Pierre Guichard, relentlessly reading my work as a 'continuist' effort to put feudalism into Islamic Valencia and Islamic structures into a 'feudal' crusader kingdom, expressed reservations about my meaning at a Rome congress and devoted an extensive article in the journal *Awrāq* to repositioning my data in a kind of rebuttal. I must restate and clarify that position here, both to curtail useless polemic and to illustrate by this Eslida tax the transculturative effect of the Valencian crusade.

Community service in al-Andalus stressed the onerous and never-ending maintenance of city, town, and castle walls, as Torres Balbás found in his encounters with *sukhra*. This continued as a Mudejar obligation after the crusade; Boswell found general evidence for it in fourteenth-century Valencia, with no Mudejar complaints of later intrusion. So important was this labor that the surrender charters need not have adverted to it when claiming the taxes owed to the previous Muslim rulers. Christians of even the highest classes were also bound, by directions of Jaume I and Valencia's law code or *Furs*, to an analogous counterpart in service or money. Mudejars indeed had a double burden in Boswell's Valencia: to work on maintaining the town walls and to do the same for their separate quarter when they had one. (At Játiva, Muslims also specialized in providing all the quicklime for this task.) Did this very real obligation come under the Mudejar imposition called *sofra*? The Chivert charter suggests that it did, as do the extra-Valencian La Aldea and Nabal charters in this century.

Most of the early Valencian documentation, however, when not merely an unhelpful *sofra*, concerns '*sofras* of wood and water,' as provisioning for castles and defenses. Such provisioning was more easily accomplished than wall work, and perhaps more easily dispensed at first by the Christians as at Eslida's first charter. If dismissed, it may have been imposed in a general way after the first revolts, either in punishment, as Guichard conjectures, or as a military caution. With the earliest documentation so sparse, and not all taxes or concessions expressly listed in surrender charters, it would be rash to proffer firm conclusions on this. The dismissals may indicate, on the contrary, a universal tax from the start, whose exemption had to be explicit. As in the case of wall maintenance, Christians of Aragon had to provision castles too, within their different socio-economic context. Nothing more can be said with any confidence about this obligation as it had existed in Valencian Islam. Not even haulage of taxes-in-kind, which can be found elsewhere in Islam, is pertinent here in its privatized Mudejar form, since not even Christians considered it a labor service, whether community or personal. I once suggested that haulage in its two separate contexts 'represented continuity' in the transcultural sense, from Islamic communal to Mudejar private forms; but there are almost no data to carry this thought further.

These early Mudejars had other labor obligations – work on the king's palace at Valencia city, construction of roads they themselves shared, and guard duty at the local tower or on town defenses. It is not clear whether any of these were associated with or related to *sofra*, in the Christian mind, even by abuse or by extension. Guichard argues that the Mudejar *sofra* obligation I had explored in Valencia must have meant provisioning at first, falling further into the Christian servile context around 1260 when one of my charters shows it as a kitchen service. This may miss a dynamic at work from the first in Mudejar Valencia. The Aragonese model, down the Ebro even to Tortosa, and clearly in the La Aldea constitutions of 1258 for Valencian Mudejars crossing the border to settle, already identified *sofra* with *opera* or various servile works for one's lord. Did Aragonese lands in Valencia read *sofra* from the start in their own customary terms? Did the crown, whose documentation dominates our data, concern itself rather with castle provisioning as the essential concern? My first presentation of the data assumed that the Aragonese homeland model prevailed by the end of Pere's reign, bringing *sofra* and *opera* into convergence. This is not really clear, and may hurry the process too much. Manuscripts from his successor Anfòs shed no further light. In any case the natural evolution would be toward the *corvée* Dozy found. In 1334 at Perpunchent it covered construction of buildings, for example, and in 1371 at Ribesalbes it meant two days' free work from each household.

The *sofra* at Eslida exemplifies the subtle operation of acculturation even in the case of a relatively inconsequential tax. From the Christian side, there would have seemed little difference between communal work on the local fortification and its provisioning; in their scheme too this easily transferred to paying a commutation, precisely as a 'service.' As a service, then, the tax under Christian control could diversify into personal labor services of several kinds already common in Europe. The Catalan borrowing of the term *sukhra* as *sofra*, and its Aragonese cognate, indicates such a transference. Since this had already transpired in the homelands which had domesticated the word, Christian lords on the Valencian frontier must have viewed the *sukhra* there as the homeland *sofra*, an attitude which would explain the assimilation of the one to the other. The division of Valencian properties among a large number of landlords could only have encouraged this evolution. More than other taxes, too, service contributions lie open to abuse and expansion. Seen from the Mudejar vantage, context rendered *sofra* immediately and vitally different. Resited, reoriented, whether expressed as provisioning or as a fee, it straightway changed a community activity into a kind of tax obligation; it tied Muslim to castellan in an alien societal structure and by performance of a sufficiently different obligation. By its name and implied derivation, however, I think it not unfair to see it as a bridging institution in this early provisioning form, no longer the Islamic obligation nor yet in Valencia a proper labor service. In this way, as I have expressed it elsewhere, *sofra* 'was a link with the Islamic past both semantically and in life.'[9]

It is not easy to explore such areas, given the current combative atmosphere of the continuist–discontinuist ideologies. Any claim to similarity, common element, or point of contact becomes suspect as betraying the unique and unitary nature of Islamic culture. But for anyone approaching from outside those ideologies, something very different catches the eye: counterparts and resonances, the functional analogies that distort the analogate in one culture under pressure of conquest by another, to bond the two while partially assimilating the victim community. Whether direct or proportional analogy, the difference between the analogates is contained in the very meaning. Such comparison by function or counterparts has nothing to do with continuity. Indeed it is through the very counterparts that a conquered society can suffer the most direct and damaging discontinuities. The aristocrat and farmer, to take obvious examples, both display this characteristic similarity-in-dissimilarity with their counterparts in another culture. When exploring cultural inter-change or cultural transformations, the concept of functional coun-terpart or element makes a useful tool. Thinking in such terms, Ira Lapidus was able to compare the Islamic city with the European commune, well aware that they are absolutely different though functionally open to comparison; Glick can even attempt to study comparatively the primitive Spanish Christian communities with the Cordovan caliphate's advanced society, city and monastery serving as functional correlatives. In thirteenth-century Valencia, and with major points of contact, this functional approach becomes much easier, as the two communities are forced into active or subtle relationships.

Such points of functional analogy, whether at the level of farmer or entertainer or castle holder, provide study-links between cultures; in case of conquest, whether of American Indians or Valencian Mus-lims, they allow each society to perceive the other as echoing in some points its own. The very perception by alien overlords would in-creasingly distort the cultural element so perceived. Rooted in its modicum of reality, such perception could work deep assimilative effect or remain as superficial terminology. The effect might leave most areas of a culture untouched directly; but distortion of even a few important elements would color the entire society's self-perception. When the Valencian crusaders deliberately kept so many elements 'as in the days of the Saracens,' these certainly comforted the conquered, lent a sense of some continuity with their immediate past, and facilitated both administration and human relations for the conquerors. Their condition was in fact a relative continuity, the formation of a subculture, a simultaneous preserva-tion and deformation, salvation and loss. At the time of Eslida's second constitution, many externals remained unchanged to the careless eye in most of Valencia. But the heart knew differently and could mourn with the poet al-Rundī, writing around 1250:

> Ask Valencia what became of Murcia,
> And where is Játiva, and where is Jaén?

ALFANDECH VALLEY: SALVAGE AND SURVIVAL

The Alfandech charter is an archival oddity. Like nearly all such surrender constitutions, it disappeared early in both its original Arabic and its crown Latin parchments, nor was any copy inserted in the crown's paper registers. It is no surprise consequently that Alfandech's first or earliest charter no longer exists, in contrast to the accident of the survival of that of Eslida. As with Eslida, however, the Alfandech Muslims revolted, playing a prominent role in the 1276 countercrusade, a circumstance which necessitated renegotiating their charter at the final surrender. On the Eslida model, this charter mirrors in briefer fashion its vanished original of a quarter-century before. It supplies an extraordinarily valuable record of the final rebellion. What remains to us today is an official translation by the crown chancery, done near the end of the century from the Arabic original and registered on paper in the crown archives as a formal record.

The Islamic community that petitioned this copy was as unusual as Eslida in its geography and strategic disposition. The hills that terminate Valencia city's countryside at the south coast enclose a long, intensively irrigated valley, its nine villages and several castles then dominated by the great fortification of Alfandech on a conical hill. The Castell d'Alfàndec itself was described in the Cid's day as 'castrum Sarracenorum in monte magno.' King Jaume does not describe the fall of Alfandech castle, but his junior contemporary Muntaner includes it among principal stages in the conquest: 'and then also he took the castle of Corbera, [and] the Valley of Alfandech with the three castles it held.' Since Jaume awarded the valley to a vassal in mid-July of 1238, some three months before the city of Valencia surrendered, the king was at least confident of Alfandech's imminent surrender. Muntaner leaves the impression that its actual acquisition took place during the subsequent overrunning of the country south of the capital. The contemporary chronicler Bernat Desclot recounts how the crusaders, after the fall of Valencia city, 'attacked castles and towns, and took fortresses and stone castles as far as the Valley of Alfandech de Mariñén,' Alcoy, and Albaida.

The economic and strategic value of the valley is clear from the status of the baron who received it in gift: Nunyo Sanç, or Nunó I, a close relative of the king's and for the past quarter-century count of the Roussillon and Cerdagne regions of southern France. A hero of Las Navas and Muret, and a main pillar of the Balearics crusade, Nunyo was among the most powerful magnates at the king's side when Valencia city fell. His death in the final days of 1241 or the first weeks of 1242 marks a *terminus ad quem* for Alfandech's transfer to the Christians. Like so many grants, and in the case of this strategic set

Alfandech de Mariñén (Valldigna) Valley. In this compressed view
Tabernes de Valldigna lies at the far left (c), Benifairó de Valldigna next
(b; castle not shown), Simat at front center (a), the nearby Valldigna
Cistercian monastery at the right (d), and the Vacas River. Compare
with map (p. 53). (Cavanilles, *Observaciones sobre el reyno de Valencia*, 1795)

of defenses very understandably, the count's claims lapsed. At about
this time too the crown sited the region as a component in the wider
civil jurisdiction of Alcira city. During al-Azraq's revolt shortly after
the close of the crusade, Muslim forces may have retaken Alfandech;
in 1249, immediately after the revolt, King Jaume attempted to
settle the valley with some 250 Christian families, including forty
crossbowmen from Tortosa and forty immigrants from his native
city Montpellier. The effort seems to have been abortive, Muslims
continuing as the dominant population. Of Alfandech castle itself,
Islamic and Christian, today only remnants of the walls and central
homage-tower ride the ridge under the modern name of Castillo de la
Reina Mora.[10]

From the beginning the valley's *aljama* was prosperous, a main
source of Mudejar rents for the crown. For a time it formed part of
the crown's dowry-security for Constança, the Hohenstaufen wife of
Prince Pere. When Pere himself became hopelessly entangled in
debt, King Jaume assigned Alfandech's revenues as a major relief.

73

When war clouds gathered in spring of 1276, Jaume on 3 March prudently ordered Alfandech castle to be strengthened. Three weeks later 'many' castles had revolted, and the war was spreading rapidly. As late as 1 April Alfandech either lay at peace or was under protection of truce, while the royal armies concentrated far to its south. In mid-April, with hostilities more than a month advanced, Jaume assigned the region's revenues to support the armies led there by his bastard Pere Ferran; Alfandech's Muslims were to pay rents and taxes directly to Pere Ferran. A revenue document in mid-May included the Alfandech area with no notice of war; yet by mid-August it had become a main center of resistance. A general truce between the Muslim rebels and the crown on 29 August expressly excluded Alfandech de Mariñén and fifteen other places: Alfandech led this list of districts where the war would continue to be pressed. A clarifying letter a week later reduced the list to three clusters of hard-core resistance: the castles of the $qā'id$ Ibrāhīm, Alcalá castle of al-Azraq's family, and 'Alfandec de Marynnen.' A separate copy of this broadside went to 'Gil Martínez [de Oblites] and Sanç de Llacera and all the others in the siege of Alfandech.' The two barons had already distinguished themselves elsewhere in the rebellion, and their siege is one of the few for which records survive.

While the general truce extended for three months from early September, Alfandech's siege went forward with vigor. King Pere himself stayed at the siegeworks from 23 to 26 September. Preliminary negotiations for surrender probably began on that occasion. A few weeks later Pere was promising estates there to various individuals, 'when we partition or grant the Valley of Alfandech for Christian settlement.' Since this was the king's only visit, either during the rebellion or throughout his reign, the surrender charter published below may plausibly be dated from late September. If it is dated later, the only reasonable choice left is October, which month Pere passed at Valencia city; thereafter the king felt confident enough to leave the Valencian kingdom for the first time since joining his father in stemming the revolt, and traveled up to spend the next months in highland Aragon.

Though Alfandech was pacified, the war went on. Alfandech itself had been too close to the capital city and too strategic a crossroads to leave in enemy hands long. Nothing further is heard for a year – a circumstance emphasizing the success of Pere's pacification, since in a war the absence of news is good news. Then a crown letter at the end of 1277 ordered ten Muslims, seized by Christian raiders in the valley, to be set free. The final notice of defeated Alfandech turns up in a list of September 1278, a guideline for tax collectors about the fees paid by some hundred *aljamas* for confirming their *ante-bellum* privileges. Nearly all those areas had actively participated in the revolt. Alfandech's community must have suffered severely in the war; it could only scrape together half the fee required. Settlement meanwhile proceeded apace, with Alfandech soon getting its own parish church with rector.[11]

Near the end of the century a distant echo came from Alfandech's moment of military glory, an episode which would occasion our most valuable record of Alfandech's crusade days. The Conqueror's grandson King Jaume II, returning by way of this valley from a successful raid against the Muslims, decided to raise a Cistercian abbey here in gratitude, and renamed the region expressively Valldigna. The Muslim tenants, still the valley's majority population, apparently anticipated erosion of their privileges when the castles and lordship would pass from crown to monks. In the year of the monastery's foundation therefore (15 March 1297), the *aljama* made 'humble supplication' that Jaume II 'concede, approve and confirm' their treasured surrender constitution.[12]

In acceding, Jaume staged a solemn ceremony involving himself and five great barons on the Christian side, with undoubtedly a cast of local notables representing the *aljama*. King Jaume described the original document brought by the Muslims as 'a certain privilege written in Arabic letters, sealed with a pendent seal of the illustrious lord King Pere of famed memory, our father.' Jaume II caused this original to be 'transcribed faithfully from Arabic into Latin, at our command.' His scribes omitted the date of the original, along with signatures and other accidentals. The new version described itself as 'faithful,' but apparently in substantive rather than slavish fashion, since at one point the Latin hurries past the details, with the phrase 'as is more fully contained in the aforesaid privilege.'

The document opens with amnesty: 'the same lord King Pere, our father, forgave the Saracens of Alfandech Valley all offense and damage which had been committed by them in the time of war.' By further proviso, 'any Saracen who had taken himself off to the war zone, or outside our realm, can return to the aforesaid Valley of Alfandech and remain there safe and secure.' Nor can anyone 'presume to demand anything from him as ransom-of-war'; local author-

75

ities may have claimed returning rebels as prisoners, demanding some small ransom or fee, until the amnesty clarified this point.

The bulk of Alfandech's charter provisions is traditional, serving to illustrate my thesis that Mudejar privileges expressed a basic and continuing policy. Details are fascinating, however, and in a number of ways novel. Items registering Islam as an established religion within the Christian realms of Aragon are, as always, the least original and the most interesting. The valley's Muslims 'continue and are established in the Law and Sunna.' They may 'teach their children in the mosque from their books,' and maintain a *ṣāḥib al-ṣalāt* (the main functionary or imam at a mosque, who led congregational prayers). 'Alms' and 'prayer' remained 'just as had been the custom in the time of the Saracens'; this would have included community tax collection like the *zakāt*, and public manifestations like pilgrimage and the muezzin's call, both of which appear explicitly elsewhere in Valencian Mudejar privileges. Above all, the charter guaranteed the *waqf* or endowment which financed the community's religious institutions: 'the supporting properties which used to belong to the mosque remain and apply to that mosque just as was the custom in former times.'

Intra-community autonomy, both in governance and law (already touched on), were covered by the provision 'that they can elect from among themselves the *qāḍī* and the *amīn*, according to their will and counsel.' Since the crown frequently imposed its own *qāḍī* and its *amīn*, this concession was significant. A further privilege provided 'that none of them be arrested or detained by reason of someone else's crime or [unpaid] fine, but that each be charged with his own crime or offense.' Like other Mudejars, 'they can carry weapons throughout the whole land and jurisdiction of the said lord king.' Rents and taxes played a minor role in this constitution, simply continuing the Almohad practices as they had been 'in the time of the Saracens' and 'as the custom had been.' Among these customary levies only *almagran* was specified, meaning here the basic tax on irrigated land; tax lists show *almagran* as Alfandech's single most important revenue. The salt monopoly of the crown was qualified: 'they can buy salt as was the custom in past times' – a freedom from regulation not normally accorded. Right of pasture was affirmed for 'livestock large and small' anywhere in the jurisdictional countryside of the valley.

They could 'live on and hold their farms and possessions, according as these were apportioned among them and delivered.' To maintain the ethnic identity of the group, the charter forbade 'that any of these Saracens sell or alienate their farms or holdings to anyone except only to Saracens.' Any Muslim here 'can leave his properties to another Saracen,' following past Islamic custom. Finally, 'all the aforesaid Saracens, both men and women, are to remain safe and secure with all their goods, under the protection of God and of the same lord king, without any deception,' and no one may presume to harass them with accusations. This solemn confirmation by Jaume II, given according to the best understanding of the valley's Muslims, was witnessed by five of the highest barons of the crown. The barons included Bernat Guillem d'Entença (Bernardo Guillermo de Entenza) lord of Alcolea, Chiva, and other castles, unsuccessful claimant of his father's seigniory of Montpellier, and majordomo of Aragon, who regularly undertook international missions for the crown; a notable soldier, he made his last will in 1300 and went off to Cyprus to be a Knight Hospitaller. After Bernat in the list of witnesses came Jaume II of Xèrica (Jérica), son of the Jaume I (Jaime Pérez) who was in turn the son of King Jaume I and his commoner wife Teresa Gil de Vidaure; Jaume II of Xèrica served as standard-bearer (*vexillarius*) to his cousin King Jaume II. Pero Martínez de Luna and Artaldo de Luna also witnessed. They represent branches of one of the most powerful lineages of the highland kingdom of Aragon proper; both appear prominently and regularly in the affairs of Jaume II. An intriguing witness is Gausbert or Jaspert V, viscount of Castellnou or Pyrenean Vallespir, who had lost his country by backing King Pere III against Philip III of France and Jaume II of Majorca. The document's scribal superintendent, appearing at both the beginning and the end of the list of witnesses, was Gil de Jaca, later the general bailiff of the kingdom of Aragon. Alfandech's Muslims treasured this talisman for a long lifetime, before again expressing communal anxiety and discontent. During the wartime years of 1364–5 they fled *en masse* from the monastery's jurisdiction to neighboring lords, despite crown penalties.

My transcription and analysis of these Alfandech and Eslida finds were presented in an address before the international conference of Mediterranean studies at Barcelona in 1978. Shortly afterwards an intriguing companion constitution came to light. Barceló Torres has discovered a translation of 1355, from Arabic 'into Romance or the language of the Aragonese,' of the charter given in March 1277 by King Pere to the rebel Muslims of Alfondeguilla and Castro. The original is lost, but this Aragonese version was prepared 'and diligently examined' by Ibrāhīm b. Shuʿayb (Avenxuay), *qāḍī* of Uxó and *manescal* or veterinary of the queen. The castle and districts involved bordered Eslida on the south and are today reckoned as the single *comarca* or district of Alfondeguilla. King Jaume had noted their haste to surrender to his passing army, as part of a general collapse of the castle system dependent on the Vall de Uxó. After the surrender in spring of 1238, Jaume gave the town of Alfondeguilla to the knight García de Vera. History is silent about both places until 1272, when Jaume awarded them to his son Jaume of Jérica as part of the barony of Jérica. The region is obscure enough; the great Solde-vila twice even annotates the appearance of this 'Alfandec' in Jaume's autobiography as being the more important Alfandech de Mariñén. Its very obscurity underlines the generous conditions, of standard Mudejar type, routinely restored by King Pere in 1277. Not even the vulnerable fiscal provisions, as Barceló Torres notes, suffered any considerable erosion. Doubtless further such finds, embedded in revised charters of a century or more later, will turn up and expand our growing knowledge of early Valencian Mudejarism.[13]

Meanwhile the Alfandech and Eslida constitutions greatly extend our meager supply of this documentary genre, and reveal more clearly the institution of Mudejarism. They also illumine the countercrusade of 1276 with valuable new information. On the human level they afford another glimpse of that Islamic society in Valencia, evanescent, poised for its devolution toward the Morisco tragedy two centuries later. The provisions of these charters, modifications of the Mudejar treaty pattern, conferred on the conquered a public identity and dignity. Moderate taxes placed them in a status equivalent to their Christian neighbors in terms of tax burden. Homely details preserved their Mudejar religio-social, economic, and administrative community structure, and show that both the mountain and the valley communities enjoyed prosperous autonomy. The circumstance that each community actively guarded these charters of privilege, and that the alien overlords confirmed the charters with ritual solemnity, reveals the nature of the contracts as a community's strong wall of protection and simultaneously as a bridge joining Islamic and Christian societies. The charters afford us a close focus, a chance to analyze closely a significant moment in the lives of two colonial communities, contemporary but very dissimilar.

Since the documents belong to a genre (indeed, allow us to define more exactly that sparsely documented genre), they reveal a contemporary mindcast – what the conqueror willingly conceded and what the conquered adamantly required. At the same time, these charters are radically historical, presenting individuals of a specific place and time in their idiosyncratic ambience. Such historical exemplars, handled with archeological patience, can be made to speak volumes. When all is said, however, these are structural and legal witnesses, which leave more unsaid than they reveal. A larger frame of englobing circumstance suffused this apparently idyllic situation with psychic pain, personal and communitarian. To explore that, the historian must eventually climb up from the limited ambit of the surrender charter to vantage points offered by a very broad range of documentation. The following chapter undertakes to summon up that wider, more distressing world.

3

Christian–Muslim confrontation:
the thirteenth-century dream of conversion

The surrender constitution formed a bridge between Christian society and its enclaved Muslim communities. Threatening movements
now passed over that bridge to assault the inner citadel of Islamic
integrity. This was not a phenomenon proper to Mudejarism at all,
nor were the movements involved rooted in Spanish experience.
Valencia's conquerors were medieval Europeans; to appreciate their
motives and movements one must reckon with the wider world of
which they were components. If a European movement was like a
tune which each country or region rendered after its own style,
Valencia and its parent realms of Aragon merely embodied that
music or movement according to local needs and manner of expression. One such refrain, rising to dominance in mid-thirteenth century, was Europe's preoccupation with converting the infidel. Isolating this theme, hearing it in its universal as well as its local context,
can reveal much about the direction and changing mood of European–Islamic relations in the colonial kingdom. It reveals much also
about the mutual causality by which this frontier affected Europe as
a whole, even while Europe set the themes and rhythm which deeply
affected Muslim and Christian in this distant south.

NEW DIRECTIONS: A CRUSADE FOR CONVERTS

In both eastern and western Mediterranean, crusader spokesmen
entertained some hope of converting enemy Muslims, though for
long their concern remained minimal. War hysteria, especially during the early crusades, hardly provided the propitious atmosphere.
Christians, steeped in generations of propaganda against a relentless
foe, made poor messengers of the Gospel. Some priests proved so
hostile toward Muslims as to argue against their conversion. Custom
and expediency combined, as we have seen, to dispose of conquered

populations by establishing their religion and social order as a kind of privileged enclave, while unconquered regions militantly opposed any infiltration of Christianity outside their own similar enclaves. As the twelfth century wore on, dissent against armed crusading grew, the *chansons de geste* echoed with references to Muslims converted singly and *en masse*, and the first stirrings of a literary and intellectual rapprochement with Islam made themselves felt.[1]

Dissent did not slow the military machine or its essential popular support, and the early study of Islam yielded little more than a closet literature for parochial Christian intellectuals. A new orientation nevertheless emerged, gathering strength especially in the western Mediterranean, where political and military circumstances favored for a time the Christian side of the crusade-Holy War balance. This orientation relates to a wider vision of converting India, Tartary, and China, and to the embassies sent to the Mongols from 1234 on. Crusading itself became more secularized in the thirteenth century as the expansionist ambitions of rulers assumed increasing priority over the common aims of Christendom, and legal scholars briskly constructed a new philosophy of relations with non-Christian societies. In that century, consequently, 'the overall strategy of Christendom underwent modification'; the battle now was 'not only military but doctrinal, through a dialogue of controversy.'[2] Nowhere does this spirit of combative dialogue appear more visibly than in the kingdom of Valencia.

The Christian fever for converting Muslims can be charted, in its ups and downs, in both pre-crusade and crusader Valencia. Important in itself as a little world of Muslims ripe for the harvest, the Valencian kingdom served also as a beachhead or gate through which the proselytizers sought to penetrate North Africa under the aegis of Aragon's king. Islamic Spain and North Africa lay open to some such penetration, the Almohad unity of the area for ever fragmented into mutually suspicious or inimical principalities since the disasters that followed Islam's defeat at Las Navas in 1212. The most important of these fragments for a time was Ifrīqiya – roughly Tunisia and part of Algeria – whose Hafsid dynasty after mid-century appropriated the awesome title of caliph. Christian powers, especially the realms of Aragon, enjoyed a range of entry into the North African states. Christian merchants frequented Tunisian and Moroccan ports, sometimes residing in mercantile enclaves; Christian nobles, townsmen, and even borrowed army groups served the sultans' battlefields; and a succession of ransomers, slavers, diplomats, and other visitors lent their varied presence. A reverse flow carried Muslim merchants, diplomats, ransomers, Berber troops on loan to the Christian king, and immigrant farmers and artisans invited by king, church, nobles, and townsmen. This swirl of movement offered chances to influence or proselytize, though always with discretion and on sufferance. In Morocco the Dominican bishop was martyred in 1232, as were Franciscan groups in 1220 and 1227. From 1246 to 1250 a knight of Zaragoza, become a Franciscan, was the bishop for 'Africa' as well as papal envoy to the caliph at Marrakesh. The *ecclesia marrochitana* of these men was by intention missionary rather than a chaplain adjunct to the Christian merchant and military groups, and it roused opposition from the merchants.

On the diplomatic level contacts between North Africa and Christian states evolved in a variety of patterns, occasionally assuming more universal significance. In the power struggle between empire and papacy Tunis became a center for the wavering Hohenstaufen cause, a place where agents of the crown of Aragon helped nurse it back to strength. The career of Ibn Sab'īn illustrates in its own way such wider dimensions. From North Africa he influenced the Islamic rapprochement with Frederick II and Louis IX; 're-presenting in those years the conscience of Islam,' after the fall of Baghdad in 1258, he worked in the East for a truce with Western Christians so as to confront the Mongols while preventing the imminent recapture of Constantinople by the Byzantines.[3] The Muslims even sent an embassy to the papal court to have the pope force Castile to respect its provisions of the Alcaraz treaty concerning Murcia. Similarly in 1257 the pope intervened for Tunis, as ally of Aragon, against the crusading fleet of Benet de Rocaberti, archbishop of Tarragona.[4] Political and commercial interchange served to underline the continuing influence upon Europe of Islamic literature, philosophy, and learning. Poets and wandering musicians broadcast the literary wares of Islam throughout Spain and into other lands. The brilliant contributions of Toledo's twelfth-century school of translators, reflected in lesser centers of translation like Tarazona, continued into the thirteenth century, when Alfonso X made his large additions to this treasury.

Years before summoning the First Crusade, on the occasion of restoring the primatial dignity to captured Toledo in 1088, Pope Urban II had urged upon its incumbent archbishop, Bernardo de

Cluny, a policy of conversion. 'With warm affection we exhort you, reverend brother, that you live worthy of so high and honored a pontificate, taking care always not to give offense to Christians or to Muslims; strive by word and example, God helping, to convert the infidels to the faith.' Gregory VII, leader of the Gregorian Reform, anticipated Urban's program by dispatching a mission to Spanish Muslims in 1074, hoping to convert the ruler of Zaragoza, Aḥmad I al-Muqtadir. Abū Ja'far al-Khazrajī, in his history of the caliphs, rails at the 'low, dissolute, and contemptible Muslims' who joined the Cid shortly afterwards, 'most' of whom converted to Christianity. These eleventh-century efforts may be related to the wider work of French Cluniac monks in Spain. They found an echo in limited but significant efforts at conversion during the First Crusade.[5]

Hope for Islam's conversion, from eleventh-century stirrings, took on strength by the middle of the twelfth century. The first translation of the Koran in any language, sponsored by Peter the Venerable and completed by a team of collaborators about 1141, found an echo in the translation of Marcos of Toledo in 1213 under the patronage of Toledo's great archbishop, Rodrigo Jiménez de Rada. Later King Pere IV of the realms of Aragon commissioned two separate translations into Catalan. Pope Lucius III, promulgating regulations for the crusading Order of Santiago in 1184, sounded the same note as Urban a century before: he 'stringently commanded that they aim at one thing alone in their fighting against the Saracens – not love of worldly praise, not desire of shedding blood, not greed over land acquisition – but either that they defend Christians from their onslaught or else that they may be able to draw these [Saracens] to practice the Christian faith.' (A contrary school of canonical thought increasingly stressed the crusades as the continuation of Rome's struggle against intruding barbarians and saw the infidel as belonging by rights under Christian colonial control.) Less than a decade later, in 1192, Pope Celestine III asked the Toledo archbishop to dispatch a bilingual missionary for preaching to Christians in 'Morocco, Seville, and other cities of the Saracens.' Presumably such a missioner also served the dreams of conversion.[6]

In the twelfth century Peter the Venerable had urged winning the Muslims 'not as our people [so] often do, by weapons, not by force but by reason, not by hate but by love.' An even more prestigious contemporary, St Bernard of Clairvaux, the organ voice of Christendom, had urged that energy be channeled into converting Muslims and 'masses of pagans' instead of trying to influence Europe's Jews, who were protected by a providential time lock – the Jews 'have their set time [for conversion], which cannot be advanced.' At the opening of the thirteenth century the great Pope Innocent III, inclining to a popular belief that the world might end around 1284, envisioned a final crusade effort in East and West to prepare the mass conversion of Jews and Muslims. Jacques de Vitry, preaching and baptizing converts in the crusader Holy Land, informed Europe from 1217 to 1221 that 'many' Muslims, 'if they heard sound doctrine, would easily be converted'; 'many' already had their children baptized out of superstitious hope for health; 'frequently a number of Saracens cross over' into Christianity, only to return to 'the customary uncleanness of the pagans' because Christian life was too demanding. As the end of the world neared, he claimed, the sword would consume the recalcitrant while the other Muslims would convert.[7]

In the 1260s Roger Bacon hungrily eyed the multitude of Muslims, Mongols, Buddhists, and pagans ripe for conversion, and especially their philosophers, specifically including among them the Muslims living in the midst of the Christians of Spain. Crusading alone was ineffective against Muslims and must be supplemented by an army of learned men; these 'men wise in all knowledge' should preach by persuasion. In the 1270s William of Tripoli undertook to refute the Koran directly, so as to bypass philosophy and persuasion alike: 'and thus by the simple word of God, without philosophical arguments, without weapons of war, like simple sheep they ask for Christ's baptism and enter God's sheepfold.' At the far turn of the century a student of Aquinas, Pierre Dubois, confected an elaborate program for mass conversion of the infidels.[8] By that time contacts with the Mongol world had widened the range of hope for conversion – merchants were traveling regularly into China; the convert from Peking, Rabban bar Sauma, had arrived in Europe in 1287 and had given communion to Pope Nicholas IV and Edward I of England; and John of Montecorvino, after a tour of baptizing through India in 1291–2, had founded his diocese at Peking. Meanwhile the theme of the baptized Saracen haunted Europe. In folk literature his archetype was Renouard, a convert–crusader of heroic legend, whom Dante places among the epic warriors in Paradise; Marco Polo's opening chapter spins a long tale revealing the 'secret' conversion of the caliph of Baghdad and 'many' followers. For North Africa the dream waxed the strongest in the middle of the thirteenth century and again at the century's end; then it waned and for ever died.

Thirteenth-century crusading popes like Honorius III, Gregory IX, and Innocent IV encouraged conversion of Muslims by persuasion; from time to time the program tended to focus on a promising princely candidate. Internal dislocations rendered plausible the widespread Joachimite belief marking 1260 as the beginning of the millennium; as part of this vision Joachim of Flora had persuaded many that Islam, the seventh head of the beast, would be conquered less by fighting than by preaching. The chiliastic branch of Joachimism was exegetical rather than prophetic; it saw Islam as ordained by God, to be met by the faith and prayers of the Christian remnant; from 1268 the infidel masses would convert, leaving only fringe peoples as the army of Antichrist, with the Franciscans as Joachim's monastic preachers to the Gentiles and Jews. Arnau de Vilanova, physician to several kings of Aragon, became a leader in elaborating this view in the last decades of the century.[9] The noble 'Abd al-'Azīz, described by Emperor Frederick II as a relative (*nepos*) of the Tunis sultan, created a sensation when he arrived at Rome to be baptized.[10] Gregory IX entertained hopes for converting the sultan of Tunis, much as he hoped to convert the sly sultan of Damascus and the Almohad caliph Abū 'l-'Alā'. St Louis, king of France, directed his crusade toward Tunis partly because contemporaries believed in the possibility of winning the current Hafsid ruler. At mid-century St Ramon de Penyafort informed Rome that North Africans were inclining toward the faith, 'especially the politically powerful and even the king of Tunis.' After the last Almohad fled from Morocco to the court of Jaume I, bearing along a gaggle of relatives and retainers, to become pensioners of the crown at Calatayud and Valencia, some of these relatives became Christians. In 1285, as the duel projected at Bordeaux between Charles of Anjou and King Pere of the realms of Aragon captured the imagination of many European knights, who vied for a place in the lists, a son of the sultan of Morocco asked to accompany the party of Aragon; he promised to turn Christian if Pere overcame the Angevin.[11]

It is likely that the king's namesake who appears in a document as 'Peter of Tunis, son of the sultan of Tunis,' was the son of the dethroned caliph Abū Isḥāq Ibrāhīm, and the godson–protégé of King Pere.[12] Five years after the last Valencian revolt the sultan of Bougie (Bijāya), Ibn al-Wazīr, offered to become a Christian as well as Pere's 'man and his godson and his vassal.' The king shared this good news with Rome.[13] At the end of the century the Hafsid caliph's cousin and counselor, Abū Yaḥyā Zakarīyā' I, al-Liḥyānī, conveyed the impression that he was about to convert; he continued these maneuvers after he became sultan in 1311, confiding how he was a Christian at heart and had postponed baptism only from motives of prudence.[14] Don Fernando Abdelmán (Castilianized from 'Abd al-Mu'min), son of the emir of Baeza, lived in Seville's Moorish quarter as the convert spokesman and protector for its Muslims. Even the leader of Valencia's revolt, al-Azraq, came to King Jaume 'and told me he wanted to become a Christian,' suggesting marriage to a relative of the powerful lord Carròs, admiral of Catalonia. Abū Zayd made a particularly fine display because he was not only *wālī* over Valencia and eastern Spain but a prince of the blood, descended from the great Almohad founder. Complacent in the winning of such men, Spanish observers easily saw Islamic potentates as likely targets for the lightnings of grace.[15]

Of Abū Zayd's several sons, Muslim and Christian, one presented an adventurous horizon for the dreamers of conversion. This son was 'Zeit Aazon,' a Latinized name probably standing for 'the *sayyid* al-Ḥasan.' Older authors speak of Abū Zayd's having two sons baptized at Murcia in 1241, with St Fernando of Castile and Prince Alfonso present as godfathers, under the baptismal names Fernando and Alfonso, the latter eventually becoming a Knight of Santiago. The son Fernando poses no problem and may have received his baptism at Murcia under some such conditions; Abū Zayd had briefly been the king's vassal, after all, and is said to have accompanied him on the Seville crusade. Alfonso, on the other hand, seems to be the al-Ḥasan who appears abruptly in a papal bull of 1245, an adult Muslim preparing for baptism and transferring to the Santiago order his 'kingdom of Zala' in Africa. Innocent IV approved the transaction, with its expressed hopes of basing there an easy conversion of North Africa.[16] The puzzle of this grandly named principality can be clarified by reference to a parallel case in the early fourteenth century, the pseudoconversion of a 'king of Africa' who proves to have been merely governor for the Tunisian town of Mahdia (al-Mahdīya). In converting, the son of Abū Zayd was probably conveying title to the coveted Moroccan port of Salā, against which Alfonso X launched a crusade in the late 1250s. Allied with such projects for princely baptism was the conviction that mass conversion would issue concomitantly. This had been a pattern in convert-ing large areas of non-Islamic paganism that now lay safely within Christendom. Jaume's son King Pere told the pope that by extend-ing the crusade into the region later called Algeria (western Ifrīqiya) 'the greater part of the population will become Christians.' Four local 'chiefs and lords,' describing themselves as 'blood relatives' of the Tunisian king, swore to Pere that 'fifty thousand persons – men, women, and children' – would welcome baptism.[17]

The obsession also gripped Valencian crusaders. King Jaume took the Cross hoping 'to convert' the Muslims of Valencia to Christianity.[18] A highly symbolic act, performed under the walls of besieged Valencia city, was the public baptism of Muslim converts. To set legal precedents for a court test over metropolitan ownership of the proposed Valencian diocese, the bishop of Albarracín, under armed guard and with economy of movement, improvised an ordination, a confirmation, and a grant of indulgence; though no baptismal font stood at hand, the essential concern with conversion was signified when the bishop baptized two local Muslims in the church of Sant Vicent just outside the enemy's walls. Three years before the close of the Valencian crusade, when most of the kingdom was in his hands, Jaume formally reversed the customary policy of benignly neglecting and even discouraging the conversion of con-quered Muslims: they could now convert 'freely and without opposi-tion from anyone, notwithstanding [any] statute or agreement or even rooted custom about this by our predecessors or anyone else forbidding the same.' Not long after this crusade Penyafort could report to the pope from Barcelona on the great success of his Domini-can convert-makers in Spain. The groundwork was laid, the door stood open, and now only a sufficiency of clerics was needed to bring in the souls. With Ramon Lull, he believed that the accumulating sheaves proved the harvest was ripe. Rational dialogue and disin-terested love would conquer all.[19]

The convert movement in the conquered kingdom of Valencia has left ample traces in surviving documentation – individuals, colonies of converts, neo-Christians as a social problem and as a class, organized programs of conversion, baronial resistance to the move-ment, and even a guild or confraternity of converts. Elsewhere I have itemized their numbers and explored the dimensions of the move-ment, including the preaching program; and in a separate study I have demonstrated the lively prejudice felt by local Christians toward convert and Muslim as alike.[20] The methodology of the movement remains to be examined, particularly those approaches that gave the movement its tone and that strike the modern student as bizarre. Facing an Islamic country, the medieval missioner had the option of five tactics: secret conversions, via commercial, chaplain, or other contacts; fanatic confrontation, designed to precipitate a dramatic response; infiltration via metaphysical dialogue with whatever Islamic savants came to hand; diplomatic maneuvers toward winning a potentate, in whose footsteps many subjects could drift into Christianity; or, finally, cracking the military carapace by conquest, to expose an Islamic region to public proselytism.

FRANCISCAN CONFRONTATION: THE MARTYR MOVEMENT

In the use of all five methods during the thirteenth century the new mendicant Orders stood to the forefront. This was logical, since they constituted the mobile and main missionary force of a Christendom grown too suddenly complex and expanded. They combined the zeal of freshly founded orders with the new learning of the universities, and because they fitted their times so aptly they drew into membership some of the most promising spirits of the day. They formed efficient international organizations, disciplined, with high *esprit* and with novel vision and techniques. Mendicants advised on crusade projects, spurred the fighting forces to greater efforts, and planted priories when the smoke of battle cleared. They roamed the conquered countryside with programs of preaching. Within Islamic lands they contacted princes, served as chaplains to merchants or mercenary troops, sought to expand discreetly the body of native Christians forming in conjunction with such alien nuclei, and met in heady argument with Muslim sages. Taking advantage of the tolerance Muslims felt for professional holy men, they ventured to act openly at times and even to preach in public. The situation was more hopeful in the crusader East, where native Christian bodies confused the scene and Byzantine polemic had prepared some foundation. North Africa, on the other hand, entertained a special awe for the holy fanatic.[21]

Prominent among new techniques, or techniques given a new dynamism, was the Franciscan tactic of confrontation. Outrageous, consciously ineffective, yet designed to engage the forces of heaven at some mystical level, it seized the imagination of contemporary Christendom. Much like the Christian 'Martyr movement' of the ninth century, which disconcerted early Spanish Islam, the new protest movement proposed to preach boldly in mosques and Muslim crowds the iniquity of Islam and the triumph of the Cross.[22] The preacher hoped for miracles but settled for the more probable martyrdom, and successful use of the tactic required prior commitment to death. In this end-of-days, the essential note of Franciscanism proposed an eschatological conformity to Christ's own suffering, a new Age of Martyrs. This movement differed significantly from the earlier Spanish outburst. The Cordova movement, as James Waltz notes, had come partly from alarm over the cultural and religious erosion of Spanish Christians, and partly from enthusiasm for the novel Carolingian ideology of a *respublica christiana* around which to polarize. Franciscan scholastics like Alexander of Hales and Bonaventure in our period explored the many aspects of martyrdom without clarifying the Cordovan or the obsessive thirteenth-century form. The Franciscan Martyr movement did have approval of church authorities, unlike the Spanish movement, and could bear an orthodox interpretation. This was underlined in the summer of 1970 when Pope Paul VI canonized four such Franciscan martyrs of the fourteenth century. Adverting to the traditional refusal to canonize in cases of provoked martyrdom, a position formalized by Benedict XIV, the pope distinguished between intended provocation and the exercise of a preaching ministry despite the inevitably consequent martyrdom.

St Francis of Assisi made three such martyrdom forays. He journeyed to convert the Almohad caliph of Western Islam in 1213, but fell sick in Spain. An attempt to reach the Syrian Muslims foundered when contrary winds drove his ship on to the Dalmatian coast. He traveled boldly to Damietta in Egypt in this spirit in 1219, where against all probability he charmed the sultan al-Malik al-Kāmil Nāṣir al-Dīn. Dante exalted 'the thirst for martyrdom' that drove Francis to 'preach Christ in the presence of the arrogant Sultan'; Giotto immortalized the scene in his painting at Santa Croce in Florence. The stigmata or wounds of crucifixion that marked the saint's body, as a surrogate martyrdom, related to this obsession.

Moved by the victory of Castilian—Aragonese armies over the Islamic world at Las Navas in 1212, St Francis envisioned a campaign of conversion. At Islamic Seville, for example, a band of

Franciscans tried to force entry into the central mosque and had to be deported. Pushing on to Morocco, all five won martyrdom in 1220. This episode had a Valencian connection. The band found a patron in a Christian general serving in the Almohad armies, the exile Prince Pedro of Portugal who would soon help King Jaume conquer the Balearics and then Valencia, and who would become briefly in turn 'feudal' lord of Majorca and lord of Valencian Morella–Castellón–Segorbe. In deference to this luminary, the Almohad ruler twice packed these disturbers off to Ceuta for embarkation. The Almohad could not prevent their return and murder, but did allow Pedro to send their relics to Coimbra. A separate band at that time entered Tunis and was ejected. The Franciscan order dispatched seven more in 1227 to Ceuta, where they successfully found martyrdom.

Two Italian Franciscans, the priest Giovanni of Perugia and the lay brother Pietro of Sassoferrato, penetrated Valencia around 1228, while it was still an immemorially Islamic region, to court death at the capital city of its *wālī* Abū Zayd. The Almohad had them publicly executed, to the lasting edification of the neighboring realms of Aragon; his own conversion, not long after, was popularly attributed to their blood, while their field of execution became a Valencian holy place.[23] The bizarre episode marked the start of Franciscan commitment to the conversion of the Muslims in the crusader kingdom of Valencia. Ramon Lull on Jaume's Majorca, central figure of the Franciscan mission to the Muslims, meant to set off for North Africa in the same spirit of martyrdom, recoiling from violent death but deliberately courting it. Lull, an eminently rational man, devoted to philosophical argument as a prime means of conversion, nevertheless viewed even his missionary schools of language and polemic as concomitantly schools of martyrdom. Legend, echoing his lifetime thirst for martyrdom, has him killed by a mob while proselytizing in North Africa.

DOMINICAN DIALOGUE: RATIONALISM IN DEBATE

More prominent in the long run were the Dominicans of Valencia and North Africa. A dynamic new order, fresh from successes in Albigensian Languedoc and at the universities in Europe, the Dominicans distinguished themselves in their missionary activity by a novel double tactic – the rationalist argument enthusiastically resounding in the university centers, combined with cultural adaptation by means of language schools. The first element, when turned against Islam, marked the culminating phase of a polemical approach that had come hesitantly to the fore in the early twelfth century under the aegis of writers like Peter the Venerable. Its thirteenth-century expression, more metaphysical, bore the stamp of the Arabic philosophers who so heavily influenced the initial century of transfer of Aristotelian treasures to the West before 1240. The school of Averroës prevalent then among philosophers of Western Islam accepted three modes of persuasive argumentation: rhetorical – to move ordinary men of sound intelligence; dialectical – by argument and counterargument within any common frame of suppositions, as academics use; and demonstrative – proceeding without presuppositions and from first principles, such as rare thinkers or philosophers use. So fashionable had polemics of every kind become among Christians in the realms of Aragon, and so dangerous in the eyes of authority, that King Jaume's conventicle at Tarragona during the Valencian crusade had to forbid laymen to dispute about the faith publicly or privately under pain of excommunication.[24]

The Dominican bishop of Antioch asked Thomas Aquinas for 'moral and philosophical arguments, to which the Saracens give a hearing'; Aquinas' missionary handbook of 1270, responding to this plea, rebuked the concomitant tendency to reduce life and revelation to understandable, provable categories. He admonished his colleagues that, though Muslims were open to argumentation, one could not convert by reason; philosophy served 'not to prove the faith but to defend the faith.'[25] The warning was needed. A Christian rationalist, inhumanly rational, might bend his energies to force the adversary's mind, proceeding without regard for the Muslim's values, limitations, insights, or faith-structure. Such an intellectual, or verbal, confrontation sharpened issues, emphasizing more starkly the irreconcilable points of difference between two exclusivist faiths. Limited initial success was bound eventually to harden the opposing group. Ironically, since philosophical dialogue easily becomes aggression, more could have been achieved by a deliberately non-intellectual and tolerantly pragmatic approach.

On the other hand, if the Franciscan tactic amounted to confrontation in the politico-social ambience, the Dominican approach constituted an infiltration of circles that moderns vaguely designate as the establishment. In the relatively undifferentiated, or rather

91

interpenetrating, Islamic society, to influence a sage was to have an impact on religious, academic, governmental–administrative, and mercantile spheres. Louis Massignon has advanced the theory that in time of crisis, as tension mounts unbearably, cultivated men seek a resolution in ecumenical or unitive directions, while the common man becomes intransigent toward external and internal enemies. Massignon sees this principle working itself out during the thirteenth century both in the East and in southern Spain. The idea can be nuanced to suggest that the euphoric dialogue of conversion between Christian and Muslim academics – so fruitful in Spain according to thirteenth-century Dominicans – created stiff resistance among other Muslims of the same class. The very success of such an effort undoubtedly triggered hostility, polarization at both extremes, and effective countermeasures. This may explain the bad feeling so evident in the riots in Valencia in 1275.[26]

The Franciscans did not wholly disdain the tactic of rationalist discourse or the founding of language schools to promote it. The most eminent single wielder of the method was the Franciscan tertiary Ramon Lull, troubadour turned mystic and scholastic, whose efforts in this direction merit a special word. The pen of this pre-eminent publicist of the conversion movement poured out tireless propaganda, largely directed to Christendom; 243 works have been authenticated, in prose and poetry, in Arabic, Catalan, and Latin, with conversion a major preoccupation. On one occasion Lull requested King Jaume II to forward from Barcelona for his use at Tunis a small library of fifteen books of his disputations with Muslims. Ignorance seemed to him the main hindrance to conversion; he reported in a sermon that though he conversed widely 'with eminent and scholarly Saracens,' he had never met one who grasped Christian beliefs rightly. In his *Doctrina pueril* Lull argued that the savants were skeptical about Muḥammad, and consequently open to conversion; if the most important came over, the masses would follow. Again in the novel *Blanquerna* he insisted that Muslim sages did not believe the Islamic religion about which they were so skilled, and were vulnerable to friendly argumentation. Lull thought Muslims 'nearer the Christians than any other unbelieving people' but reluctant to engage the problem with their intellects because of the sacrifices involved in conversion. Though many refused all controversy, many others 'follow arguments and love proofs'; Christians ought therefore to pursue them with logical syllogisms.[27]

A scene from Lull's novel *Blanquerna*, though dealing with Jews, particularly captures his fantasy of rational conversion. The holy bishop of his story, brooding over the Christian stoning of two Jews, concludes that he could play the peacemaker by reducing differences to a single religion; forthwith, he preaches and holds seminars every Saturday in the synagogue until he absorbs both Jews and problem into the Christian unity. Fellow Franciscans like Roger Bacon shared this Lullian enthusiasm for persuasive or philosophic polemics as the prime tool of conversion. Lull himself came to this scene a bit late, since his religious visions and consequent alteration from troubadour—seneschal to mendicant—philosopher began only in 1263. As the son of a Majorcan crusader, and seneschal to the Conqueror's son Prince Jaume on Majorca, he brought to his task a young lifetime of observation from the highest vantage points. Abandoning his wife for the consuming labor of preaching to infidels, some say he found himself attracted initially by the Dominican style, only later assuming the status of Franciscan tertiary.

Lull's astonishing productivity and the impact of his fascinating character have made his single Franciscan school of language more celebrated than the whole Dominican program. The school was the significantly titled Trinitat, founded by Prince Jaume at Miramar on Majorca in 1274, endowed with 500 gold florins annually, confirmed by Pope John XXI in 1276, and preparing continual relays of thirteen Franciscans until its sudden demise in 1292. In *Blanquerna* Lull describes at length this founding 'in perpetuity.' Proud of its success, he turned up at Rome a decade later to advocate establishing five more such schools. The language apostolate intrudes into *Blanquerna* a number of times, as does Lull's larger preoccupation with Muslim conversion. In one chapter the fictional pope keeps a converted Muslim as his 'scrivener of Arabic'; in another 'he sent for the friars who had learned Arabic' and who had 'converted the Saracen king and a great multitude of people.' In other chapters four friars learn Turkish and leave for the East; two, skilled in Arabic, write to the pope, and the pope determines to resolve language differences, which underlie wars and sects.[28]

After the turn of the century the aged Ramon Lull described to the ecumenical council at Vienne how a great number of Muslims 'were subject to Christians and most of all in Spain'; he outlined a program for preaching to Muslims on Friday and to Jews on Saturday. Still sanguine, Lull wanted only syllogistic arguments. With a sustained program, he claimed, 'it would necessarily follow that the Jews and Saracens would come to the way of truth.' At least one Muslim, the great Muḥammad al-Riqūṭī, found humor a bulwark against such an aggressive approach. Teaching at Murcia's purely secular school of Arabic under the patronage of Alfonso the Learned (a colleague there was the convert Bernardo de Arábigo), he declined the invitation to turn Christian, arguing that since he already found himself deficient in his duties toward one God, he foresaw the measure of his failure toward a Trinitarian three![29]

Another Franciscan, not a tertiary like Lull but the friar Roger Bacon, harped upon the theme of Arabic conjoined to philosophy, with special reference for the Muslims in Christian Spain. 'Arabic serves little use for theological study, but for philosophy and for conversion of infidels much,' he wrote; philosophy in turn was vital for preaching to the infidels. Nor did mere conversational ability avail: 'many men can be found among Western Christians, who know how to speak Greek or Arabic or Hebrew, but very few who know the literary structure (orationem grammaticae ipsius) or how to teach it – I've put many of them to the test.'[30] Despite the eminence of Bacon and Lull, Franciscan labors in this direction remain poorly documented. Their more usual approach was less formal and structured; their forte was a mission of heart more than of head.

The Dominicans, like the Franciscans, saw the Spanish and North African regions as a unified apostolate. In 1256 the master-general, Humbert de Romans, surveying progress and opportunities, hailed Spain and North Africa together as the bright spot for Muslim conversions. Like Humbert, Pope Alexander IV joined the two areas in his bull of 1256 to the Dominican provincial of Spain, giving faculties for specialists to be sent 'to the lands of the Saracens of Spain [and] over the whole kingdom of Tunis'; here 'Spain' meant Murcia and Granada. The standard monograph on Dominican missionary efforts in the thirteenth century divides the universal Muslim mission into six geographical areas, two of which comprise Spain and two North Africa; the distribution reflects the emphasis given these conjoined regions.[31]

St Ramon de Penyafort was this apostolate's leading spirit. A portentous figure in thirteenth-century Europe and moral commentator for his times, the great lawyer became general of the Dominicans in 1238. Already passionately concerned with converting Muslims, he was now able to channel the energies of the young order in that direction. The central part of his life's work in the missionary movement, however, came after his resignation from the generalate; there is reason to think he resigned precisely to concentrate on the promising areas of Tunis, Murcia, and conquered Valencia. From headquarters set up at the Barcelona friary he managed a far-flung program for the conversion of Jew and Muslim in which the Valencian kingdom figured prominently. A friend and executor of his last wishes composed a brief biography recording how Penyafort attracted Muslims by his 'sweet and reasonable discourse'; he begged 'means for their support from kings and prelates'; Moors came to him 'as to a unique refuge.' Another colleague characterized him as 'enthusiastic for spreading the faith among Saracens.' The crowd of kings and nobles gathered to pay tribute at his funeral testified to the influence at his disposal during his life.[32]

PHILOSOPHICAL SCHOOLS OF ARABIC

Polemical preaching, common and programed in Valencia, was not the only weapon in the mendicant arsenal. Equally important as a convert-making technique was the institution of schools of Arabic studies to train specialists in controversy, especially with Muslim academics. These centers applied to the Valencian and North African situation a long-standing Dominican policy. As early as 1235 the master-general, writing from Milan to all the order, called for men 'prepared to learn Arabic, Hebrew, Greek, or some other outlandish language.' Penyafort transformed the Arabic schools into something special. They did not aim to instruct in the elements of Arabic; students undoubtedly knew the language before arriving. The mass of Dominican missioners from whom they came learned their Arabic without counting it anything special, probably working under veteran colleagues in the Near East. Relatively few profited from these advanced centers designed to give facility in polemical conversation. The ideal graduate was a man like Ramon Martí, described shortly after his death as 'philosophus in arabico.'[33]

Most of the records for these schools have disappeared, though minutes from Dominican general and provincial chapters, along with references from the lives of leaders, supply some information. A converted Moor, the Dominican Miquel Benazar (Ibn Naṣr), may have created the first such philosophy and language school shortly after the fall of Majorca; if so, it soon foundered. This Benazar, to whose name the title Blessed is popularly prefixed, is said to have been the son of the Ben Aabet (perhaps Ibn 'Abīd) who figures in King Jaume's memoirs as surrendering and then helping conquer part of Majorca peacefully. The Dominicans placed their central schools for work with Western Muslims at those spots within the area that combined density of Muslim population with maximum opportunity – Tunis for a while, then Játiva, Murcia, and Valencia city, with Barcelona as the home base. Tunis was the first center established from Barcelona. It dates from the early 1240s, at the latest from 1245. An assignment of eight friars in 1250, often mistaken as the founding, shows it in full career. Apparently it died just before 1259, though a promising phase of Dominican activity ensued there after the peace of 1270. The provincial chapter at Valencia city in 1259 decreed an Arabic school for the Barcelona priory; instead the Valencian school, continuing or briefly reopened, seems to have absorbed the Tunis people. Alternatively, the Murcian school may already have taken up the slack of the Tunisian loss; it was bilingual, providing also a chair of Hebrew.

Five Dominican language schools, to all appearances, developed by the end of the thirteenth century. José Coll, their keenest historian, challenges this common conclusion, arguing rather that centers appeared and died in a broken pattern defying neat analysis. Játiva was the most constant, Murcia the most celebrated. Coll certainly defers the Murcian foundation too long, however, choosing 1266 on the feeble grounds that only then did the Christians conquer Murcia. Actually Murcia had been a tributary of Castile with strong internal Christian influences for two decades. Penyafort recorded many Murcian conversions for this earlier period. The definitive conquest by Jaume I in 1266 undoubtedly demanded the school's reorganizing and strengthening. Penyafort himself decreed the Murcian *arabicum*, the contemporary Pere Marsili reported, 'arranging to send selected Catalan friars, who progressed to the great advantage of souls and to the honor of his countrymen (*natio*).'[34] After the troubles connected with the 1275 war, this establishment broke up, the Hebrew section moving to Barcelona and the Arabic to Valencia city.

A school apparently opened or flourished at Valencia city by 1250. Friar Miquel moved down from Lérida that year as professor; eight other Dominicans were posted to the city and a Valencian removed to Majorca. This school may have been merely theological, but one hears nothing further of any kind of studies here until abruptly encountering a full *arabicum* shortly after the death of King Jaume. The Dominicans, with priories already in six cities of Jaume's realms and shortly to open seven more, had worked at Valencia city for over a decade by the time of the notice in 1250 and had nearly completed their second complex of large church and other buildings.[35]

A letter from the master-general in 1256 may help clarify the murky academic scene at the capital city. Humbert praised 'the friars in the region of Spain who for many years already have studied in Arabic among Saracens [and] are wonderfully proficient in the language.'[36] Though contemporaries often reserved the term 'Spain' for Muslim-held areas, the Dominican province of Spain comprised the Christian countries, Valencia city not yet belonging definitively to a particular one of its eight vicariates. Assuming that Penyafort organized the Spanish studies of this letter along the same lines as the Tunisian, since he was directing both projects from Barcelona, the most plausible conclusion is that schools existed from before mid-century at Murcia city or Valencia city or both, a conclusion that advances our knowledge of the origins of the language schools by more than a decade.

The Valencia *arabicum* may have continued unbroken from before 1250 until it emerges again into the documentation after King Jaume's death; or if one follows Coll's theory that the Murcia school did not take up the work of the abandoned Tunis center until 1266, then his conjecture is reasonable that the Tunis men filled in at Valencia rather than Barcelona, creating a school for the period 1258–66. A third thesis is possible. The Valencian establishment may have gone to Játiva around 1260, combining with the Hebrew chair brought down from Barcelona. The Valencia city school reappears at least by 1276 or 1277, this time either replacing or consolidating with the translated Arabic chair of the Murcian school. No Dominican *acta* survive to trace the history of the schools during the subsequent five years. In 1281 Joan de Puigventós is discovered in charge of the Valencia city *studium arabicum*, with five friars assigned as new students – Pere of Tartary, Nadal, Martí Seriol, and from the Cordova friary Juan Serrano and García Arceiz. The Estella chapter that year dispatched two Moorish converts to the Valencia enterprise, the friars Salvador and Domingo Sancho. This activity, often carelessly cited as a founding, no more marks the beginning than does the notice of 1250, both apparently episodes in the school's mature life.[37]

The Játiva school must have persisted, though no document survives for the thirty years up to 1291. It seems to have been the most continuous, and in the first decade of the next century it proved the most active. Its location owed much to Játiva's status as civil administrative center for southern Valencia, as former capital of a Muslim subprincipality almost like that of Valencia or Murcia, and as retaining after the crusade a larger Muslim population and more native atmosphere than the forcibly emptied Valencia city. Of all the kingdom's main towns, Játiva at first kept its Islamic administrative–social structure most fully; intellectually it became the center of Mudejar Valencia. The Játiva and Valencia priories, though part of the same Dominican province, quarreled over respective jurisdictions for preaching in the new kingdom. In a compromise settlement Valencia took the northern half from Morella to the Júcar River, and the Játiva house got from the Júcar to Bañeres. The division reveals a natural zone of apostolate for each and a further reason for an Arabic center at Játiva. The school's timetable seems not to have related to the development of the Dominicans' priory at Játiva for their more general work. King Jaume had given them land there in 1248, but they were still projecting a house in 1285 and may not have commissioned this until after 1290.[38]

At the end of the century, when the peninsula ceased to be a single Dominican province and Aragon joined Navarre as a separate province, a general chapter decreed that Játiva should no longer receive students from all over Spain. In 1302 the Aragonese provincial chapter balanced this, urging superiors to facilitate attendance by volunteer students at Játiva. The next year Friar Pere Escarramat came as teacher, while the Játiva prior got orders to 'hire and maintain one Jew who is also schooled in Arabic, or some Saracen, so that he may teach there along with the said Friar Pere'; he later became *Vicarius Africae*. In 1304 the provincial chapter assigned another group of students to Játiva.[39] Shortly afterwards Queen Blanca, the wife of Jaume II, provided a scholarship fund in her will for 'the Dominican friars at Játiva studying in Hebrew and Arabic, to support them as long as the aforesaid *studium* exists – on its demise the said revenues to go to the nuns of Santa Maria Magdalena at Valencia city.'[40] Blanca de Anjou, daughter of the king of Naples, had been a close friend of Ramon Lull; her will was drawn at Valencia city, two of its six designated executors being Valencia's bishop Ramon Despont and the king's Dominican confessor Guillem

Arinyó. These circumstances may explain the legacy, since other Valencian wills usually ignore this apostolate. The will's proviso for transfer of the legacy indicates that reorganization of the language school system, and phasing of its independent entities into the theological program a few years later, was already in the wind.

The language centers had been Catalan in inspiration and in early personnel. What of Castile? Jaume the Conqueror reproached his colleague of Castile, Alfonso the Learned, for plunging into bookish pursuits while neglecting conversion of the Mudejars. Alfonso could not avoid involving himself in the Murcian foundation, however, since it was for Castile that King Jaume had helped so much in conquering that territory. The contemporary Nicolau Eimeric records how Penyafort 'with the help of the lord king of Castile and the lord king of Aragon saw to the establishment of a school of Arabic language' at Murcia. When Alfonso established with the utmost solemnity his *studium generale* or university of Arabic and Latin studies at Seville in 1254, he by no means intended a missionary but an academic enterprise, springing from the king's fascination with Arabic culture and with university learning; its charter bore the confirmatory signatures of three Islamic 'kings.'[41] The language-center movement never broadened its base. Under the urging of Lull, Pope Clement V at the ecumenical council of Vienne in 1312 ordered two chairs each in Arabic, Hebrew, and Chaldean for the universities of Paris, Oxford, Bologna, and Salamanca, as well as at the papal curia, 'so as to lead wanderers into the path of truth.' No record survives to prove that any of these began or, if they began, that they lasted long. From 1248 at least, and probably earlier, Paris boasted a college of 'Arabic and other' Near Eastern languages that instructed relays of ten 'young men' (*pueri*) or 'clerics' from overseas, but we know nothing about the establishment beyond that bare fact.[42]

METAPHYSICS, BOOKS, PERSONNEL

Critical for the success of polemical efforts at conversion was a metaphysical theology with which to meet the Muslim savant on his home ground, and if possible some handbooks to facilitate its deployment. The Catalan Ramon Martí composed his *Pugio fidei adversus Mauros et Iudaeos* for this mission. With these areas in view the Catalan Penyafort requested a similar work from Thomas Aquinas and so prompted the master work of Aquinas, the *Summa contra gentiles*. Lull conceived his similarly titled *Llibre del gentil* for this crusade of philosophy, probably after the disputation in 1263 with the Jews at Barcelona, but he confected other works for disputing with Muslims.

A direct or causal connection between the labors of Martí and Aquinas, argued persuasively but then abandoned on grounds of chronology, is once more being sustained. The two Dominicans had sat together as students under Albert the Great, their works display parallels and borrowings, and their separate interest in the Arago-Catalan mission is clear. Earlier arguments by Miguel Asín y Palacios for direct borrowing by the *Contra gentiles* from the *Pugio* had been frustrated, however, by the separate works of Luis Getino (1905) and José Llovera (1929) that dated the *Pugio* at 1278, a decade after the time commonly assigned to the work of Aquinas – 1261 to 1264, or even 1258 to 1263.[43] Evidence of a connection remained strong, so that in 1969 José Casciaro fell back upon informal pre-publication interchange between two friends as the explanation. Meanwhile Pierre Marc, in his 1967 introduction to the critical edition of the *Contra gentiles*, grappled anew with the dating problem; external and internal evidence led him to reverse previous conclusions and to assign the work to the last years of Aquinas' life, roughly 1270–3. There now seems little doubt that Aquinas used Martí's earlier *Capistrum* (1267), while Martí later drew upon the *Contra gentiles* for his own *Pugio*; further interchange, along Casciaro's line, also seems probable. Some historians of Aquinas such as Weisheipl are dismayed at the prospect of redating his entire corpus, however, and are not at all comfortable with Marc's arguments.[44]

Unaware of this future revolution in dating and innocent of the complexity of Mudejar Spain, certain older scholars had expressed skepticism over the missionary motives of Aquinas, seeing only the 'gentiles' of the Paris academic scene as his target. Thus M. M. Gorce rejected the witness of a junior contemporary, the Catalan Pere Marsili, Penyafort's fellow Dominican and biographer, on the grounds that 'except perhaps for some teachers or rabbis' in the realms of Aragon, 'one cannot see very well what profit' could be drawn 'from this work of extreme erudition and real philosophical difficulty.'[45] The puzzlement betrays ignorance of the high civilization flourishing in Valencian and Murcian Islam during the centuries leading up to the crusade; it also rests on a misunderstanding as to the nature of the Dominican schools for which the work was desired. Besides, Marsili was a man eminent in the Islamic mission, distinguished in letters and learning, a counselor to Jaume II, and well placed to know the facts. When he put his account together at the Barcelona center, thirty-five years after the death of its director Penyafort, many who had known that great man were still alive to dispute irresponsible claims. His witness is definitive. Today one can even point to the moment when Penyafort's appeal was conveyed to Aquinas – during Martí's trip to Paris, in November 1269 to March 1270. Aquinas surpassed Penyafort's request for a handbook, of course, creating a master work useful against not only the Greco-Arab views in their Parisian and varied Islamic forms but against the full range of *errores infidelium* facing Christendom.

Careful survey uncovers forty students at our language schools during the lifetime of King Jaume, surely a fraction of the total. The contemporary Marsili records that at Murcia alone 'twenty friars or more of the order of Preachers were taught in that [Arabic] language.' From study of available names, the great majority at all schools appear to have been Catalans. This reflects political realities of both crown patronage and geography; the school areas lay under King Jaume's control as at Valencia and Játiva, his influence as at Tunis, or his special relationship due to conquest and partial settlement as at Murcia. Each group of six or more students studied for two or three years at a center, receiving at the end a kind of university degree, the *licentia disputandi* required for formal public controversy and issued by the Dominican provincial. Friars could return for a refresher course. A school might be an *arabicum* alone, as at Valencia, or bilingual, as at Murcia and Játiva. Bilingual *studia* could be coequal or, as apparently happened at Játiva when the Jewish controversies threw emphasis upon the Hebrew faculty, a *primarius* in the one language could control the school while a subteacher of the other language functioned under him. The pattern has confused some moderns, causing them to see a founding at Játiva when the Lérida chapter in 1312 'establishes a *studium arabicum*,' the prior to provide a professor. Actually this represents an administrative upgrading of the subordinate faculty.[46]

The *studia* required libraries, always an expense to collect. An indication of how the precious books were acquired comes from the testament of Ramon Despont, the last bishop of Valencia in the thirteenth century: as benefactor of the local Dominicans he left them a large amount of money, a scholarship at the University of Paris, and for the Játiva center sets of both *Summae* of Aquinas. The majority of language instructors were not Dominicans or even converts but Muslims, especially during the early decades. A life of Penyafort by a near-contemporary says that 'many of these, particularly the erudite, inclined to accept the truth of the Catholic faith, and the teachers of the brothers in the Arabic language were almost all converted by the industry of these [Dominican] students.'[47]

Three Dominicans stand out in the apostolate of polemical schools in Valencia. Ramon de Penyafort loomed as the moving force until his death in 1275. His junior contemporary, Joan de Puigventós, crown overseer for the wider popular mission to the kingdom of Valencia's Mudejars, received the habit at Valencia city's priory and probably took his Arabic training at Murcia. He taught at the Valencia city school, where according to a document of 1281 he held the Arabic chair, and he served as subprior of the local Dominican residence. His extensive work among *aljamas* of the Valencia kingdom caused many to regard him as a saint. He died in 1301. Closer in age to Penyafort was the famed 'philosophical Arabist' Ramon Martí, 'beloved intimate' not only of Jaume I of Aragon and Louis IX of France, Marsili records, but also 'of the good king of Tunis.' From Subirats near Barcelona, Martí entered the order during the opening years of the Valencia crusade and was one of eight assigned to strengthen the Tunis school in 1250. In 1257 he composed an *Explanatio simboli apostolorum* for work with Jews and Moors. His *Summa* against the Koran in 1260, now lost, culminated the Islamic phase of his work and provided the Dominican schools with a solid text. A Hebrew student, he was diverted to this new field by public controversy with the Jews of Barcelona in 1263. In 1264, as one of a trio appointed by King Jaume, he examined Jewish books; in 1267 he composed a polemic work for use with Jews along much the same lines as the Muslim polemic. Aside from a briefer mission to Tunis in 1268 and 1269, which won him an appearance in King Jaume's memoirs, Martí continued this specialization. In 1278 he finished his celebrated *Pugio fidei*, whose first selection was directed to Muslims, and in 1281 took the Hebrew chair at the Barcelona *studium*. He died after 1285.[48]

Men of lesser stature, such as the teacher Pere Escarramat, played their roles. It is probable that friars like Sans Boleya (Sancho de Bolea), ambassador to Tunis in 1299 and polemicist, involved themselves with the Mudejars of Valencia. Francesc Cendra, active in the Tunis *arabicum*, as a diplomat in Africa, and as prior of the Barcelona house, must have shown interest in the sister centers. Blessed Pere de Cadiret, another product of the Tunis school, became by 1257 inquisitor for the realms of Aragon including Valencia. Bernat de Bach held vicariate powers over the Catalan–Valencian–Murcian region from 1275. Bernat de Peregrí from Lérida, student at the Valencia *arabicum* from 1269, and later crown inquisitor, fostered the Játiva center; he died in 1309. Most of this elite band, however, remain unknown as individuals; a handful appear as bare names receiving assignments.

The approach of the schools marks a trend away from older concern with the dogmatics of Islam. Metaphysical dialogue comes to the fore as much as theological confrontation. In short, metaphysics constituted a specialized apostolate concerned rather with the ranks of Islam's erudite. The broad front represented by compulsory attendance at rationalist preaching was only indirectly connected with the schools' apostolate to the intellectual elite. Specialized teaching undoubtedly filtered down to the ordinary theological student or friar in the Valencian kingdom's priories, but it supplemented background and tactic rather than providing the content of sermons. A double movement of conversion, in which the dramatic concept of the schools overshadows the mendicants' wider, quiet work, progressed in a parallel manner. Acquisition of conversational vulgar Arabic, perhaps with the aid of vocabulary handbooks like that by Ramon Martí, was as easy for the young friar as for the merchant or adventuring knight. Because of confusion between the two apostolates, Dominican success on Majorca caused Coll to postulate an early Dominican school there.[49] Under both guises the unremitting crusade of polemics, continuing far beyond the crusade of the sword, had a measure of success.

From one point of view, therefore, the schools had a limited focus of attention, unrepresentative of wider missionary work; from another angle they constituted the most formidable direct attack on Valencian Islam. The acculturative effect of converts from this class upon the Muslim community had to have been traumatic. Academic Spanish Islam, heir of Averroës and Avempace, wrestled with the sons of Albert, Aquinas, and all the array of thirteenth-century scholastic genius. At this level the mendicant effort appears in a more favorable light than it does as the arrogant rationalism it became when more widely diffused. Enthusiasts for philosophy saw themselves taking the only ground on which Muslim leaders could meet them. The long life of this conviction suggests that metaphysics still enjoyed some position in the Valencian Mudejar intellectual scene.

Ironically it was a pious Muslim, not the busy Dominicans, who left us our only glimpse into the system actually at work. Ibn Rashīq al-Mursī, a beardless adolescent assisting his father in drafting notarial documents at Murcia city around 1250, fell into controversy with a priest at the local center. He later recalled how a routine oath in connection with a lawsuit between a Muslim and a Christian brought him to the ample residence (*dār*) and church of the infidel missionaries. They constituted 'a group of priests and monks dedicated, according to them, to the devout life and to studying the sciences, but interested above all in the sciences [learning] of the Muslims and in translating them into their language.' The 'object' of these clerics, Ibn Rashīq continues, was 'to criticize – may the most high God frustrate their projects!' These clever aliens 'were eager to engage in polemic with Muslims, intending to lure the weak to their side.' This description hardly fits the short-lived *madrasa* patronized by Alfonso the Learned, whose chief ornament was the Muslim Muḥammad b. Aḥmad b. Abū Bakr al-Riqūṭī al-Mursī, a school where Christians and Jews enrolled along with the Muslim student body; nor did diocesan authorities in this era have at their disposition such a body of learned 'priests and monks.'

Ibn Rashīq encountered there 'a priest from Marrakesh, eloquent, widely knowledgeable, and moderate in discussion,' who not only knew Arabic perfectly but was versed in the Koran, Arabic literature, and scholasticism. The Muslim found him patient, tolerant, and free from fanaticism. This may have been the great Martí, or less probably the diplomat and archdeacon of Morocco García Pérez, or merely one of the local Dominican staff. The priest praised the boy, remarking that he had heard of his father's erudition and of the youth's promise as a bright student. Invited to enter amiable debate, Ibn Rashīq plunged into an extended discussion of miracles and related themes. The experience impressed the young Muslim profoundly. Years later, perhaps after he had become *kātib* to the emir of Ceuta or after his subsequent return to Granada, he composed a record of the long dialogue, preserved centuries afterward in a chance copy by another scholar. Beyond the bleak administrative records, this episode reveals something of the manner of approach and inner strength gracing these institutions.[50]

THE END OF THE DREAM

The duration of the Valencian schools, continuing into the opening years of the fourteenth century, betrays the survival of a larger class of erudites than historians have supposed. The future of the schools apparently fell under dispute before the end of that century's first decade; after 1313 they mysteriously disappear from the provincial records. The *acta* of the provincial chapter of 1313, perhaps critical for our knowledge here, have disappeared. Training continued as before, Coll argues, but dispersed now in the Dominican philosophy faculties of the realms of Aragon. The reorganization, carried through only a short time after the upgrading of the Játiva *arabicum* in 1312, marks a coming of age for the schools and a passing of the crash-program phase. It may also mark a diminution of the Mudejar erudite class in the Valencian kingdom. It probably represents a reorientation away from special mendicant concern for the Spanish frontier toward fresher fields. The academic reshuffling, however, did not terminate the importance of Játiva and Valencia city as local centers of conversion.

There is room for a more pessimistic view. Charles Dufourcq contends that the dream of converting North Africa dimmed in the first quarter of the fourteenth century and that now more Christians were being lost than Muslims gained: an era of harsher military crusading and commercial problems was at hand. If his interpretation is just, Christian attitudes in the Mudejar regions and Dominican attitudes in general must have reflected the change. Some commentators, assessing the whole enterprise of medieval intellectual missions, complain that the polemicists never really entered the Islamic mind as sympathetic ecumenists. The schoolmen would have thought the reproach irrelevant, since their specialized mission assumed that the Muslim intellectual at bottom could hardly take the dogmas of Islam seriously.

Despite the substantial numbers they won for Christianity, the Dominicans could not shift Valencia's Islamic communities. The reverse *dhimma* condition protected and fortified the Muslim's faith, a faith already rooted in this region as a universal phenomenon for half a millennium, according to Epalza's thesis. This faith not only

resisted external transformative pressures now but reacted communally to turn such overt intrusions into a strengthening experience.
In the final analysis, Islam's traumatic losses here represented individuals; whatever the value of the schools to those individuals,
institutionally the schools were a failure in terms of Dominican
goals. Besides its inability to move from isolated individuals to some
general effect, the Dominican approach suffered from another weakness. The Aristotelian revolution had swept over Europe's Christian
and Jewish communities at the very time when it was waning in
Western Islam. Almohad rule had been friendly to philosophy, and
had held at bay the conservative fideism of the Malikite theologians;
a golden age had ensued for metaphysical speculation until the death
of the great Averroës shortly before King Jaume's birth. Almohad
collapse then revived Malikite power and discouraged metaphysics
at the very time when Jaume's crusading hosts were advancing. Ibn
Ṭumlūs of Valencia, who died in the year young Jaume first besieged
Peñíscola, had helped turn speculative minds toward the safer field
of logic. Metaphysics survived sufficiently to attract the Dominicans
as a tool for proselytizing, but it was far less compelling and widespread in Spain than previously.

Dominique Urvoy has noted a more radical defect in the philosophical approach: neither language nor metaphysics addressed the
basic 'cultural presuppositions' of the Muslim, so that the Dominican skills could not penetrate Muslim psychology. A psychological
rather than merely linguistic–speculative accommodation was required. Applying psycho-sociological and more pragmatic sociological techniques to such data as biographical sketches, Urvoy is
exploring the expressions of Islam peculiar to eastern al-Andalus in
the pre-crusade generation. She concludes that metaphysics had lost
much of its relevance there, not only for the generality of Muslims
but for a great part of the cultivated. A baroque religious sufism had
instead captured their enthusiasm. This doomed the Christian
approach through metaphysical rationalism, whose day had largely
passed. On the other hand, al-Andalus on the eve of the crusade
lacked the solid and aggressive self-confidence which was to shield
North African Islam from Christian penetration. Within the narrower field of polemics, one might add, conservatism prevailed, and
certain themes recurred even in later Morisco polemics against the
Christians. Cardaillac thought the themes employed by Aquinas
enjoyed continued relevance in that context. Polemic has limited

uses, however, and its thematic relevance does not cancel out Urvoy's socio-psychological findings, especially as applying to the atypical mindcast of this section and generation of al-Andalus.

It is likely that the work of the language centers influenced the complimentary view Ibn Khaldūn took of Christian philosophical activity. He first drafted his major work in Tunisia from 1375 to 1378; though he wrote a lifetime after the *studia* disappeared, his focus was that of a Tunisian with chauvinistic pride in his Spanish origins and a sharp awareness of the Valencian crusade era. As diplomat to King Pedro of Castile in 1363 and 1364 he was offered his family's Seville property, which had been confiscated at their flight over a century before. Tunis, he reminds us, had served as the central receiving area for Valencian and Murcian Mudejar emigrants. It had also housed the main Dominican schools that later retreated to the Valencia–Murcia territory. Ibn Khaldūn understood 'that the philosophical sciences are greatly cultivated in the land of Rome and along the adjacent shore of the country of the European Christians.' The 'adjacent shore' included, but must have stressed, the realms of Aragon. Ibn Khaldūn used the term 'Rome' in traditional fashion for Byzantium, but more often as the capital city and symbol for European Christendom. His shorthand use of it here for Europe is peculiarly just, since the philosophic apostolate among erudites was commissioned and encouraged by the popes, who showed lively interest in the conversion of Tunis. The philosophical sciences 'are said to be studied there again and to be taught in numerous classes,' Ibn Khaldūn continues; 'existing systematic expositions of them are said to be comprehensive, the people who know them numerous, and the students of them very many.' This paragraph reflects the brief but real rupture in the mutual insulation of Muslim and Christian intellectual societies, a bridging of learned languages and alien mentalities. Ibn Khaldūn exhausted his interest in Christian metaphysical activity in those sentences, breaking off with the pious tag: 'God knows better what exists there.'[51]

As time passed, the dream of conversion flickered, fitfully dimmed, and died. It could not survive the harsh realities, for it rested on unfirm foundations – that Muslims stood at the brink of conversion, that their savants could scarcely credit Islamic beliefs, and that key princes inclined toward Christianity. It rested, too, upon an aggressive optimism – sometimes upon an eschatological euphoria, including influences from Joachimite ideology and from the Mongol irruption – that faded as the factors constituting the medieval balance shifted at the turn of the century, giving way to problems, doubts, rebuffs, and general decline of spirit that the crisis of the Black Death at the following mid-century merely culminated and crowned. The dream rested, too, upon a situation within Islam, shattered and shaken and on the defensive, which inevitably readjusted, reacted, and grew again in strength. Lull again came reluctantly to admit the need for armed crusade, making of war a second foot for holding up the crippled dream. For a moment of time, nonetheless, influential people had favored sheathing the sword, sitting down in dialogue with the immemorial and hated enemy; for a moment, many men had groped for some common ground that was not a battlefield. The dream failed. It had amounted to a reaffirmation of a traditional, more profoundly Christian approach to the dissident. Paradoxically, however, its aggressive rationalism and polemical proselytism, like some virus introduced in Christendom's bloodstream, heralded a new age of self-righteous harassment and discrimination. By the end of the century Christendom had put on an armor of inquisition and was entering an era of punitive harshness, but the memory of the century-long effort remained quiescent in mendicant tradition. New Worlds, a century or two later, revived the dream in fresh forms; for the moment anyway it had entered the Western spirit as a corrective tropism. And if it contributed nothing more lasting than to encourage Aquinas in elaboration of his open-minded *Contra gentiles*, mankind is the richer.

4

Piracy: Islamic–Christian interface
in conquered Valencia

The passion for conversion just observed reveals the role of Europe's new mendicant friars in the shaping of Valencia's dual society. The preacher had much in common with the next object of our attention, the pirate. Both adventured forth seeking their respective prizes far afield; each disdained death in his pursuit; neither was so lonely and unaffiliated a figure as at first sight he appears. Both fitted a pattern perfectly understandable within the context of the other's society. Both operated just outside routine civil and ecclesiastical establishments, yet as an independent arm or function of those more prosaic authorities. And both served as multiple points of contact between Christian and Mudejar society as well as between the realms of Aragon and the external Islamic societies. Mendicantism and piracy alike interfaced the two peoples.

CORSAIR–PIRATES: THE SHADOW OF COMMERCE

Whether as privateering or bloody robbery, piracy was a constant in Mediterranean history from ancient into modern times. A cross-cultural phenomenon, corsair activity was the shadow of commerce, an unceasing form of guerrilla warfare, a frontier of opportunity for the upwardly mobile, the crusades at a grassroots level, a kind of kidnapping or mugging, and a routine investment. Repugnant to modern sensibilities, in medieval times it wore the face of respectability, reflecting the realities of a war-torn world. It was in fact a form of commerce, or in Dufourcq's phrase 'a veritable industry.' City councils, sultans, and kings commissioned it; fishermen, knights, and merchant venturers made it their seasonal avocation. Banks backed it; businessmen drew up contracts, crews hired on, and investors realized a healthy return (after taxes) from this high-risk enterprise. So conventionalized and profit-oriented was this medieval activity, that some historians are reluctant to apply terms like pirate or corsair, with their demonic image.

The pirate turned privateer when he could get a commission, whether direct or implied; the privateer easily turned to piracy when peace came; the merchant diversified into either activity or into smuggling and contraband, as his opportunities and conscience might counsel. The pirate was ecumenical in his choice of victim, the privateer indiscriminate as to his licensing contractor. The pirate saw targets of opportunity everywhere; the privateer flourished in those petty wars between city-states or regions which flared around the horizon like Northern Lights and now go unremarked in most histories. The Muslim privateer–pirate had the Christians as target; the Christian, the Muslims; but each group was as much a scourge to its own people. Corsairs and pirates formed an interconnection between Islamic and Christian societies – a regular contact for all classes, and an international conflict carried literally to the front door of coastal populations. As endemic as the plague, they shuttled populations of kidnap victims between the two societies in what Fernand Braudel calls 'a concentration camp world,'[1] its trauma accepted with resignation as part of life but affecting the sensibilities of corsair and victim alike. Even in its renegade or pirate form the phenomenon was beyond control. Central authority remained weak throughout the medieval Mediterranean, merchantman and war-ship were readily convertible, and sea actions involved darting about on the riverine seas in short bursts of activity. At the end of the thirteenth century Genoa did indeed establish a ministry of piracy to channel complaints from Muslims, Jews, and Christians wrongfully attacked by Genoese ships; this Office of Robbery soon foundered under the volume of claims.[2] Only much later would strong monarchies, heavy taxation, and a technological revolution in ships and armaments create Alfred Mahan's 'sea-power' and true navies, able to impose control.

Like the hermit and the slave, the medieval corsair was far more important than his place in historical consciousness suggests. He left no archives or memoirs but must be run to ground (or into port) from oblique references and random documentation. Once ubiquitous, he now lurks at the periphery of the historian's vision. Nor can he be discovered by assembling notices from different eras and regions. The piracy–privateer industry was always in dialogue with its surroundings, answering to economic cycles and political shifts, waxing or waning, and assuming novel guises. It must therefore be studied minutely in its local context, as expressing local needs, strengths, weakness, technology, sensibility, and politics. Conversely each period can be studied in its pirates. Every generation gets the pirates it deserves.

The golden age of piracy was to be the seventeenth century, when the breakup of Spanish, Turkish, and Mogul Indian empires, with the Ming decline in China, fostered 'the great pirate belt' from China to the New World. For the Mediterranean, perhaps the sixteenth century saw at least a silver age. More mysterious, because its details have not been gathered or a synthesis attempted, is the world of medieval Mediterranean piracy during the freewheeling period of final expansion and affluence, from about 1100 to 1300, when the medieval Commercial Revolution expanded privateering and piracy as a by-product. Authors like Dufourcq, Favreau, Gazulla, Goitein, Lopez, Mollat, and Ramos y Loscertales have contributed chapters toward this eventual study, but the field of pre-fourteenth-century piracy still lies open.[3] Braudel suggests that the neglect is due to psychological factors, a reluctance to see our ancestors in this role; it more likely comes from our lateness in discovering that the center of the medieval world lay at the Mediterranean, with the tribal north of England, France, and Germany as fringes. Though Braudel believes that the word 'pirate' did not enter common usage in the Mediterranean until the seventeenth century, Catalan records show it to have been a normal medieval term for illegal privateers.

VALENCIA'S NAVY: THE KING'S CORSAIRS

Any bloc of Mediterranean littoral might serve equally well for assembling notes illustrating thirteenth-century corsair activity at a local level. Mediterranean Spain makes a particularly good laboratory. Corsair documentation on this littoral is mostly unpublished, and maritime interaction there with Islam was constant. The very expansion of King Jaume's realms was triggered by Muslim piracy. His stunning amphibious seizure of the Majorcan island kingdom, as Mario del Treppo notes, was 'born as an operation of vigilance against Saracen pirates and to defend Catalan sea traffic.' Matthew Paris, the thirteenth-century English chronicler reporting on Jaume's conquest of Majorca, says the island had been 'crammed (referta) with pirates and robbers,' and had been a major danger to 'merchants and pilgrims' but especially to Christian merchants between Spain and North Africa. The crusade against Valencia itself, Vicente Salavert argues, 'had among other purposes the objective of securing the right flank' of the valuable coastal trade to North Africa against this plague of pirates. Conversely, Adolf Schaube concluded that Jaume's own mature pirate-power had made possible, and then encouraged him to turn outward and undertake, his island and coastal crusades of conquest. Corsair activity was not a by-product or merely the naval arm of the Valencian crusade, therefore, but its very occasion, technology, and to a large degree purpose.

Even after King Jaume's further conquest of Valencia, however, his searoads remained dangerous, his frontiers weak, his navy nearly nonexistent except for licensed entrepreneurs, and each conquered territory vulnerable both by its extensive coastline and its dissident Islamic majority. As in all such regions, individual cities and lords financed and licensed privateers against the general enemy. Merchants contracted for raids in the same spirit and jargon as they signed to haul wheat. The crown, while mounting its own expeditions, tried to oversee the general activity or at least to control its excesses. Regulation of corsairs formed one of the oldest sections of medieval Catalan law. By the thirteenth century this legislation had become ample and traditional. The codes of Valencia and Tortosa gave it attention; and in the last quarter of the century crown statutes laid down details on the pre-deposit, license, exclusion of royal officials, protection of accused corsairs from imprisonment until convicted, and similar conditions. The king's share from every corsair act became a major financial resource for the crown treasury. And Jaume's power and reputation at sea grew until he won the international title from the papacy: 'admiral and captain-general of the church of Rome.' (Historians have hitherto believed that the 'captain-general' title was held in Aragon only much later, by Jaume II.)[4]

As Goitein pointed out for the earlier Middle Ages, there was 'no clear-cut distinction between piracy and war.'[5] Nor did naval forces exist as moderns know the term. Sea-power of a country consisted largely of the number and quality of merchant vessels which could be licensed or else drafted and armed in an emergency, and the number of galleys the authorities then franchised to be built, whether by commission or popular subscription. Against local pirates the common folk might even contribute toward an 'alms galley' (*galea de l'almoina*). Further complicating the scene, from the late eleventh century the spirit of crusade had grown universal at sea, with greed and cruelty the companion of piety. Indulgences were offered for privateering in support of crusading in Spain, and these applied also to almsgiving which funded such voyages. Within the larger framework Christians still fought Christians, Muslims fought Muslims, unexpected cross-alliances formed and dissolved, hoodlums from both Christian and Islamic worlds joined together, and there would have been more than a few cases like the mutiny of 1323 when a Catalan crew killed its captain and set out as pirates, crying 'Let's go plunder everybody!' ('anem a robar de tot hom').[6] At the same time, a countervailing need for peace and stability united merchants with crown in an effort to secure trade agreements outlawing piracy between signatory countries. Catalan–Muslim truces fluctuated, broke down, and were initiated anew.

Individual corsairs can be discerned from time to time in the thicket of King Jaume's documentation. His powerful vassal and close relative Nunyo Sanç, count of Roussillon, around 1230 'armed a ship and two galleys to go privateering (*entrar en cors*) in the regions of Barbary.'[7] This does not seem a random action but part of the naval pressure the king was bringing to bear on North Africa. That very year he named Carròs de Rebollet, a German crusader (probably by way of Italy), to be his admiral, soon sending him also to harry the North African coast. In 1234 an ambitious naval attack in force attempted to destroy the Muslims' corsair base at Ceuta. The count of Ampurias made his principality particularly attractive as a corsair center. In 1260 King Jaume warned him not to let Genoese and other foreign corsairs, outfitting at and sailing from Ampurias, attack ships of the crown's ally Tunis; otherwise the king would indemnify Tunis by attacking Ampurian property. In 1264 King Jaume noted that the citizens of Barcelona had 'armed two galleys against the Saracens,' and he generously waived any share or taxes which might accrue to the crown from their raids.[8]

Several licenses or privateering patents by the crown have survived from 1263 to 1264. Guillem Grony, crown vicar of Barcelona, could 'wreak all damage' on the subjects of the rulers of Islamic Tlemcen and even Tunis; his raiding crews were to have a year's moratorium on all debts. Berenguer de Trepó or Tripó could arm a ship to recover losses sustained to the Tunisians. Bernat Cancull could attack all Muslims with his two ships, 'on sea and land,' except for ships or even passengers traveling from friendly Egypt. Ramon Marget held a commission to attack Granadan subjects and apparently also Moroccans. The Barcelonans were authorized to arm galleys 'and any kind of ships or sea vessels,' and were promised over two years of truce-free hostility. Bishop Arnau de Gurb of Barcelona outfitted his own ship. The Tortosans contributed another. And the king appointed his son Pere Ferran de Hijar to command a separate royal fleet, which other privateers could join if they chose. The highest prelate in the realms, the archbishop of Tarragona, Benet de Rocaberti, metropolitan over the Catalan, Aragonese, and Valencian dioceses, in response to King Jaume's 'urging' outfitted and armed 'one galley to wreak damage and harm on the Saracens.' Three canons of Barcelona acted as agents of the archbishop in these arrangements; the king waived his share of any privateering profits, in favor of the prelate. Obviously the 1264 raids formed part of a general effort amounting to sustained war.[9]

A decade later the town of Cartagena sued King Jaume: his corsairs had entered their (Castilian) port, boarded a Genoese ship, and borne off Muslims and Jews from Islamic lands. That same year the knight Romeu de Castellet and Master Bonifaci received license to hit all Muslims, and also Christian ships carrying contraband to Muslims. Earlier the two men, operating out of Tortosa under the titles respectively of admiral and captain with a 'galley' and a 'ship,' also got a license good for only one round-trip, to plunder the subjects of Islamic Tlemcen. Since the permit included Jewish subjects, King Jaume followed this with a hasty amendment designed to protect 'any Jews who wish to change residence from the land of the king of Tlemcen to our land to take up settlement.' Jaume soon had to cope with a lawsuit against Castellet for having seized 'a certain old Saracen' of Murcia. He also closed a loophole: seizures at the port of tributary Ibiza island.[10]

Archbishop Benet of Tarragona, mounting his own profitable raids, on one occasion overstepped himself, loosing his ships in 1257 against merchantmen from Hafsid Tunis, then under truce; King Jaume brought charges of 'piracy' ('piraticam tirannidam exercendo'), the sultan sued for damages of 30,000 silver besants, and the affair had to be settled by papal arbitration. Another embarrassing case happened in 1274, when Hugolí Pelós of Majorca raided Málaga; the *ra'īs* there seized Catalan merchandise in reprisal, and King Jaume had to arrange an understanding between the Muslim and Pelós. When Romeu de Castellet's two ships raided Cartagena, however, the king's inquiry absolved him of fault; Romeu had sensibly freed the two ambassadors of Tlemcen's ruler he had caught among more legitimate prey. A subdivision of corsair activity was licensed reprisal, as when Bernat de Llorach was authorized to capture up to 6,000 silver besants' worth of Granadan shipping in 1258, to compensate for seizure of his own ship by Muslim pirates on the high seas.

Jaume's successor Pere licensed reprisal in 1280 against the king of Castile because 'certain pirates (*pirate*) of the said king carried off merchandise and other belongings' of Abraham Abingalel 'our Jew of Valencia.' This may be the Abraham ben Gabel encountered below in chapter 6 as a friend of the Tunis ruler; alternatively the present diplomat's name may be Arabic Khalīl with Hebrew co-name Hillel. Abraham 'was coming back from the king of Granada, to whom we have sent him' on a mission, when the pirates struck. Castile had rejected Pere's protest, so the king licensed Abraham to seize Castilian properties, hold them a month to force restitution, then if necessary sell them for recompense. Abraham was not to target 'any merchants of Castile coming with merchandise at Valencia,' or to take any action which might diminish Valencian customs duties. King Pere had another touchy case on his hands when Macià (English Matthew) of Poblet, 'on a voyage he made in the parts of Barbary as a corsair,' captured some Muslims who admitted being Moroccans; 'but when Macià brought them back to Valencia,' they claimed to belong to Granada (then being conciliated by Aragon) 'in order to get free.' Pere set up a crown investigation. Five years later a bold piracy occurred in Pere's own Valencian port of Denia. Ferrer or Ferran de Santacília (Sancta Cilia de Jaca) ferried 'twenty-three men and women Saracen merchants' to Denia from Algeciras in Granada (less likely from Algiers, as the archival catalog gives, though both names were identical in Arabic and the scribe gives *Algeer* plus a curious flourish). 'Pere de Ribalta and his accomplices, with his armed galley (*lleny*), seized these Saracens in the port of Denia' along with their seventy gold pieces, their silver, and their merchandise. Angered at this breach of mercantile courtesy, the king ordered their release and restitution immediately.[11]

CROWN CONTROL: PIRATE ETHICS

The most famous of Jaume's documents in this field has been universally misunderstood. In 1250 he promulgated a law said to have outlawed privateering and even to have signaled a turning point in his North African policies. But his policy remained much the same: maximum commercial advantage and control, especially through his truce-ally Tunis, via diplomacy, treaties, and control of international European quarters in North African cities. The privateering document, probably as ineffective as most such resounding promulgations from Jaume's throne, seems designed to center in the king's hands all licensing to outfit and raid: 'Because I see and know for certain that great harm comes to my country by the outfitting of corsairs, and can come again, therefore I wish and firmly and severely order you not to permit any military outfitting to occur by any corsairs or any other men of my jurisdiction, against any men not of my jurisdiction.' Far from outlawing corsair activity, Jaume let it go merrily forward; a quarter-century later we find him addressing a circular letter to 'fidelibus suis corsariis,' asking that they refrain from attacking the ships of Prince Manuel of Castile, which were under Jaume's protection. The presumed condemnation merely closed to seignorial, municipal, and other authorities the licensing of privateers, without excluding crown activity whether directly or through a licensing bailiff. Some thirty years after its promulgation Jaume's successor Pere designated or reiterated the bailiff as the crown's sole licenser: 'going or coming,' those who outfit naval expeditions at Valencia were to channel any dealings 'with Our officials' through 'Our bailiff of Valencia or his lieutenant, and with no one else.' King Jaume also established precise fees for domestic and foreign pirates putting in at Valencian ports, if they were operating against Islamic enemies; done in 1243, as the conquest of the Valencian south was winding down, it became a permanent statute. Some months before Pere's clarification, Bernat of Solsona misunderstood the king's invitation to outfit privateers and proceeded to act as a free entrepreneur. Arrested, he was allowed to continue because 'he had hired the greater part of the men necessary for that arming, and had paid them the greater part of their salary,' and anyway did not mean to attack anyone under truce or peace with the crown.[12]

Details of privateering operations become more regularly accessible from documents of a generation or two later, when the crown maintained a special codex on 'Wars with the Saracens.' One of its documents forbids privateering against the Islamic states of Tunis, Bougie, and Tlemcen, with whom a truce had been signed; it allows all attacks on Granadan ships; but since the Moroccan truce is not fully signed, privateers must attack Moroccan ships only at sea, never along Catalan coasts. Earlier the crown apologized to Tunis for the pirate Pere Bernat, explaining that he had been proscribed now for eight years but had taken commission from the king of Sicily. A moral dilemma rose when the Valencian Ramon Terrades seized seven Muslims of Bougie during truce: since the Muslim ruler had fortuitously died meanwhile, Ramon was able legally to have the seven certified as prizes of war! A more complicated case involved jewels and fine cloth, belonging half to a merchant of Majorca and half to the ruler of Morocco; a team of one Genoese and three Castilian ships robbed these from the Majorcan carrier.

Other documents tell of death and wounding in defense of one's ship; of Ibizan Christian pirates stealing four Moroccans (the crown will return the ransom and punish the pirates); of two Muslims illegally kidnapped by Barcelona pirates from a Genoese ship; of the ruler of Granada arresting the viscount of Roda (a tourist returning from Santiago) in reprisal for Catalan seizure of a Granadan ship in the port of Tunis; of thirty-four Muslims being restored to Granada, and then twenty-four more; and of a Granada–Aragon treaty agreeing that 'corsairs or robbers' (*corsaris*, *robadors*) of either party were outlaws and legitimate prizes of war when hostile. One breach of this peace involved three captains: Bernat de Puig of Majorca, whose ship had forty oars, Anthon Puig of Ibiza with sixteen oars, and Bernat Tamarit with eighteen. These worthies had captured a Málaga wheat barge with its ten Granadan subjects, plus a commercial transport belonging to two Muslims of Valencia, as well as four Muslims from Almería. Forestalling such incidents during an earlier truce with Morocco, the crown had warned authorities at Ibiza that adventurers were arming ships there, intending to take privateer commissions: they could be licensed only after swearing not to attack Moroccans, both because of the current truce and because the crown was trying to recover its own Barcelonan, Majorcan, Valencian and other subjects from Moroccan clutches.[13]

Similar incidents could be multiplied from the intramural piracy between Christians. Needless to say, such entries concerned major trespasses and rich cargoes; small operators with negligible profit margin were not worth pursuing. Four thirteenth-century cases may stand here for all. In 1272 King Jaume demanded that Genoa make good the losses suffered by Pere Ferran de Coll of Barcelona at the hands of Giovanni de Monterosso (Monterubeo) of Genoa 'in the sea of Turkey.' A crown committee, under the Hospitaller master and a baron, heard witnesses and concluded for the victim; the king sent nuncios, who ultimately returned empty-handed. Finally the king authorized Pere Ferran to recover by violence 8,000 'Saracen besants' in goods from any Genoese merchants anywhere in his realms on land or sea. King Pere in 1276 complained to Marseilles that 'your fellow citizen Guillem Cornut robbed Berenguer Cortina and his partners at sea'; meanwhile three other Marseilles pirates had plundered Miquel Febrer, Pere d'Alcarràs, 'and some other citizens of Tortosa,' stealing their cargo of 'arms and other things.' Two years later Francesco Grimaldi 'and some other accomplices,' operating an armed ship out of Nice, 'violently seized' a ship of one Badoc (or Badós) of Barcelona and the ship of Bonamich de Pala-frugell; their cargoes of wheat and general merchandise belonged to the Barcelonese Ferrer Olivar, Guillem Lull, and his son Guillemó, and had been loaded at Narbonne for Provence. In 1251 even the pope protested to King Jaume when 'some of your sons of iniquity despoiled' Pandolfo of Genoa; Jaume's refusal of restitution, Innocent IV scolded, 'did not become the royal dignity.' Accounts of such episodes from the thirteenth century must be treasured, since they afford glimpses of the activity surveyed in general terms by treaties, law codes, and *obiter dicta*.[14]

The early period cannot compete with the fourteenth and especially with the fifteenth and later centuries for colorful detail. For that reason an early charter in King Jaume's archives is especially valuable.[15] It is at once a labor dispute between a privateer and his captain, a rare notice from the sea campaigns which paralleled the land Reconquest of the thirteenth century, and a glimpse of the summary discipline which held sea raiders together. It is also an exercise in legal history, from a period celebrated for its bulldog barratry and love of legalisms.

MORAGUES: CORSAIR CAPTAIN AGAINST ISLAM

It brings on to the stage of history a neglected naval captain, Pere Moragues, one of the many creators of Catalan sea-power in the thirteenth century. Discovery of this hitherto unknown captain, and his corsair role on the Islamic–Christian frontier, prompted a further search of the royal archives for information as to his person. The king's registers yielded two more documents that reveal him first as an international merchant and then as a significant admiralty bureaucrat. Three years after the privateer episode discussed below, 'Pere Moragues of Valencia' appeared as the victim of an international dispute. He had bought 118 rabbit pelts in Castile, paying the export fees, only to have a certain García Sánchez de Santa Cruz seize them at (then Castilian) Requena on the Valencian frontier. King Pere of the realms of Aragon intervened, demanding release of the shipment under threat of reprisal. Moragues appears here as a merchant, a normal role for all Catalan classes from high to low. The wide range of prices for rabbit fur, from a few sous to 50 or much more apiece, obscures the exact worth of the shipment, but it could have been a luxury commodity of high value.[16]

Somewhat later, nearly a decade after the privateering feat examined below, this same 'Pere Moragues, resident of Valencia' received an appointment to serve indefinitely at the king's pleasure as secretary 'of our fleet at Valencia,' to take effect as soon as the fleet was built.[17] This office combined the functions of quartermaster and general accountant, requiring its holder to serve as legal overseer and authentic witness for all decisions or negotiations, a kind of commissar who kept the official register of shipboard happenings. In this position Moragues was entitled to a tenth of all booty or prize money. The open-ended tenure increased the value of his appointment. The access to the king enjoyed by Pere Moragues in these documents argues a relatively elevated burgher status. The Moragues or Moragas (plural of Moraga) were in fact a knightly Catalan family, with a green bush on silver field as a coat of arms. An occasional representative can be discovered earlier in the history of Catalonia, one of them settling at Tortosa. Three others appear as beneficiaries of land distribution after the Valencian crusade; but a certain Guillem is the only one of these who stands clear as a personality, a counselor to King Jaume in the compilation of Valencia's law code or *Furs*.

Pere's ship was a substantial but relatively modest specimen of galley called a *lleny* (Latin *lignum*). Alfonso X of Castile classifies galleys among the small or light ships. By the opening of the thirteenth century they had replaced the clumsier double-banked

Pirate galleys attacking. A falling mast has just killed the 'admiral.'
(Thirteenth-century) (Alfonso X, the Learned, *Cantigas de Santa María*,
cant. 35)

El Escorial Library (Patrimonio Nacional)

Byzantine dromon as the favorite warship. Concomitantly their size,
small sail, and expensive banks of rowers diminished their value as
merchant vessels except for luxury or low-bulk items. By the last
decade of the century a revolution in galley construction was creating the ever larger 'great galley' as distinct from the light. Pere's type
of *lleny*, though belonging to the intermediate stage of galley evolution, was distinct from a proper galley. It would have been lighter
and more heavily oared, with a single deck, one removable mast, and

on each side a single line of twenty rowers' benches, each bench bearing two rowers to a total of forty men. Muntaner twice describes *llenys* of eighty oars. This may have been exceptional, though King Jaume's personal galley, the *Montpellier*, carried that number. In a great victory over the French, only a *lleny* escaped, because 'it was better as to oars' than the Catalan admiral's galleys. Muntaner's memoirs of naval action give the impression that two *llenys* accompanied any fleet of a dozen or more galleys, serving as guard to fleet or port, as scout to reconnoiter, and especially as fast long-distance messenger ship. He describes in one port as many as thirty-six 'single-deck *llenys* of Catalan merchants.'

Llenys fought alongside galleys in battle but apparently less effectively. Like galleys they carried a contingent of crossbowmen, seamen, and marines (*aliarii*) besides their fighting rowers. Doubtless they carried the complement of offensive weapons Alfonso X describes, including lime to blind the enemy, soap to upset his footing, and pitch to set him aflame; but the special advantage of the Catalan galley or *lleny*, as Muntaner propounds at length, was the native breed of crossbowmen who could clear an enemy's deck just before the grappling. That Pere Moragues operated such a *lleny* out of Valencia city is unsurprising; by the time of transition from Jaume's reign to his son's, Valencia had become a main shipbuilding center for the realms and, with Barcelona, the place 'where there is the greatest number of seamen.' Such seamen included Muslims, especially along the Valencian coast, who were very well paid. Some shipboard positions were Muslim specialities, Boswell notes, particularly the helmsmen and the musicians who served as signal corps and whose trumpets and kettle drums rallied the attack. When good pay, booty share, or crusade appeal failed, the crown drafted Muslims and Christians alike under the rubric of their communal military obligations, and even emptied jails of their Muslim prisoners as a form of commutation. In an unpopular war, the crown could more easily draft Jews and Muslims to the fleet as its wards.[18]

In early 1276 Pere took commission with his *lleny* as a corsair and 'went privateering (*in cursum*) to the regions of [Islamic] Spain (*Spanie*) against the Saracens, with an armed ship.'[19] The timing is significant. Though dated 1275, technicalities of the incarnational calendar together with data on King Jaume's movements definitely set the year as 1276. Thirty years after the conquest of Valencia, and twenty years after the last Islamic revolt in that region, the Muslims had begun a great countercrusade to recover Valencia. The Marinid ruler Abū Yūsuf Ya'qūb in 1275 led a roll call of troops from all over his Moroccan empire to a great victory at Ecija. The new ruler of Granada, Muḥammad II, added his strength to the Marinid's. And the Mudejar subjects of Christian Spain rose in rebellion; those at Valencia took 'many' castles by mid-March of 1276, a figure soon to become 'forty,' as they awaited the Morocco–Granadan allies preparing to join them.[20]

King Jaume, now old and near death, hurried in person to the Valencian frontier to counter these blows. Moving his available forces to best advantage, the king summoned his feudatories on 13 March 1276 to a grand rendezvous in Valencia city's irrigated countryside or *huerta* at Easter. The ambassador of Tunisia's Hafsid ruler Abū 'Abd Allāh Muḥammad I would soon be in Barcelona, and would hurry south to confer with Jaume at Valencia concerning this common threat. In the interim the king's best hope, aside from a defensive screen of soldiers, was action carried to the enemy by sea: small blows rained disconcertingly, to keep the aggressor off balance. This included sending municipal squadrons, as when he ordered Tortosa's townsmen in June 'to send galleys to give help at Denia.' As the war continued, this action at sea widened; Jaume's son and successor King Pere authorized a special sea campaign, even during truce, against the bothersome Muslims of Orcheta castle in Valencia who 'have armed their ships and wreak damage on the Christians.'[21] Moragues' raid, a year earlier, had been an opening gun in this crusade and countercrusade at sea.

ALQUER: SUMMARY NAVAL JUSTICE

Oarsmen at that time were not slaves but free citizens usually hired for wages or shares. Among the crew taken on for this adventure was 'Alquer,' who signed for the full enterprise as a rower at salary. The single name confuses; even if it were the Catalan family Alquer or Alqué, surnames alone are not correct form. One is tempted to see a Mudejar here, perhaps a corruption of 'Algerí' for Algerian. Then, too, Alguer is a rare Catalan personal name, either from Visigothic Aldeguer or a form of Alguerès from Alguer in Sardinia; it might also represent a variant of Alguaire near Lérida. This man of the single name, from the lower classes, therefore, 'stole food' on the voyage. (The imperfect tense may indicate a continued crime, not discovered at once.) The need to steal food during a regularly commissioned raid suggests a naval expedition of some length, in enemy waters so dangerous as to preclude hasty reprovisioning. Since the king's document, our only record of the raid, came at the end of a formal inquiry by committee, and since anywhere from a month to three months would have been a reasonable duration of the voyage under the circumstances, Moragues may have cleared Valencia's port early in January. Four months made a normal tour of duty here for a galley, with provisions and armament self-sufficient except for water. Winter waters on this coast were punishing and usually avoided, but in crises the galleys did go out. In mid-fourteenth century Pere IV codified traditional privateering behavior at the end of a voyage; each privateer had to return to his home port first, and within four months (in some cases five) reimburse crown expenses and surrender the royal share of booty.

Local law gave a captain competence to deal summarily with malefactions such as Alquer's. The *Furs* of Valencia applied directly to Moragues' ship, since that was his port of origin. That code stated: 'Captains may arrest sailors who steal from merchandise or supplies of galleys or other ships, [and] make restitution to owners; the city council may punish them as thieves.' The punishment decreed elsewhere in the code was severe for all thieves: loss of 'the right ear' for the first offense, of a foot for the second, and for the third hanging. Christian and Islamic law were equally harsh on a crime so abhorrent to medieval Mediterranean men. The common source of this punishment was the immemorial law of the sea. For Mediterranean Spain this was reflected not only in the Valencian *Furs* but also in the customs of the sea, already being codified but soon to receive their definitive redaction in the next century as the celebrated *Llibre del consolat de mar*.

The *Siete partidas*, the posthumously evolved version of King Alfonso the Learned's *Espéculo*, an ideal code rather than the law of Castile then, devoted attention to shipboard food and its theft. Every warship is a vulnerable castle which should carry 'many victuals,' it says, specifying biscuit, salted meat, cheese, vegetables, onions, garlic, vinegar, and fresh water, but forbidding wine. (Catalan warships routinely carried wine.) The captain, who holds over his ship the punitive powers of an admiral over his fleet, must set a guard for the food and be ruthless in punishing its theft. The code notes that from ancient times the penalty for common seamen stealing food was loss of ears and hands, and for a second offense death, though the king himself favored rather branding the face.[22]

Moragues was in effect a naval captain on a combat mission; consequently he assumed the role of arresting officer, judge, and executioner. In the spirit of the law, Moragues 'cut off his ear with a knife.' At the expedition's close, with crew and captain again under landlubbers' law, Alquer apparently threatened suit. Moragues countered by petitioning the crown directly, seeking an injunction or waiver of prosecution. His nervous anticipation of trouble was not unwarranted. Whatever disciplinary power the law conferred on a captain at this time, both merchant and wartime crews resisted concentration of power in one man, and law encouraged a democratic organization at sea. Venetian war admirals, for example, could in theory behead recalcitrant captains and heavily fine insubordinate sailors; but in fact enforcement even of the fines depended upon the city fathers back home. Moragues may well have acted in a technically correct but practically over-harsh manner.

Moragues had obviously neglected to provide himself with a prior charter explicitly authorizing drumhead justice, as some more prudent colleagues had done. Romeu de Castellet and Master Bonifaci, encountered above on the eve of their corsair raid, held such a document in 1273 giving full powers over 'any of those you hire or who will go with you at pay,' in the matter of 'any crime or delict while they shall be in the aforesaid armada'; Castellet could 'exercise due justice, as it shall be necessary, after the manner that admirals are accustomed to do.' Though an admiral or fleet commander, Castellet had felt this provision advisable. Another admiral, the king's son Pere Ferran, similarly received in 1265 the king's 'full jurisdiction over the men who will be in the galleys' then going on raid against Muslims; this included 'complaints, evils, or injuries of any kind.' Pere Ferran 'can judge and do personal justice, as the custom is,' on land or on sea. Two years after the Moragues episode, the ex-Sicilian courtier Conrad Llança led a four-galley punitive fleet out of Valencia, to reimpose tributary status on Tunisia; his commission for the 'office of admiral in our kingdom' imposed obedience on 'all captains (*comites*), sailors, and seamen,' with Llança 'doing justice both on land and on sea to each and every one drafted to the said armadas, both in civil and in criminal matters.' At the same time the king empowered Pere Pisà or Pietro the Pisan: 'if any men, of those who follow you on the voyage or raid that you are about to make for us, happen to commit faults or crimes, you can impose a penalty and punish them in body and possessions, as seems good to you according to the quality of the crime.' For good measure the king sent a charter to the crew, commanding obedience to Pisà as to the king himself.[23]

In the case of Moragues, King Jaume and his legal advisers did not address themselves to the facts of the case but only to the underlying principle. The king's investigation concluded that 'every captain of an armed ship (*lleny*) is allowed to correct and punish the men of that ship, while it is on its raid, for any crime committed.' He forestalled legal harassment by decreeing that, if Moragues had indeed 'cut off the said Alquer's ear,' the crown 'pardons' the act and dismisses any legal action or recompense, and any civil or criminal penalty which might threaten. Corsair captains carried no malpractice insurance, and the Valencian region (where the petition and its response were datelined) was notoriously overrun with Roman lawyers in that very decade.

The episode, revealed at random by a captain's maneuver to protect himself after a voyage, is particularly valuable in disclosing a hitherto unknown naval expedition as the opening movement of King Jaume's response to the Mudejar countercrusade. Presumably this was one component of a more extensive naval campaign, via corsair commissions to entrepreneur shipowners – not only because this was the normal pattern of war among the maritime powers then, but also because naval action is briefly but explicitly treated by King Pere not long afterwards as part of the same war. King Jaume does not bother to advert to such naval activity in his several documents about the war or in the brief recapitulation in his autobiography, so that this single glimpse of the sea crusade may well be all that remains in the surviving records. The episode also offers an insight, not otherwise accessible for the time and place, into crew–captain relations in wartime. Finally, within the legal context so characteristic of the period, it recalls vividly that wider world of thirteenth-century corsairs whose documentation awaits full presentation.

5

King Jaume's Jews: problem and methodology

As the dust of battle subsided, the Homeric struggle between Islam and Christendom on this Mediterranean frontier settled into the deeper, more significant phases of psychic readjustment, shifting autonomies, and sporadic rebellion. Had the invading minority imported a static society, this process would still have proved complex and painful. European Christians were redefining their own psychic shape, unfortunately; they were riven by reform, legal, and conversion movements, greedy for places in the commercial–corsair sun, and reckless for power that was assuming ever new patterns and balance at the international, royal, feudal, and civic levels. In exploring this turbulent interplay of Muslim and Christian, it is all too easy to overlook another grand participant, an entire society which bridged the other two. Here the northern bias decried in the first chapter has done the historian particular disservice. The royal–feudal territorial blocs of northern Europe had little place or patience for the Jew and more easily marginalized him, whereas the Mediterranean world valued him as a significant and active component of its central activity. Hostility continued, but differently experienced and differently expressed.

The kaleidoscopic political scene in the south makes it unwieldy, as the historian contends with powers like Marseilles or Genoa, Majorca or Malta, whether bundled loosely as with Jaume's entities or wholly autonomous. If powers like Toulouse or Ragusa fall out of the historian's frame of reference, how much more easily does so diffuse a political phenomenon as the Jews. This political pluralism of the Mediterranean paradoxically facilitated the unity and prosperity of the dispersed Jewish cosmos.

THE SUCCESSORS OF BOFARULL

The Mediterranean world formed a socio-political ecology consisting less of territorial blocs or nations than of multiple small unities, loosely federated at best, resembling the ancient cosmos of commercial city-states. A world so fragmented must be bonded into larger unity by shared movements, patterns, experiences, psychology, and sets of similar institutions. It will be a dynamic world, with energies freely flowing between its separate points. This interaction within western Mediterranean Christendom was paralleled by multilevel interaction *vis-à-vis* the Byzantine, Islamic, and Jewish communities. Recent works like that of Shelomo Goitein's *Mediterranean society* leave no doubt that a cohesive Jewish Mediterranean community, non-territorial but self-conscious, functioned within the interstices of the more visible Byzantine, Islamic, and Western cultures, at once identified with and transcending each host culture.

Recovery of the Mediterranean vision, which lifts our eyes beyond the parochially national boundaries of an older historiography, has occasioned an accompanying reappraisal of the roles of Muslim and Jew within Europe. Mediterranean Spain is a particularly crucial country for such study, both because of the close interpenetration of the three communities precisely as Mediterranean and because of the ample documentation surviving. And the century of King Jaume is the central or culminating period for examining the convergence, before the less hospitable fourteenth and fifteenth centuries restricted the open role of Muslims and Jews in Christendom. Francesc de Bofarull i Sans, near the end of his distinguished career as head of the Arxiu de la Corona d'Aragó, did not hesitate to proclaim that the golden age for Europe's Jews came 'in the reign of Jaume the Conqueror,' a time which for them 'surpassed all epochs and all countries.' Within that geographical and chronological area, a particularly promising field of study is the kingdom of Valencia – a *tabula rasa* where Christian, Muslim, and Jew converged most vigorously, and where all three were actively sought as valuable immigrants.

Over half a century ago, in the first of the congresses on the realms of Aragon, Bofarull i Sans read his seminal 'Jaime I y los judíos,' presented modestly as 'una mera noticia histórica.' His introduction rapidly surveyed the Jews of the realms of Aragon from the eleventh through the thirteenth centuries, offered short biographies of ten prominent men, and touched on a pot-pourri of random topics under geographical headings. The meat of his contribution, however, was the documents filling the bulk of his 125 pages. A mere dozen or so of this treasure pertained to the kingdom of Valencia, and those mostly from the final years of King Jaume's life. Bofarull's landmark collection was paralleled simultaneously by Jean Régné's descriptive catalog of over six hundred documents from Jaume's reign; fewer than a hundred touched on Valencia, a percentage double that of Bofarull. The final foundation stone toward serious documentary study of the Jews in the realms of Aragon was Yitzhak Baer's first volume of source materials in 1929. Later the Jewish entries in the catalog of general Valencian documents of Jaume I, by J. E. Martínez Ferrando in 1934, served to supplement and for Valencia to supplant Régné. A glance through the footnotes of Baer's more recent history of the Jews in Christian Spain, or the six-page bibliography on Jews in J. Lee Shneidman's history of the thirteenth-century realms of Aragon, or the indexes and book reviews of *Sefarad*, reveals the great progress achieved in recovering Jewish history and letters in the realms of Aragon since the first congress. The scholars who have contributed in half a dozen languages are too numerous and their contributions too complex to allow summation in a few paragraphs. But in this luxuriant growth, one empty space stands out: the kingdom of Valencia during the critical decades of transition under King Jaume.[1]

Leopoldo Piles Ros, who has done excellent work on Valencian Jews in the later Middle Ages, and who once projected a history of the region's Jews, now recognizes that more basic work must come first: recovery and exploitation of the essential documentation, a task requiring 'numerous researchers.'[2] The lacuna of materials is most noticeable for the period of Jaume and thus explains the gap in historical work there. This seems puzzling at first, since the mass of more accessible material in the registers at the Arxiu de la Corona d'Aragó has long been organized by the catalogs of Régné and Martínez Ferrando. But the very success of these catalogs has inhibited archival investigation. Except for a rare individual like David Romano, whose well-known articles on notable families in the reign of Pere the Great touch also on the Valencia of Jaume, the best of scholars seems content to browse and borrow from these brief descriptions of Jaume's manuscripts. Even this has not been done systematically. An industrious licenciate thesis might well be devoted to pulling together all the published documents and notices, collating the whole into a coherent synthesis. It would lack depth and detail, but would at least organize our present stock of superficial data.

Piles Ros has shown, on a small scale, what can be done using only the Martínez Ferrando catalog entries, in his articles on Alcira and Burriana. Manuel Grau Monserrat has done the same for Morella. Haim Beinart follows the Martínez Ferrando catalog for much of his Valencian information, as do Shneidman and often enough Baer. Francisca Vendrell Gallostra draws on Régné for her thirteenth-century episodes of Cavalleria family history. Abraham Neuman, whose history like Baer's is a model of scholarship, has woven whole sections of his two volumes cleverly from Régné. Even Ferran Soldevila, who transcribed valuable unpublished materials on Vives b. Vives and other Jews in his biography of Prince Pere (recently left unfinished by the author's death, just as Pere ends his vicegerency of Valencia and succeeds his father Jaume as king), unaccountably relies sometimes on Martínez Ferrando catalog items.[3]

FROM CATALOG TO DOCUMENTARY ARCHEOLOGY

The temptation to press catalog information into the service of scholarship on the Jews of King Jaume's Valencia is a general affliction among the few who approach this field at all. Yet reliance on Régné and Martínez Ferrando holds special dangers. Régné threw his collection together in haste, missing documents, skimming, and at times misleading: Romano has analyzed these shortcomings of Régné's enterprise.[4] Martínez Ferrando was more leisurely, more careful, and chronologically more concentrated; but he too worked rapidly and·in good part from the manuscript notes of previous catalogers, with consequent superficiality, omissions, and errors. The labors of both men remain invaluable, but they should not be expected to stand in for the documents themselves. The best of catalogs makes a feeble foundation for research. Their short paraphrases lack context, detail, nuance, the impact of the original language, or the corrective subsidiary information of the full text. Reconstructing the history of the Valencian Jews under King Jaume will therefore require heavy archival labor. The obvious place to apply this first is the series of registers which cover the last twenty years of the king's life. The registers should supply at least a hundred documents significant for the purpose.

When the documents are finally in hand, the reader must appreciate that the transcription itself can be faulty; it is always wise to check suspicious wording, crucially important phrases, or lacunae against the manuscript. The lacuna in Bofarull's document number 25 (9 May 1262), for example, can be closed by diligent use of the quartz lamp: Jews imprisoned anywhere in the Valencian kingdom on tax charges were to be paroled on Friday evening and all day Saturday up to 'tempus quando stella apparebit, singulis diebus S⟨abbati⟩ vestris.' Even when such additions advance our knowledge only a little, they at least assure the reader that no surprises lurk below the line of printed dots. In Baer's great collection of Jewish documents, to take another example, number 108 on Valencian and other taxes is not what it seems. Comparison with the manuscript reveals this transcription to be a selection from various folios compressed to form a mathematical or paraphrase presentation, without indicating *dimisits*.

Sometimes a reasonably transcribed document incorporates serious flaws. The massive and well-researched history of Morella by Ortí Miralles devotes its section on the Jews to a transcription, translation, photograph, and explanation of one long document of 10 February 1264. A dozen small errors obscure the reading, a few of them seriously, and two cause misinterpretations in the explanatory portion. The editor read 'unumquamque hostacium' for 'unumquodque hospicium,' and 'viginti solidos terni' for 'viginti solidos tantum'; this led him to explain the household tribute as *cena*, and also to miss an important aspect of the privilege. The best of editors nods, and strange readings can invade their pages. Even when the editor is careful, however, the scribe can have heard or seen a word incorrectly, or simply have made a mistake. The editors of Valencia's *Repartiment* have reported correctly on 'Muḥammad Alondi the Jew,' as examination of the manuscript proves; this may be a convert to Islam, renamed as usual, who had retreated when the Muslims left Valencia, but just as probably the scribe has nodded.[5]

Departing for a moment from the formal problems to the substantive, that Morella charter deserves closer examination for meaning. Commentators see it as the beginning of a Jewish presence or community in Morella. It is both more and less. It invites Yaḥyā b. Maymūn (Catalan Maimó, the Arabic translation of the Hebrew name Asher, or 'fortunate') and all Jews to come settle Morella, setting as their constitution henceforward the customs and privileges of the *aljama* of Valencia city. Those who 'will newly settle there' ('ibi noviter populabunt') are to receive full exemption from crown taxes the first year, plus commutation during the next four years to a flat sum of 20 sous per household. The editor sees this as the beginning of Jewish settlement in Morella; it seems rather a stimulation and programed expansion, elevating the juridical status appropriately while offering a tax incentive. The context of similar documents places it as part of King Jaume's determined program to import more Jews into all parts of his new kingdom. Only those 'newly settling' would get the tax break, while the older residents presumed by this exclusionary wording would at least benefit by the more liberal constitutions and extended area for housing.

After effecting a full transcription (not avoiding any necessary application of the quartz lamp), the investigator should not rest content with the substantive information in a document, but bring to it the patience and some of the methods of the archeologist. Meditating on it as a whole and in each stray detail or implication, he must interrogate it relentlessly for any clue. He should then interrelate these small points, with each bit of data illumining others, into larger 'models' and hypotheses, supplementing a given piece of information with anything remotely pertinent or revealing in the full range of documentation. Reflectively and continuously he will sift both whole and part into the background of known Jewish society of the time, both locally and in general, not neglecting insights from analogy.

The results must be sited in turn within the Mediterranean world, Christian and Islamic, of which it was an integral part; they may also be marinated in whatever non-historical erudition a given historian possesses, for deeper insights. These stages are not necessarily successive; mutual causality and parallel operations are more likely. But at all costs the transcription must be lodged in its *Sitz im Leben*. Such an approach promises results on a scale that justifies the investment of so much patience and time. Its application to Mudejar materials in these same registers – materials scarcer and less revealing than those about Jews – made it possible to reconstruct in two books of some nine hundred pages the social structure and activities of Valencia's Muslims during the generation after the Valencian crusade. Much more can be done for the Jews.

THREE STEREOTYPES: THE URBAN
MONEYLENDER

Transcription of manuscripts is the first necessity; once this foundation has been laid, many hands can build upon it. All the registered documents about Valencia by Jaume I will eventually appear in my *Diplomatarium regni Valentiae*. As *entremeses* for this larger feast, a collection of twenty-five transcriptions on Valencia's Jews is presented below in appendix 3. Our next chapter will take up the stories within each document. Half these manuscripts were selected from the earliest five hundred items in the registers; the remainder were chosen at random from the general run. Chronologically well over half fall within the first decade of the registers' span, the others within the last decade. Geographically they involve some two dozen towns or their countrysides. They show many properties owned or controlled by Jews, such as modest farms, extensive estates, vineyards, a public bakery, baths, watermills, salt mines, a luxury shop, and a wine-warehouse business. They touch on topics as varied as a prison, a palace, excommunication by the *aljama*, the henna industry, important families hitherto unknown, a passport, a homosexuality trial, and (with the supporting documentation in the text) a caliph's gift, women's fashions, markets, and an assassination.

The dominant subject matter of the documents may be variously categorized. One scheme might divide them as concerning: immigration and settlement in various regions, a Jew hanged for murdering a Muslim, a Jew assaulting and wounding a Jew, construction of a mill, protective defense for an individual's property, immunity from officials entering a home, extensive property purchase from a knight, transfer of debt, exemption from commercial fees, rival factions within an *aljama*, use of Jewish taxes to develop Valencia's irrigation system, indefinite reduction of a community's taxes, collecting crown taxes from Muslims, operating a salt utility, clarifying an individual's tax obligations to his community, rectifying a property muddle between rival owners, and a grant of property. Some of the documents about property reveal the names and quality of immediate neighbors. Some of the manuscripts concern a whole community, others an individual or family; some involve men of status, others ordinary people. A document may contain much more than its face topic would suggest. The murder case, for example, involves the widow of the culprit recovering at law both her dowry and her late husband's gifts to her; by 'the laws and privileges of the Jews' she won from the court a third of the joint property, and purchased back the confiscated portion for 4,200 sous. In this episode the property was bounded by holdings of affluent Christians; and the amount of her highest bid suggests that the Jewish community refrained from competing for the widow's inheritance. Régné has described some of the documents given here, has noted others, and has missed yet others. All but one have a limitation: they concern Jews directly. Many of the most valuable entries in the registers, easily missed by catalogers, concern some neutral matter which reveals in a passing phrase or fugitive glimpse a community, a dignitary, a merchant, or the *iudaria nova* of Valencia city.[6]

Perusal of such documents in context can lead to surprising conclusions. Three such conclusions may be presented here by way of illustration – one of broad scope, one of middling rank, and one a small yet significant detail. The first concerns the stereotype that Jews controlled the finances of the crown as lenders, collectors, and tax farmers. This has become indeed an orthodoxy hardly requiring proof, and readily repeated. But it is false. The assumption arises from reading too exclusively in materials directly relating to Jews, ignoring the wider general context. Jews did indeed take a lively role at all levels of loan and collecting, a role perhaps disproportionately larger than that of other groups; at the very top, where the regional or central treasurers stood, the Jew was probably the active agent. But Muslims and Christians also loaned money to the crown, farmed taxes, and collected. As in Europe generally, in fact, the financiers and collectors for the king in Valencia were predominantly Christian.[7] So jumbled is the tax documentation that this situation only comes to light after extensive reorganization of the data.

This conclusion can in turn serve as a premise, to redefine the role of the Jew in the Valencia of King Jaume. He was not so isolated a figure as he once seemed, cut off in an onerous financial role, presumably an object of resentment and envy. Shneidman and Romano are probably right in arguing, on altogether other grounds, that baronial efforts to remove Jews from the office of bailiff under Jaume's son King Pere relate to dissatisfaction with growing crown influence rather than to any feeling against the Jews in themselves or as moneymen.[8] (Similarly, the role of Jew and Muslim as moneylenders, with a higher 'usury' index, needs to be rethought; but that is a separate problem.) Even as financier and tax collector in Valencia, the Jew was in the mainstream of a common Christian activity. His operations there assimilated him to, rather than divided him from, his fellow Valencians.

The second point also concerns a stereotype: that the Valencian Jew was urban rather than rural. Here the misunderstanding is due partly to the modern dichotomy between country and town. In Valencia the grant of a house frequently (perhaps usually) involved also a small farm in the countryside; even when this was worked by one's *exaricus* or Muslim 'partner–tenant,' it gave the townsman a stake in and experience of the country. Jews had such properties and *exarici*. But even in the role of straight rural dweller, whether affluently presiding over *exarici* or as working his own small farm or mill, there were far more Jews than are allowed for by historians. Any number of towns, too, amounted to little more than villages set in their fields, with a rhythm of life rather rural than urban. Again, award of a property could be by town name, since Valencia was organized by town-cum-countryside units, without indicating a commercial and urban existence for the settler. A definite conclusion must await full publication of the documents, but it should also include a rethinking of the categories themselves. A Jew with extensive properties may have been a country squire like his Christian counterpart, despite his town residence. Again there are implications to be drawn and pondered about the relations between the two peoples in Valencia.

The final illustration is more a matter of detail. So strong is the identification of financier with Jew that at least one prominent lender in Valencia has long been presumed a Jew on that ground alone. Encountering this man's large loans to Prince Pere, the erudite dean of Catalan historians Ferran Soldevila concluded that 'he must have been a wealthy Jew who speculated widely.' Juan Torres Fontes, the eminent historian of medieval Murcia, makes the same assumption. It will be helpful to clarify his status and move him into the Christian community; the point is important in itself, but also reinforces the theses just posited. His very name has seemed mysterious; Miret i Sans calls him Ada, and Martínez Ferrando prefers Ade, with an alternate Adam. His real name was Adam de Paterna and also Adam de Castellar. (Ade is merely the genitive and dative of the usually indeclinable Adam, by patristic precedent here in the first declension.) He had two sons, Pelegrí and Bartomeu; Pelegrí's early death made Bartomeu the guardian of his brother's four children Arnau, Elvireta, Ramoneta, and Jaumeta. Adam was influential enough to secure a crown pardon for a ward of his own, Joan Sanç, who had 'wickedly killed' a Valencian Mudejar. Adam died just before 1270 and was buried, alongside Pere Adam de Paterna, in Valencia city's Hospitaller church. His heraldic device seems to have been a bell or perhaps a pear.

Some two dozen documents in the registers show him owning important properties in the kingdom of Valencia, including the castles of Segart and Beselga near Murviedro, and the town of Benifallim. To recover his loans he managed the revenues of castles and districts like Alfandech, Pego, and Tárbena. His loans to the crown were large and continuous. One bond, for 18,000 sous, has two members of King Jaume's household swearing that the royal debtor will repay on time. Another gives Prince Pere 20,000 sous without 'any open or concealed interest'; 15,000 more were loaned partly in cash and partly in wine and cattle (perhaps for the Murcian wars); and the total owed by the prince to Adam soon rose to 38,000 sous. Prince Pere's wife secured a loan of 35,000 from Adam by handing over her crown, of Islamic workmanship. Adam contributed 3,000 sous to help outfit a warship at Valencia, and made large loans to the queen and to the Valencian baron Carròs de Rebollet. The king's complex of loans from him was not fully repaid until a decade after Adam's death.

King Jaume could well thank Adam, as early as 1258, for 'the many and valued services' he rendered the crown and was continuing to do 'daily.' It is astonishing that so prominent a figure has remained obscure to historians and has been so long assigned to Valencia's Jewish community. In sorting out Valencia's Jews, paradoxically, scholars will inevitably recover important elements of Christian Valencia. Adam's long obscurity demonstrates the need for basic research in Valencian Judaism. A census of names alone would make a good beginning, with their proper transcription and equivalents, as well as a map of holdings and distribution, and a scale of importance according to wealth, position, craft, and frequency of citation.

With the documentation so much richer in the fourteenth and fifteenth centuries, its social context clearer, and its archival distribution so conveniently wider, there is a tendency for scholars to turn to that later time. But the significant period of transition was in this earlier era; the foundation for the Jewish communities lies back there; and the more-or-less golden age is there if anywhere. When the pogroms of 1276 shook the kingdom of Valencia from end to end, to be punished mercilessly later by the crown, it is significant that the mobs never disturbed Valencia's Jews. Church legislation and separatist status alike bracketed Jew and Muslim together, but here the bonding failed. The equilibrium between Jew and Christian, and the factors of shared experience, for the moment outweighed the elements of difference and hostility. The Valencian documents in the registers of Kings Jaume and Pere are a key by which we can unlock the puzzle of how this equilibrium came into being and was maintained. The mini-cartulary in appendix 3 is a small contribution toward recovery and presentation of that full documentation.

It is important to remember that hostility did remain an element in the balance, as we saw when discussing the *dhimma* context in chapter 2. Jaume's son Pere, for example, was doubtless sincere when declaring in 1279 that 'our intention and purpose is that our people be supported by justice, Jews and Saracens as much as Christians'; but he felt it necessary to send charters to this effect to twenty-four major towns, including six in Valencia. He also had to dispatch a concomitant rebuke to twenty-three Franciscan headquarters, including those in Valencia, because 'when some of your friars preach in the synagogues of the Jews, they try to lead those Jews to the Catholic faith by threats, violence, and invective, with the result that the [Christian] populace (who go to those synagogues not for purpose of preaching but rather for self-deception and scandal) might seriously hurt and kill the said Jews,' which would 'exceedingly disturb' the king. 'The Jews,' he concluded, 'must be attracted with sure initiation and with rational and gentle persuasion, since no one is to be forced to our faith unwillingly.'[9] As chapter 1 explained for the Mudejars, we do not have here a 'dark side' and a 'bright side,' to be 'balanced' with some tilt to one or the other, but a life-situation essentially painful and distortive, within which a courageous people maintained for themselves a Jewish subculture and a practical *modus vivendi*.

PREPARATIONS FOR THE DIG

Before we meet individual Valencian Jews, it may help to know something of their numbers, names, and location. Almohad persecu-

Murviedro castle and town. (Cavanilles, *Observaciones sobre el reyno de Valencia*, 1795)

tion had recently driven many Jews north into the Christian states and disrupted the long-established communities. Eliyahu Ashtor believes, nevertheless, that 162 families remained at Valencia city at the time of Jaume's conquest; if so, many may then have moved out with the city's evicted Muslims. Valencia's *Repartiment* or property division lists some hundred Jews receiving grants in the city. By the end of the thirteenth century, we have the names of 250 tax-paying Jews there (presumably mostly heads of families); later in the four-teenth century their quarter had to be enlarged. King Jaume vigor-ously encouraged immigration; frontier opportunities drew Jews as well as Christians, but risks and dislocations inhibited the flow.

Places like Castellón, Játiva, and Murviedro, the largest Jewish *aljamas* or communities after the capital, soon had perhaps fifty families each. Of twenty-seven Arago-Catalan *aljamas* contributing in 1274 for Jaume's trip to the ecumenical council of Lyons, only five were on his Valencian frontier (Valencia city, Alcira, Gandía, Játi-va, and Murviedro or Sagunto), and Valencia city's sum exceeded the other four together. For comparison, Barcelona is usually said to have had some 200 Jewish families. Baer estimates the tax-paying

Jewish families in Jaume's realms as over 3,600; he assigns the leading communities at Barcelona and Zaragoza 200 each, Gerona a somewhat smaller number, and Lérida 100. Spain had the largest Jewish communities in Europe, but two hundred to four hundred families represented maximum *aljamas*; fifty to a hundred families was a large *aljama*. Valencia city at our period held perhaps fifteen thousand individuals, with the Jews perhaps a fifteenth of the total. At Valencia city they lived under the privileges or constitution of Zaragoza from the start, acquiring shortly those of Barcelona and their own special privileges as well.

Dufourcq estimates that the kingdom of Valencia by the end of the thirteenth century held 50,000 Christians, 140,000 Muslims, and 10,000 Jews. Thus one in six non-Muslims on this frontier was a Jew. This compares with his estimated 25,000 Jews in Catalonia as against a mostly Christian population of 400,000; and with 20,000 Jews in Aragon proper, where there were 50,000 Muslims and 100,000 Christians. Valencia like Catalonia had some ten Jewish communities then, by his reckoning, with about fifteen in Aragon. The very largest communities, as at Valencia, Barcelona and Zaragoza, had some 2,000 souls (perhaps two to three hundred extended or 'patriarchal' families). If one Valencian in six among the non-Muslims was a Jew, apparently concentrated at a handful of cities, their influence and impact had to have been considerable. This was no negligible minority but an inescapable intimate presence.

In the episodes from Valencian history discussed below, personal names and surnames of Jews will be given in Catalan. Many Spanish Jews kept an echo of their antecedents in al-Andalus by incorporating the form 'ibn' as in 'Abenafia' or in the Arabic–Romance amalgam Ibn Vives; 'ben' can also be used, as in the case of the great Ibn Adret or Ben Adret. I tend to standardize such names with 'ben,' as less confusing to the reader in a mixed Mudejar–Jewish–Christian society. As examples below will illustrate, it was common for a Jew to translate his private Hebrew name into a Romance and/or Arabic equivalent or cognate; alternatively he might simply add a non-cognate Romance or Arabic name. These extra name-forms served for his public and business life in the world at large.[10]

Though one function of the appended documents, besides their intrinsic interest, is to warn against reliance upon catalogs, this should not be taken as a criticism of those catalogs or of their compilers. Valencian historians owe a great debt to Martínez Fer-

River confluence at Forcall. (Cavanilles, *Observaciones sobre el reyno de Valencia*, 1795)

rando; his catalogs for Jaume and Pere opened new horizons and stimulated lasting interest in a region too long neglected. My own researches have been constantly facilitated by these products of his labor; it would be petty and thankless to search out their errors and shortcomings gratuitously. In handling a large volume of documents – especially in the notarial hand, highly abbreviated, on deteriorating paper, and affected by problems of dating and anthroponomy – any historian will accumulate his share of errors. A cataloger must not only expect the percentage of error to rise higher, but because of the very volume of his material must resign himself to a kind of impressionistic superficiality. Short documents and very clear documents fare best in such work; longer, complicated, or deteriorated documents often come through badly. If one is relying to some extent upon previous indexers, as Martínez Ferrando was, their shortcomings are in turn incorporated. In short, a catalog must not be expected to assume the role of source material, nor does a cataloger intend this.

One valuable category of documentation on Valencian Jews is that which mentions them peripherally, so that a catalog simply

Jewish physician (*al-ḥakīm*) inside his street-front office, in dialogue with a Christian. (Alfonso X, the Learned, *Cantigas de Santa María, cant.* 108)
El Escorial Library (Patrimonio Nacional)

omits them from its description. Thus document number 19 of our appendix is dismissed in the Martínez Ferrando catalog as part of a set of 'notes about crown taxes'; but it shows Salomó (English Solomon) b. Lavi of Zaragoza's dominant Cavalleria clan, with the mildly honorific *En* or Sir, in his capacity as head bailiff in Valencia for Valle de Almonacid, Vall de Uxó, and Segorbe. His colleague and perhaps subordinate at Almonacid is Ramon Ricard – an eminent Barcelonan who had directed the Catalan merchant enclaves at Alexandria, Tunis, and Bougie for the crown, conducting embassies and loaning very large sums to King Jaume. The companion report here is by Bernat de Cascall, a knight from Bergua, mentioned in a codicil to King Jaume's will. (Bernat became embroiled in 1269 in an accusation of adultery with the wife of the lord of Bergua, from which he offered to purge himself in ordeal by battle with that lord, but was instead protected by Jaume as being a crown vassal.) Our brief note adds only a little to knowledge about Salomó perhaps, but the company he keeps in this business affair illustrates how Jews and Christians of the highest ranks worked in common for profit and community service. Salomó continued prominently in Valencian fiscal affairs, installing himself 'in the castle of Murviedro' in 1273, for example, as bailiff 'of Murviedro and Segorbe, Onda and Uxó, and Almonacid, as long as it pleases' the king.[11]

The archeologist on his dig, however many fellahin may be substituting at the shovels, remains restlessly alert for the telling trace, the significant minim embedded. His resurrected trophy, whether stone wall or vase shard, when cleared, cleaned and set on public display, retains no hint of the niggling skills brought to its recognition, of the prosaic hours under the sun, or of the labyrinthine technical report justifying the terse explanation posted there. Some kinds of history proceed in an analogous fashion, where alien documentation must be 'worked,' clues fleetingly sighted, bits shaken from between the lines, or an item turned up by routine perseverance. The student of Valencia's Jews must show the archeologist's pertinacious fortitude, the same delight in a universal singular recaptured for display, the same lawyer's liking for educing, marshalling and presenting evidence, and the same satisfaction with his seemingly small contribution to the larger picture. This is how cities and citadels are unearthed, their stony emptiness repeopled, and our past recovered.

6

Portrait gallery: Jews of crusader Valencia

If the archeologist is fortunate, he may turn up an entire house, sheep pen, or roadway, even the beginning of a city. The archival historian who works by indirection among recalcitrant alien documentation may likewise unearth such a larger object. Led by catalog or by chance, he examines his find scrupulously, brushes away irrelevancies, cajoles meaning from its more discreet sections, and gives it context. The cases presented in this chapter are of that class. A single document, or several at times, lonely items enough, can evoke by one episode a sudden, self-contained world. Each story contributes toward a larger social history, while proving valuable in its own humanity.

THE CAVALLERIA CLAN

The Salomó de la Cavalleria encountered at the end of the previous chapter was one of four sons of a more portentous figure, En Judà or Jafuda b. Lavi, patriarch of the Cavalleria clan, bailiff of Zaragoza, and 'treasurer of the realm' of high Aragon. Judà de la Cavalleria had many official connections with the kingdom of Valencia, reflected in seventeen documents from the beginning to the end of King Jaume's registers. He owned properties at Valencia city in the Jewish quarter and outside it, and had the privilege of grazing a thousand sheep tax-free. He sent one of his sons to serve the legal requirement of personal residence for his basic Valencian estate. The first document in our mini-cartulary catches him in action, in a routine bit of fiscal rationalization. Small though it is, it illustrates one moment in the articulated series of Jewish loans which helped effect the consolidation of Christian Valencia. Pala(h)í de Foces, member of a powerful Aragonese family, squire and companion to King Jaume intermittently from 1236 to 1263, had run up a debt of

3,000 Jaca sueldos in connection with expenses of his tenure of Alpuente castle to the west of Valencia city, his creditor being Judà. Since the crown properly owed this debt, the king formally assumes it here, issuing this debt bond for Judà to recover it from his bailiate or tax administration of Zaragoza. It seems likely that Judà had loaned Palaí the expense money directly, and that this clumsy circular loan is being rationalized.

Judà appears also in documents 10 and 11 of 1263 in appendix 3, respectively a generous grant of land and an immunity from intruders on his property. The grant involved a *plaçia* – not the urban square or *plaza* (*platea*) but an expanse or area or esplanade in Valencia city's irrigated countryside. It connected two properties Judà had previously purchased 'from the sons of the deceased Bertran de Vallers,' and fronted directly 'on the public road (*via publica*).' Another road or street (*carraria*) ran to the estate of the wealthy Valencian financier (later the city justiciar) Arnau de Font, to another property Judà had bought from Sanç de Vall (probably a familiar of King Jaume), and to a *regale* of the king. We can see that the area is desirable, well located, owned by affluent and powerful men including the king, and familiar to Judà from the three parcels he already held.[1]

The Martínez Ferrando catalog reports all this carelessly as a grant 'of some lands' in the countryside 'bordering on the *real* or garden' of the king. This loses the impact of an extensive *plaçia*, as well as missing its context and also its function in joining Judà's other parcels. More important, it too easily assumes that the *regale* is the celebrated Real or royal park and palace lying across the river from Valencia city. Careful examination of the phrasing, together with consideration of document 11, makes this doubtful. That document, issued a week later, protects the *regalia* of Judà: the bailiff and justiciar must not 'allow any person or persons to enter the buildings of the *regalia*' of Judà 'or to dwell in them' except by the owner's permission. Intruders will be punished with the penalties provided by the *Furs* or law code of Valencia. Negligence in thus protecting Judà will bring down the king's 'very great displeasure.' The same four properties owned by Judà in document 10 are referred to by the plural *regalia*; moreover that document calls the king's property *regale sive ortum* and all but one of Judà's properties each an *ortum* (farm).

From document 10 alone it would seem that *regale* and *ortum* can be synonyms; document 11 assures us that this is so by applying *regale* to each of Judà's farms, including the *plaça*. It is well not to demand an exact meaning for every use of words like *ortum*, *hereditas*, or *regale*, since the documents use them generically and even carelessly; but it is evident at least that *regale* is similarly generic and in this case probably not 'the garden of the king.' Not only was *reial* (Castilian *real*, English royal) confused by popular usage with the identically spelled word to approximate Arabic *raḥl*, but the Islamic original encompassed both farm and country estate. Judà's documents warn us not to oppose such Latin approximations as *rafal*, *rahal*, *raal*, and *reallum* to a supposedly purer royal *regale*. This philological aside, while clarifying the nature of Judà's holdings in document 11 and cautioning about catalog information, is not the main point. A simple land grant has allowed a view of the Zaragozan's land purchases in Valencia, his securing of a crown grant to join them, his ability to win immunity and privileged privacy, and something of his social standing and economic role in the development of the new kingdom.

MUBĀRAK THE MURDERER

An enigmatic but obviously important local figure emerges from a set of three documents of May 1258.[2] One calls him Mechadanus, another Mubarich Machadani and Megadanus, and a third Megadanus and Mechadanus; his wife is Ceta or Cita. Martínez Ferrando makes the couple Mubanch and Cote; Régné read their names as Mubarich Machedan and Cota. Since Jews often carried Arabic names in Valencia, it seems likely that these given names are Mubārak (blessed) and Sitt (mistress, lady). Goitein has noted how surprisingly prevalent in Mediterranean Jewish communities was the feminine name Sitt, usually in combinations like the 'mistress of the West' or 'ruler of the men.' In later medieval Barcelona, one of several Jewish women physicians was Na Cetia, obviously a Catalanized expression of Sitt.

The husband's surname might be a personal element like al-Ma'dānī, but is more probably the office of *muqaddam* (head man). The nominative form in these documents rather than the genitive, whenever Mubārak is nominative, and the freestanding use of this 'second' name, reinforce the conjecture.[3] *Muqaddam* in the Near East designated the elected leader of a Jewish community; in Spain in the

Landforms of Ibi: town and part of castle-district. (Cavanilles, *Observaciones sobre el reyno de Valencia*, 1795)

thirteenth century it was becoming popular as meaning one of the board of elders of a local Jewish *aljama*.[4] The Arabic name-forms suggest a family bridging the Islamic and Christian worlds, perhaps a Jew left over from pre-crusade days or (in view of his extensive lands acquired after Christian grantees had held them) a go-between or crown servant during the wars. This can only remain a surmise, since not all Jews took or added Romance names as did Vives b. Vives, and some Arabized names like Alconstantini had persisted in Romance form among Arago-Catalonia's Jews.

Mubārak was a man of landed wealth, holding 'buildings, farms, vineyards, fields,' and other properties in Mislata and Soternes alone, upriver from and almost adjoining Valencia city; specifically he had a vineyard and field in Mislata, and a newly planted vineyard and four fields in Soternes. The cash valuation of these properties, when suddenly dumped upon the depressed land market of 1258, was still between 7,000 and 8,000 sous. There is reason to think that this figure represents an artificially low estimate; perhaps it should be doubled. Mubārak also owned 'buildings' at Alcira, perhaps houses, enjoying exemption from crown taxes; their minimum, and probably merely nominal, value was 200 Valencian sous. He had extensive debts as well, though not encumbering these properties, a circumstance which hints at mercantile or tax bond investments. To judge from the crown's interest in his posthumous affairs, especially in protecting the widow from his creditors, the Mubārak family must have had influence in government circles – or else sufficient local influence to encourage their community to intervene in their interest. 'A Jew of Valencia,' Mubārak was a resident (*habitator*, not *vicinus* or citizen) of Alcira to the southwest. The description is ambiguous but seems to make him a member of the Alcira Jewish community, with 'Valencia' standing for the kingdom rather than the city.

Mubārak's properties obviously lay in choice locations. If their value and their siting on the irrigated *huerta* did not reveal this, the neighboring farms of substantial Christians and the access roads for markets would strongly suggest it. The four fields at Soternes had previously belonged to Christian landlords; the vineyard at Mislata adjoined that of the town's governor (*alcait*). Actual farming here would have been done by tenant–owner *exarici*, both on Mubārak's land and on his neighbors'. One neighbor was the important Mudejar castellan al-Tīfāshī. At each place Mubārak's holdings were closely grouped. Some twenty-five neighbors are given by name, to bound the properties accurately; with patience, these interlocked properties might be rearranged to reconstruct their original pattern. A very early settler and at the height of his career, little more than a dozen years after the close of the Valencian crusade, Mubārak now tumbled into complete disaster. He engineered or in some way became responsible for the murder of the Muslim 'Avingamer' (perhaps Ibn Ghamr). Was the victim a Valencian Mudejar, or a foreign dignitary? We have no details or even a clue. The Mislata–Soternes district was heavily Mudejar, and this Muslim may have been a local leader; there was a *qāḍī* of that name somewhat further south, and the syllables might be bent to fit various tribal names. These were troublesome times all over the Valencian kingdom, with al-Azraq's revolt in full swing, so the occasion may well have had semi-public overtones. King Jaume, 'executing justice' in this case involving a Muslim victim and a Jew, 'caused him to be hanged' and then confiscated his property.[5]

There the matter would have ended, the person and crime of Mubārak hidden from history's eyes, except that the widow Sitt sued for her share of the confiscated property. Though a party to the suit, the king was also the appropriate font of justice here. He heard the claims, examined 'the deeds which your aforesaid husband drew for you' (probably in Hebrew), and consulted 'the Law and the privileges of the Jews' on this matter, rendering judgement that 'you had a third part in the aforesaid goods.' Sitt should also have kept the value of her dowry, 250 morabatins. Before the case could be settled in court, but roughly at the same time, the crown bailiff had duly put the confiscated properties up for auction to the highest bidder. This proved to be the widow herself, perhaps because there was a glut of Valencian properties on the market or perhaps because the local community declined to challenge the widow. The sum offered was 4,200 Valencian sous, a price which the document hints was below the true value. In lieu of payment after the court decision, the widow substituted her dowry and third-share claims on her husband's goods, set by the court at 3,533 sous. Sitt paid only the balance, 566 sous.

Subtracting the dowry of 250 morabatins or 875 sous should reveal the third-share of Mubārak's property, perhaps some 3,325 sous. Multiplying this by three would give his assets as 9,975 sous (plus his wife's dowry and including her share). A complication is the ambiguous word morabatin. The official exchange in Valencia at this time was 4 Valencian sous to the gold Josephine morabatin, $3\frac{1}{2}$ to the Christian pseudo-Josephine, and 6 to the Castilian Alphonsine. The middle figure is used here as the rate for calculations. The sale to Sitt includes a long formula guaranteeing any surplus worth of the property to her, and waiving the crown's claim.

Sitt apparently lacked personal resources, with the disappearance of her share and dowry in the general confiscation, so that she could neither recover the Alcira properties (which went to Pere Barceló) or offer cash or credit for the Mislata–Soternes purchase; instead she had gambled on the court's awarding her a sufficient amount to cover almost all of the high bid she had made. Does this mean that Sitt bought back less than a third of her husband's properties, or that her bid had been carefully measured not to exceed by much the likely award from the court, or rather that some previous understanding had been reached between king, widow, and a compassionate community in order to restore the family fortunes in this pat fashion? The rent she owed for that year alone on the Soternes buildings and land was 200 sous, an indication that her total profits for that place amounted to anything from 600 to a more probable 2,000 sous per annum.

The episode reveals an affluent family of a local Valencian community shortly after the conquest, the dowry and property rights of the wife, the pattern of landholding and a hint of wider commercial affairs, the interaction of Muslim and Jewish community in law before the king's court, and what seems to be a merciful arrangement (or an expedient in a land glut) to convey much of the property back to the widow, who would presumably manage the vineyard and other *huerta* holdings.

THE BARBUTS AND THE HENNA CONSPIRACY OF BEN VIVES

A fascinating glimpse of family rivalry, the perils of high office, and an undiscovered clan of Valencian notables are all found in document 20. Martínez Ferrando notes it briefly as a waiver of charges against Ibn or Ben Vives; but it is much more. Vives b. Josep (or Jucef) b. Vives, called in the Latin records Vives Abenvives, appears in the registers from 1261 as an affluent 'Jew of the city of Valencia.' His Catalan name and surname were commonly used by Jews as equivalent to the private Hebrew names Hayyim and Yehiel, as 'life' or 'may you live.' Invariably combining the Arabic ibn with Romance Vives, his very name reflected the bridging function of many Jews in Valencia. He rose swiftly to prominence from 1267 as a loan financier to the crown and especially to Prince Pere, appearing as bailiff especially at Alfandech de Mariñén, Alcira, and Pego, once holding bonds from the prince to a total of over 100,000 Valencian sous. He supervised the fortifying of Jaume's palace at Valencia and served the crown in other projects during a remarkable public career. The document of 1274 in the appendix finds him at Alfandech in full course. Three Jews brought charges of peculation and immorality against him: Salimah or Salāmah Barbut, Abraham Samaria, and Abraham Gerundí or de Gerona. (Barbut is Catalan for 'bearded one'; since Jews with the name Solomon in Islamic lands not infrequently assumed the compatible Arabic substitute Salāmah as its 'translation' rather than Sulaymān, Barbut's first name in Hebrew may well have been Solomon, Catalan Salamó or Salomó.) A fourth colleague, Isaac Barbut, drafted the charges and may have been scribe–adviser rather than a principal. They associated as fellow plaintiff a Muslim named 'Abd Allāh b. Dā'ūd – perhaps for appearances, since the alleged victims were the valley's Mudejars. They accused Ben Vives of fraudulently purchasing henna at a third to a half of its fair price from the Muslim farmers, loaning them 'pennies and other money' at illegally high usury, and practicing homosexuality.

King Jaume first heard witnesses on the morals charge, found it unproved, then dismissed the companion charges – either as wasting his time or as embarrassing his regime ('We do not wish to carry on the inquiry'). Jaume then issued this recapitulation and protection from any future civil or criminal prosecution. He included in the waiver subordinates, in all their financial dealings with the valley's Muslims during the tenure of Ben Vives. A deletion in the manuscript makes it clear that the king had first issued it on 3 August 1274; the enemies of Ben Vives must have made a flank attack through the court of Prince Pere, since King Jaume recalled the document, added a paragraph of royal protection for Ben Vives and his men against any legal action by the prince, and redated the whole as 9 August.[6]

The commodity in which Ben Vives was accused of speculating deserves notice. Henna had a role in the textile industry as a basic dye; it was in demand as a cosmetic, especially to dye hair and beard, and for processing leather and skins a reddish yellow; it also had medical and perfume applications. Valencian references to the plant during the post-conquest period of King Jaume are scarce – just enough to hint at its production and sale: a place in the tariff lists for Valencia city and its district in 1243 (ranking 51 out of 79 items), in lists for Alcira in 1250 (number 64 of 66), and in a combined list for Biar, Burriana, Játiva, and Murviedro. The Valencia city notice moved into the law code of the kingdom. The earliest tariff was 20 pence per donkey-load (càrrega), but more generally ran to 8 or 10 pence. Our document of 1274 reveals that Alfandech Valley was a center of production. Alfandech was also a Mudejar nucleus of strength, confirming a suspicion that henna was a specialty of Islamic regions as its derivation (al-ḥinna) suggests; the geographical concentration of henna tariffs in reconquest Valencia supports this impression.

The standard price for 1274 is also given, since Ben Vives was paying 2 sous, instead of normal range of 4 to 6, for each arrova. (Arroves were components of a load, each about 10½ kilograms.) Since this was the only product illegally manipulated by Ben Vives, or conversely selected by his enemies as an accusation, it must have been highly profitable and a major resource of the Alfandech area. Of the many charges against his bailiff, Jaume details only a select three: the henna racket, high usury, and homosexuality, with henna both heading the list and having the most detail.[7]

That Ben Vives was not without resources himself is shown by a document of 6 September in which Mateu and Salāmah (but not Isaac) Barbut, Abraham Samaria, and Abraham Gerundí won from King Jaume a charter of protection against Ben Vives 'or any other Jew of his kin' confiscating their properties or setting afoot any charges or inquiry. Ben Vives can pursue debts or complaints only by going to court. This charter widens the context of the first document. We see that the former plaintiffs were debtors to Vives and to a serious degree. The appearance of yet another Barbut, and the protection from the whole family of Ben Vives, makes it probable that we are witnessing an episode in the faction fighting between wealthy Jewish families then common in Jaume's realms. His second instrument clarifies the surnames of the two Abrahams, and identifies all parties to the dispute as 'Jews of Valencia.' A further clue to the hitherto unknown Barbut clan is the random appearance of Genton Barbut in 1271. His personal name is a distortion or approximation of Yom Ṭob; he was *argentarius* or silversmith to the king and held a crown shop at rent in Valencia city, to which Jaume chartered protection.[8]

A year and a half after the Barbut–Ben Vives quarrel, a further document (number 25) conceals as an *obiter dictum* the information that Isaac Barbut had owned a mill in the Gandía countryside, and that he is dead. In that document, one Vidal de Favàritx received permission to build a mill on a minor stream named Villalonga, and 'always to receive the water needed for it' from the stream – 'namely [the distance] from the mill of Isaac Barbut the Jew, [now] deceased, downwards.' (Apparently this guaranteed exclusive use of the power generated by the flow along that length.)[9] No Barbuts appear in the generous indexes of the histories by Baer, Neuman, or Shneidman, or in the itinerary of Miret i Sans; Martínez Ferrando lists only 'Salema' in his index, and in one of those two abstracts only Mateu. Isaac, the scribe who drafted the original attack on the great Ben Vives, appears nowhere. The bits and pieces we have just seen, therefore, constitute the historical resurrection of an important clan of notables from the pioneer days of Valencia city's *aljama*.

THE SCARLET DRESSES OF BEN SHUNANA

Before leaving Vives and his adversaries in the Valencian community, we can notice a business associate who appears in document 5,
and who introduces a hitherto unnoticed Valencian family of some
affluence. He had appeared in Régné's catalog, a bare notice repeated in the itinerary by Miret i Sans with attribution to Régné, and
finally in the catalog of Martínez Ferrando. A related, unpublished
document states that 'Aczmel Avenczunana,' a Jew of Játiva, had
received a passport of protection from King Jaume in April 1268 'for
himself and his family.' Ismael's surname may translate as Shunana
or Zunana. The routine protection, available for people who had the
influence or the fee, contains a valuable glimpse of the Jewish
community's own sumptuary laws. Ismael's wife 'can wear clothing
from any materials except scarlet Persian, notwithstanding [any]
statute of the Jews passed or to be passed.'

Discriminatory clothing laws of Christendom affecting Jews had
only feebly entered Jaume's realms, and they would not touch the
kingdom of Valencia for a long time yet. But Jewish *aljamas* were
themselves concerned about conspicuously extravagant or frivolous
clothing, with its divisive or impious impact on the community. The
notice about Ismael's wife is probably our earliest record of this
concern in the new kingdom. Another was to come in 1283 when
Játiva's Jewish community forbade to its members ostentatious
clothing and accessories. The cloth for which the conjectural translation 'scarlet Persian' is given in our own case was the rare and valued
presset (occasionally *perset*) *vermell*. An import from the Near East, it
rarely figures in Catalan import lists and never in Valencian; Christian sumptuary laws mention it. It was popular with wealthy Spanish
Christians and Muslims alike, especially for capes and shoes; in his
surrender treaty the Valencian *qāʾid* of Bairén had demanded from
Jaume red clothing for fifty of his entourage, and for himself alone an
outfit of scarlet Persian. This unusual clause in Ismael's charter
reinforces the impression that he was wealthy.[10]

Neither Régné nor Martínez Ferrando mentions his family elsewhere, but Martínez Ferrando does record the sale 'of some houses
and farms' to one 'Abentuinayna' (Régné's 'Abentuyayna'). Publication of our appended document 5 reveals this to be a Zunana or
Shunayna. If *faquimus* is his title, he could even be our Ismael seven
years earlier. The truncated form of the word, and the lack of a first

name, both persuade that his personal name was Faquim; the derivation of name and title will be considered below. Faquim is 'the son of Josep' (English Joseph) and like Ben Vives was a Jew 'of the city of Valencia.' He and Ben Vives are seen here buying 2,700 sous' worth of properties 'in the territory (*terretorio*) of the city of Valencia'; for this considerable investment they are receiving 'all the buildings, farms, vineyards, and the whole estate' at suburban Melilla near Ruzafa, as more fully described in a separate 'public deed of sale.' The former owners now selling are Martín Sánchez de Lóriz, 'knight' of Aragon, and his wife María Díaz. If the surname links Ismael, Josep, and Faquim as contemporary relatives, another family of Valencian notables has been discovered; if the rare surname improbably belongs to two different families, each was affluent and surely important to the capital's *aljama*.[11]

THE RISE AND FALL OF DAVID MASCARAN

More eminent than Ben Vives, though an Aragonese rather than a Valencian figure, was the oligarch Daviu or David (al-)Mascaran. His early career, during the reign of King Jaume, was relatively quiet, consisting largely of financial transactions connected with Prince Pere. After Pere came to the throne, David rose to power and general influence among the Jewish *aljamas*, becoming identified with oppressive taxes and high-handed arrogance. Brought low by factional in-fighting in the *aljamas*, David had his case referred by King Pere in 1285 to the most celebrated jurist of the realms' Jews, Barcelona's rabbi Salomó b. Adret, who also headed a bench of three Jewish judges to try David in 1286. An enemy in the *aljama* assassinated David in 1290. King Jaume was employing him as early as 1271, referring then to his father: the two Mascarans had been managing crown finances at 'our castles of Guadalest and Confrides and Penáguila and Castell.' Jaume also gave to David that year an exchange table or bank, 'five and a half Valencian palms long, before the ark of the [Torah] scroll of the synagogue of Valencia,' located alongside other banks. Since a synagogue at this period was as much community center as house of prayer, the ark did not dominate the interior; it was probably located in a niche or an apse in the eastern (Jerusalem) wall, with the *bimah* or platform at the west. David's stall, just wide enough to accommodate one customer at a time, must have formed part of a small exchange in the street or *plaza* facing this eastern wall.[12]

The few details which can be gleaned about David Mascaran in Jaume's reign are precious, because he was then a Valencian rather than the national figure he became under King Pere. To discover that his father likewise was a financier and involved seriously in Valencian crown finances strengthens the supposition that David was not an *arriviste* but had links with a family of this name a century or two earlier. His possession of a bank shows that local eminence had been achieved long before he stepped on to the wider stage of history. Document 22 offers in intriguing detail another turning point in David's life. It is the more welcome in being a surprise, nowhere revealed in Martínez Ferrando's catalog note about a Christian receiving land at Algirós. In fact the Christian was not receiving but surrendering that land. In this transaction of 1275 Ermengod de Selga and his brother Mateu have given back to the king their charter for holding eleven jovates or plowlands 'in the district of Algirós' near Alcira; in exchange King Jaume is awarding an obviously richer if smaller property of eight jovates advantageously located on the 'canal of Alcira' – either on the main irrigation trunk or (by popular usage) in that irrigation network. To clear this valuable land of any lingering claim by a former owner, King Jaume explains that 'David Almascaran the Jew was holding by our grant' those irrigated eight jovates, and that the crown had confiscated them 'because the said David does not keep personal residence on the said estate' as the general law for such grants demands.

In fact, David 'has gone to settle at Orihuela.' The fertile *huerta* beyond the Valencian kingdom's southern border in Murcia had been reconquered by King Jaume from Muslim rebels, on behalf of its tributary overlord Castile in 1266, a decade before; the ensuing land rush had gobbled up half of Murcia's Mudejar-owned farmlands by 1272, and most of the remainder during the next decade. Many settlers were Catalan, though Orihuela itself would pass from Castile to Aragon only toward the end of the century. David was not only part of this movement, but abandoned a fine estate in the Alcira *huerta* for his adventurous new residence.

Since he was active in Valencian financial affairs in 1274, a year before our land transaction, one might conjecture that David had moved south out of Valencia only very recently. But an earlier complaint and confiscation by the king in this same area indicates that David and his father were gone, perhaps long gone, in 1273; Jaume notes there that he had opened the 'new irrigation[-network] of Alcira' on condition of personal residence, that among the beneficiaries had been 'the Jew Abraham Almascaran and his son David,' that their default both of residence and of labor had forfeited their estate, and that four of these jovates were now going to the son of Simó de San Feliu, the king's scribe. From this document we discover the name of David's father, and see one stage in the dismantling of their joint estate near Alcira. Considering David's strenuous activities in the service of King Pere and in intra-*aljama* struggles, he could hardly have remained long resident in Orihuela after the new king took power.[13]

SHASHON: BATHS AND MILLS OF AN ARISTOCRAT

Another intriguing figure is Astruc(h) Jacob Xixó(n) or Shashon. We have two dozen documents, from Jaume's registers alone, tracing his career as bailiff of various local Valencian revenues of the king or Prince Pere from 1260 to 1275. Using the surface data in Martínez Ferrando's catalog, Ortí Miralles has outlined a bit of his activity; but much more can be discovered about him. The manuscripts present his name variously: Xixon is common, both declined and undeclined, as is undeclined Xixo and (less usual) undeclined and declined Sexon. In several Catalan areas Xixons is a modern family name; it seems likely that Astruc's surname was an equivalent of Arabic Shashon or Sashon (Sasson or Sassoon), a Romance approximation for Hebrew Shoshan or 'lily'; it may also relate to Arabic Sha'shu'. His Romance first name, Astruc or Strug, from late Latin for 'star,' common to Catalan Jews and Christians, was a favorite equivalent for one's private Hebrew name of Mazal Ṭov or of Gad. A loan of 1263 calls him 'a Jew of Tortosa,' while a tax instruction of 1285 characterizes his heirs as 'Jews of Morella.'

Peñíscola, Morella, Tortosa, Segorbe–Onda, and Burriana define his area of loan operations, some of them involving impressive sums; at various times he ran the salt monopoly of Peñíscola, helped finance a counterweighted catapult for the army, marketed for the crown tens of thousands of sous' worth of produce collected as tax (perhaps as the crown share of church tithe), served as paymaster in the elaboration of Peñíscola's fortifications, and extended his reach through his 'lieutenant' (*locum tenens*) Musquet (Mus'ad) Mordecai. He owned mills at Campanar in the Valencian *huerta* and built a public bathhouse there; on another property he built a synagogue. King Jaume exempted him in 1266 from regalian taxes and from the private or Jewish taxes of any *aljama*; no court could hear a case involving him except the king's personal or delegate court, nor could any *aljama* 'put him or his under a ban (*in vet*) or a communal ordinance [*in tacana* = Hebrew *taqqānā*] or any other restrictions besides, except only in excommunication [*in herem* = Hebrew *ḥērem*], for informers [*molsenuch*; cf. Hebrew *malshinim*].' Astruc was obviously a highly important man.

What can our appended document 24 add to this? To begin with, it can correct the impression left by the catalog, and openly narrated by Ortí Miralles, that Astruc's wife was Dolça and his brother Guarner: on the contrary, these are the family of Mateu de Montreal, a knight and loan financier himself to both King Jaume and King Pere. It also corrects the catalog statement that Astruc was buying properties only in Valencia city, and it adds a wine-cellar to those properties: 'an oven, baths, cellar, and mills located in Valencia city and its [countryside] districts.' By supplying the price, 30,000 sous, it reveals the magnitude of the transaction. And finally it tells us that the knight Mateu and his wife and brother had petitioned that the crown go on record as 'guarantor in perpetuity' for everything itemized in the (now lost) bill of sale, the king and his successors and crown officials to protect Astruc and his heirs 'in court and out of court everywhere.' A phrase toward the end reveals that the three sellers had their own warranty (*guarencia*, Catalan *guarença*) to this effect, and they were passing the burden to the government. This is no simple sale, therefore, but an extensive transaction involving expensive public utilities, consolidating Astruc's previous interests in the *huerta*; thus it counteracts the impression that he was a rather parochial figure confined to northern Valencia. By publication of this document Astruc loses a wife and brother but gains universality as a figure in pioneer Valencian history.[4]

THE SALT MINES OF SAMUEL AND SALĀMAH

While Astruc managed the salt works of seashore Peñíscola in 1263, Samuel the son-in-law of Salāmah of Daroca took over the salt mines of (then) Valencian Arcos de las Salinas on the mountainous west–central border (document 7). The catalog entry for this transaction simply states that Samuel rented the Arcos salt works for four years. Details within the document, and external context, have a fuller and fascinating story. Salimah or Salāmah of Daroca, 'a Jew of Monzón,' was one of many occasional investors in crown loans. The present arrangement, unlike Astruc's, which aimed to recover a loan and its interest, was a straight sale (by the usual bidding at auction) of the administration of a regional salt monopoly to Samuel, who could expect a minimum salary of ten percent of total crown profits. Consequently he had to budget the complex of prior encumbrances on this revenue – interest to bondholders, pensions assigned, and debt-bonds rather like checks issued to creditors. Regular encumbrances he was to pay at three set times each year; but a special schedule controlled the larger debts. In the first of his four years he would disburse 9,000 sous to the archpriest of Daroca, plus 700 in connection with the monopoly process itself, and 2,300 to his father-in-law Salāmah toward reducing a large debt owed him by King Jaume. During each subsequent year Samuel would pay 5,000 to Salāmah, and 7,000 to creditors the crown would progressively designate.

The fixed price of salt over the Teruel district was high, so profits were great. The price per *faneca*, or about 40 quarts, 'raw or processed,' was set here at 15 Jaca pence or 1 Valencian sou, which was also the ceiling decreed in 1250 by an *Aureum opus* privilege everywhere in the Valencian kingdom; the salt bailiff had to supply wholesalers at the mines for 3 Valencian pence and in Valencia city for 5. Samuel had contracted to lease his monopoly for 12,000 sous per annum; he therefore expected a minimum collection of his price plus ten percent (to a total of 13,200), plus the salaries and expenses of the industry, the marketing, and the tax administration. From other documents we know that Salāmah had previously loaned 5,000 gold Alphonsine morabatins to the king, for which he had in 1257 assumed direction of Arcos castle and the salt monopoly. Four months after Samuel's appointment in May 1263, the crown's total obligation to Salāmah was expressed as 8,850 gold morabatins, translating as 53,000 Valencian sous or 55,000 Jaca sueldos. The September document itemizing this debt is misreported by Martínez Ferrando as 3,850 gold morabatins, because he read only the item in the opening lines.

King Jaume had stopped for a single day at Monzón, audited all his current obligations to Salāmah, contracted to ignore all assignations or encumbrances on Arcos salt after Easter 1264, and committed the full crown revenues of those salt works to retiring the debt. This did not void Samuel's tenure as bailiff; it merely rearranged his budget or schedule of payments. At this time, the agreement notes, Salāmah was serving as bailiff for crown revenues from 'the Jewry of Lérida, and from the profits of pasturage and of the oil building [warehouse?] of the oil-press of Lérida and of the marketing of linen [or flax] and wool of Lérida.' While it would be naive to think that Samuel had taken over the salt works by coincidence, without influence exerted by his financier father-in-law, the terms of his purchase indicate a straightforward sale of that bailiate, with Samuel as entrepreneurial administrator. If Teruel was forced by law to buy Valencian salt from Samuel, it also contributed more directly during that same year to the new kingdom's economic development. Document 6 is cataloged only as an assignment of taxes to the 'repair' of Alcira's irrigation network; it was in fact an assignation of 'all the revenues and profit' received by the crown from 'the Jews of Teruel,' plus the *portatge* or transients' toll of that city, toward 'paying the necessary expenses' of that Valencian system as it expanded and adapted to incoming settlement. Small though the detail is, it forms part of the mosaic of Jewish contributions to the building of the kingdom of Valencia.[15]

SONS OF THE *ḤAKĪM*

The tangled situation in documents 8 and 9 must have recurred frequently during the rapid settlement of a conquered area. King Jaume had given away to different parties the same piece of land. With settlers relatively scarce and many not bothering to take up the required residence, one might suppose that such errors were easily fixed by granting fresh lands to one party; but that solution overlooks the attachment resulting from holding the property over a decade or two, the improvements introduced, and the plans or dreams which had arisen, and especially the tenacious individualism and pride which instigated so much medieval barratry. The catalog entry for document 8 says only that the sons of Joan de Garrigues got the property previously held by the king's *alfaquim*; for document 9 the entry notes that the loser's son received 3,000 sous as compensation.

In fact a civil suit had been brought by Samuel and Isaac, sons of the deceased courtier–physician of King Jaume, Aaró (English Aaron).

Aaró had received from Jaume an estate at Játiva, with the proper documentation. The king gave the same property to the (unnamed) heirs of Joan de Garriga or Garrigues – the documents employ first the plural form of this name, then the singular. Apparently the Garrigues party took over the property, precipitating a series of suits initiated by the sons of Aaró. King Jaume says Samuel and Isaac 'have sued in our presence many times, petitioning that we return to you' the estate. Both sides presented documentation and argumentative claims during a final appearance at Lérida in the summer of 1263. The king 'adjudicated the said estate to the said sons' of Garrigues, ordered 'impediments' or harassment to cease, and 'annulled every charter of the said sons of Aaró.' About a week later, still at Lérida, King Jaume restated the case. He did not reverse his decision, but he admitted that chronologically 'we gave that estate [of Aaró] to Joan de Garrigues afterwards, whence it is clear to us that we made the grant of the said estate to your aforesaid father.' The king made royal amends: 'not wanting to cause you any injury, we promise and undertake [that] we will give you, in compensation or replacement of the said estate' another estate at Játiva 'worth 3,000 Valencian sous.' If Jaume failed to find and deliver this prize before six months were out, he obliged himself to pay Samuel and Isaac the 3,000 sous in cash. Considering Jaume's canniness with money, and the surplus of free land, one surmises that he shortly presented the patient pair with a new home.

Aaró's title *alfaquim* derived from *al-ḥakīm* (Castilian *alhaquín*) or medical man-of-science. The crown office of *alfaquimatum* was filled by Jews identified by that title, some of whom appear as beneficiaries of land grants in the Valencian *Repartiment* after the crusade; specialists in Arabic learning, they often headed the Arabic section of Jaume's chancery. Historians have tended to allow the role of savant to 'decorate' the *alfaquim*, because of his frequent appearance as Arabic secretary. David Romano currently insists that he was merely a physician as *alfaquim*, and rejects extension of the term itself to include erudition as a savant in Arabic. This would reduce the history of word-usage to etymology; in a region where King Jaume referred in 1270 to 'the Sunna of the Jews,' one must be more cautious. In any case, the current controversy rests on basic misunderstanding by both sides. The traditional education of the Islamic *ḥakīm* was as much philosophical as medical, or more so, so that his capacities as man of learning outweighed his medical value and opened posts at court to him in both the Islamic and Christian worlds. Whatever his practical services in diplomacy or chancery or medicine, Aaró had been by very status therefore a splendid figure at Jaume's court. In his person he joined the three cultures now interacting in Valencia.[16]

THE BONJUEU STABBING

Sometimes a catalog entry supplies the basic data while missing the main point of the document, as in number 16. Salomó (English Solomon) Vidal, 'a Jew of Burriana,' had been wounded, and Salomó the son of Bonjueu or Bonjudà de la Torre had been implicated somehow in the crime, perhaps as an instigator. Of the two principals, only Vidal is identifiable. He will appear in King Pere's records as bailiff of Villarreal and director of its Muslim and Christian immigration, from at least late 1276 through early 1281. Villarreal, whose founding by King Jaume was at least two years in the future at the time of the attack on Vidal, was the region bordering Burriana at the west; Vidal, at Burriana, must already have been in the service of Prince Pere, since our document comes from Pere and concerns his rights in the episode.

What Salomo b. Bonjueu sought from the prince was not (the catalog's) forgiveness or dismissal of charges, but a waiver of all Pere's own claims as a possible party to the case. For this Salomó settled out of court, paying Pere 200 Jaca sueldos (250 Valencian sous). No 'lieutenant or official' of Pere henceforth can cite Salomó to court in this matter, or confiscate his properties, or make any demands. The document clearly states, however, that the culprit must 'answer at law in this affair to [any] suit' which Vidal might bring against him. The connection with Prince Pere was incidental, a happy accident which preserved for us this notice about an internal *aljama* dispute, quite possibly a faction fight between local families; had the episode represented something external, such as opposition to Pere's agent, the settlement would have conveyed more detail or sense of outrage, instead of this brusque, routine attitude. The effect of Pere's dismissal was to confine the case to the jurisdiction of the courts of Burriana's Jewish *aljama*.[17]

THE FAMILY OF THE ḤAKĪM BAḤYA

An unpretentious item in the catalog has a confirmation of the inheritance of Salomó, from his father the *alfaquim* 'Bahiel' – Zaragoza vineyards, and lands near Murviedro and Alcira. Salomó's brother and his uncle Salomó the *alfaquim* had also been in the will. There is a related confirmation, a few folios back, for the brother Moisès (English Moses), which the catalog misinterprets as a division of Murviedro and Alcira properties among the three heirs. The central figure here is familiar from his appearances in King Jaume's autobiography, but not in his wider family and community background. The *rāv* or rabbi Baḥya had been the patriarch of the Alconstantini clan when the Balearics and Valencian crusades were fought, the rival for *aljama* power against the dominant Cavallerias in Zaragoza and therefore in the Jewries of high Aragon, and the leader of the pro-Maimonidean intellectual currents. As Arabic secretary to King Jaume he arranged the surrenders of Majorca, Játiva, and Murcia; his brother Salomó did the same for Minorca. Baḥya's name has puzzled historians from Gayangos (who argued for Babiel) to Soldevila (who with the Marsili manuscript preferred Bahihel); it appears also as Bafiel, and it invites conjecture as to some form of Hillel. It seems, however, to be an Hispano-Arabic diminutive of Judeo-Arabic Baḥya; in Spain the Latin suffix *-ellus* affixed itself even to Arabic names to yield bastard forms like Muḥammaḍāl.

Baḥya appears in the *Repartiment* or land division of Valencia with generous grants, as do his brother Salomó and his son Moisès. Of the two sons the younger, Salomó, had the less vaulting career, including profitable bailiates over Murviedro and Montesa in Valencia, and nomination by the queen as crown rabbi and chief justice for Aragon's Jews. Moisès, something of a rascal, cut a grander figure, becoming treasurer and Arabic secretary to the crown, bailiff of Valencia city for five years, and head judicial authority for that city's Jews from 1258. But he made a serious mis-step during intra-*aljama* quarrels, forging a document (which cost him half his wealth confiscated), and involving himself in the beating of a rabbi who had testified to King Pere about the faction fights of Zaragoza. Jews and Christians allied to oust him from his Valencian posts on charges of unscrupulousness. Later he won pardon and restoration of confiscated properties, but died six years afterward. Though the adult career of Moisès spans the whole crusade and resettlement of Valencia, his peak and best-documented period was under King Pere.

The appended charters 13 and 14 involve no lawsuit or major surprises, but they do convey new information. There were more than two brothers; both documents refer to other 'brothers' as plural. Since no court fight or delay intervened, Baḥya seems to have died recently. As younger son, Salomó got a smaller share – a vineyard, a field, and an unspecified estate or farm. The catalog badly identifies their locales. The first was not 'some vineyards in the *arrabal* [or Jewry] of Zaragoza,' but 'a certain vineyard' in the irrigated area of the Zaragoza countryside called Raval then and Rabal today. The second property or 'estate' comprised at least two pieces of land, one of Conillera (Castilian Conejera) and the other in the area called Gausa, both of them in the countryside or jurisdiction of Murviedro (modern Sagunto); Gausa is a small but fertile area in the northeast section of Valencia's Sierra de la Calderona. The catalog item 'some fields in Alcira' was actually 'one field in the district of Alcira in the place called Alcanessia,' perhaps Alcanyissa.

Salomó had a charter already from Baḥya, as did his brother Moisès, so that the king was confirming not the last will and testament but 'the partition' as more fully described in what seem to have been separate copies of the same charter. Moisès received 'some buildings and vineyards in Murviedro and its districts, and the hamlet in Albacet [near Murviedro] with its appurtenances, and vineyards in the place called Raval in the district of Murviedro and [also] in Conillera, and buildings in Valencia [city] which belonged to Ḥamzah [?] the Saracen, and the estate which you have in Alcira – namely fields you have in Barralbés, and the farm you have in Alcanèssia, and the mill in the place called L'Alfàs in the Alcira district, and buildings in Alcira.' Assuming that the unnamed brothers of Moisès and their uncle Salomó the *alfaquim* received between them at least the same amount as either of the two whose records have come down to us at random, some idea can be formed of what the rabbi Baḥya held in the kingdom of Valencia alone.[18]

WELCOME TO THE FRONTIER: JEWISH PIONEERS

A cataloger's haste can invert the meaning even of a short document; number 12 of our appendix illustrates this. The Martínez Ferrando entry sees an 'exemption granted to the Jews of Murviedro, freeing them from paying at Christmas the 500 sous to which they were obliged.' The document says the opposite, in fact; but the reservation of its real meaning to the final or *nisi* clause can mislead the careless. King Jaume is here reducing the usual 500 sous, an arrangement he is establishing now and for the future 'for as long as it shall please us.' This was not a case of an *aljama* directly farming or buying its own revenues – a common procedure by which a community acted as its own bailiff, thus avoiding or at least acquiring for the communal chest the ten percent bailiff's salary. It seems instead the straightforward kind of reduction or reassessment one encounters in the king's lists under the rubrics *dimisit* and *remisit*. The sum itself is too large to be a poll tax or a household tax (probably neither existed here as a regalian exaction anyway).

At first it seems too low to be the sum of a year's taxes, since the king will be collecting 2,000 from Murviedro's Jews (again as 'tribute') and 12,000 from its Christians a decade later, and in 1275 apparently took 1,000 from its Jews. The word 'tribute' in Valencia could mean poll tax (as with the Mudejar besant), or commonly the agricultural rents, or simply the complex of taxes in general. A closer look at the figures suggests that the previously assessed 500 sous was a lump-sum for the body of Jewish taxes by the crown here. The 2,000 seems part of the war fund for the king's Holy Land crusade, quickly amassed by waiving future taxes for three years, to a total of four years. Játiva's Christians would thus pay 3,000 sous per annum as the norm; her Jews paid the 500 which was reduced to 300 in this earlier period, very probably to attract more Jewish immigrants. Since the Jews of Valencia kingdom paid no municipal taxes, aside from their private contributions to intra-*aljama* expenses, the total of taxes directly to the king would appropriately fit the concept of tribute.[19]

The amount collected also casts doubt on Baer's thesis of a poverty-stricken Murviedro *aljama*, an interpretation more appropriate to the parlous period a century later from which his evidence comes. A companion document, issued to the Jews of Játiva a decade after our Murviedro privilege, decreed 'that every year from now on, you give and are bound to give us and ours 600 sous of Valencia for tribute,' half at Christmas and half on the feast of John the Baptist. The document contains nothing to justify the catalog's description of this action, however, as 'a reduction' as at Murviedro. The two documents together suggest that Murviedro's *aljama* was roughly half as wealthy as Játiva's, but that King Jaume envisioned future growth at Murviedro in 1263.

Document 4 illustrates the immigration policy of Jaume, and the tensions and bickering it caused within the Játiva *aljama* as early as 1261. From mid-century, when the king had negotiated a shift of the Banū 'Īsā dynasty's political center from Játiva to the castle of Montesa, he strove to increase both Christian and Jewish immigration at Játiva. The privilege to Moisès Avengayet (Judeo-Arabic Giyāt, Gayyāt) in 1253 represents a standard inducement: freedom 'from all tax or tribute and from whatsoever other crown obligation' for five years, an immunity now extended in 1258 for an additional two years. This was not a rare concession, as the Martínez Ferrando catalog gratuitously states, 'for his services to the king.' Nor was it yet another of the abusive personal privileges irresponsibly conferred, as Neuman is misled into believing by Régné's catalog.[20]

Tax exemption, not only for the accepted traditional classes such as professional scholars or the poor but for the prosperous elite who served the crown locally or generally, was an enduring problem for any *aljama*. The problem was particularly acute when the exemption extended from crown taxes to the vital private taxes of the *aljama* itself. In the kingdom of Valencia this perennial situation existed alongside a very different drama. King Jaume actively pursued a program of importing as many Muslims and Jews as he could attract, using as a major lure temporary exemption from all crown taxes. The program varied slightly at different locales. At Burriana the standard exemption for the pioneer Jew, for example, was the first four years; in document 17 for 1271 or 1272 Samuel Sa Real or Sarreal 'our Jew' receives this status 'just as is granted with fuller detail to our Jews settling at Burriana.' The wording dissipates the impression left by the catalog entry that this was a random personal exemption. It ran 'from the day you began to keep domicile in Burriana up through four complete continuing years to come,' and included 'every *quèstia*, *peita*, or common or any other exaction' demanded in the king's name. Like all the immigration exemptions, it did not mention *aljama* taxes nor extend to them.

Returning to Játiva, it becomes clear from a series of documents which includes our number 4 that Moisès b. Gayyāt fits this immigration pattern. Starting with that document, we find King Jaume in 1261 responding 'to the whole *aljama* of the Jews of Játiva' with the clarification that 'no Jew among you, by reason of exemption granted by us, can withdraw himself from meeting communal obligations (*vobiscum facere vicinaticum* [Catalan *veïnatge*]), and he must respond to the public 'alarms' just like the other Jews of Valencia. When the exempt years are over, each exempt resident must take up his share of 'all' the crown taxes. The situation had been general enough by 1260 to have prompted the *aljama*'s grievance and the crown's redress or clarification. A class of new settlers had grown during the period following the king's 1252 settlement which had confined the Muslims to a section of Játiva and had begun the new epoch. They had probably arrived within the last five years of the 1250s, since other documents indicate that length of time as the usual exemption; some may have arrived earlier and have illegally prolonged their exempt period, since the king insists on payment of taxes by those whose charters have lapsed. The moment of crisis and appeal would have been 1260, since the king's resolution of the problem came in early January of 1261. Thus the catalog description of the king's letter as 'defining the scope' of the *aljama*'s liberties is inexact and misleading.[21]

This view of Játiva's pattern of Jewish settlement, at the midpoint of its evolution under Jaume, takes on added meaning in the context of later, related documents and at the same time clarifies those later privileges. Seven years after the king's order that exempt settlers pay intra-*aljama* taxes, Jaume issued a general privilege formally exempting all Jewish settlers during their first five years. Our only copy of this 1268 charter turns up within a related letter of 1274 applying its terms to a particular settler. A further charter of 1274 spelled out in more detail the range of exemptions and their limits. These documents are incorrectly presented by the catalogs. Martínez Ferrando saw the settler's document as merely an extension of the *aljama*'s five-year exemption to a new member, and he missed the enclosed charter of 1268. Régné confused the issue by a previous notice in which the Játiva *aljama* received these privileges within a few weeks of their being applied in March 1274 to that newcomer. Relying on Régné, Baer had the king issue the first known 'charter' for this community in 1274; since this is extraordinarily late, only two years before Jaume's death, both Baer and Beinart call it 'a new charter.'

Taking these three documents in order, the 1268 general privilege exempted 'each and every Jew who wants to come settle at Játiva – from the day he wants to arrive up through five subsequent full years' – from all regalian taxes, fees, or obligation. By late summer of 1273 the first five-year period had ended, so the Játiva *aljama* refused to apply it to the newcomer Isaac b. Yanāḥ, 'a Jew of Toledo, who came to settle at Játiva because of the said exemption.' The king came to Isaac's defense, applying 'the aforesaid privilege specially' to him and dismissing 'any charter granted to the *aljama* of Jews of Játiva to the contrary.' Perhaps Isaac had arrived within the original five-year period, or perhaps King Jaume was declaring the 1268 privilege to be open-ended and continuing. To keep the settlers coming, in any case, the king issued a general privilege only a month before Isaac's final sentence came from his appeal. By this privilege 'any Jew who will come into Játiva to settle' would be exempt 'beyond those five years during which we granted that Jews settling there would be exempt, by our charter as contained therein'; presumably this continued the five-year periods. The privilege required that any Jew now settled or later to come, who removes himself or his domicile elsewhere within eight years, 'is bound to pay his share in levies and other crown taxes and obligations paid by the said *aljama* in the time during which he stayed in Játiva'; thus removal before completing eight years would have been prohibitively expensive. Within three months of arrival, moreover, Jews had to swear to pay their share without exemption 'in the communal expenses, legally and properly.' Any infraction of this charter could bring a fine of 100 morabatins.

The three documents tell us a great deal about the Játiva Jewish community, where before we had only the catalog's tax exemption of 1274. It would be instructive to relate these privileges to the wider privileges given to the Jews of Jaume's realms in 1268, to the very late settlement patterns and importance of Játiva (the Mudejars' political and psychological center during the post-crusade period of revolts), to intra-*aljama* factions elsewhere, and to patterns of immigration – since Isaac was 'a Jew of Toledo.' Did he receive special consideration simply because the king normally served as final court of appeal in intra-*aljama* appeals, and especially of course in the application of a crown privilege; or does Isaac's provenance denote some connection with the court of Castile?

Some communities evolved faster than others. While Játiva remained to some extent the kingdom's Mudejar center, with the crown anxious to flesh out its Christian and Jewish colonies, Valencia city already was strong enough to dispense with exemptions of the immigration type. In spring of 1269, obviously after negotiations with the capital's *aljama*, King Jaume decreed 'that all Jews residing or who from now on will reside in the city of Valencia' must pay their share of crown taxes and services. This covered real property and moveables, including all moveables elsewhere in the kingdom of Valencia (on which local taxes would cease and Valencia city's claims take precedence). The only exception were Jews of Valencia city already holding exemptions 'with our charters, as contained in those.' Jaume promised that he would issue no further exemptions. 'If we do exempt anyone of those men or women Jews from now on, that enfranchisement or exemption is prejudicial to you and cannot be used to their advantage; indeed that exemption is to be considered void.' What is more, the *aljama* itself is encouraged 'to place under ostracizing ban [*in herem* = Hebrew *ḥērem*] and minor excommunication [*in nidivi* = Hebrew *niddui*], and to forbid burial to them in your cemetery, and to deploy the whole range of your Law, until they pay their part in the aforesaid – excepting of course the exempt cases already made and conceded by us.'[22]

MAÏR IN THE PALACE

Among a number of glimpses of the Játiva Jewish quarter and of men now obscure to us is the appended document 18. In 1272 King Jaume gave life tenure of a farm or fertile plot (*ortum*) to Pere Ballester, which had belonged 'to the Jew Maïr [Meir], deceased.' The odd form of temporary tenure, proper to an office, indicates that Maïr had previously been so installed; in any case he was one of Játiva's earliest Jewish landowners. The location intrigues: Maïr's property 'is inside the *aljaferia* of Játiva,' a word which conjures up the celebrated Moorish palace called the *Aljafería* for which Zaragoza is famous and whose syllables are said to derive from the name of the ruler Abū Ja'far b. Hūd. Ballester already held by similar life tenure 'our buildings of the said *aljaferia*,' an ambiguous phrase which accommodates the idea that this was the palace of the Banū Īsā family, abandoned when the *qā'id* Yaḥyā b. Muḥammad moved to his consolation prize of Montesa twenty years previously; if so, Maïr apparently held adjoining gardens or grounds. The Jew's property 'faced the summit of the greater castle of Játiva' and stood 'on the road which goes to the said castle'; on another side it flanked 'the Jewish quarter of Játiva.'

The deliberate destruction of the city and much of the castle in war in 1707, as well as the odd lie of the town's streets along the slope of a ridge, make it difficult to place all this. The double castle of Játiva – the greater and the lesser – were joined in an enveloping wall along a mountain crest. Does the neighboring Jewry point to a site for Maïr's property outside this complex, somewhere in the walled town which sprawled down the hillside? Or does the vicinity of the Jewry, in accordance with a common pattern in Spanish Islam by which that quarter lay within the walls and close to the *alcázar*, indicate that the *aljaferia* was indeed the castle complex and that Maïr held or administered for life-tenure the grounds between its two fortifications?

We know nothing more of Maïr; if he is to be identified with a namesake who had been bailiff of Gandía, then he was dead by spring of 1268. Martínez Ferrando had difficulty with his name, presenting him in the catalog items as 'Mayno,' and twice in the index as 'Mayrino.' Examination of the manuscripts shows all three names as Maïr ('Mayr,' 'Mayrius,' and genitive 'Mayrii').[23]

THE CALIPH'S GIFT

Maïr is not the only such figure of mystery in King Jaume's new realm. Other Jews, obviously men of substance and public service in their own day, flit past us now in a random phrase or in some document apparently without clarifying context. Take for example 'Abraham Avingabell.' Martínez Ferrando's catalog follows the lead of an earlier archivist who had scribbled a title across the top of the manuscript; he reports a routine rental by Abraham of 'a shop situated at the entrance to the Jewry' of Valencia city. It was something very different. This is a key record in King Jaume's diplomatic *entente* with Islamic Tunis, and our only memento of the Jew who obviously had played some role in it. Jaume had maintained close trade relations with Ifrīqiya or Tunis for a quarter-century, despite troubles, and had sent a splendid embassy to the Hafsid capital in 1274 (complete with thirteen esquires, two trumpeters, and a flautist) to repair the alliance. One result of this maneuver was a return embassy from the caliph al-Mustanṣir in the spring of 1276, three months before Jaume's death. Those were parlous times: Marinid Morocco had invaded the peninsula in 1275 and was preparing its 1276 invasion; Tunis had recently thrown back the crusade of Louis IX of France, and was a staging ground for Hohenstaufen refugees ambitious to replace the Angevin Guelphs in nearby Italy; and the kingdom of Valencia was in the throes of a revolt so extensive and threatening as to consitute a countercrusade.

Our document shows that the caliph's ambassadorial party, after their landing at Barcelona, had 'just now' arrived in the king's battle headquarters at Játiva. As part of the ceremonial pleasantries, the ambassador had requested favors, presumably for friends of Tunis or of its officialdom. Three such favors were granted here at Játiva and entered into the registers: a pardon and waiver from prosecution for Ramon de Vulpelleres (now Vilalba Sasserres) 'on account of the death of Bartomeu Romeu whom you killed', a life-tenure for Guillem d'Arquers as bailiff or administrator and tax superintendent 'of our mills of Barcelona' with the usual salary of a tenth of the district's income from this public utility, as 'the other bailiffs of the said mills had been wont to receive,' and a workshop at Valencia for the Jew Abraham b. Gabel. It is clear that Abraham was, in his own way, an important man. It is also obvious that his 'shop' must have amounted to more than the standard rental item assumed by the catalog, since it was a caliph's favor in the same class as the pardon and the tax sinecure. Latin *operatorium* at Valencia encompassed every type of establishment from a modest workshop to the most elaborate industrial premises available; like *domus* it was pressed into use by the scribes for various kinds of buildings.

The document also shows that his place stood among the shops reserved to the crown, 'at the entrance to the Jewry' from inside the city – that is, in the center of Christian Valencia and at the point of heaviest traffic for Jewish Valencia. It faced the entrance to 'la Soc' or 'La Açoc,' probably a local *sūq* or market and possibly 'the' neighborhood market of the Jews; on another side, it stood 'on the public street of the Fig Tree *plaza* (*platea de La Figuera*).' Crown shops bounded a third side, and a 'certain shop of Guillem de Porciá.' Guillem had recently been justiciar of Valencia city; he leased expensive crown shops here, including the *qaysārīya* luxury shopmall; his name in the document reveals something about the complex of workshops where Abraham was locating. The setting proclaims the king's bounty; one can assume that the rental of 40 sous, or perhaps more accurately the license fee commonly treated as a rental, had been reduced for Abraham by a similar generosity; King Jaume, for all his carefulness and even stinginess with money, was paradoxically open-handed when lavishing gifts on any ceremonial occasion. We know nothing more about Abraham b. Gabel. But we do know now that he was a substantial and even leading citizen of the Valencia city *aljama*, strategically located to become ever more affluent, and that his past involved some public service or private connection with the Hafsid court at Tunis. If Abraham ever surfaces in the interstices of some future transcription, scholars must be alert to learn more about him.[24]

ATTRACTING THE JEWISH IMMIGRANT

A jejune entry of the catalog, noting only an 'exemption granted by the prince to the Jews of Gandía,' can be specified by consulting the appended document 15. Prince Pere there extends 'to all the Jews of Gandía present and future' the same 'liberties' which King Jaume had already conferred on the Christians of that town, concerning tariffs and transport taxes (*lleuda* and *peatge*) on the merchandise they handle. It applies to Gandian Jews everywhere in the kingdom where the privilege runs, and in its details is an application of that same privilege. Since these two constituted the main taxes on imports and especially on the domestic markets of the Valencian kingdom to which Gandía merchants traded, such a concession was expensive for the crown and of great importance for Jewish or other merchants. We do not have the text of Gandía's Christian privilege; but since all Jews of the Valencian kingdom had been exempt from both taxes on their persons and pack animals since 1247, this later and local grant must have covered a range of specific merchandise.[25]

An equally jejune catalog entry, described only as a favor exempting Valencia city's Jews from the justiciar's court, conceals a program designed to increase Jewish immigration. The first clause does assure 'the *aljama* of the Jews of Valencia [city]' that they need no longer 'answer at law for anything' to the justiciar; he is never to be the arresting or detaining power. The second clause then confers upon the crown bailiff jurisdiction 'over all charges which will be brought against you [Jews] or any individual among you in whatever matter.' The bailiff alone can arrest men or women Jews 'who for any reason have to be arrested,' and hold them 'in our prison at Valencia.'

The city's *aljama* had its own courts for criminal and civil matters, of course, staffed by Jews expert in their traditional law; as with every Valencian *aljama*, the city's legal system was self-contained, with appeal or reserved cases in the king's hands, despite abortive efforts to erect a Jewish chief justice. But when Christians brought charges against Jews, the municipal court of the Christians had hitherto taken over, under its novel justiciar who was elected annually from local men. Besides the disadvantage of a parochial court under local personnel, the alien court tended to maximize its own jurisdiction, to be less sensitive toward the Hebraic legal aspects of a given case, and even to encourage some Jews to escape from the rigor of their own courts. Since Jews were wards of the king, too, the justiciar's claim to handle mixed Christian–Jewish cases could be made to seem unbecoming. In the Valencian kingdom the Moors had already won some transfer, especially in capital cases, from the justiciar to the bailiff. For both Jews and Muslims the shift to this more universal and less explicitly judicial figure had the advantage of emphasizing their own traditional law, escaping local pressures or prejudice, and facilitating appeals to the crown. It also filled the king's treasury, rather than the city's, with fines and confiscations.

The document is presented, however, in the non-legal context of encouraging immigration, and this purpose undoubtedly enjoyed priority among the king's motives. His third clause assured 'Jewish men and women who come to settle at Valencia' that neither the king nor his officials will 'disturb' them (*inquietare*) or put obligations upon them (presumably beyond the customary taxes); and it forbids any legal investigation against a settler 'in connection with any crime or misdeed or debt' he had been involved in 'outside our land before he moved to Valencia.' The next clause goes further: all Jews 'who flee from our land because of any crime for which they were [officially] charged, [but] in which sentence was not delivered or which could not be proven by sufficient witnesses,' can return and settle safe and secure. They cannot be put to the question or tortured; but if new charges are brought, they must stand ready to answer the plaintiffs at law and to post the usual guarantees. A final paragraph, dealing with pledges, bail, and confiscation, protects Jews in all the kingdom from having their Muslims seized 'as long as other goods' are available, despite any laws to the contrary. The most intriguing sections of this document, including its very context, escaped the confines of the catalog paraphrase as lifted from the opening section of the manuscript.[26]

These twenty-five documents have been chosen almost at random, from among the many as yet unpublished, having regard only for some variety. Yet each opens a vista upon the Valencian kingdom's *aljamas* – sometimes a glimpse or an insight, sometimes a larger view. When set even roughly in their more general contexts, each reveals much more than its mere surface data. Thus they illustrate both the need and the possibility of an intricate, widely ranging history of the Valencian Jewish community, seen simultaneously as a cosmos in itself and as an integrated element in the functioning of the Christian–Muslim–Jewish society.

Too narrowly political or ideological a study of this phenomenon can obscure the social reality. Concentration on only those documents explicitly concerned with Jews as individuals and groups will overlook the vital details necessary to tell the story. And focus on Jewish history alone, with the other communities adverted to only as a framing periphery, will make it impossible even to study that history adequately. Painstaking recovery of seemingly negligible details, transformation of these details by setting each in ever widening circles of context, and patient interrelating of parts to parts and of whole to parts can achieve at last the much needed and long awaited history of Valencia's Jews during the reign of King Jaume the Conqueror.

7

The language barrier: bilingualism and interchange

Jews in Jaume's realms commonly spoke Romance as their primary tongue; an indeterminate number knew Arabic. Bilingual Jews with classical Arabic, such as the king's Arabic secretaries and his dragomans or translators, provided a formal bridging service of particular significance between Valencia's three communities. But what did the Muslims speak? This might seem an artificial or foolish query, if so many authors did not teach that of course they spoke Romance. Among a culture's primary boundary-maintaining mechanisms, shields to its very identity, language stands high. If language is completely common, so will much else be shared. A common language, even as a bilingual's second language, would have provided the two societies uneasily co-inhabiting the Valencian kingdom with a solid foundation for transfers and progressive assimilation. If the two stood isolated at the elementary level of language, however, conditions for forbearance or fusion were very different.

THE PROBLEM: ROMANCE, BILINGUAL, OR ARABIST POPULATION

A number of Muslims must have spoken some Romance; while numbers of Christians had some Arabic. But did the generality of people communicate readily across the religio-cultural lines – in the cities, on the farms, or at the aristocrat–notable level? The meager and ambiguous evidence throughout Islamic Spain has produced two schools of interpretation, neither of which applies to thirteenth-century Valencia satisfactorily. One line of historians and linguistic specialists affirms that Spain's Muslim population was significantly bilingual, with Romance the more dominant or domestic tongue. Another holds that the Muslims generally spoke only Romance, with Arabic the preserve of a negligibly few erudites and officialdom.

Valencian sea-coast from the Sierra de Engarcerán. (Cavanilles, *Observaciones sobre el reyno de Valencia*, 1795)

Some express this in terms of class division, separating the exclusively Romance-speaking masses from Arabic-centered upper classes. Others phrase the opposition as Romance-speaking rural areas versus cities more hospitable to bilingualism. A number of authors see a chronological distinction: deepening Arabization from the late eleventh century, under the brief Berber dynasties; they too are reluctant to surrender a considerable survival of bilingualism. Many representatives from the different schools cherish bilingualism as a characteristic peculiar to Spain within medieval Islam, a symbol and vehicle of deeper continuities.

Few voices have challenged the consensus of the traditionalists. Three have recently spoken from a background of Valencian studies: the essayist Joan Fuster, the structuralist historian Pierre Guichard, and the Arabist Míkel de Epalza. For the essayist, the almost exclusively Arabist culture of sixteenth-century Morisco Valencia argues a fully Arabic pattern before the thirteenth-century crusade. For the structuralist, the early victory of Arabic in Valencia flows logically from the dynamics of his total model. For the Arabist, a 'macrohistorical' approach sites Islamic Valencia in the wider Shiite–Sunnite religio-cultural struggle of the tenth century, revealing wholesale Arabization of the masses. In widening these more general attacks upon the fundamental premise of the traditionalists, an historian ought to search now for data by regions and by time-periods, sensibly allowing for variety and evolution. The kingdom of Valencia during the crusader generation provides such a laboratory for closer investigation.

If the consensus for Romance dominance is impressive, the same cannot be said for the evidence invoked. There is little enough of it for a region like Valencia, so the linguist snatches at historical scraps, while the historian borrows conclusions from linguistic and literary analysis. Worse, the historical evidence lies scattered over a disconcerting sweep of centuries, so that it must be stretched forward to cover very different eras, while the literary conventions or toponymical–anthroponymical sources are by their nature inconclusively achronological. Anecdotal fragments play a major role. Ibn Ḥazm found it strange that some Muslims near modern Aguilar and Morón in eleventh-century Castile 'did not speak Romance but exclusively Arabic.' Ibn Sīda of Murcia, writing in that mid-century and apologizing for his inelegant Arabic, seems to blame the dominance of Romance speech on his environment; but Dolors Bramon, correcting Ribera's widely quoted mistranslation, shows how Ibn Sīda intended an ethnic jibe, not a linguistic description, against the 'non-Arab' Muslims of the region. Some probative fragments can be fitted into contradictory interpretations, as when the Cid late in that same century had Mozarabs guard Valencia's walls because they knew the ways of Muslims 'and spoke as they did.' Such examples might also be made to reflect an eleventh-century transition into a more extensive Arabic, a stage in evolution away from bilingualism.

In assessing such evidence, perhaps more attention should be paid to total ambience: the symbiosis between city and countryside in Islamic Spain, the sharp differences in regional background and development, the mobility so striking within the Mediterranean Islamic community and its drift of population, and the precise impact of the Berber dynasties. Perhaps the historian and linguistic scholar would be wise to search out comparative analogies from other areas of medieval Mediterranean Islam, as well, and especially to borrow concepts and findings from the behavioral sciences. The language problem involves so much hypothesis and conjecture that no source of light should be disdained. Meanwhile the work of Bramon, Fuster, Guichard, Sanchis Guarner and recently Barceló Torres and Epalza has dealt a terrible blow to the traditionalist position.[1]

For the non-Hispanist medievalist, coming to the problem from the outside, the very terms Romance and Arabic with their variants can be confusing. Classical Arabic in its medieval form was a universal or mandarin instrument serving the literati, bureaucrats, and religious figures (groups more interpenetrating than differentiated), with city children frequently learning its rudiments. Vulgar Arabic, at times so debased as to be useless for understanding the Koran, existed in various Spanish dialects; this is the Arabic in question here as a popular speech orientation. Federico Corriente has laid out for us in a pioneering study the phonology, morphology, syntax, and much vocabulary of this vulgar Arabic 'Spanish dialect bundle.' He notes that it was 'the first Arabic dialect ever to have risen to full-fledged status as a vehicle of a popular and universal culture.' For its Valencian manifestation at least, this elevation came very late, as L. P. Harvey notes, during a brief half-century before its collapse in early modern times. The bundle of peninsular dialects evolved through the interaction of native and immigrant elements in 'a melting pot,' especially in the ninth and tenth centuries, Corriente finds; Valencia particularly developed 'local features.'

Imported Berber, which made some places briefly trilingual and which undoubtedly gained strength during the Almoravid and Almohad years prior to the Valencian crusade, did not take root in Spain; Guichard does argue for an early, intense Berberization of the Valencian region, but this need not have impeded subsequent Arabization. Literary Arabic is the most accessible of the Islamic languages of Valencia, in a legacy of carefully wrought literature; samples of less elevated work, though rare, are not lacking – for example, a Mudejar contract of marriage. Some scholars see an echo of vulgar Valencian Arabic in the word-list attributed to the Dominican linguist Ramon Martí, presumably composed in thirteenth-century Valencia or at least in eastern Spain as a handbook for convert work among the conquered Muslims. In 1566 Martín de Ayala, the archbishop of Valencia, published an interlinear *Doctrina cristiana en lengua aráviga y castellana* for newly converted Moriscos; clumsy and straitened in Latin characters, it offers clues to the pronunciation of Granadan vulgar Arabic. Valencian was a distinct dialect, despite the high degree of homogeneity of Spanish vulgar Arabic.[2]

What was Romance among Spanish Muslims? Though some describe its early form as a single language, resembling 'perhaps Galician and western Leonese more than any other,' it was a congeries which varied and evolved by regions. Aprioristically one might expect in thirteenth-century Valencia some form of Castilian, Aragonese, Catalan, or native Valencian. The Valencian crusaders called such tongues Latin, and a Romance-speaking Muslim a Latinate. Romance was also called in Catalan *aljamia*, from *al-'ajamīya*. (Only in the later Mudejar period did that word assume its modern meaning of any Romance language as written in Arabic or Hebrew characters; the phenomenon itself began earlier and has analogs in other Mediterranean countries.) The corresponding generic term for Arabic was *algaravia*, from *al-'arabīya*.

Local chauvinism adds a complicating factor in the case of Valencia. Was Valencian Romance merely a dialect or subform of imported Catalan as it declined into variant shape among the multilingual post-crusade settlers? Or is it a more ancient and honorable form, reflecting immemorial pre-crusade Romance of the Valencian region, a linguistic bridge proudly uniting over the centuries a common Valencian people who were separated at another level by the accident of Islamic and Christian religions? This latter vision reflects, in local and linguistic form, the wider battle of interpretations about the nature and evolution of Spanish culture: did European Spain absorb and transmogrify its few Muslim conquerors, or did a radical discontinuity intervene, profoundly orientalizing the Spaniards?

PROTAGONISTS AND POSITIONS

Representative opinions on bilingualism, first for Spain as a whole and then for Valencia, can illustrate and elaborate the several schools. The great Evariste Lévi-Provençal concluded that Romance dialects deriving from Latin persisted alongside Arabic in Islamic Spain from the ninth to the fifteenth century; 'a kind of Romance–Hispanic *koine* prevailed in almost all regions,' though more in country than city, over Arabic or Berber. Henri Terrasse sees Islamic Spain as becoming 'Arabized only little by little and remaining bilingual,' with Romance serving as 'the language of women, the language of the home, often enough that of inmost thoughts.' Emilio García Gómez argues that Romance lyric poetry continued, enjoyed presumably by Mozarabs and at least a stratum of bilingual Muslims. Following Julián Ribera Tarragó, he puts Romance as the familiar language of all classes from emir to rustic.

An older historian so widely read as Andrés Giménez Soler taught flatly that the Spanish Muslims 'had not adopted the language of the Arabs' and consequently that Mudejars 'never spoke Arabic'; one or other erudite mastered it, of course, but the common language remained native Romance. Later historians such as F. Arranz Velarde contrast the exceptional literary Arabic with the widespread Romance. Among current authors the Arabist Anwar Chejne has 'widespread bilingualism' yield only to the armies of the Reconquest and thus 'become less prevalent' from the late eleventh century; because of this 'linguistic conquest' the Mudejars forgot their Arabic, and 'the language of the Moriscos was Romance.' Titus Burckhardt more cautiously states that 'a large number of the townspeople (we do not know how great a proportion) spoke Romance at home and in the streets'; though literary Arabic was 'thoroughly alive,' some Muslims had no Arabic beyond their prayers. Corriente assumes the traditional bilingualism for al-Andalus, though the Granada kingdom was or became monolingually Arabic; he sets the thirteenth century as 'the turning point' for decisive loss of Romance, as a reaction against the disconcerting Christian advance Corriente presents no evidence for this timetable or for late bilingualism. Reyna Pastor de Togneri, analyzing the shift from Islamic to Christian Spain, finds 'a certain Romance–Arabic bilingualism which was distributed equally' among Muslims and Mozarabs; unaware of the frequent phenomenon of bilinguality in the Islamic world, she sees this as unique to Spain.[3]

The authority of Ramón Menéndez Pidal, potent in problems of Spanish history, adds weight to the bilingual case. In his study on the origins of Castilian, he divided bilingualism into three stages. During Spain's first two centuries of Islamic rule, Romance 'predominated'; except for 'extreme cases,' educated Muslims and Mozarabs were bilingual, while 'Romance doubtless dominated' the masses. During the tenth and eleventh centuries, despite the flowering of Arabic culture and concomitant languishing of the native spirit, he sees the balance of evidence as favoring the thesis that the previous linguistic situation persisted. From 1099, with Berber influence increasing and Mozarabs leaving *en masse,* Romance still retained 'considerable social and even literary value,' and bilingualism 'continued very strong in all Islamic Spain.' Fragmentary for each stage, his evidence grows progressively weaker until the third stage rests on episodes such as Pope Celestine seeking a missionary knowledgeable in Latin and Arabic to visit the Mozarabs, Jacques de Vitry reporting that Mozarabs used Latin as a learned language, and the dubious biography of the Valencian Mozarab St Pere (Pedro) Pasqual. Persistence of Romance nomenclature in botany, and the odd phrase or final verse of Romance mixed into a poetical form (perhaps the performer's melodic key, of no linguistic relevance) add little reassurance.[4]

The reader begins to suspect that the Berber dynasties found a fading bilingualism, already minimal or spotty, and further discouraged it – partly by hostility, partly by diminishing and isolating the Mozarabic enclaves, partly by presiding over a far larger influx of Arabic speakers than has been admitted, and mostly by paralleling a continued linguistic acculturation whose origins and momentum anteceded them. In that scenario the Glick–Bulliet thesis of mass conversion not long before the year 1000 would supply a supportive reason; the resultant 'fall' of the caliphate, amounting rather to a sudden Islamization or dispersal of Arabism to the masses in the provinces, would have hurried Arabic acculturation drastically. Romance had endured long enough to influence a mixed Arabic for Spain's masses, however, the kind of Arabic garble which evoked contempt from the otherwise Hispanophile Ibn Khaldūn: owing to contamination from Romance languages 'the entire urban population' of fourteenth-century Granada 'had come to speak another language, one peculiar to them,' an Arabic which seemed 'no longer Arabic.'

For Valencia, and indeed the wider *sharq al-Andalus* including such territories as Murcia and Tortosa, Epalza proposes a very different evolution. Chapter 1 noted his thesis of rapid mass conversion there, due to lack of bishop-centered communities capable of entering *dhimma* or protected status. Carrying his story forward chronologically, and arguing from the wider Maghribian scene as well as from local indications, Epalza sees the Valencian and neighboring regions transformed in the tenth and eleventh centuries into 'one of the most Arabized zones of the peninsula.' The occasion for this shift was the Fatimid threat from North Africa, not only military but as a religio-social expansion of Shiite Islam, a threat particularly against the vulnerable Mediterranean regions of eastern al-Andalus. The Cordovan Sunnite reaction took more direct administrative control of those regions, introduced a system of very heavy fortification, and especially undertook a program or 'grand campaign' of politico-religious indoctrination of the masses through the ubiquitous Sunnite (Malikite) *faqīh*. The end result was 'a general Arabization and Islamization of the masses.' This convulsive cultural revolution was reflected in the flowering of Arabic letters and learning in the region's cities and towns, which notably graced the post-caliphal petty principalities here. This explains as well the elevated power of the local *faqīh* and the triumph of Malikism. It corrects the image of an artificial court culture in the eleventh-century principalities in this region as though it were a superstructure unrelated to an unchanged rural or city society. The action had particularly aimed at our Mediterranean regions, and also affected the Berber groups there. In a great surge, this relatively backward area became thoroughly Arabized at the grassroots level and expressed that universal movement in its court cultures. In the thirteenth century, Jaume's crusaders would confront a populace immemorially rooted everywhere in the Arabic language and culture.[5]

The narrower battlefield of Valencian linguistics has its special alarums and excursions. Francesc Carreras i Candi, half a century ago, in his monograph on Valencian (englobed within a multi-volume standard reference work), summed the older positions and bibliography from the chronicler Beuter up to Simonet, concluding that 'the Arabic tongue was little known by our Muslims, even among the highest social classes.' He conceded a negligibly few bilingual Muslims plus a general familiarity with the Arabic language, and insisted (despite 'ancient prejudices') that 'the Iberian Romance language' held the field alone in the Valencian region up to its conquest by King Jaume. Nicolau Primitiu applied this position to the post-crusade Mudejars so exuberantly as to misread an important document and make a convert *faqīh* abandon his Arabic to learn Valencian so as to preach to the Muslim masses. The current champion of the traditionalist view, Antonio Ubieto, insists that the Islamizing of eastern Spain was merely 'a religious conversion but not a change of culture (*raza*) or of language'; Valencia's Muslims spoke Romance as their basic tongue, the educated adding Arabic. Consequently 'the Valencian region suffered no change in its human structures,' either from the eighth-century Arabic conquest or the thirteenth-century Christian Reconquest. Current events have politicized this desire to legitimatize Valencian as an ancient and perduring language which dominated Islamic Valencia. Fortifying a growing mood of regional autonomy, Vicente Simó Santonja has published a large volume of eloquent argumentation on the antiquity, superiority, and perennial dominance of Valencian; its impact locally has been strengthened by a reissue of Ubieto's 1975 book with added chapters of linguistic arguments. An academic curiosity has transmogrified into a political polemic.[6]

This legitimation of modern Valencian as a direct descendant of a Visigothic and Mozarabic language shared by Muslims and Christians is firmly dismissed by Manuel Sanchis Guarner, whose work in historical linguistics of the Valencian kingdom is now the standard. While the Arabic invasion did freeze the several Visigothic dialects we lump together as Mozarabic, Valencia's dialect was 'very different from the present Valencian language,' which is 'nothing else than the Catalan imported by the Reconquest' and modified by regional morphological–phonetic elements and some Arabic and Mozarabic vocabulary. Sanchis Guarner does leave room for a residually bilingual Islamic and Mozarabic upper class. But the influence of Fuster, the feebleness of Mozarabic as a literate language (so that educated Mozarabs 'preferred Arabic,' while the masses could hardly resist the steady pressure of Arabic as a superior vehicle), and the significance he attaches to the bilingual Mozarabs as intermediaries between Islamic and Christian regions up to the very invasion by King Jaume – all lead him to incline to the general triumph by Arabic.[7]

Was a community of Romance-speaking Mozarabs on hand to welcome King Jaume and his invaders? The thesis is popular but untenable. A negligible scattering of Mozarabs, especially among the lower classes, may have survived the persecutions and mass emigrations under the Almohads, to influence the alteration of the crusaders' Catalan into a Valencian form. The abundant crusade sources are thunderously silent on any such survivors, nor did they ever serve as intermediaries during or after the crusade. Their church of Sant Vicent just outside Valencia city's walls apparently stood abandoned by the time of the crusade and was probably serving as a mosque; during the post-crusade lawsuit over metropolitan possession of the diocese, witnesses testified that it lacked a baptismal font and that both church and cemetery had to be 'conse-crated' by the first bishop to reach it. Since the consecration formed part of a careful dossier of liturgical acts designed as proof that Toledo exercised earliest actual possession, it was not likely to have been an unnecessary proceeding. The one text commonly cited, to demonstrate that a Mozarabic community actually survived there, is a pre-crusade grant of 'the place and church' of Sant Vicent to the Aragonese monastery of San Victorián; but this phrase is merely the dual construction or repetition common in Latin (*sive* serves as copula twice here, *et* once), and in any case no people at all are in view. Any Mozarabic presence or influence in crusader Valencia was subterranean and officially invisible, by scattered individuals now unknown.[8]

The Valencian historian Roque Chabás, concluding that the rare Romance documents prepared by the crusaders for Muslims here were in Castilian, suggested that the generality of Valencian Moors had for long been out of contact with their Catalan-speaking neigh-bors but in touch with Castile. The Arabist Ribera Tarragó arrived at the same conclusion concerning Valencian Muslims, via his ex-amination of surviving words. José Lacarra, speaking for the Ebro Valley residents he has researched so thoroughly, who constituted the immediate pre-frontier of Islamic Valencia, believes the Mus-lims there spoke 'a Romance idiom.' The archivist Enrique Bayerri, in his monumental volumes on the same region, argued that 'the normal thing was to ignore the Arabic language of the rulers,' except for a handful of useful phrases, even the local intellectuals falling back on Romance in their private lives.

Against the range of Romance-dominant schools, Fuster proposes that Valencian Muslims were Arabic-speaking at the time of the crusade, and were bilingual only by exception. Where the scholars of Romance persuasion argue forward from a much earlier linguistic state, Fuster is driven to his contrary conviction by the obviously unilingual Arabic speech of the Moriscos and assumes that this must represent a pre-crusade cultural condition rather than a brilliant cre-ation by subjugated Mudejars. Guichard, in his application of struc-turalism to the society of Islamic Spain and especially to Valencia, touches lightly on language as a basic structural factor. Of Valencia's Mudejars he concludes: 'contrary to what is sometimes thought, they spoke [only] a vulgar Arabic dialect,' so that individual con-tacts with Christians 'appear to have been relatively limited.' Epalza, as we have seen, has Valencia 'one of the most Arabized zones of the peninsula' by a convulsive tenth-century mass movement, with no hope of surviving Romance bilingualism. Each position, aprioristic, aposterioristic and macrohistorical, achieves only plausibility unless solid contemporary evidence can be unearthed.[9]

DRAGOMANS, ARABIC CHARTERS, AND COMMON SPEECH

Some evidence from the crusade generation is ambiguous; in arranging surrender formalities in Arabic, for example, the Conqueror just might have intended a courteous regard for the official language. Taken as a whole, however, the evidence indicates that the two peoples could not normally understand each other, and that the barrier was Arabic. In such surrender, King Jaume refers to interpreters. Negotiations with Murcia involved his sending first a ransom-official knowledgeable in the enemy's language (the Christian *exea*) together with a Mudejar. This encounter led to a second, conducted for the king by Domènec Llop (Domingo López), a settler of Murviedro who 'knew Arabic,' and by Astruc Bonsenyor, 'a Jew who was my secretary of Arabic'; the word each time is *algaravia*. At his subsequent secret meeting with the Murcian envoys, Jaume kept at his side only Astruc 'who was a *trujaman*' – that is, crown dragoman or interpreter. Such dragomans formed part of the entourage. Ibn Faraḥ (Abenferri), the envoy from Játiva, had to conduct his business 'before my [the king's] dragoman.' At Minorca Jaume sent three agents 'and one Jew whom I had given them for a dragoman.' He had his message to Elche carried 'by one of my dragomans, with the *exea*.' Jaume's agent negotiating with the ruler of Majorca spoke through an accompanying dragoman. Even so unceremonial an occasion as settling a quarrel over irrigation rights between the Christians of Bairén and Benieto in 1244, involving testimony from a local Muslim, required the use of 'a dragoman.'[10]

All the Valencian surrender treaties still extant originated as Arabic or Arabic-cum-Latin documents. Sometimes the authorities prepared matching copies in each language (as they did also with Majorca's book of post-crusade land division); at other times they preferred an interlinear system. King Jaume's son Pere has left a description of the charter given by Jaume in 1242 to the Muslims of Eslida and its neighboring towns, the whole being preserved in a copy of 1342. 'The document was written in Latin words, interlineated with Arabic or Saracen letters.' Only the Latin, the copyist noted, was being transcribed for preservation, a circumstance explaining why copied charters usually survive in Latin. The same result came from dividing a bilingual chirograph or double document torn across a line. Uxó's 1250 pact was in Arabic, and the crown's lost copy doubtless in Latin. King Pere's 1283 military directive in Arabic to his Valencian Mudejars was subsequently put into Catalan copy. The restoration of treaty privileges to Alfandech, after a revolt, survives in Latin; but a notation by Jaume II in 1298 attests that he had seen the original Arabic letters, complete with Pere's seal, and had caused this faithful Latin translation to be drawn from that Arabic. The surrender by al-Azraq near the end of Jaume's crusade was done in Arabic; owing to unusual circumstances, its counterpart was in Castilian. A 1236 contract of vassalage by the ex-*wālī* of Valencia, Abū Zayd, comes down to us in Latin but still has the Muslim's approval appended in Arabic along with his titles and the date by the Islamic era. The transfer of fealty by the Muslim ruler of Murcia from King Jaume to Castile, five months after Jaume's conquest, is annotated: 'written in Latin and Arabic (*en arábigo*).'

Jaume had the charter for Chivert drawn in both languages; our transcript of 1235 witnesses that the original filled 'thirty-seven lines of Saracen letters, of which I the undersigned notary wrote none in the present copy.' The thirty-seven lines of lost Arabic at Chivert disconcert at first; the Latin requires over 170 lines of print in a modern book just for the body of text. The Latin of the original however, as the notary betrays in discussing damage to its last lines, ran to no more than forty lines at most; if the Arabic was more compact than the Latin, the correspondence of forty lines to thirty-seven indicates an interlineated original. The disparity between forty manuscript Latin lines and 170 printed derives partly from the wholesale abbreviations then prevalent and partly from the oblong shape of the parchment which easily reduced the total of original lines. Any number of humbler, private documents may have had an Arabic counterpart or original now lost. Mudejars sometimes transferred land titles to Christians by means of an Arabic deed, as at Alcira in 1245. King Jaume referred to such a 'Saracenic instrument' in 1261 when confirming the conveyance of a Carbonera property by the Játiva *qā'id* to the settler Domènec Marquès. So rarely does an early Valencian document actually survive in its original Arabic, however, that King Pere's brief agreement of 1277 with the rebel *qā'id* of Finestrat now appears extraordinary.[11]

The intermediary role of bilingual Jews in Valencia assumes the existence of a language barrier. The 'secretariat of Arabic' was an institution long established in the realms of Aragon, used mostly for foreign contacts but also where necessary for domestic needs. Its incumbents were Jews, valued for their language skills. In 1220 Pope Honorius III had rebuked King Jaume for 'rarely or never' sending diplomats to the caliph at Marrakesh except Jews, who might betray Christendom's plans and secrets. Prince Anfòs had his own Arabic 'office,' to which in 1284 he appointed the Jew Bondavid Bonsenyor with instructions 'to cause documents to be drawn or read in Arabic.' Men like Samuel the *alfaquim* drew local instruments in Arabic for Valencia, in their capacity as 'writers of Arabic' for the crown – a safeguard for the Muslims of Carbonera, for example, or 'a certain Saracen parchment of Guadalest.' The Christians' use of Jews as the ordinary intermediaries with Islam oddly enough found no echo among the enemy; Valencian Muslims of the crusade era did not employ Jews as interpreters in surrender negotiations, either because the inimical Berber domination had discredited their use, or because they found it more acceptable to communicate in Arabic while relying on the known institution of royal dragomans. The single use of a Jew occurred at the surrender of Petrel castle – and he had immigrated there only recently when Castilian tributary overlordship had been accepted; Jaume expressed surprise that 'the Saracens had done him no harm.'[12]

Several times in his memoirs King Jaume directly names the language of the Valencian Islamic kingdom and of the offshore island principates. He has the Murcian ruler of Majorca address the *aljama* 'in his Arabic (*en sa algaravia*).' When Peñíscola unexpectedly sent its offer of surrender in writing, Jaume had to find a Muslim at Teruel 'who knew how to read Arabic (*algaravia*)' in order to decipher it; the Romance of this bilingual go-between was Aragonese. The first surrender feelers from Almazora came through Miquel Pere (Miguel Pérez), an esquire of the Aragonese Pero Cornel, who used to bargain for the release of prisoners there because 'he knew Arabic.' A message from the *qā'id* of Bairén, conversely, came by a 'Saracen who knew our Latin [Romance]'; and at Villena the king treated with 'two Saracens, one of whom knew Latin [Romance].'

Long after the crusade, in 1282, a bill of sale for a Valencian slave thought it worth identifying her specifically as 'a white, Latin-speaking Moor, by name Fāṭima.'

Of these insistent cases, one has occasioned confusion. King Jaume had been at Teruel when he received the Arabic offer of surrender from Peñíscola and had it translated by a local bilingual Muslim; he then rushed in reckless haste to the Valencian coast to parley under the walls of Peñíscola, taking with him only seven companions. 'Because we came so hastily,' he told the Muslims, 'our secretaries were not here.' The only sentence he quotes directly from the Peñíscolans is in non-Catalan Romance, a device Jaume sometimes employs to signal the language of the speaker. Authorities as formidable as Martí de Riquer and Joan Coromines have suggested that this speech was Valencian Mozarabic, indicating a Valencian Muslim community bilingual in Arabic and Romance. A more obvious conclusion is that Jaume, having been unable to translate the original message except through a talented Aragonese Muslim luckily at hand, had snatched him along on the day's wild ride, so that he could concede verbally in detail 'those things they demanded,' without waiting for his Arabic secretaries. The sentence is by that Aragonese Muslim translator, and reflects rather Aragonese with hints of Mozarabic locution. Sanchis Guarner has elucidated these Mozarabic traces; their presence is not surprising, given Teruel's border situation as a haven for Valencian refugees in Almohad times. The episode is cast as a lightly prosified song incorporated into the narrative, and doubtless had enjoyed a wide audience via wandering jongleurs.[13]

The word commonly used in King Jaume's memoirs to indicate the speech of the enemy was *algaravia*. To the king this was a synonym for Arabic and for 'the Säracen's language.' He also used *aràbich*, as when he sent broadcast to the *aljamas* of his Valencian kingdom 'letters and messages in Arabic.' His son Pere similarly issued tax instructions 'written in Arabic (*in arabico*) to all the Saracens of the lord king in the realm of Valencia.' These words signified the natural speech, and to all appearances the only speech, of his Muslim subjects. In the surrender documents, a species of permanent constitution for rural as well as urban areas, this *aràbich* was demonstrably Arabic. The more ambiguous term 'Saracenesque' (*sarrahinesch*), counterpart to 'Christianesque' (*cristianesch*), must mean Arabic. When King Pere during a North African adventure sent ashore a sailor 'who knew Saracen very well,' the language was probably Arabic; the Muslims reciprocated by finding 'a Moor who knew how to talk Romance (*pla*).' A clearer context was the reception of Mudejar tax accounts at Orihuela in 1317 in *murisch* and their translation into *christianesch*.[14]

On the spontaneous and popular level also there is evidence that the Muslims of eastern Spain spoke Arabic. The ruler of Islamic Majorca heartened the defenders in the hurlyburly of a Christian assault by shouting encouragement in Arabic; King Jaume, catching the hortatory imperative, exhibited his knowledge of Arabic fragments by recording how the Muslim 'cried to his men "roddo!", that is to say "stand."'' On another occasion a surrounded Muslim, invited to surrender rather than be killed, proudly chose death with the cry 'Le, mulex'; King Jaume interpreted the phrase: "which is to say, 'No, lord'." A less pertinent but nonetheless useful episode comes from Valencia's Granadan periphery after the turn of the century. When the Arago-Catalan forces attacked Almería in 1310, Prince Ferran of Majorca was attacked by the son of the ruler of Guadix, who kept shouting to him: 'Ani be ha soltan' (probably the colloquial *anī ben as-sulṭān*, for *ana bnu 's-sulṭāni*). Ferran had to learn from the interpreters (*los torsimanys*), with him on the battlefield, that this meant he was a king's son. Such incidents, involving spontaneous speech, suggest that one should apply literally the observation in the *Chronica latina*, written by a contemporary Castilian prelate, that Spanish Muslims were 'a people of a different religion and language.'[15]

The attitude of missionaries in this region may convey something about the language. Ramon Lull deserves a passing nod: though his immediate milieu was the analogous Majorca kingdom, his wider horizons embraced nearby Valencia. He learned 'lo lenguatge aràbic,' in which he wrote some of his books, from a bilingual slave purchased on Majorca; rather defensively he explains to God in one passage that praising Him in Arabic is a good thing, and that he fears no man for doing so. More to the present point were the famous Arabic language schools set up at both Valencia city and Játiva. The Dominicans concentrated precious manpower there after the crusade, confident of an eventual harvest of Muslims. Though the language schools envisaged an apostolate among the intellectuals or influential figures, and served an area broader than this conquered kingdom, their very location at so early a date, the successes they reported, and the institutionalizing of the missionary efforts as schools of Arabic, point at least to a numerous Mudejar group who handled Arabic familiarly, and imply that Arabic was the only tongue by which they were accessible.

A particularly valuable witness, this time to the Arabic unilingualism of the common man, comes from the last decade of the thirteenth century or the first decade of the fourteenth. By that time the Muslim educated and notable classes had suffered depletion both by loss of real power and by emigration, while adaptation to the conquerors' patterns would have been most intense and as yet unrestricted by legislation or other pressure. Yet the Dominican bishop of Valencia, a saintly scholar–statesman distinguished for his peacemaking services on the larger Mediterranean scene, found the weight of Arabic in Valencia a discouraging incubus. Speaking of the heartland of the new kingdom, where Christian settlers clustered in greatest intensity, he complained in a sermon delivered before his metropolitan that half or over half of the mixed Muslim and Christian population in his diocese spoke only Arabic. This speech was reported to Pope Benedict XII by the metropolitan of Tarragona, Arnau Sescomes, as an eyewitness. Though dated 1337, Arnau is quoting 'the late' bishop of Valencia. This was not the reigning Ramon de Gastó (1312–48) but Ramon Despont (1289–1312), former governor of the Ancona march at Rome, chancellor and intimate of the kings of Aragon, protector of the poor, who brought the twenty-year war of the Sicilian Vespers against France to a close and helped resolve a number of lesser difficulties. His experience and stature, as well as the official nature of this communication, lend weight to his witness. Bishop Ramon may have exaggerated for effect, and his proportions leave room for the increase of bilingual Moors expected by that period; but he makes clear that even then the majority of the Mudejar community was unilingual and confined to Arabic. Boswell's researches into the later fourteenth century found that in Valencia 'the vast majority of the Muslims did not speak the language of the dominant culture,' though 'they were the backbone of society there, manufacturing its goods, constructing its buildings, even fighting its wars.' He notes that the authorities needed Muslims, Jews, and Christians as translators to convey royal instructions, collect taxes, and in general serve as language go-betweens, a situation the exact opposite of that of the Arabic-ignorant Mudejars in the other realms of Aragon.[16]

THE MORISCO EVIDENCE: *TERMINUS AD QUEM*

Without this accumulating evidence, the later Morisco unilingual Arabism would come as a shock, a language revolution unnoticed and unrecorded until long triumphant. By culling the evidence lying neglected in Boronat's old collection of documents, Fuster has called attention to this phenomenon of triumphant Arabic in the sixteenth century. He realizes how improbable it is that the late Mudejars or early Moriscos forged a universal and exclusive language for their community in the intervening two centuries, with acculturative pressures steadily increasing and the rural classes early coming to predominate. Cardaillac, studying the genre of religious polemic developed in Arabic by the Moriscos, was equally impressed by the role of language as the wall of religion and culture in the Valencian region. Ana Labarta is even tracing the culture of books and letters Valencian Moriscos supported. Fuster shows not only that the Moriscos here spoke Arabic exclusively, allowing for a stratum of exceptions, but that both their own leaders and the Christians' saw this as a defense for their communal identity and for their religious preferences. Transforming the forced pseudo-conversion of the Moriscos into genuine conversion would have required learning their language, as zealous ecclesiastics urged; but this, the civil authorities countered, would only consolidate the foe. Destruction of the language itself, as the inner fortress of the Morisco 'nation,' had higher priority than conversion. Eventually the crown launched what Fuster describes as 'a war' and 'a systematic offensive' to extirpate Arabic. One effect of this linguaphobia was the incidental documentation about the tenacious strength of Arabic in Valencia.

At a post-rebellion treaty in 1528 the Valencian Moriscos reminded Charles V that 'in the said kingdom the greater part of the Moorish men and almost all the women' were ignorant of Romance (*aljamia*), and that to learn it would require 'a very long span of time,' at least forty years. The emperor fatuously gave them ten years to learn Castilian or Valencian. The parish rectors in 1550 found communication impossible because Valencian Moors 'do not know' Romance; some thought their isolation from Christian contact to blame, but Morisco attitudes indicate that the isolation was sought to protect the language and way of life. The bishop of Orihuela found Moorish women especially 'stubborn and resistant to our language'; he considered 'their language an impediment to their conversion,' a device of the local *alfaquís* who thereby sustained the whole fabric of Moorishness. Moriscos in Aragon proper, who had lost their grasp of literary Arabic, sent their children to Valencian parts to study it. One Morisco commoner, on the other hand, though he could 'read and write [vulgar] Arabic,' confessed that he understood 'little or nothing of the book of the Koran.' A Moor of Chiva, who 'had never spoken or written except in Arabic,' seems to represent the norm, with bilingual Moors the exception.

At that time the Valencian *aljamas* still kept in Arabic such intra-*aljama* records as contracts, marriages, and sales. A number of Valencian Christians fell into the Arabic speech of their neighbors, so that later the government was able to use them as spies. Converts wrote religious books in Arabic for their reluctant fellow Moors; Muslim pedagogues countered with classes in Arabic. Fuster points to 'a veritable public documentation [in Arabic] which guided the daily life of the *aljamas*.' He describes 'the fight against Arabic' waged grimly by sixteenth-century Christians, and sees all this as a key to understanding the Morisco problem and the tension between the two peoples.[17]

The accumulating evidence impresses. Even if it did not lead inexorably to an exclusively Arabic-speaking populace, it would demand readjustment of currently held theories, a revision which nuances also the traditional understanding of Spanish Muslim society. The Arabic-speaking stratum in Valencia was, at the least, far more numerous than previous commentators allowed for; it must have included not only the professional and administrative classes, and the average horseman in battle, but the generality of people who were not at the lowest level of proletariat and rustic. The tradesmen, the elders of a smaller town, the multitudinous owners of farms – all those most visible as the people of a place, all those not faceless, in short the generality of folk with even moderate influence – were Arabic-speaking.

This might theoretically leave room for conjecture that some stratum still clung to a garbled Romance – poorest *exarici*, the lowliest laborers or workers in the city, perhaps sheepmen, minstrels, fishermen, and muleteers. Their language could only have survived in life's backwaters. Sealed away in their lowly anonymity, incapable of real communication in Arabic beyond the necessities of the market-place, they would have been useless as translators and unacceptable to both sides in responsible public actions. If the speakers of Arabic had some grasp of Romance, to cope with such classes, it must have been as rudimentary and ineffective as the Romance-speakers' Arabic, at the level of the tourist or resident colonial. Most probably these rural masses had already lost their Romance too and spoke Arabic. If Epalza's arguments are accepted, this probability becomes a certainty.

In a cosmopolitan region like the eastern coast, special 'Latinate' or bilingual Moors surely were at least as common as Arabic-speaking Christians. From their ranks came the interpreters, the friars' language instructors, and the Moorish members of a Christian lord's household. As Ibn Kammūna observed, in a treatise written at Baghdad at this time (1280): 'when a linguistic minority is in contact with a linguistic majority, the minority learns the language of the majority, while the majority does not learn the language of the minority or, at best, learns it much later.'[18] In the Valencian context, the dominant Christians constituted the effective 'majority'; the more numerous but intimidated Muslim 'minority' produced its share of adaptive linguists, but such individuals can shed no light on the language of the populace at large. The full picture of thirteenth-century Valencian society, as reconstructed in the light of fresh evidence, shows an Arabic-speaking, not a bilingual population. Arabic was the common coin of the Valencian world encountered by crusaders, merchants, churchmen, administrators, and settlers.

CONCLUSIONS

The full revision of the accepted traditionalist position can be presented in several conclusions. (1) The Arabic-speaking classes constituted at least a very broad sector of the population and not a small elite, in pre-crusade Valencia. (2) The Romance-speaking masses, if any, were nearly invisible in public affairs; they must have had at least a bilingual grasp of vulgar Arabic. But the evidence suggests that the masses were already confined to Arabic, just like the generality of the upper and middle classes. (3) After the crusade, when the literate and administrative classes emigrated in dispropor-tionate numbers, while the farmers stayed as prized resources for the Christian landlords, it was precisely the masses who clung to Arabic, with an intransigence obviously owing less to their increasing isola-tion than to a proud, deliberate sense of cultural identity. (4) After the crusade the incidence of Romance may have risen somewhat;

occasions for its use multiplied as Christian settlers moved in. By the late 1250s a full generation of Mudejars had grown up under Christian rule, some of them doubtless absorbing the conquerors' language. As Ibn Khaldūn saw clearly, the conquered tend to imitate their conquerors.[19] The young, the facile, the adaptable, the opportunist, and to some extent all those thrown into closer contact with the Christian neighbors who constituted the new establishment, would either acquire or sharpen Romance. This in turn set the stage for that minimum transcending of religio-cultural differences which triggered restrictive legislation and polemic. Could it also have amplified a minuscule residual 'Mozarabic' element, the old Valencian some would see as legitimation and bridge for a modern Valencian language independent and non-provincial? (5) After the post-crusade revolts, the picture may have changed. The destruction of political hopes by the conquest of Montesa, the increasing absorption of Valencia into a European mood as immigration and Catalan institutions worked their influence, the increasing loss of leader classes by emigration, the growing isolation and eventually the active search for cultural islands by the more zealous Mudejars now in retreat from the pressure of Christian presence – all would have combined to discourage neo-Romance except among that minority who kept a foot in both worlds or who drifted into the European orbit for opportunistic reasons.

It is difficult to say when the Arabist orientation had begun to predominate in pre-crusade Valencia. The region had long been a unique corner of Spanish Islam, something of a frontier far from the feeble heart of the Cordova caliphate. It had assumed its cultural and linguistic forms by slow evolution, with a turning point probably under 'Abd al-Raḥmān III in the tenth century. A seaboard community, linked horizontally with the Near East and vertically with North Africa, its non-peasant elements lay unusually open to external Islamic influences and population drift. Whatever Romance dominance or binguality one might conjecture for the earliest Muslim generations must have eroded badly in the tenth and eleventh centuries, if not before. The flight of the Mozarabic remnant in the twelfth century would merely have confirmed in a small way the already settled Arabic pattern, now presided over by the Berber dynasties. Epalza's thesis of the lack of a native Mozarabism from the start, the mass absorption of Valencia's population by Islam as a consequence, and the convulsive Arabization even of the masses in the tenth century, supports and intensifies these conclusions, moving both Islamization and Arabization on a radical scale to a very early generation. In any case, and for our purposes, Valencia on the eve of the crusade was not bilingual. Arabic also continued as overwhelmingly dominant through the fourteenth century, Boswell concludes. If the arrival of Christian settlers had posed any threat to Arabic, other factors would soon have countered this: increasing isolation in the countryside, increasingly restrictive legislation, and reflexive zeal by the Muslim community leaders. The protective ramparts of Arabic, a barrier to ready communication with the Christian settlers from the fall of Valencia city on, eventually became the Morisco barricades.

Even if one were to concede the traditionalists' near-universal Romance dominance, or a maximum binguality, their understanding of the life-situation would still be wrong. A special form of language barrier would still have stood between Muslim and Christian; the thin stratum of classical Arabic-speakers among the upper class would still have posed a disproportionate obstacle. In anthropological terms, the Arabic of the dynamic establishment figures, in both city and countryside, constituted a main boundary-maintaining mechanism for Valencia's Islamic culture. This was more true for Arabic in Islam than for the role of Latin in Europe, because of the interpenetrating nature of the Islamic establishment. It was more true also because Arabic was a language essentially sacred in a sense that Hebrew, Latin, or Greek were not. In such a situation of Arabic–Romance bilingualism, basic communication between Valencian Muslims and Christians might indeed have been easy; but the linguistic–cultural frame would have emphasized the separateness of each world, so that the very communication paradoxically would only have intensified the sense of alienation.

Language was a problem in post-crusade Valencia, and entered the texture of the conquered kingdom's larger social problems. When all the evidence is brought to bear it seems reasonable to conclude that the role of Arabic here went far beyond the framing function of a formal or mandarin tongue, profound as the implications of such a bilingual situation would have been. It was a problem in the very mechanics of daily living. Each people spoke a different language in Valencia, without a significantly diffused binguality. Language had to have been the primary perceived difference and alienating factor between Muslim and Christian in conquered Valencia.

8

Bounding the Moorish frontier: territoriality and prosopography

Jaume's strange new kingdom, with its symbiotic triple society, has been explored in the previous chapters from a variety of interrelated aspects, each one novel, neglected, and fundamental. This chapter touches on a number of the same themes but from a vantage itself novel: a genre in documentary typology, the real-estate trial to determine local boundaries. The actual physical bounds of one's village, city, valley, or farm during the unsettled transitional period became a principal concern drawing together Muslim and Christian before the king's court. A surrender constitution guaranteed little, unless boundaries fairly and securely contained its privileges. Any hope of conversion was fatuous unless the colonial power could maintain justice in so simple a public affair, handling the basic administrative problem of who owned what and where. At bottom the problem was legal and best settled at law, itself a profession and ideology coloring all of Valencian reconstruction. Muslim, Christian, and Jew, pirate and preacher, eventually encountered the king's law; all three peoples become embroiled in it for land quarrels petty or grand.

INFRASTRUCTURE, *COMARCA*, AND *TERME*

When the last bastion of Islamic Valencia fell in 1245, King Jaume had doubled his coastline holdings, swallowing an extensive commercial principality of some fifty walled towns sprinkled over some twenty-five traditional regions or districts. So impressive was his prize that Jaume established it as a separate kingdom with its own money, parliament, and law code. In this he went far beyond the mere multiplication of sovereign titles for new conquests, a phenomenon common to Islamic and Christian rulers in Spain. A cornucopia of wealth and power, destined to reorient the evolution of

Arago-Catalonia, the new kingdom also posed massive problems. The dense population of Muslims remained firmly in place; the sound and look of the land stayed unchanged, as muezzins called from minarets and Muslim merchants jostled their loaded donkeys through the maze-like alleyways. Christian settlers, relatively few despite the king's best efforts, huddled by preference in the bustling port cities or in nuclei at strategic villages in the Muslim countryside.

Colonial assimilation involved a complex of component problems, including defense, administration, urban reorganization, and the Europeanizing networks of parishes, civil courts, and commercial institutions. In this reconstruction a normative principle was maximum profit with minimum dislocation. To achieve it, some traditional policy often guided the handling of a sub-problem, for example the policy of semi-autonomy for conquered Muslim communities. One such tradition was acceptance of, or adaptation to, prevailing geographic–administrative units. This applied less to the great regions making up the kingdom than to the component districts or countrysides claimed by every city and town; under crusader rule, this would extend to the least village. Each small entity, with its own district, fitted into the larger district of some other entity, like those hollow dolls which contain smaller hollow dolls in descending inner sizes to the smallest. The Valencian conquest, as it appeared initially to the settlement programers who drew up codices of land distribution, held some two dozen basic districts of Christian settlement, each with its inner and smaller entities. In a given case, the underlying defining principle might be geographic, as with an irrigated plain or a valley; economic, as with a crop or a river dependency; military, as with a strategic node; or wholly human, as with a pattern set by tribal or linguistic inheritance. Most of these larger divisions owed their existence to a combination and interplay of such factors, dominant and recessive, which admitted of flexibility and redefinition as the contributing element weakened or began to function differently. The whole system framed the human geography, or rather constituted an interacting ecology of geo-social systems, more varied in its forms than anywhere in Spain, through which the crusader kingdom of Valencia existed.[1]

The Latin and Catalan word *comarca*, used today to describe any of the two dozen larger districts which have evolved and modified out of these districts of thirteenth-century Valencia, did not take on that meaning until early modern times. Only its ancient meanings of boundary and frontier zone prevailed in crusader Valencia. The more common word *terminus*, Catalan *terme*, referred to the boundaries or limits belonging to a city, castle, town, or activity (as with a grazing, or tax-collecting, or parish circumscription). By the same token, *terme* meant the area or district so enclosed; in an administrative sense it can at times be translated also as jurisdiction, which it implied. Jurisdictional or administrative bounding did not necessarily jibe with the underlying socio-economic zone later conceptualized as a *comarca*. A 'natural' *comarca* often contained a package or juxtaposition of local *térmens*; where the precise boundaries of a *comarca* might elude the historian (and probably the contemporary inhabitant, if he had used the concept), the boundaries of a *terme* were ascertainable if necessary by a court of law. Larger districts or *térmens* did in fact tend to approximate the 'natural' *comarcas* we still discern today.

The entities of thirteenth-century Valencia at issue here are not the *comarcas* as such, whatever formal existence they may have had then apart from the district or district-complexes. To what extent *comarca* and *terme*-complex coincided is a problem which must wait upon a study of the crusaders' bounding policy, and must then proceed by comparison patiently at each local level. Nor are we concerned with the larger administrative structures designed to pull the entire new kingdom into some semblance of unity, while multiplying royal presence and sharing out the tasks of central government. Nor is this the occasion to apply the geographers' deeper Central Place methodology of a radial city with dependencies (giving a dynamic boundary always in process, especially where radial cities nearby exercise their evolving attraction), and its geo-ecological frame (a set of relationships, including man and his produce, in a landscape). We shall concentrate instead on the *térmens* or districts characterizing every population center.

Historical forces were eventually to modify the whole system of Valencian boundaries. Demographic evolution, split-offs, new services, decline of castle power, expulsion of the Moriscos, and arbitrary intervention by rationalizing government authorities are among the factors which gradually glossed the past, elevated new 'feudal' regions into super-districts, and reduced some units to more plainly geographic or economic meanings, until the inner boundary map shifted significantly. Despite all this, the basic two dozen *comar-*

cas and many of their component districts remain, as a recent survey puts it, 'clear at their centers, if confused at their peripheries.' Today Valencian planners and historians are working to conceptualize a systematic and balanced comarcal map, revising each immemorial unit around a dominantly natural or geographic unit, with history and economics as subordinate integrators, refined by linguistic, ethnographic or other factors, combining districts as needed. In June 1971 the civil authorities specified ten districts for the south-ernmost or Alicante province, nine for Castellón de la Plana province, and nine for Valencia province; each of these twenty-eight holds a roll call of inner village or town districts, numbering from a few to forty or more. More recently a counter-polemic seeks to liberate Valencia from its historical geography–typology, proposing instead an anti-comarcal structure and integrating the region by designated social and partly historical 'zones.'[2]

Beneath all schemes, lies the boundary infrastructure carried over into the crusader society. Considering what we know of territoriality as a force in human affairs, it is astonishing that historians have paid so little attention to the origins and interrelationships of these basic blocs in crusader Valencia. At best, an occasional antiquarian has assembled pertinent data as background to a local history. Interest has centered instead upon the later results of such divisions: the marvelous patchwork of contrasting character and behavior from district to district or from valley to valley throughout the kingdom of Valencia, so richly evidenced in popular sayings, costume, defects, habits of mind, language, and celebrations.

As with modern nations, inter-district or even intra-district disputes about borders during the post-crusade generation could arise from a multiplicity of sources. Claims to privilege or dominance within a district or over a district-complex were asserted or challenged; irredentist bits of territory were discerned; sectional vendettas led to district invasions; conflicts erupted over passage or pasture or irrigation. Even in Islamic days a certain imprecision must have troubled the system. Village chauvinism could disincline a hamlet to count itself administratively subordinate to an overweening neighbor, for example; thus several Mudejar villages in the Sierra de Eslida kept bothering the Christians to disengage them from the Eslida Muslims and attach them to another unit.[3]

Arrival of Christian settlers could disrupt or alter the rhythms within any district or its relation with neighbors. New crops acceptable to the conquerors' palate, a traversing street through the tangle of an Islamic town, suppression or conferral of a district market, conjunctions of districts under a favored vassal, a program of expanding the network of roads or of irrigation channels, fragmentation of an estate–farm as component mill and oven and lands dispersed to separate owners, tax privileges, overlordship by a military Order, or the inrush of a body of Christian or of immigrant outsider Muslims as the crown plotted rational development: these and dozens of rearrangements affected the local units.

As first organized by the crusaders, for example, Penya Cadiel or Benicadell castle supervised a district composed of two inner zones, Carbonera castle and Rugat castle, each with its villages and district. The fortifications designated 'castles' by the Valencian crusaders ranged from a few mighty edifices through modest links or district refuges to simple fort–towers. Guichard stresses the role of such structures in Islamic times as normally auxiliary in the respective district and as military–defensive under the state's governor or ruler, contrasted with the administrative–governmental centrality often conferred by the crusaders on even minor local defenses. Some historians identify Benicadell castle itself with Carbonera, or see it as a system of four linked castles – Beniatjar, Carbonera, Carrícola, and Otos. Within a few decades these castles were abandoned ruins, and district life centered in the towns. Though Carbonera and Rugat castles clearly divided the Penya Cadiel region by their respective districts, its local historian believes that no precise frontier or zone of influence can be traced between them. It is more exact to say that no occasion arose for verifying the border by settlers' witness, so as to end disputes and remove the ambiguities arising from normal ongoing change, as will be seen in the cases below. Rugat controlled eight or more villages, Carbonera perhaps six. A few regional rights, mainly military headship and judicial appeal, were invested in distant Játiva; transient tax-franchises for creditors were allotted here, and under King Jaume's son a jurisdictional species of barony was superimposed.

Another example of post-crusade rearrangement lies at the far north of the kingdom, where the castle and town of Castellón de Burriana presided from Magdalena hill over a district roughly that of today's Almazora and Castellón, with a half-dozen villages. As a consequence of revolts in 1247, King Jaume ordered the town moved to some suitable locale within its district but on the plain, leaving the castle to languish. Thus Castellón de la Plana began its rise to be the premier city in the northern third of the kingdom. Gandía, on the coast a good distance south of Valencia city, affords yet another example. At the moment of conquest its irrigated plain or *huerta*, ringed by mountains, held three towns and thirty-five hamlets or nuclei of population, some with tower defenses, over which five castles or forts watched from five mountain passes. Gandía itself, little more than a market town, received an influx of some seventy Christian settlers and very soon became the hub of this little world of hamlets and castles. By 1305 a town wall was under construction, and a governing board of jurats guarded their small archives of privileges. The crusader castles slowly assumed ancillary status during this reorientation. In 1282 King Pere sent two outsiders, Biar's castellan and Játiva's town secretary, to decide on a border between Gandía and Palma, 'personally visiting and inquiring for counsel from Christians and Saracens.'[4]

Change influenced the basic units indirectly, too, by decisively modifying or replacing or reorienting the more artificial larger regional boundaries of the kingdom. An overlay of jurisdictions bonded the mosaic of units into a variety of alliances or relationships: a diocese or a parish system, a tax collectory, a system of judicial appeals, a 'feudal' loyalty, a customs arrangement, the holdings of a monastery or military Order, or a traversing set of sheepwalks. The precise outline of the kingdom itself, at its west but especially along its southern border, required tinkering and international accords. The continuance of a few super-regions, essentially the natural administrative or social hegemony of a major city like Valencia, Játiva, or Alcira over a fairly large set of its basic local units, involved shrinkage and redefinition. All such larger outlines or jurisdictional overlays did not alter the units themselves; like building blocs they reassembled into new configurations without losing their individual shapes and integrities.

Thus the castle and town of Cullera, owned by King Jaume and the Knights Hospitaller in commonalty on a half-and-half basis, identified with a small or particular territory as well as with a wider or general territory. The general rather than the particular district defined Cullera with its dependent villages and hamlets. The general borders ran up to the confronting borders of other general districts: Corbera, Valldigna, and Valencia city. 'Below' or within Cullera's general district, a village like Sueca enjoyed its own tiny range; and 'above' Cullera the regional leader Alcira held a certain jurisdiction. Thus Sueca's district was englobed within Cullera, Cullera within Alcira, and Alcira within the new kingdom, each relationship involving obligations and privileges. The basic unit was still Cullera – Sueca being a relatively unimportant and dependent village, and Alcira having a very loose and limited set of claims on Cullera. Some distance south of Cullera, Denia began with a particular district, comprising the modern districts of Jávea and Denia, but with a more characteristic general district of twenty-six village units (ten of them today long defunct). Denia's parish, as well as its tax collectory and defense network, covered the general district.

Where markers or natural features defined a Valencian territorial unit, the penalty for disturbing one arbitrarily or slyly was severe in the law code of the new kingdom: 5 Alphonsine gold morabatins as a fine plus loss of one's holding. The law even forbade a farmer to 'put boundaries or remove those [already] in place' for his own farm, 'because bounds ought to be placed or removed with the [neighboring] landowners present and agreeing.'[5]

FRAMEWORKS FOR A NEW KINGDOM

The conquerors retained something of the kingdom's framework, so the land continued to wear an Islamic aspect uncomfortable to the Christians. Some of this appearance came from the demographic weight of the Muslims remaining, and some of it from the colonial authorities' inefficiency in devising enough ways to Europeanize (new money, calendar, Gothic churches, institutions, and practices). But in good measure it was deliberate, to facilitate orderly transition as well as continuity, in keeping with traditional policy of the crusaders' predecessors. 'As it was in the time of the Saracens' recurs in King Jaume's documentation as a normative principle for activities as varied as allotting irrigation water or tracing a right-of-way. This was not an antiquarian respect for immemoriality but a practical tool, so a modifier was sometimes precisely stated: 'at the time when we conquered them.' Surrender constitutions for many Islamic *aljamas* reinforced the impression of superficial continuity during the early decades of assimilation, amounting to alien enclaves, until rebellion and colonial brutality eroded and then subverted the initial agreement. For at least a generation Muslims and Christians could share many experiences, and the average Muslim remained ensconced in a relatively familiar physical environment. Acculturative pressures were inexorable, but what remained of the geographical backdrop to the Muslim's daily life lent comfort and strength.

By way of background to the study of internal boundaries, tribal and Roman antecedents may be bypassed, and the Islamic and Reconquest divisions roughly sketched. Of some twenty-one provinces constituting the caliphate of Cordova, two had centered respectively on Valencia city and on Játiva to its south. When petty principalities replaced the caliphate, the basic divisions remained much the same, with maritime Denia replacing inland Játiva and with parts lost to Zaragoza and Alpuente. The Valencian region, with Valencia city its brilliant center, later became one of the five Almohad provinces in Spain, but on the eve of the crusade a series of civil wars again disintegrated its unity. The Englishman Walter of Coventry, as he described the English king's passage along the coast of eastern Spain in 1190, had divided the Almohad waliate of Valencia into Valencia city, Játiva, Alcira, and in the north Burriana and Peñíscola; of two odd spellings, 'Oedeeb' must stand for 'Iatib,' a cross between Latin *Iativa* and Arabic *Shāṭiba*, while 'Stuve' seems a corruption of Arabic *Shuqr* (Júcar), a name for Alcira.[6]

Arabic cosmographers from al-Idrīsī to al-Ḥimyarī depicted Valencia as a set of such city districts, usually about nine. al-Idrīsī in mid-twelfth century showed this region as an Alcira–Denia–Játiva–Bocairente zone, a Valencia–Burriana–Murviedro–Cullera castle zone, and a northern zone featuring places like Peñíscola. He describes Valencia city as one of the more important in al-Andalus, with many merchants and much shipping. In the thirteenth century Yāqūt gave special notice to Valencia city ('famous,' its residents called 'the Arabs of al-Andalus'), Alcira (among the world's 'notable and excellent' cities), Denia, Játiva, Murviedro, Onda, and below this *madīna* category the 'marvelous' castle of Cocentaina and the 'well-defended' frontier castle of Castielfabib. al-Ḥimyarī's list of significant centers of al-Andalus adds Alpuente, Bairén, and Onda, with Ondara previously 'a great city.' al-Waṭwāṭ in the thirteenth century includes Almenara, Bairén, Cullera, and Morella in his list of a dozen regional centers. The adventures of the Cid touch on many of the same places; he collected great revenues from centers such as Murviedro, Liria, Jérica, and Segorbe. Ibn Khaldūn in the fourteenth century summed his predecessors by depicting Alcira–

Valencia and Denia–Játiva axes. Presumably such places enjoyed an administrative–fiscal role locally for the central state.

The incoming crusaders arranged land distribution around twenty-three centers listed in as many small books containing land-distribution information, plus Valencia city, Burriana, and Morella. As my *Islam* noted, these included north of the Júcar River: Almenara, (Burriana), Liria, (Morella), Murviedro, Onda, Peñíscola, Segorbe, (and Valencia city). South from the river were: Albaida, Alcira, Alcoy, Almizra, Bocairente, Calpe, Castalla, Cocentaina, Corbera, Cullera, Denia, Guadalest, Játiva, Jijona, Luchente, Onteniente, and Rugat. For regions under crown control, my count of items entered in Jaume's registers by quantity stresses Alcira, Játiva, and Valencia city; half that amount concerned Burriana, Gandía (the Bairén district), Morella, and Murviedro; half that again concerned Cullera, Denia, Segorbe, and Peñíscola. The eighteen other places coinciding with the land books continue as next in quantity among the registered items, but add eight more: Alfandech, Altea, Beniopa, Gallinera, Pego, Penáguila, Tárbena, and newly founded Villarreal. The administrative and defensive circumscriptions of both Islamic and crusader Valencia at the period of transition would appear to coincide at least in a number of centers, after eliminating one or other as holding unique importance for the crusaders and allowing for a few omissions like Jérica. Guichard has noted that most such blocs display pre-Islamic (sometimes pre-Roman) names, in contrast with the usually Arabic toponymy of the hamlets within each. Despite total change of social structure and function, some physical–strategic geography perdured, a simultaneous discontinuity in continuity.

For non-local taxes, crown judiciary, and other larger administrative purposes, the crusaders divided the new kingdom at the Júcar River, Valencia focusing the lands to the north and Játiva those to the south. Thus the procurator general or crown lieutenant over Valencia had a lieutenant of his own *citra Xucarum* and another *ultra Xucarum*. (From 1304 the Jijona River became a further interior boundary, separating new lands acquired at the far south; the Uxó River, about a third of the way down the kingdom, served at times for further demarcation.) Similarly for taxes a supervisory bailiff held responsibility north of the Júcar, another to the south; eventually a general bailiff would preside at Valencia city. Under King Jaume's two successors a special Valencian tax region or collectory surfaces, called 'the Mountains' (*Montanea*); this particularly visible regional enclave comprised the Islamic or Mudejar communities of Denia, Jalón, Tárbena, and other places, with its own bailiff. The name persisted into the seventeenth century, when it seems to have encompassed most of the area south of the Júcar; at that time the chronicler Gaspar Escolano devoted a chapter to it, as extending from Játiva to the Alicante border and from Castile to the sea. Valencia city from the first held pride of place in the crusader kingdom's governance, though it was not a capital in any modern sense. Játiva's semi-independence for more than five years after formal surrender, and its character as rallying point for Muslims of the realm (still the majority there), paradoxically strengthened that dominance. Whatever reasons of military security may have counseled this division at the Júcar, the historical role of Játiva made it seem natural.[7]

The kingdom as a whole expressed its framing outer boundaries early, though the southern frontier was to be the subject of international dispute and arbitration more than once. These boundaries were formulated in general terms at first, in 1242 as 'the whole kingdom of Valencia from Biar to the Ulldecona [Sènia] River, and from the Albentosa River up to the sea, and according as the district of Requena borders Castile, over to the sea.' The 1251 law code for the new kingdom opened with a similar design: 'from the Ulldecona River to the Biar district, and from the sea over to Albentosa and Manzanera and Santa Cruz de Moya and the limit of Requena district, which close the region as it faces Castile.' A more elaborate formula also went into the code, dating from the reign of the Conqueror's grandson but probably representing in its essentials our earlier period.[8] The crown could adjust these outer frontiers as policy dictated. Thus King Jaume decided in 1273 to include Castielfabib, on the far western border, in the new kingdom rather than leave it in Aragon. This accords with Almohad siting of this castle, in the geography by Yāqūt written on the eve of the crusade, as in the jurisdiction (*min aʿmal*) of Valencia. Jaume's privilege notified 'each and every man' of Castielfabib 'that you are to be of the territory of the kingdom of Valencia,' for taxes, law, defense, and geography; 'and you are bound to act according to the code of Valencia and not according to the code of Aragon or Teruel.' Even at that outer rim, local squabbles had long made Castielfabib's own immediate boundary obscure; Santa Cruz de Moya had claimed some of the territory of Castielfabib's small village Arroya Cerrezo, until King

Jaume sent the Valencian cathedral precentor Vicent to settle this 'contention,' and in 1270 ordered Moya to respect Vicent's settlement.[9]

The city of Valencia was given a generous district comprising its irrigated *huerta* plus all land 'up to Murviedro district which borders Puzol, and to the districts of Olocau, of Chiva, of Buñol, of Torres and to Montserrat, and to the districts of Alcira and Cullera; and it is to extend from the seashore for a hundred [statute] miles out to sea.' Alcira not only had its own small district but received an honorific set of neighboring districts around five castles, including Cullera and Alfandech; all fell, at least in theory, within 'the district and jurisdiction of the town of Alcira,' under the same kind of jurisdiction Valencia city had for its larger region. Játiva too received a regional as well as an inner municipal district, roughly from below Alcira on the Júcar south to Onteniente, west to Almansa, and east to the sea. Thus the Albaida Valley by a decree of 1250 had to follow the Jativan standards to war whenever summoned, send its trials before the justiciar of Játiva, and share its pasturage. These large, artificial regions meant in fact mostly that certain tax obligations, judicial organization, and privileges could affect the wider region; much later the crown transferred Alfandech under Játiva, for example, only to rouse bitter resistance in 1297 at the prospect of Jativan sheep browsing into that seaside valley.[10]

The most artificial of boundaries were those superimposed for some *ad hoc* purpose, ecclesiastical or civil. Pre-crusade commitments gave ecclesiastical control of the northerly sector of the new kingdom to the extra-Valencian diocese of Tortosa, all the rest of that kingdom constituting a diocese of Valencia, except for a wedge of Castilian-sponsored diocese of Segorbe attempting to intrude at the center. Each diocese busily plotted its networks of parishes (a parish usually having more than a single church), of archdeaconries, and of tithing collectories.[11] Like military Order commanderies or monastic seigniories, of course, these did not constitute the integrity of the district units. Agglomerations of units into some ambiguously 'feudal' barony, while not characteristic of early Valencia, did occur. Prince Pedro of Portugal briefly held Morella, Murviedro, Almenara, Burriana, Castellón, and Segorbe (1244–50). The Cistercian monastery of Benifassà controlled a *tinença* or holding of seven distinct elements, five of them castle-cum-district units. Such configurations did not nullify the component inner blocs, with their old boundaries. The *tinença* of Cuevas, commonly seen as a unit, actually comprised seven quite separate towns, which in the event always chanced to fall under a single lord.[12]

'AS IN THE TIMES OF THE SARACENS': MUSLIM WITNESSES

In granting any of Valencia's dozens of 'castles-with-towns' or its hundreds of lesser places, the charters spoke mostly of rights, obligations, and limitations, noting only that the place included its proper 'district' or 'bounds' with all Muslim and Christian inhabitants. Since these districts could echo the Muslims' geo-historical past, some charters made an allusion to that fact without further detail. The important town of Burriana in 1235, for example, 'is to have its boundaries just as was the custom in the time of the Saracens,' while the smaller and more obscure 'castles and towns' of Culla and Cuevas de Vinromá similarly kept their boundaries 'integrally, just as the Saracens had and held and possessed those castles and those towns.' Cervera del Maestre 'castle and town' went to the Hospitallers that same year 'with absolutely all boundaries and rights' which belonged to it 'ever in the time of the Saracens by custom or by law.' King Jaume gave his notary Pere Sans (Pedro Sánchez) in 1242 Montornés near Castellón 'with the boundaries belonging to the said castle in the time of the Saracens.' He confirmed to Onteniente's settlers in 1250 'all those boundaries which the Saracens of Onteniente had and held in the time of the Saracens.' And in 1274 he conferred Chulilla and Garx 'castles and towns' with their 'fortifications' on the diocese of Valencia with all 'frontages and boundaries as ever they best belonged and ought to belong to the Saracens.'[13]

The same formula could appear in the surrender constitutions which guaranteed semi-autonomy for the Muslim communities; the Moors at Uxó, for example, kept 'their hamlets and their boundaries in the said valley, established and consigned before the Muslims left the land,' as well as 'all their boundaries according as these were already decreed to them in the time of the Moors.' Most land grants fell back on a summary version, such as 'with its boundaries,' or 'with all else which pertains or ought to pertain to the said hamlets' (for three places at Onda in 1245), or 'with all else generally expressed or unexpressed, which belong or ought or can belong to the said place and its boundaries' (for Foyos in 1247).[14] In this same spirit, it was not uncommon to define a locale's boundaries simply in terms of the encircling districts. In awarding the 'castle and village' of Bicorp and the adjoined hamlet of Benedris, for example, the king declared that 'the boundaries of Bicorp border on the boundaries of Pallás which belongs to the kingdom of Castile, and with the borders of Cortes [de Pallás] and of Millares which belong to the kingdom of Valencia, and with the mountain-range of Zaydan [Sierra del Caroig?] and with the borders of Putri [?] and along the division of boundaries between Castile and our kingdom of Valencia; the boundaries of Benedris village border on the Guadalaviar [Turia] River.'

A prudent landlord might anticipate difficulties, or an alert grantee might get wind of problems even before taking possession. In that case he could petition the crown for an antecedent investigation in full. Since this followed the same laborious procedure as would a contentious lawsuit, aside from legalistic formalities, it must have been a rare expedient and expensive. In 1261 Pere Ennec (Pedro Iñiguez), 'procurator of Our Beloved Prince Sans [Sancho],' did just that. Having secured by crown grant the village of Benisanó in the district of Liria on the Valencian *huerta*, he took pains to get a companion document assuring him that the village keeps 'all the boundaries and waters that it had in the time of the Saracens.' The key concern must have been the water rights, so precious and jealously guarded in that region: control of every scrap of irrigated land which fell within the village environs. Four days later the king dispatched an order to the castellan in charge of the Liria district, informing him 'that we have given boundaries to the village of Benisanó' for Pere Ennec, 'namely those which it had in the time of the Saracens.' On receipt of this notice, the castellan must 'receive the testimony of Our Saracens of the Moorish quarter of Liria, who are knowledgeable about those boundaries, in the matter of those boundaries'; particularly was he to take 'the testimony of Halaf [= Khalaf?] a resident of Ribarroja and of the *faqīh* Alayelli [= al-Khalli?]'. After this process the castellan was 'to install the said Pere Ennec in possession of the boundaries of that village, according as you shall discover them through the testimony of the said Saracens.' This may be a special privilege; but nothing is granted, as we shall see below, that was not due to every village. It may denote an antecedent dispute, being settled outside the normal legal channels.

Or it may be a relatively common privilege, conceded to petitioners at the start of their incumbency.

Glick has noted how the 'time of the Saracens' formula persisted in property and especially irrigation claims into fifteenth-century Valencia, mixing in with a 'time immemorial' formula. Contenders in legal disputes cited the 'time of the Saracens' phrases directly from King Jaume, in an almost incantatory fashion. One case of water division in 1421 asserted typically a continuance 'from the time of the Saracens and from the time much before this kingdom was conquered by the most excellent king, Jaume the First, of glorious memory.' Since it was obvious that customs gradually change, this 'documentary' approach was buttressed by an appeal to Muslim workmanship and surviving elements as a clear proof of origin of an irrigation component in the *temps de sarrahins*.[15]

Several general conclusions can be stated. It is clear that each population center could claim its own district or range, the smaller as components of larger entities. (The less defined situation of the smallest unit, the *qarya* or hamlet, and the boundaries assigned it by the conquerors, will be considered below.) These districts were usually not arbitrary administrative conveniences, changeable at will and of no social significance, but rather a range for human action, clearly known to and defined by their immemorial Muslim settlers. As with any boundaries, they were susceptible of challenge, ambiguities, and violation. They were not usually identified with the 'natural' *comarca*, except in the case of the largest, being rather component elements of a given *comarca*. They could be assembled in a variety of packages for mapping as a small-holding, a large barony, a tax collectory, or a parish; but this left unchanged the town-cum-castle district or the city district as well as their interior village districts. The entire system was sufficiently precise, and so jealously guarded by the communities involved, that crown lawyers and judges could deal with internal border disputes as a routine class of cases with a routine methodology for resolution. The key to such resolution was community consensus of the oldest local Muslims.

SUE YOUR NEIGHBOR: ROMAN LAW AND REAL ESTATE

As settlers jostled into the conquered kingdom – townsmen and castellans and abbots and villagers – they found that their 'Saracen boundaries' could not easily be translated into exact landmark rocks and hollows. Even back in the homeland, uncomplicated by an alien frontier, boundary disputes remained a recurrent nuisance. The very border between Aragon and Catalonia, despite divergence on either side in language, economy, institutions, and history, was under litigation at Jaume's court at this time, to the king's undisguised exasperation : 'without reason, by certain not very bright people.' Teruel in Aragon was also experiencing difficulty in finding its border with Villel to its south; both sides cited 'many men' to testify in court, so that the judge was able eventually to walk and mark the boundaries, heaping 'a great marker of stones' at one spot.[16]

In Valencia the newly formed city councils took each other to court; landlord rose against landlord, monk against monk, military Order against king, and leagues of villages against larger towns. All this constituted a category of communal activity impressive in its range and significant for the settlers. As a given case dragged on, it provided the pioneers from disparate backgrounds, legal traditions, and even languages or dialects, with their earliest sustained activity as a group. The phenomenon recalls the analogous participation in public quarrels which provided practice in political sophistication in Italian and Languedocian towns two centuries earlier and hastened the development of their communes. Numbers of boundary cases in Valencia rose upon appeal to reach King Jaume's court, in effect usually the court of a judge-delegate dispatched by the crown. Few of the decisions, however solemn, were entered into the royal registers; most went down on parchments which then scattered into ill-fated communal or family archives. Enough did survive in crown records, for one accidental reason or another, to direct our attention to the whole genre and to show its unique importance. Fleshed out by boundary details from other kinds of charter, they shed great light on post-conquest settlement.

This activity can best be seen in representative cases; a random example, on which to concentrate in depth, is reserved for the next chapter. Sub-types include the problem of one's own district borders, the problem of a dividing border between two districts, the problem of including a given town or hamlet within one's district, the problem of settling one border only to have a neighbor cry injustice, the problem of long pre-emption of a village rightly belonging to another district, and the problem of confecting partly artificial borders to accommodate a newly created settlement. Crown judges, traveling even to uncomfortable hinterlands, presided over these cases, panoplied in the procedure of Roman Law. From one aspect, this was a chapter in the spread of Roman Law at grassroots level, and a pulling together of Islamic practice, variant local customs of the Aragonese or Catalan settlers, and the procedures which had been so passionately studied by King Jaume's swarm of jurists at Bologna. Each case saw its Latin *libellus* prepared, its Roman judge and procurators, sometimes their canonical counterparts, its review of witnesses 'according to the form set by law for receiving witnesses,' and its sentence. Often enough the king himself, rather than his judge-delegate, heard the final stages.

Jérica became such a center of dispute. In 1261 King Jaume presided over a concluding reconciliation, the sharp language of his sentence forming our only surviving record. The occasion of the dispute may well have been Jaume's gift of Jérica in 1255 to his clandestine wife Teresa Gil de Vidaure and to her potential offspring, a gift confirmed in February 1261 on the eve of this trial after the birth of their son Jaume. The son Jaume of Jérica enters the king's records decisively now, with grants of castles to him in 1260 and of clothing in 1263; some historians see Teresa as the king's mistress, but neither the pope's attitude nor Jaume's (he sought a divorce) supports this. The king declared the results of the trial personally 'in the presence of the plaintiffs,' namely 'the justiciar, jurats [executives], and whole council of Teruel,' an impressive audience. The Aragonese commune of Teruel on Valencia's northwest border had played a major role in the crusade, both as staging center for the main invasion and as militia reservoir. Among its handsome rewards had been segments of the new kingdom which the crown claimed as proper to Jérica. The present litigation established that the district for Jérica's castle and town ran from 'the hill or fortification called [El] Toro, as the waters run from Montalgrao (*Mons Algarau*) toward the settlement of the crossbowman,' and so through various natural features and 'straight lines' plotted between landmarks such as a stream or ravine (*rambla*). The Teruel officials formally acknowledged that 'they nor theirs nor the town nor its villages of Teruel had or have or ought to have any claim or ownership in any way or form in these,' but the whole belongs to Jérica.[17]

One of the fullest bounding records, especially from the procedural side, has survived rather by accident and only in a later authorized translation. The town of Cocentaina, at the southernmost part of the kingdom in the Alcoy mountains, found its boundaries challenged by a league of eight neighboring towns. All hands forestalled further legal entanglements by requesting a royal boundary commission. This duly sat, in the persons of 'the judges-delegate' Domènec Marquès and Berenguer Escrivà, both of Játiva, and rendered its decision. The crown registers contain only the king's confirmation in 1268 of this sentence 'concerning the boundaries about which the people of the said places quarrel among themselves.' Chance has preserved much more information about this episode and the procedure involved. Copies of pertinent documentation, kept in Cocentaina's archives, eventually disappeared. Authentic copies had been drawn in 1420, however; before these in turn could be lost or destroyed, a crown secretary–translator in 1764 made a Castilian version of the whole record. We see there the appeal to the king by the contending parties, then the instructions for the two commissioners to investigate 'personally' and carefully, and 'with some other persons' to make final disposition of the boundaries. The inquisition took the better part of a year; the two judges received their mandate in early April of 1268 and had their judgement confirmed by King Jaume in late January of 1269.

The report of their procedure is long. They 'had examined all the witnesses which any [of the nine towns] wanted to present.' They had eventually traveled over the landscape, point by point, 'posting markers,' presumably semi-permanent in character. Between Cocentaina and Travadell, for example, they had established a line of eleven such markers, connected by imaginary 'direct lines.' Each was described. 'The first divider is on a bank of Penáguila River, at the far end of a certain gully called Almorig (*Almorroig*); item, the second marker is on the place called Cayod, at the rocky point of the said gully named Almorig, near a pile of stones.' Each region had an analogous network of markers, with their Arabic names attached, and with features such as olive groves, a riverbank, roads, many gullies, 'spots' with proper names, and hills. This chance survival via double copying is our only record detailing the athletic activities of commissioners in the field.[18]

Sometimes the lord of a town resisted assimilation into the district of a larger neighbor; a wealthy lord could hold such a neighbor to a lengthy, expensive lawsuit. Blasc or Balasc Ximèn d'Arenós (Blasco Jiménez de Arenoso), son of Jaume's lieutenant over the kingdom of

Valencia, claimed Alcublas de la Pedrosa (in Catalan, Les Alcubles), a town some 51 kilometers west of Valencia city on the swelling edges of its *huerta*. 'The commune of Liria' claimed this for its own 'as [in] the district of Liria,' and had been 'agitating' Blasco for some time about this and several of his other villages. Alcublas was something of a prize; King Jaume had awarded it as a gift to his wife Teresa Gil in 1257. Faced with Blasco's demands that 'a certain district, Alcublas,' be left to him, Liria took its case to the king. The town's procurator Bernat Espanyol (Bernardo Español) persuaded Jaume to issue the usual triple summons for a civil case, complete with Roman Law *libellus*. Blasco refused to respond, even by agent. The king therefore declared the baron 'remiss' and 'contumacious,' forfeiting his claims ('if in fact he had any') by this refusal to defend. The king voided Blasco's own case, in effect awarding Alcublas to Liria. This sentence was given at the royal palace in Valencia city, in the presence of various citizens of that capital and of at least two excellent Roman Law experts acting as assessors, the Marseilles patriot Albert de Lavànya and Guillem de Belloch or Bell·lloc.[19]

On the very day that the king delivered the sentence, he cited Blasco to defend himself at law in person or through a procurator against yet another attack 'by the men of Liria,' this time 'concerning the matter of the demand which the men of Oset, Pedriza, and Rafal Abinhazmon make on you.' These towns are obscure and perhaps long disappeared. No further details on the action survive. A decade later there was a sequel under Jaume's son and successor Pere. Obviously a residue of the quarrel still simmered, as 'the commune of the men of Liria' appealed to the crown to enforce its decision that Alcublas belonged to Liria. The next year Teresa's son (King Pere's half-brother) announced through the king his willingness to compromise 'on the business of the Alcublas district and of certain other places' under contention with Liria. The king allowed this 'as long as you do not come back to me again by reason of this arbitration.' Here the actual process of bounding was not at issue, but rather the existence of an autonomous enclave allowed within the town's larger boundaries. Such enclaves occasioned serious quarrels, like the decades-long struggle between Liria and Benisanó over water rights.[20]

An analogous case (undoubtedly representative of many, but again with only the king's sentence left instead of a trial record), was the lawsuit 'between Don Gil Garcés de Azagra on one side and Don

Gil Ximèn [Jiménez] de Segura on the other, about the towns of Gayanes and Fontizeles,' which Garcés de Azagra claimed for 'the district of Perpunchent' but Jiménez de Segura insisted 'never were of the Perpunchent district but were always towns by themselves.' The Perpunchent Valley, not far from Cocentaina, boasted a castle and several villages of Muslims. It had remained by treaty in the hands of the Muslim warrior–emir al-Azraq from 1245 until the suppression of his revolt in 1258. Some twenty Christian house-holders had settled here in 1248, and as others arrived a church went up. The knight favored with this frontier castle, after revolt had returned it to the crown, was Gil Garcés de Azagra, cousin and intimate of the independent lords of Albarracín. He turns up as a minor but significant figure in the king's circle some ten times between 1221 and his death in 1273, notably at the abortive siege of Peñíscola in 1225 before the crusade itself. Of the various properties he acquired in the conquered kingdom, the centerpiece was Per-punchent, awarded in March 1260 in lieu of properties like Planes castle promised to his father.

By marriage to Toda or Tota Ladrón de Vidaure he was an in-law of King Jaume; his daughter Milia married one Guillem de Biga. At Garcés de Azagra's death, when his executors put the castle up for thirty days' public auction, 'many' hurried to bid on it. In seeking to dominate the two relatively insignificant hamlets in his little hold-ing, Garcés de Azagra was dealing with an equally eminent knight, the Aragonese Gil Jiménez de Segura of Teruel, holder from 1258 of Margarida, another of al-Azraq's castles, not far from Perpunchent, and crown bailiff for the kingdom of Valencia north of the Júcar River. He would be one of a team of two chosen by King Jaume in 1270 to review all land grants ever awarded above the Júcar. Jiménez de Segura also seems to have died shortly after the dispute; he transferred the two hamlets of this document to his son Pero Jiménez and drops from sight. The son in turn rocketed on to the international scene; elected bishop of Albarracín–Segorbe, he led an invasion of Valencia, taking the Segorbe church by force for his diocese, to King Jaume's embarrassment and papal displeasure.[21]

King Jaume handled the preliminary stages of this Perpunchent case at Cocentaina, ordering the collection of witness from elderly Moors 'about the situation in the time of the Moors.' The king's term *ancianos* is not merely a translation of 'sheiks' here. His orders make clear how old these 'elderly' should be: 'the oldest and most elderly

Moors from the [farmer] locals, of seventy and eighty and ninety years.' The disputants agreed to a commission headed by two residents: the knight Ximèn Pere d'Orís [Jimeno or Eximino Pérez de Oriz] and 'Don Roderic [Rodrigo] the rector of the church of Cocentaina.' If this took place in early spring of 1266, the process required two years before the final sentence of the king; the alternative possibility, based on Jaume's itinerary, would allow little more than a month, all within 1268, perhaps sufficient in the case of two mere hamlets. At any rate, Jaume summoned the two commissioners at Alcira in 1268, along with 'the testimonies which they had received,' and had them 'read before him.' Collating these evidences, 'the one with the other,' with the help of 'experts,' the king concluded: 'we are certain that in the time of the Moors there had been no castle in Perpunchent in former times,' and the little towns had stood 'by themselves.' He therefore pronounced these findings formally as a sentence, enjoining Garcés de Azagra from further disturbing Jiménez de Segura in his holding of the two places, and then affixed his seal in the presence of 'many' assessors. This large quarrel over a very small prize thus produced a document useful not only for details of a boundary trial, but also for information on two important knight-settlers from Aragon proper. It also reveals several other settlers, as well as information otherwise lost to us, especially the existence of a parish and rector this early (with his name) and the fact that the castle did not extend very far back into the Islamic era, at least with any administrative–defensive relevance.[22]

One case became a classic in European legal history, between the Cistercians of Benifassà in northern Valencia and the Knights Hospitaller, as to whether the small town of Ros(s)ell had immemorially belonged to the castle of Cervera. 'For a quarter century it exhausted the Hospitallers and Benifassans.' Brought to a halt first by Pope Innocent IV in 1250, it was definitively arbitrated before a papal judge-delegate and Jaume I in 1268: 'that the said place Rossell and the said mills are and were of the district of the castle of Cervera.' A jingle entered lawyers' folklore: 'Per mal libell, perdé l'abat Rosell' ('By a badly presented case, the abbot lost Rossell'). This furious clash of two international bodies, each panoplied with jurists and accustomed to legal battles, escaped into the canonical stratosphere, beyond the normal process of settlement used by civil authorities in Valencia; Muslim witness counted for less, consequently, than the barrage of pre-grants, grants, and other paper evidence. The monks had energy to spare, engaging in a boundary dispute with the knight holding Herbés in 1258, with the commune of Morella over wood-gathering and grazing jurisdictions in 1259, with the Knights of Calatrava over another boundary in 1272, 'violently' with the Templars over Refalgari in 1278, with Tortosa and Peñarroya over their common borders until 1280, with the crown bailiff of Peñíscola over the hamlet of Irca until 1281, and industriously on a number of allied fronts.[23]

The boundaries of Morella in the northwest corner of the kingdom were traced early and with great care. The Aragonese high baron and royal majordomo Balasc d'Alagó (Blasco de Alagón, encouraged by a pre-grant of 1226, had led one of the first recent invasions of Islamic Valencia. King Jaume demanded Blasco's Morella conquest for himself, as being so large and strategic as to equal 'a county' and thus too dangerous to tolerate as a relatively autonomous fief. The two men arrived at an agreement which left the place in Blasco's hands for a decade or so until he died. Within a year of his conquering Morella, Blasco and the king had convoked its Muslims and established a boundary board consisting of four of their oldest and most knowledgeable. Their names seem to be Muḥammad the *amīn* (Aman), Mūsā b. Mas'ūd (Muça Abenmaçot), Ibn 'Abbās (? Baço), and the *ṣāḥib al-ṣalāt* or imam (Çareiçela, probably a miscopy for *çavaçela*). The results of their labors are sketched in a dozen terse lines in Blasco's charter of the next month (April 1233) and at great length in King Jaume's charter in early 1250 after he had inherited the region. Jaume's description requires some thirty-five lines of modern print and over sixty lines in the printing of another transcription, as it tracks from valley to hillside to ridge to farm, past peaks and down more valleys, up to 'the watchtowers (*talayas*) of María,' into 'defiles' (*angostas*) and past such landmarks as 'a little bridge,' 'the shaded gulley' (*barrancum umbrosum*), a tower, a road, a stream, and 'the small field of Domèneç Sanç.' This elaboration is particularly valuable, not only for its toponymic detail, but as merely confirming the careful boundaries set by local Muslims nearly twenty years before, so that henceforth 'the residents of the castle and town and villages' of this northwest corner could develop their land without fear of further challenge.

Challenges nevertheless came. Muslims of one sector could assess their own farther boundaries too generously, or a neighboring district could bellicosely dispute some barren sector and force an arbitrated compromise. Shortly after Blasco's Muslims ran his boundary for him, the Knights Hospitaller at Cervera del Maestre castle entered counterclaims; eventually both sides came 'to perfect agreement about boundary posts,' in a settlement of April 1235, based largely on dry run-off gullies. 'Cervera castle fronts on the main mountain ridge which is above the place called Chert according as the waters run toward Cervera in time of rains, on another side on the main ridge above Barzella as the waters run off toward Canet in time of rains, and on another side on the main ridge above the peak called Bel as the waters run and double back toward Cervera in time of rains.' The 'perfect agreement' held for nearly a hundred years, but with increasing unsteadiness. The Morella commune, the Hospitallers at Cervera, and the equally aggrieved neighbors the Cistercian monks at Benifassà all joined in appointing four umpires to settle their mutual frontiers; by this time the arbitrators had to rely on 'old and trustworthy men' as witnesses, a pattern that would recur as the century wore on. By 1328 the supply of elderly Moors familiar with pre-conquest Islamic Valencia had been exhausted.

Even before the king could issue his 1250 boundaries for Morella, the Templars of Cantavieja sued to recover lands from Morella: 'they suffered injury concerning the boundaries of Cantavieja, a great part of which he [the king] appropriated to the districts of Morella.' The Templars joined this with a request that 'the boundaries of Albentosa [then Valencian, on the Aragon border] be established for them and bounded just as they were established and bounded in the time of the Saracens.' King Jaume agreed in principle in 1247 to give Cantavieja, just across the border in Aragon, its proper district but without violating 'the boundaries which Morella ought to have.' The Cantavieja–Morella conflicting claims may well have derived from disagreement among local Muslims, since the area was a jumble of mountain country susceptible by its very nature to frontier disputes.[24]

Another example of relatively late inquiry into borders was a case conducted by Jaume's son Pere in 1282. To avoid expensive court action, the districts bordering on Onda had to present their evidence to the king, with their charters; witnesses included the lord of neighboring Borriol. Some two decades later, when Jaume II established a monastic seigniory over Valldigna in the late 1290s, Cullera refused to accept his understanding of the boundaries. Cullera resisted 'the said division and partition, made to the prejudice of the said district of Cullera' and to its 'great diminution.' The king then, 'having seen with [my own] eyes these districts, which I personally visited,' marked off the boundary in great detail, including sites such as the field in which five fig trees stood – 'and a marker-stone (*moylo* [Catalan *mollo*]) ought to be put in it.' Cullera was also among seven town districts squabbling with Valencia city nearby, 'because boundaries do not yet exist between the city and the aforesaid places, nor are any marker-stones positioned or fixed there.' The king eventually dispatched a 'commission' in 1321 to call witnesses, and 'summarily' and informally to settle the business. There seems no end to the passionate barratry.[25]

FRONTIER BARRATRY: CASE STUDIES. THE AMORPHOUS *QARYA*

A category of bounding, not encompassed by the normal rules, affected towns founded by the conquerors. Such foundations were rare, since the kingdom of Valencia was a cornucopia of towns and castles already functioning and requiring care. The only notable place so established by King Jaume was Villarreal, a district and town carved out of Burriana. In 1273 he addressed himself conscientiously to arranging its boundaries, presumably confiscating bits of district from its neighbors by right of eminent domain. Jaume opens his declaration with the principle that 'it belongs to kings and princes to assign fixed boundaries to the settlements they found' and to give the settlers there 'laws or customs' to live by. He therefore declared that the boundaries of Villarreal, 'which I decided to make in the district of Burriana' as an independent district, were to run 'from the main irrigation channel of Burriana facing the same settlement,' a clumsy way of saying that the line ran south from the Mijares River along the main irrigation canal called today the Villarreal channel; the *populacio* here is Burriana. The description continues: 'and thence as it abuts the frontier of Nules,' which the Burriana frontier intersects at the south; 'and thence [northwest] as far as the ancient ruins called Misquitella which is opposite Bechí.'

Misquitella puzzles commentators but is merely the landmark remains of a Roman settlement at La Torrassa, in the sector of that name in Villarreal's subdistrict Pla Redo, at a spot apparently called 'the little mosque' (from Catalan *mesquita*); the place and its function reappeared in a sixteenth-century repair of the boundary marker

near 'some enclosures called in olden times Mesquitella.' The Catalan phrase *al antigor* intruded in our Latin text can mean 'in olden
fashion,' which does not fit well in the word order unless a clumsy
adverbial sense is presumed; Catalan *antigó* and *els antigors* means
Roman or pre-Roman ruins and matches the wording of Jaume's
document better. The penultimate stage follows in Jaume's declaration: 'and thence from the covered [marker-]stone on the elevation in
which rock is quarried,' and 'all the way to the Mijares River.' The
description here proceeds with relative brevity by a few fixed points
of reference, because the triangle of land based on the river was
following a course artificially chosen, just as the town was artificially
created.[26]

The smallest units in rural Valencia were the village or hamlet
called a *qarya* or in Catalan *alqueria*, and the private estate or farm
called a *raḥl*. As on Majorca, the crusaders sometimes had difficulty
distinguishing the two, indicating that at least some private estates
physically resembled farm complexes with mills and with *sharīk* or
hired-labor housing. Thus the crown spoke of 'the *alquerias* which are
called Villela and *raal* Alcortoix.' The crusaders' Latin term *alqueria*,
as Poveda's findings caution, may include any number of *raḥl*-type
farms. One can only make educated guesses, or rather sociological
models, as to what the Islamic *qarya* had been like on the eve of the
crusade, who inhabited it, what size it averaged, and what internal
patterns (tribal, sharecropper, free farmer as actual cultivator) characterized it. Such models begin with sparse clues from crusader
documentation but essentially proceed from analogy, similar situations in al-Andalus or the wider Maghrib, previous or later periods,
an 'Asian mode of production' posited, or toponyms as presumed to
reflect homogeneous and unchanging patterns through many centuries. Chapter I touched on the dubiousness of the 'Asian' mode, on
the folly of supposing a European-type landlord in Islamic Valencia
or a properly feudal lord in crusader Valencia, on the probability
that 'share tenants' and hired laborers also worked under free-
proprietor owners, and on the meaning of rural castles. That chapter
warned of the need to distinguish the strict Mudejar tenant, created
by radical surrender in the Castellón and Valencia city *huertas*, from
the free-proprietor tenants elsewhere under treaties guaranteeing a
kind of personal ownership. It also presented my own Islamic rural
model, involving a complex of various levels of free proprietors with
their share tenants, and a variant more homogeneous model.

From a juncture of archeological and documentary evidence, Guichard has posited a tentative pattern of rural organization in the irrigated countryside around Valencia city just before the crusade. It differed in nomenclature from the more usual situation as at contemporary Cordova, where fifteen administrative districts held 800 rural villages (the *qarya*) as well as 301 towers (the *burj*), and 148 castles (the *ḥiṣn*). Muslims in Valencia applied the term *qarya* generously to all non-administrative rural localities, he thinks, grouping them into the clusters dependent upon some town or center. Some of these Valencian hamlets were sizeable, some had a defensive tower, others again were very small and unprotected. He concludes that the towers signal a pattern in which a fortified village served as strongpoint to its surrounding open hamlets and private properties, each such rural ensemble being a little defensive and perhaps tax district. The fortified village huddled within a rudimentary and probably wooden outer wall, while an attached stone tower with its small enclosure served for serious protection. The crusaders perceived the varied range of *alquerias*, from insignificant hamlet to small town, according to their own objective ranking by size and degree of fortification. They assigned the village towers as though tiny castles; the larger fortified villages they described and treated as 'castle-and-town' centers. Guichard believes that the Christian immigrants into Valencia city's countryside tended to gravitate around the towered villages, while Muslims choosing exile emptied countless of the minuscule open villages. Crusader settlement thus reorganized the human geography of this particular area, he argues, not merely transforming its nature from village communities to feudal lordships. This pragmatic redistribution elevated the larger fortified villages like Bétera or Manises into castles-with-towns rank, and such intermediate tower villages as Moncada into seignorial centers. The terms were not hard and fast, especially among the crusader authorities, and betrayed imprecision as well as a degree of interchangeability. This scheme, concerned with rural places below the rank of secondary cities and main towns or castles, claims as yet the modest status of a study plan toward further exploration. In revising it, account must be taken of the anomalous effects of my distinction about radical surrender in that city's *huerta*.

Jaume's documents describe the possible dependencies of such a crusader hamlet as fields (*camps*), farms (*orts*), communal bakeries and mills, a 'tower,' waste or pasture lands, waters, and plots of land with names ('a place called Arnales in the district of Ador, *alqueria* of Palma,' for planting vines), and the ubiquitous *rafal* or *raḥl* now sometimes reckoned by the invaders as components of an *alqueria*. The dependencies within any rural mini-district, down to the least farm, received boundaries assigned by the crown surveyors, who formed a significant sector of the early Valencian bureaucracy; but those boundaries were private, not jurisdictional. How could a public boundary be set for a unit so small and amorphous as an *alqueria* containing a few farming families, which enjoyed the barest minimum of any public role and which often lay isolated in an undeveloped countryside? Where such a hamlet had evolved sufficiently to muster a community and to seem a significant settlement to its neighbors, a sense of its limits may already have been established; the crown could verify these, as in the case of Benisanó seen above, by the usual commission of inquiry among Muslim locals and neighbors. Even then, the boundaries originated less as territorial than as functional designations, frozen in a moment of evolution by the arrival of the crusaders.[27]

A major discovery I made about the Valencian *qarya*, when preparing my *Islam*, was that it had no 'fixed boundaries.' This did not mean that it was not a recognizable unit, or that central government could not reckon taxes or defenses in terms of its community, but rather that it was by nature amorphous. From one viewpoint, it may be seen as including those farms the hamlet-dwellers cultivated, and thus limited in its expansion by travel distance. From another angle, that assumed by Lévi-Provençal, in Spain it was a response to defense needs, the farmers coming in off their fields to fit into a protective system of defended and open hamlets. From the aspect of a water community, the cooperating and disputatious cultivators had to keep their skilled presence permanently close to the individual mini-farms, while banded into villages for consultation, support, and cooperative water distribution. Whatever tribal or intra-village relationships existed, the limits of village expansion must have responded to such functional mechanisms. On a lush *huerta* like Játiva's, where King Jaume says the *alquerias* were thickly set, expansion must often have been defined by the multiplied presence of other hamlets all around. The relevant document quoted in my *Islam*, which will now be analyzed in depth as a case history, did not say that the Islamic *qarya* was without a sense of what pertained to it, but rather that there were no 'fixed' and publicly recognized boundaries, merely private properties and a community of convenience or necessity.[28]

The case which gives expression to the principle for bounding hamlets involved relatively humble contestants in the valley of Albaida. Baldoví de Baldoví (Castilian Balduino, English Baldwin), citizen of Játiva and owner of a small castle called Xíu, was disputing 'vineyards and farms' held by Cresques of Gerona 'and certain other residents of Játiva.' Baldoví claimed that these belonged to his grant and civil jurisdiction 'and are of the district of the village of Xíu,' a position he wished the crown to vindicate. To Baldoví's charges, the defendants retorted that these properties, which they had held 'in peace and without any contrary voice for three years and more,' lay in the Játiva district and 'are not in the district of the said village, nor did the said village in Saracen times have fixed boundaries.' In this document the toponymical specifics are less important than the general principle the crown now enunciated, though we do learn that the disputed land fell 'within Puiggròs or across the river called Albaida and below the road to Barxeta,' a town on the Játiva plain northeast of the city.

King Jaume, after hearing arguments from both sides, took counsel with 'the high magnates and knights and others' about the disposition of similar cases 'already decided in the kingdom of Valencia.' He concluded 'that any village (*alqueria*) of the kingdom of Valencia has no fixed boundaries except only those boundaries which the Saracens of the said village were accustomed to work, returning from them that same day from their plot to that village.' Accordingly Xíu 'has for a district only as much as the Saracens of the said village of Xíu used to work and now work in the area around the said village at the time we got Játiva from the Saracens,' the disputed farms not included. Conversely 'the other vineyards and farms which the said residents of Játiva have there' belong to them and to 'the district of Játiva.' The Latin here is not at first sight unambiguous, for so vital a general decree, and a classicist might hesitate over *cum fuerit* as possibly future temporal, or *aliqua* as indefinite rather than inclusive, or *casu simili* as singular rather than representative. The text itself, checked against a companion text in the Templar–Montesa archives at Madrid, is sound. The abbreviations can only be extended plausibly in the direction taken. And if read in the framework of similar chancery usage, the meaning emerges as given here. Finally, a finding-aid scrawl by some archivist of an earlier but modern era confirms one's own impression: 'nota de terminis omnium alcheriarum regni Valencie.'[29]

Where a surrender constitution for some locality had guaranteed independence for external farmlands or properties in various other districts, so that the Muslim community controlled through its members a scattering of property enclaves abroad, the king exempted these also as an immunity from local control. Thus King Jaume gave the bishop of Vich in 1238, confirmed in 1241, the two hamlets of Labeirén and Cunillera in the Valencian district of Murviedro, modern Sagunto: but he excepted 'from this grant all lands and properties which the Saracens of Murviedro work, hold, and possess in the districts of the said hamlets at that time when I conquered Burriana with my army.' He added that 'all the rest of the districts and holdings of the said hamlets, whether or not there were Saracens there at any time' went to the bishop's jurisdiction. This did not really affect the principle of establishing limits for a hamlet by tracing the immediately pre-conquest farming pattern; it merely removed certain of the Muslim-held elements, after that reckoning, from the jurisdiction or rents of the local Christian authority.

Besides the revelation about a class of such mini-disputes, with the clear general principle stated, a number of facinating side-details emerge from the Xíu decision. The principal plaintiff, Baldoví, was 'a medical doctor' at Játiva, a rare reference to a profession then burgeoning at Jaume's University of Montpellier and soon to produce the great Valencian physician Arnau de Vilanova. Jaume's ample documentation tells us nothing else about Baldoví, but his owning a township indicates a relatively high social status. Baldoví must have died at about the same time as King Jaume: our only other notice of him comes in April 1277, concerning 'Baldoví de Baldoví, resident of Játiva, defunct.' In his last will he had designated a rising Jativan landholder, Ximèn Sabata (Jimeno Zapata), as guardian of his minor children and executor for his properties. The new King Pere, needing Zapata's services as a busy crown functionary in Valencia, 'withdrew' him from that guardian obligation, 'since he is a knight and occupied with my affairs,' and appointed another Jativan. Zapata went on to become lieutenant to the royal procurator of the kingdom of Valencia, and in 1282 was commissioned to settle the boundary dispute between Gandía and Palma, as well as a three-cornered boundary problem involving Mogente, Carmogente, and Enguera. The name 'Baldwin' is intriguing; an unusual first name in Jaume's realms, it was surname for a number of personages in Aragon proper and for several crusaders or settlers in the Valencian kingdom. The physician in question along with his brother Joan de Baldoví had received the village in March 1248 from the king, who was then in the neighborhood putting down a Muslim revolt and besieging Luchente.[30]

The few historians adverting to this place have trouble with its very name. Miret i Sans read it as 'Tiu' and elsewhere as 'Chin'; Huici saw 'Thiu'; the catalogs of Martínez Ferrando and Javierre Mur both simply retained the manuscript's 'Chiu.' It is in fact the Islamic castle of Xio or Chio, today a few ruins near Chiva de Buñol in the Albaida Valley, a treacherous spot where the crusader king was to receive a military reverse from his Muslim subjects in the final year of his life. Near the end of the century the Knights of Montesa, successors to the Templars, held it, with a copy of our sentence in their archives. Baldoví's adversaries and victors were led by Guaresques of Gerona. This strange name must be Cresques, common among Catalan Jews as a cognate for messianic Hebrew Zemach or 'branch.' That a Jew should be a major landholder and even the leader of a party (presumably Christian here) is not an oddity for the time and place; but it does suggest wealth or personal charisma. The *Repartiment* in 1248 reported that he already held buildings in Játiva, on a corner bounded by two 'public ways'; it confirmed these and granted as well $\frac{1}{2}$ jovate of vineyard plus $2\frac{1}{2}$ jovates of farmland 'by the road which goes to Valencia and by the Canals River.' As a final item in this trial record, we note that sentence was delivered 'in Játiva in the church of Sant Feliu'; this is the charming, side-porticoed chapel below the castle, a Reconquest relic identified even today with Játiva's image. Sant Feliu had fallen into disrepair at mid-century but seems to have been presentable enough by now for such a gathering.[31]

Other cases offer variant models. 'The knight Ximèn Pere d'Orís [Jimeno Pérez de Oriz]' held 'the village called Alfafara located in the district of Bocairente.' Though he already had a charter from the king's judge-delegate assigning his boundaries, he took care to have them reviewed and confirmed by the crown. King Jaume assured him that he and his successors were to keep 'those boundaries assigned by the said prior [Sans Ximèn (Sancho Jiménez)] with a public charter drawn by Domènec de Cepiello [Xapell?] notary public of Cocentaina, as contained more fully there.' This Catalan knight, whose name and provenance have confused good historians, will appear in fuller context in chapter 9, as does Prior Sans; the only other figure named is an obscure notary. Alfafara is not the more important Alfafar in the irrigated plain of Valencia city, but another Mudejar town on the slopes of the Sierra Mariola near Bocairente in the modern province of Alicante, later a huddle of houses around its church. From the principle enunciated by King Jaume above, that any Valencian *alqueria* kept only those boundaries set by the distance Muslim farmers had been able to walk to work and to return after work that same day, it might seem that Ximèn needed no formal surveying. The knight had secured special consideration from Jaume, however, as well as an eminent jurist skilled at boundary work; he had also troubled to have this confirmation of his longer and detailed personal document issued, and a copy registered at the Barcelona palace. Alfafara hardly seems worth the trouble. Ximèn may have harbored ambitions for its expansion, which would have outrun the simple walking-to-work limits around his village; or he may have feared the greedy expansiveness of larger neighbors like Bocairente, who might find obscure pretexts for annexing his modest holding. Or the crown may be using the term *alqueria* loosely here.

A strange situation had developed in the hinterlands, where 'the noble' Gabriel Dionís and Pere del Bosch had long been locked in 'controversy over the boundaries of the castles of Navarrés and Bolbaite.' Both were influential and wealthy men. Bosch had been justiciar of Játiva and a delegate of that town in regional affairs; Dionís, grandson of an Hungarian count, and relative of the king of Hungary, was about to carve a prominent career as financier in the new kingdom. Apparently their respective Muslims were reluctant to give testimony in this quarrel, perhaps cowed by threats. By 1280 King Pere's patience was exhausted. He summarily commanded 'all (*universi*) Saracens, as well the sheiks as the others, living in Montesa, Enguera, Chella, Quesa, and other places of the same vicinity,' to give their witness on this matter. Dionís and Bosch had chosen the arbitration board, consisting of the bailiff of Denia Simó Guasch, the secretary for Játiva's municipality Berenguer Escrivà, and the distinguished citizen of Játiva and financier Ponç de Malferit. They must 'receive testimonies from those [Muslims] who ought to know.' The king warned the Muslims of these districts 'to give testimony to the truth in this business whenever you shall be required [to do so] by those arbitrators.' He threatened that 'otherwise we give license to those arbitrators to compel you to [do] this, as shall be necessary.'. The severity of tone here, and the wholesale dragooning of Muslims from all sides, as well as the recourse to arbitration, indicate a bitter and long-term quarrel finally being forced to a decision, as the arbiters 'terminate and decide the said controversy.'[32]

HEIRESSES IN COURT: THE LADIES ORIA AND SANCHA

A complicated case involved the district of the small castle of Gaibiel and two heiresses. The plaintiff was Oria Pérez, daughter and heiress of the defunct Aragonese knight Pero Garcés de Rueda (Catalan Pere Garcés de Roda), acting through her husband Pere Noves. Since King Jaume had given to Garcés, his familiar and fellow crusader, the castle of Gaibiel in Valencia in 1237, Oria now claimed the adjoining towns of Matet and Pavías. Acting as defendant was the estate of another defunct Aragonese knight, Rodrigo (Catalan Roderic) Díez. Rodrigo's executors, the brothers Sans and Pere (Sancho and Pedro) Roís de Corella, speaking through their lawyer Arnau Escrivà, refused to release the towns. They rejected the assertion that King Jaume meant to give them to Garcés, or that these places had ever stood within the boundaries of Gaibiel. They also argued that Garcés and his daughter and heiress Oria or Auria had resided away from the kingdom of Valencia for decades, thus forfeiting their land grant. On the positive side of their defense, the executors gave evidence that the towns belonged rather within the boundaries of Almonacid Valley; besides, Rodrigo and his predecessors had certainly acquired title at least by prescription.

More than ownership was at stake. Oria charged that Rodrigo had profited unjustly from the two places over the intervening thirty years; she was suing for 500 sous income for each lost year, presumably to the imposing total of 15,000 sous. The figure, from two negligible hamlets, is a clue to the immense profits being reaped throughout the conquered kingdom. The crown's judge-delegate heard the witnesses for both sides, then set a date for final presentation before the king at Albaida. To judge from his itinerary, King Jaume seems to have made a special, rapid trip to Albaida to hear this case. Because the witnesses agreed that the two towns lay 'within the district or territory of the castle of Gaibiel, and are of the district of the castle of Gaibiel,' King Jaume awarded them to Oria.

He also acknowledged her claim to damages, but reduced the total by two-thirds, to a more manageable 5,000 sous, plus 200 sous in court costs.[33]

The principals here are significant figures in the settlement of Valencia; so little record of their lives remains, however, that this trial illumines both family and general history. Rodrigo held the castles of Almonacid and Benaguacil in Valencia; he left the first to his daughter Sancha, was being posthumously sued for it by the diocese of Barcelona, and had only begun to pay tithes to the Valencian church on any of his holdings two years earlier, having secured in 1268 an advantageous personal lease on his own tithes for life. He may well have been one of the first canons (often laymen in that era, seeking absentee revenues) of the cathedral of Valencia city; if so he was its illiterate Rodrigo. Rodrigo's executors, the brothers Roís de Corella, were knights who disposed of considerable capital; Sans held Olocaiba and temporarily Buey castles in Valencia, and was bailiff of Gandía at this time, loaning large sums to the crown. The Corella, a Navarrese family named for their castle Corella on the Aragonese frontier, had received lands in the Valencian crusade, though later chroniclers never quite untangled the individuals involved. Our two were the most prominent in this century, in effect the knights who founded what was to become a celebrated local dynasty. Pere Garcés de Roda turns up in the king's entourage between 1235 and 1238 – for example, signing King Jaume's document of acquisition of Morella and taking part in the siege of Valencia city. His daughter's name Oria or Auria evokes the Navarrese origins of the family, though they were then connected with Rueda in Aragon. Her husband, Pere Noves, briefly had a minor role at court; he appears as signatory to a monastic privilege in November 1270 and with eight others as witnessing the grand confirmation of all land grants of Valencia in April 1271. Arnau Escrivà, the last member of this cast, was most prominent of all, though of humbler antecedents; his father held distinguished posts for the crown and for the Valencian municipality, and Arnau was to be procurator general of the new realm.[34]

Another woman now puts in an appearance, the daughter and heiress of Rodrigo Díez, Sancha. She stubbornly continued to claim Matet, and two years later had Pere Roís de Corella present to Prince Pere 'a charter of grant which the lord king our father had made to Ximèn Pere de Humet of the village of Matet, and the charter also which the same Ximèn Pere made to Fernando Díez concerning the sale of the same village of Matet.' This passage clears up a number of points. This 'predecessor' of Rodrigo Díez had been favored with a grant from King Jaume, a claim he later sold. The purchaser had been Fernando Díez, majordomo of Aragon and royal counselor, a circumstance which provides a family context for Rodrigo and Sancha. The transfer status also explains reliance by the Díez lawyer on the argument from prescription, which would otherwise seem ill-advised for a frontier situation involving ambiguous claims and revisionary land-audits. Perhaps Humet held only a pre-grant, so common then, dubious unless confirmed or backed by personal conquest. Rodrigo must have inherited from Fernando, who disappears from view after filing a will at the Valencian cathedral in late 1256. In presenting this claim, Roís de Corella added two bills of debt; 'all these documents,' Prince Pere notes, 'we recovered because of the daughter of Rodrigo Díez.'[35]

The whole lawsuit illumines yet another letter. Prince Pere had received the documents just noted, but with no explanation of his own relevance to the case except perhaps as a public authority. In a final document he is shown to have had a more intimate connection and function; he closes a debt owed to him as guardian 'of Sancha Fernández, ward, daughter of the defunct Rodrigo Díez, who is under my guardianship and power.' Since women could inherit or receive castles, appointing if necessary a castellan for the brutal task of war, Sancha must have been a minor. The prince had given contractual powers for Sancha, in leasing the revenues of her castle and town of Benaguacil, to the Jew Aaró b. Yaḥyā, who then associated his brother Abraham in the collection and conveyance of the 8,450 sous profit. To one side of all this stood more lawyers, for the diocese of Barcelona. Their former bishop, the crusader Berenguer de Palou, had received Almonacid Valley and castle, which his jurist–successor Arnau de Gurb was suing to recover from the executors of Rodrigo Díez. Almonacid could also have included Matet. In March 1273 King Jaume cited both the brothers Roís to answer at law in his presence.[36]

A relatively simple boundary case, over two insignificant hamlets claimed by an insignificant castle, thus introduces a distinguished cast and has told us much about their hitherto shadowy lives. A Díez family tree emerges, with wardship link to the crown. Two women heiresses, two important Jewish officers of the crown, a lawyer from

Valencia city's most eminent bourgeois family, and a number of crown functionaries all put in an appearance. For each the boundary document is another shining piece toward our mosaic of their individual personalities and community role. The elements of toponymy and prosopography have converged once more as in all these boundary settlements, to add significantly to our knowledge of the careers and status of people whose names appear at random in other records of this conquest and settlement.

9

Real estate and literary echo:
the case of Jofre de Loaysa

Having seen sub-types of the boundary-lawsuit genre, its variety of valuable incidental information, the details of local toponymy as well as classes and individuals active, the stages by which commissions and judges processed such cases, and the serious public concern over each, it will be instructive to choose a boundary dispute at random for closer examination. The case presented here was indeed selected at random, taken to class for a graduate exercise, to test what could be discerned in its murky depths. It eventually yielded surprises, telling us much about Jaume's new kingdom and about the men around him. It serves admirably as an exemplar of the Muslim–Christian interaction characteristic of boundary cases. And it uncovers a small but fascinating chapter in literary history.

A LOST CHARTER: THE FRONTIER FORTUNE OF JOFRE AND JAUMETA

One peculiarity is its hidden nature; drafted at Bocairente on 15 July 1265, the original has disappeared, leaving only this official copy inserted within a later document of 1271. The published archival catalog consequently omits it among the 1265 entries. The catalog also miscopies the principal's name as Bassa instead of Loaysa, thus concealing its main contribution. Another surprise emerges when the double document, made to tell its extended story, supplies the context for yet another record of this genre, a bounding done in 1273 for two of the three places of the double document.[1]

The areas in dispute were Bocairente (Catalan Bocairent) and the nearby castles of Bañeres (Banyeres) and Serrella. None of the scattered literature and local histories of the region sheds any light on this episode or is even aware of it. The three places were tucked away in the Valle de Albaida region, as part of a relatively remote

227

mountain enclave. With neighboring Onteniente and Cocentaina, though of nowhere near their importance, the triad had a modest military significance as outposts in the sea of conquered Muslims, especially during the Mudejar rebellions of the late 1250s and 1270s. Despite later bellicose traditions, they probably had fallen into the crusaders' hands around 1245 relatively peacefully. Whatever isolated settlement had previously been attempted, the Catalan knight Ximèn Pere d'Orís (Jimeno Pérez de Oriz) and five colleagues in 1255 got Bocairente estates and a franchise to settle the town's district. The *Repartiment* or book of land distribution lists some twenty settlement leaders by name, as well as 170 infantry under them in anonymous groups ranging from ten to forty-seven men. Upwards of two hundred families therefore came here within a decade of the crusade's close. King Jaume prized Bocairente, or was worried about its stability, so much that he made it one of his twenty-five major target-regions for settlement with its own 'book' of distribution.

Meanwhile the allied castles of Bañeres and Serrella had been efficiently handed over to the Aragonese knight Jofre de Loaysa and to his Catalan wife Jaumeta as early as 1249, to hold as a fief with all mills, ovens, pasturages and other profitable rights. To have received a frontier defensive region, however small, so early after the close of hostilities, suggests that this knight was an important figure. Closer examination confirms the impression, revealing the gift as connected with a special service to the crown and with an emotional episode in the Conqueror's life. Jofre de Loaysa or Loaísa is a name eminent in the beginnings of Spanish literature and historiography, attached to a memoir in 'Romance' designed to carry the famous chronicle of the peninsula's primate–archbishop Rodrigo Jiménez de Rada forward through Jofre's lifetime, from 1248 to 1305; only the Latin variant, commissioned by the author, survives. Our litigant is the historian's father, building the family fortune on the Reconquest frontier. Very little is known about either figure or about the family, so this boundary document assumes special importance for Spanish letters. The two men are even sometimes confused; when the elder Jofre turns up in King Jaume's autobiography, for example, the able editor Ferran Soldevila identifies him in his critical notes as the chronicler.[2]

The elder Jofre had held the little castle and town of Petrel in Murcia, after its preliminary or abortive conquest by Castile in 1241;

this hot and rocky river-bank community with its small *huerta* lay just south of Valencia's borders, so close indeed that rearrangement of frontiers in 1296 would bring it definitively into Valencia. It had been important enough on the eve of the crusade to win a separate entry in the geographical encyclopedia by Yāqūt, as the 'castle' (*ḥiṣn*) Bitrīr. In the general revolt by Murcia's Muslims, put down by Castile with King Jaume in 1266, Petrel had an unusual role. The rebels there were willing to surrender to Jaume, on condition that he rather than Castile keep the place, because Petrel had risen precisely against 'the bad treatment' they had received from Loaysa; they still 'had fear of En Jofre.' The king explained that he could not violate his own agreements with Castile on this matter. He persuaded Petrel's envoys to surrender through him, then 'had the men of En Jofre run up my flag on the castle,' and turned it over to Loaysa.[3]

Further search reveals that Jofre had shared in the first partition of Valencia city immediately after its conquest; his prize was a public oven, a profitable monopoly in those days, in the heart of town near baths, fonduk, butchery, and main mosque. To this were added 'certain buildings and a farm at Valencia city,' a large farm or estate of 10 jovates in the city's district, and buildings in the suburb of Ruzafa. Jofre soon acquired an even more valuable gift: 'some baths located alongside the Moorish quarter of Valencia city, with their buildings and yards.' This property turns up again in the records in 1242 when King Jaume, desiring it for the crown, gave Jofre in exchange one of the city's choicest pieces of real estate, 'the *plaza* of the entrance' of the Bāb al-Qanṭara or Roteros gate in the city walls. This faced on the river esplanade, receiving traffic from one of the two town bridges, at the heavily fortified northwest corner of the walls, in whose angle the crusader settlers from Teruel in Aragon had their quarter. That was not all. Jofre received 'also the towers and moat at the barbican [in Spain an outer wall, not a simple gate-defense], which face the [Mercedarian] monastery of Santa Eulàlia' at the city's south, a description which adds to our knowledge of Valencia's walls. He also held for two years a second oven or bakery next to the church of Sant Tomàs.[4]

Like many Valencian settlers, and like settlers of new lands in modern times, Jofre looked to further frontiers. When Castile had swept into the Islamic principality of Murcia, to claim that window on to Mediterranean trade which Reconquest treaties with Arago-Catalonia had reserved to it, Jofre picked up not only Petrel castle and town but other pieces of property. On the opening pages of the Murcian *Repartimiento*, actually the third stage of that process and dating from the late 1260s, seven male members of his family appear, including his son the chronicler. Between them they hold 1,684 *tahullas* or (individually) an average of less than 5 Valencian jovates, equivalent to 34 Valencian jovates as a total for the family's males. Even though Jofre had the largest amount, and was one of Murcia's better endowed barons, the total was not impressive when judged on a Valencian scale. The second Jofre in the opening lists at Murcia may well be the chronicler. As the Murcian partitions multiplied, more lands accrued to the family. Though Murcia eventually became the Loaysa headquarters, their Valencian lands at this time seem to have been of equal weight. Jofre's first son García Jofre, who became *adelantado mayor* or governor of the kingdom of Murcia under Sancho IV of Castile in 1284, definitively centered the family and its holdings in Murcia, a movement perhaps inevitable after his father Jofre had opted to stay on at the Castilian court. For a time, however, the elder Jofre seems to have had equal loyalties and an equal division of his family properties. Even the fall of Seville to Castile in 1248 brought him mills and other good properties there.[5]

THE BOCAIRENTE FIGHT: MUSLIMS, KNIGHTS, AND LAWYERS

In the light of these findings, the two Valencian castles received in our boundary document by Jofre appear as the culmination of a career of fortune-building. By that time Jofre had taken a wife, a Catalan to judge by her name, variously Jacometa, Jaumeta, and Jacobeta, from transpyrenean 'France' according to the seventeenth-century chronicler Cascales. The two castles in Valencia also mark a turning point in Jofre's relations with King Jaume. Jofre may have been tutor or guardian of Jaume's daughter Violant for some time; more probably he received this appointment in 1246. In that year Jaume sent Violant off to Valladolid to be married splendidly to the future king of Castile, Alfonso the Learned. The marriage pact gives him as 'Jaufrid, knight and guardian of the said lady princess, and Jacobeta wife of the said Jaufrid.' His son's chronicle relates that Violant 'took with her [from the realms of Aragon] the noble man the lord Jaufrid of Loaysa and his wife the lady Jacometa, who afterwards remained faithfully with her and in her service until their deaths'; it tells us that, during this service, Jofre 'built the impressive chapel of San Juan at Burgos in the church of the monastery of Las Huelgas.' Jofre did not lose contact with King Jaume, and corresponded with him, for example in 1253; but he had now entered the orbit of the Castilian court and a future of accumulating Castilian grants, leaving his Valencian affairs in the hands of legal procurators. At the time of the boundary dispute, therefore, Jofre was a prestigious but absentee landlord. His son García Jofre would carry the family fortunes and prestige even higher; at the same time Jofre the chronicler was advancing in his own illustrious career.[6]

The town council of Bocairente had been quarrelling with the elder Jofre over the limits of their respective districts. The contest must have lasted a long time, to have made its way upon appeal before the king by 1265. It must have created serious disturbance, before that, to involve the personal presence of the king's lieutenant. The town now named four men to present its case, led by Ximèn Pere d'Orís. Three of these representatives raise no echo in surviving manuscripts: Joan de Caparrós, Sans Ortís, and Miquel de Cascant. Ximèn Pere, however, has already appeared above, in the Alfafara boundary dispute. Some time previously he had also headed the original community of Bocairente in receiving a settlement constitution. Sanchis y Sivera suggests that he was already lord there, and in fact he may have been crown castellan this early. His name and provenance have occasioned some confusion among historians. Both Sanchis y Sivera in his landmark nomenclator, and Fullana in his standard history and documents on Bocairente, gave him the name Ortiz. Miret i Sans tentatively identified him as an Aragonese, perhaps from the Huesca region. He was in fact a Catalan, whose family had spread from Lérida to Vich and elsewhere in Catalonia. In 1251 Ximèn received for himself the Valencian castle and district of Sella. King Jaume licensed him to sell his lands elsewhere in the realms in order to buy holdings in the Valencian kingdom, and in 1258 confirmed the past decade's purchases. In 1274 Jaume formally gave him 'the castle of Bocairente,' with obligations of hospitality whenever the king passed through.[7]

The crown committed this case to the Aragonese knight Jimeno Pérez de Arenoso (Catalan Ximèn Pere d'Arenós), then lieutenant of the realm of Valencia for the vicegerent Prince Jaume. The record of the trial, part one of the document, is this knight's report. He went 'personally to the places about which the said dispute' centered. The principals for Bocairente were the four men named above. For the absent Jofre, presumably in residence at the Castilian court, procurators were 'Ser Andreu his uncle and Gil Sans the castellan of Bañeres and Serrella.' Could this be Gil Sánchez de Alagón, who was briefly castellan also at Almizra and Benejama around 1263? If not, it must have been a local knight of equivalent family ranking and importance. The main agent for Jofre was a mystery man, however, Ser Andreu. The title is clear enough in the manuscript, denoting a Provençal or more often an Italian. Italians were active of course as merchants all down the coast, but few were prominent in internal affairs. Ser Andreu does not appear in the land grants of the kingdom of Valencia, either in the *Repartiment* or in more general records. He is not apparent in the king's autobiography or in the Valencian municipal privileges. He cannot have been selected as procurator therefore on account of local competence or influence; one conjectures that he stood for family loyalty, as a representative from outside, uninfluenced by Arago-Catalan concerns and unabashed before their authorities. 'Ser Andrea' does appear in the family grouping in the Murcian book of land division, as does 'the son of Ser Andrea' in the same group.[8]

The crown judge, whose charter serves as our inner document, deserves a word as well. Jimeno Pérez de Tarazona or de Arenoso was a close collaborator of King Jaume in the conquest and reorganization of the new kingdom. A specialist in Roman Law, member of the royal household, for a time steward (*reboster*) for the kingdom of upland Aragon, he appears regularly in Jaume's autobiography, as witness to important crown business from 1244 to his death in 1266, and as steward at least from 1235. Despite this public activity, he remains a shadowy figure. The Conqueror conferred on him the barony of Arenós in Valencia in 1242, raised him to the status of *rich hom* or high baron, arranged the marriage of his daughter and son (not of Jimeno himself, as is often said) respectively to the son and daughter of the last Almohad governor of Valencia Abū Zayd, and imposed him as land distributor and measurer of Valencia despite protests by the other barons that he was a commoner. More significantly, the king relied on him as vicegerent or lieutenant general of the new realm from roughly 1240 at least into 1262, a function obscured from historians by the intermediary lieutenantship of the king's sons and by several brief tenures by others. He was probably still in that office, at the time of our trial, which was among the last of his many presidings as the king's *alter ego* at litigation in Valencia. The presence of this eminent figure at this trial indicates the importance of its principals; conversely, the trial record adds a few more data to the as yet uncorrelated materials on the life of Jimeno. It is one of the very few surviving documents, perhaps the only one, from the hand of Jimeno himself; and it supplies data toward that noble's itinerary and activities. No one in the realm could have claimed so extensive an experience in boundary and distribution cases, or have been so familiar with land throughout the kingdom. During this trial he was at the height of his career and experience, and only a year from his death.

Jimeno summoned a commission of four Muslim notables to serve as expert witnesses, men 'who knew well the boundaries' of all three places and who were 'formerly' residents of Bocairente. The first was Aḥmad b. ʿAmīr (Aben Amar) as *amīn* of Bañeres; he was inspector of aspects of commercial life and at the same time the tax collector and responsible go-between for the Christian overlords. The second was Muḥammad, incumbent for the same office at Biar, the land port and bastion at the kingdom's southwest; his fuller name, 'Maomat Amnahilban,' may conceal the Muḥammad b. Sālim (Avincelim) who was active in this office at Biar in 1275. The third was Zayd b. Ḍarama (? Abintarama), not further identified here but appearing from 1261 (Aceit Abentaram) as *amīn* for life at Ibi. The last was ʿAbd Allāh ʿAbd ar-Rashīd (Abderegit). That at least three of these four held the sensitive post of *amīn* in the southern mountains testifies to their status as notables, their acceptability to the crown, and their probable capacities for eliciting and organizing information from the region's Islamic communities. Their inclusion by name allows us to add another piece or two toward the recovery and reconstruction of Islamic communities during the decades just after the crusade. No Christian witnesses were consulted. The four notables, 'gathered in my presence in that place,' were appointed 'to assess and assign boundaries' of the three towns 'according to what they had customarily been at the time when the town of Bocairente belonged to the Saracens.'

After 'advice and negotiation' this committee plotted a line from a local spring over toward a second spring, thence to the farm of 'Alexach' and to the farm of 'Hallyecen' (perhaps al-Ḥasan, or the idiomatic combination ʿAlī Ḥasan) and to the farm of Sālim 'Alaxach,' 'and up the stream which branches off from Loriga,' thence to the farm of Ibrāhīm 'Alaxach' and to the farm of Alaric and up-wards, thence to the farm of Yūsuf al-Mus'at (Jucef Almoxat) 'and to the mountain where the white earth is,' and 'thence upwards to Serrella near Bañeres.' The triple repetition of Alexach–Alaxach suggests a tribal or family concentration at these critical points. The judgement concluded that all to the south of this line as far as Bocairente belonged to Bocairente's district. 'And all [properties] from the said places and farms up to Bañeres and Serrella are and ought to be of the districts of Bañeres and Serrella.' The four town representatives and Jofre's two men 'acknowledged and approved' the findings; Jimeno confirmed them officially. The formal docu-mentation was drawn up by his scribe Pere at Bocairente on 15 July 1265; the pendant seal of Jimeno authenticated it.[9]

The dispute erupted anew, eight years later. Perhaps the circum-stance that King Jaume had been absent from the Valencian king-dom during those years, and thus unable to attend to the quarrel personally, left open the tempting possibility of a final appeal. This time the king committed the preliminary trial to Sans Ximèn (San-cho Jiménez), the prior of Santa Cristina. Here again an almost unknown but very influential figure comes to light. Our present knowledge about him derives from a single phrase in King Jaume's autobiography, sufficient to indicate his importance without reveal-ing its nature. The king enumerates seventeen nobles and prelates leading the army with which he was about to conquer Burriana in Valencia; near the end was 'the prior of Santa Cristina.' Miret i Sans identifies his priorate as the Santa Cristina at Somport some dis-tance directly north of Jaca; for lack of a better candidate, Soldevila accepts the location. In the context of this passage, heavy with the names of towns of Aragon, it makes sense. A search through the witnesses of King Jaume's charters advances our knowledge. These give us his name and show him traveling widely in the realms on the king's service from 1270 through 1273; we lack information on the intervening thirty-five years. He held a university degree in Roman Law; his signature as a jurist turns up on various crown sentences, as at Játiva in June 1273 in two civil suits, one between brothers over property. And he was the judge-delegate assigning the boundaries to Alfafara in 1271, in a case studied above.

The present trial document is therefore our earliest record of his public life. It seems to have come from a circuit of business he undertook for the king that year in Valencia, since Jaume records at the end of 1271 a bill for salary covering 'the twenty-nine days [during] which you acted for us in the kingdom of Valencia.' According to this record, prior Sans had taken up the matter with 'aged (*anticos*) Christians and Saracens there' and had concurred with the findings of the previous commission. Christians are among the witnesses here for the first time, yet only six years have passed; these can hardly be new settlers (otherwise their 'age' would hardly figure), but must be among the age group of those interviewed by the previous commission. In that case, the relatively few Christians would be testifying to the Islamic limits they had found upon arrival, since those were the limits the king wanted as the norm. King Jaume formally examined the document of 1265 and its seal, then approved and confirmed it, at Zaragoza on 5 December 1271. He thought the entire proceedings worth entering into the crown registers.[10]

This single flash illumining the dispute now casts light upon what might otherwise seem a routine order from the king, issued at Alcira almost exactly two years later on 2 December 1273. No detail connects this with the foregoing documents, but the link becomes clear from familiarity with all three. Jaume had ordered 'the partition or bounding with boundaries' around the castles of Serrella and Bañeres. His wishes had been executed by Arnau Escrivà, the distinguished crown bailiff for Valencia city and temporarily vicegerent for its kingdom, working in tandem with Pere 'Didaci.' Escrivà has already entered our story in a previous boundary trial, but his unknown companion deserves close study. Pere (Pero) Diego, Dieguez, and Díez, 'son of the defunct Roderic Munyós' (Rodrigo Muñoz), apparently an Aragonese, turns up in two dozen crown documents from 1257 to 1276 as a crown *porter* or executive agent. He advanced heavy loans to King Jaume, audited Valencian taxes at various southern towns, served as castellan at a number of Valencian castles (including Alcalá, Gallinera, Garg, and Jalón), purchased or farmed the revenues of Cocentaina's Moors, and piled up for himself a considerable body of Valencian properties, including a tower near Cocentaina. The king himself arranged Pero's marriage at this very time to Margarita, the daughter of Andreu and Nicolasa de Puigvert ('whom I cause to be given to you as wife'), and he contributed from the royal coffers toward her dowry 1,000 gold mazmodins or 6,000 sous. Pero Diego, as an important local landholder and experienced administrator, made a suitable colleague for the eminent bourgeois jurist Escrivà on our boundary committee.[11]

Miquel Senat, notary of Valencia, had drawn up a 'full' charter of details. King Jaume now approved and confirmed the operation, 'ordering that the aforesaid partition or bounding of the limits of the said castle' be observed fully by all officials and subjects. It would seem that Jofre had not trusted the charters issued in 1265 and 1271, and had requested a special review and confirmation for his own properties. A final manuscript, confused for us by Martínez Ferrando's published catalog as involving García 'Josie,' tells how King Pere 'recovered from the Saracens' rebelling in Valencia in 1276 the castle of Serrella, and 'restored it' to García Jofre in 1278.[12]

GENRE: HISTORY IN THE TRIAL RECORD

The double document is thus significant across a broad front. (1) It is an excellent, unpublished example of a neglected source category, one which mirrors a spirited form of activity throughout the conquered kingdom during its first generation of settlement. (2) It illustrates the phenomenon of the 'lost' document, resurrected only because a copy was buried within some larger and later record. Not unusual among property records, such embedded later copies are rarely sought and studied. (3) It conveys toponymical information about this distant, strategic corner of the new realm. (4) It shows King Jaume applying his Mudejar traditional policy in an intriguing context, preserving quite deliberately an Islamic ambience and summoning a commission of Muslims to investigate and achieve this. (5) It introduces an important but little-known figure from the court of Jaume of Aragon and Alfonso the Learned of Castile, with resonances for literary history because his son (about whom we know as little) composed a celebrated history of his times. (6) It also brings to light an Italian relative of these two, shedding some minor but useful illumination on their family history, and suggesting that further study on Italian influence within families of Mediterranean and meseta Spain would be fruitful.

(7) It contributes a surprising amount of early information about a hitherto obscure town, Bocairente, which held important secondary ranking in the new kingdom. It also adds to our exiguous information about the two castles. (8) It salvages four more Mudejar notables, fleshing out our picture of post-conquest Islamic adminis-

trative personnel. At the same time, its boundary formula rescues a handful of humbler Muslims in the countryside, including what seems to be a family or tribe.

(9) For Jaume's own court, it throws into relief the almost unknown figure of the Santa Cristina prior, yielding not only a glimpse of a busy member of the royal curia but also a revealing view of one more lawyer extending at grassroots level the Roman Law movement then fomented by Jaume. (10) It sketches some procedural aspects of a civil suit and of chancery practice in handling documents. (11) Because it is a document selected at random, and transcribed at first for its central boundary information, it illustrates the treasures crouched silently waiting between the lines of countless such unpublished and unexamined documents in the Crown of Aragon archives. (12) Above all, it supplies another exemplar of a class of documents demonstrating an analogous substratum or mentality among Mediterranean Christians and Muslims. The kind of 'walking the boundaries' which might be assumed to be Roman and European had been as central (each in its very different cultural context) to Islamic as to Christian perception in Spain.

This genre of document has been long neglected. Its legal format can make it formidable, a dense summary of intricate arguments and maneuvers, while its concentration on local property lines can make it seem parochial. At best, one or other such charter is examined by a local historian in antiquarian mood. As a pattern of documents, however, it can tell us much, exposing the relentless reorganizing of a colonial conquest by its administrative bureaucrats, the grassroots collaboration so often unrecorded between Muslims and immigrant settlers, the Roman legal mentality which King Jaume deliberately fostered in the new realm and to which the frontier landlord's barratry gave such ample scope, the degree to which barons and townsmen plunged into this expensive morass of lawsuits, and the keen sense of territoriality in both Muslim and Christian residents. Above all, the incidental information is precious; like a gold trace embedded in a rock face, it is well worth the rigors of mining. Astonishingly little is known about many of the important barons and functionaries of thirteenth-century Valencia, or for that matter about the household and counselors of the king himself. For some great leaders, like the prior of Santa Cristina or Carròs de Rebollet, we have little beyond their names; others fall from sight during decades of their careers. Each of these boundary disputes uncovers such men and women in action, helping us people the realm again with its proper Moors and Christians. The new information offers clues and stimulates the search for further unpublished manuscripts, while making sense of fragmentary data already available.

The value of this documentary genre for legal and for administrative history is obvious, especially in a proto-colonial context. It serves admirably the development of social history as well, whether of families, communities, or individuals. As a typology it implies a methodology for coping with its special difficulties, a convergence of skills in regional and national prosopography, topography, and bureaucracy. The searcher must patiently plunder nomenclators, itineraries, indexes of documentary collections, codices of land distribution, and especially unpublished manuscript collections. Like a birdwatcher, he will eventually sight his quarry clearly, minute yet part of a great pattern. One may change the figure into fairy-tale or even Jungian terms. Like prosaic, unprepossessing frogs, these boundary documents await only the researcher's kiss to metamorphose into proud princes in the ranks of medieval source materials.

10

Voices of silence:
al-Azraq and the French connection:
why the Valencian crusade never ended

Appropriate epilog to these explorations is an episode and document which brings all three communities on stage for final action together. In it the crusaders receive the surrender of a local Muslim ruler and install him as vassal in their European system, a transfer into the subculture of nobiliary Mudejarism. On that single page the Conqueror invokes 'the grace' of his Christian Deus, while the Muslim

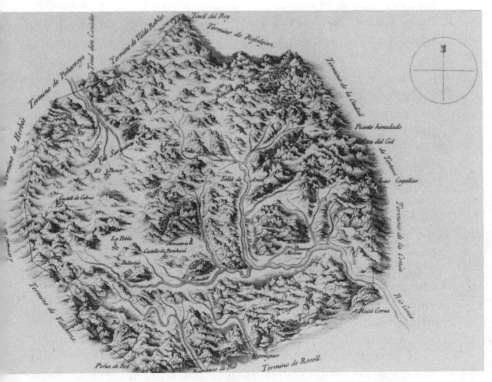

A Valencian district (*terme*): Benifazá. (Cavanilles, *Observaciones*, 1795)

239

speaks for Allah 'the Compassionate, the Merciful' and for 'our lord Muḥammad and his family.' The role of the Jew in drafting the Arabic scribe's portion of this interlinear tandem can only be presumed, as normal practice on Jaume's crusade. The king's Jewish secretary of Arabic was available, but the prince who officiated here would have had his own. The actual scribe for the Arabic was professionally familiar with the titulature and rhetorical conventions of the *dīwān*. One cannot exclude the possibility that the scribe was borrowed from the Muslim surrendering, and especially that he might have been a Jew even in that case. (Jews were embarrassingly common and even hereditary in office as clerks in contemporary Islamic bureaucracies; and a century before, the chief of chancery for the Fatimid caliph al-Āmir had been a Jew). If so, the borrowed scribe still saw the document as mandated by the crusaders, and he drafted in a thoroughly Islamic rather than European context. Deeper analysis of our document argues that he was probably a Jew rather than a Muslim, and that he was in the employ of the crusaders rather than of the Muslim surrendering.

The episode touches on most of the themes of this book and contributes to some of them: the *dhimma* experience, the problem of language, the boundaries of castles, the ritual of legalistic acceptance by either side, the ambience of violence and shifting alliances, conversion of the Muslim ruler (here in a contextual aside), the Muslims' revolt which occasioned the raid of the corsair Moragues in chapter 4, the archeological approach to the single document as recommended in chapter 1, and the surprises still awaiting investigation in the crown archives. The episode also reveals to us, for the first time, the deliberately hidden course of the Valencian crusaders' last major campaign: the way in which Jaume's crusade ended but did not end. It encapsulates as well the whole confrontation of cultures, by which the Conqueror implacably perceived in his own terms (and thus helped transform) the loser's society. As a specimen of Arabic agreements with Christian authorities on the Spanish peninsula over the course of the Reconquest the charter is less original, however singular it may be for Valencia. The place, time, and context lift it above genre and make it unique. It connects in turn with significant international developments, previously misunderstood, marginalized, and even denied; and it helps solve a major mystery in the compositional structure of the king's own autobiography.

ARABIC SOURCES: TRANSITIONAL MUDEJAR
VALENCIA

Before presenting this treasure, it is important to appreciate its rarity. It is the only public document in Arabic to have survived from Valencia's early Mudejar era, namely from the moment of final surrender through the transitional decades of Jaume's reign, except for a related but enigmatic note of 1250 introducing a rebel Mudejar embassy. Of all the agreements drafted in traditional bilingual form during the crusade or its subsequent revolts, moreover, it remains the sole exemplar. If the chronology is widened to include the reign of Jaume's son Pere, surprisingly only one further Mudejar charter is in hand, to or from the crown in Arabic – a rebel castellan's note to Pere of his intention to surrender. The collection of Arabic documents at the royal archives, these three and a Tunisian sale document aside, does not begin until after the death of both these first kings of Valencia. With half a dozen exceptions of no relevance to those reigns, the collection does not really begin until the next century. Considering the evidence for the widespread existence of Arabic and bilingual charters in Jaume's day, others may well turn up for Valencia; until they do, this almost lone survivor demands full publication and scrutiny.

The charter must be seen against an even wider wasteland. Charters aside, there is still almost no direct documentation in Arabic for post-crusade Muslim society or for Christian–Muslim interaction then in Valencia. Materials alien to the region or unsynchronic to the Mudejar experience may be intruded for atmospheric effect, general cultural elucidation, or the confecting of a plausible if static structuralist model. One may play the exegete over literary or toponymic and anthroponymic scraps to the same purpose. Indirect fragments left in Arabic are not irrelevant or negligible. Historical chronicles, though relentlessly focusing on war and politics, do carry us through the Almohad collapse and into the Valencian crusade, tracing the pattern of shifting allegiances and dating the fall of the more important cities; contemporary commentators like Ibn 'Idhārī, Ibn Sa'īd al-Maghribī, and Ibn al-Abbār are staples for this period. Independent documents also lie at hand. The poetic appeal to Tunis by Ibn al-Abbār, secretary to the last ruler of Valencia, Zayyān, can still move the reader. An eye-witness account enlivens our view of Valencia city's surrender. Letters from Zayyān to the rulers of Castile hint of wider machinations, while the reports and letters of Ibn ʿAmīra clarify relations between Ibn Hūd and centers such as Játiva. One anecdote illumines the activity of the Dominican language school in neighboring Murcia. A marriage-contract, unfortunately very late in the century, is a glimpse of life at Murviedro. Geographers, travelers, biographers, and poets have left their rich indirect legacy. The rare administrative *ḥisba* treatise such as that of the thirteenth-century al-Saqaṭī of Málaga, or the occasional genealogical description of bygone times, can be as useful as the intellectual and scarce artistic relics of the early Mudejars' immediate past.

Later historians, particularly al-Maqqarī (d. 1631) and the great Ibn Khaldūn (d. 1406), frame Valencia in the wider Maghribian scene. The most ambitious modern survey of Spanish Islam, drawn from Arabic sources by Evariste Lévi-Provençal, must be used only with caution, however, since it stops far short of the Almohad period. Equally perilous is any transfer of later Granadan or Morisco elements. All such resources at best allow us to hold up a Valencian Mudejar word or practice to the mirror of general Islamic culture. The most relevant political fragments were worried over and pulled together a decade ago by Ambrosio Huici, to fashion a conclusion for his monumental history of Islamic Valencia. Neighboring Murcia has found a similar champion in Emilio Molina López, and the Balearics in Guillem Rosselló Bordoy and Angel Poveda Sánchez. Rachel Arié and Cristóbal Torres Delgado do the same service for emerging Nasrid Granada. My *Islam* and *Colonialism* have supplied both the contextual background and interpretative amalgam for Mudejar Valencia. In both archeological and anthropological–structural modes, Thomas Glick and Pierre Guichard have been opening new vistas on Spanish Islam, with special reference to post-conquest Valencia.

However useful the Arabic resources are, their traumatic interruption in Valencia is striking. More than that, wholesale obliteration of Mudejar Arabic documents makes in itself a commentary on Valencian crusader society. Medieval paucity of records cannot explain the phenomenon, since proliferation of public records characterizes Jaume's reign more than those of his predecessors or his contemporaries in Europe. Nor can an argument be made from Christian lack of interest in confecting Arabic documents. Jaume's chancery had a special secretariat for that purpose; for Majorca there was even an Arabic version of the crown's *Repartiment* or book of land distribution. Again and again crown scribes noted that a record had been made or filed or lost in the 'Saracenic' script, until it becomes obvious that even at the highest official levels Arabic documents were not at all uncommon. Yet the conquerors never allowed Arabic as one of their several languages for registration in official copy. If a bilingual agreement entered such codices, it was the Latin or Romance version. If an interlinear parchment survived, it was invariably replaced in time by the Latin portion alone. This denotes a deliberate disengagement, a refusal of memory, an indifference or marginalizing which denied Muslim subjects relevance to one's own world.

If its language was filtered out, however, Islamic society itself was frequently and variously mirrored in the crown's records. Through these we can know thirteenth-century Mudejar society in Valencia more fully than we can know its Almohad society. By happy paradox, the invaders of Islamic Valencia are themselves transmitting to us, over a distance of seven centuries, an archives of that conquered generation. It is these manuscripts I have been plundering and publishing in transcription over the past quarter century, from the reigns of Jaume, Pere, and Anfòs. These are stray voices out of a silence, nevertheless, captive voices in an alien tongue. The charter we shall now discuss is a direct voice, a voice borne by the very parchment its protagonists handled, a relic of the instant of a culture's transition.[1]

AL-AZRAQ, SHIELD OF ISLAM

The document is among King Jaume's parchments rather than in his better-known paper registers, as a long rectangle some 25 × 40 cm, possibly designed as a scroll. It presents the surrender terms by which the Muslim sheik al-Azraq conveyed his castle districts to Jaume's son Prince Anfòs or Alfonso. Its upper portions are readable enough; the very bottom of the text, particularly the witness area, is worn and affected by damp, held together by a mounting or support of stiff paper attached down the last 12.5 cm. At least one seal obviously had adorned the lowest level, until either weight or scholarly vandalism despoiled it, leaving this end of the charter badly torn away as well as deteriorated. The seal of Prince Alfonso would have made a treasure in itself, had it survived here. A central hole

The al-Azraq treaty

suggests only that single seal. On the parchment's dorse, marginalia define past movements within archival armoires, while a modern title there categorizes it as a *carta conventionis*.

Alternating lines of Arabic and Aragonese-influenced Castilian, thirteen and fourteen respectively if signatures are excluded, begin and end with the Romance. The first composition was probably the Arabic, however; its script is larger as well as better sited on the page, neatly spaced as though inviting the corresponding Romance. The Romance script seems crowded along the top, despite blank space at the bottom, as though possession of the topmost blank was important to the crusaders; and the Romance text continues tightly even to the run-on date line, as though accommodating itself to the shorter Arabic text, without the option of distributing itself to better advantage on the page. The Romance script is the standard used at this transitional period in the chancery of the realms of Aragon, a hand until recently called French cursive or documentary Gothic, but currently the subject of controversy and novel nomenclature. It relates rather to Mediterranean script, though its strong ascender and descender stems and its crabbed lobes convey a vertical sense. Abbreviations are few and obvious. The Arabic, in Maghribī script, deserves special comment, which will be published in a separate study.

The nineteenth-century archivist Francesc de Bofarull first noticed this 'worn and blotted' document; he copied the Castilian version as a preservative caution, filing it away with the deteriorating original. The canon Roque Chabás in turn came upon copy and original during his archival rummagings, and published the Romance obscurely in his personal, short-lived journal *El archivo* in 1886, along with a brief commentary. The essential Arabic was missing, presumed to be a copy of the Romance. Noting that the Castilian and Arabic versions were dated a year apart, Chabás opted for 1244, to tuck the episode within the Biar campaign of that year, the traditional ending of the crusade. Subsequent historians rarely noticed the Romance transcription, much less analyzed it. A few local historians did make it a footnote to the career of its Muslim signatory al-Azraq; the best of these, Francisco Momblanch, recapitulated in 1970 the comments of Chabás, reproduced his transcription, and chose 1245 as fitting the mass surrenders which King Jaume said Biar's surrender had precipitated. My *Islam*, reconstructing early Mudejar society, exploited the document as an illustration of Muslims being received into the Christian 'feudal' order.

245

Only after my doctoral student Jane Wilman drew the parchment to my attention again at the crown archives, as a striking exemplar of the bilingual charter, did I approach it as an integral whole, confronting the scandal of such conflicting dates, the new data in the Arabic, and the crucial interpretative context. It soon became clear that the Arabic is in many ways a different document, much more significant than the Castilian. For that reason, but also for its importance as a unique survival, my colleague Paul Chevedden has prepared a translation (below, in appendix 4), as well as a transcription of the original and an extensive stylistic study to appear separately. Since the Bofarull and Chabás transcriptions of the Romance suffer from eccentricities and a lapse or two, I provide my own copy in the same appendix.

Before taking up the content of each text, we must meet their subject, Abū ʿAbd Allāh Muḥammad b. Hudhayl, known as al-Azraq. The editor or the scribe in al-Azraq's 1250 letter to the queen erroneously closes the name as al-Shāhir b. al-Azraq, probably for *al-shāhir* (in place of *al-shahīr* or *al-maʿrūf*) *bi-'l-Azraq*. Our other protagonist, Jaume's son Prince Alfonso, will appear more fully below. Since al-Azraq and his fellow military adventurers in post-Almohad Spain might seem 'feudal,' instead of semi-autonomous rulers or perhaps administrative figures thrust into prominence by the collapse of central power, it will be useful at this point to consult the sections in chapter 1 on feudalism, on these local lords, and on castles in Valencia. These include the tradition of such local takeovers in the Maghrib and al-Andalus, the relation of such a ruler–lord to the local Islamic community, and the indications and evidence for such a development before and during the crusade there. In the case of al-Azraq, as we shall see, disappearance of any effective state or even hope of help thrust that independent role upon the local communities and on the leader they followed.

Whatever the extent of the phenomenon, and the extent therefore to which it facilitated Jaume's immediate take-over in 'feudal' guise, al-Azraq can serve as classic exemplar. We see him controlling a number of castle regions, negotiating his own diplomacy, disposing of agricultural rents on a public scale, and hiring armies with his wealth. The crusade's advance had eventually ensured his *de facto* autonomy, though circumstances suggest a longer tenure of public power. During the rebellion soon to come, as Jaume tells us, the other Muslim leaders in the Valencian kingdom recognized his power and skill: 'they made al-Azraq the leader (*cap*)' over all. During the crusade his influence centered on his castle al-Ḥamrā' or Alhambra in Pego and on his castle at Alcalá de la Jovada, with their many valleys and sub-castles, stretching west toward Alcoy, northwest toward the Albaida country, and south and east toward Altea, Callosa, and Jalón. After the surrender in our document, according to the contemporary Desclot, the Muslim would still hold 'ten strong castles.' By that time, reverses had counseled him to fall back farther into this triangular massif beyond the Denia seacoast; King Jaume says he then 'had his main residence (*alberg major*)' at Alcalá. al-Azraq may possibly have received his influence over this formidable tumble of mountains from his father Ibn Hudhayl during the post-Almohad chaos; he would pass its diminished Mudejar remnants on, not to his brothers Abū Saʿd (dead by 1263) and Bāsim, but to Abū Jaʿfar the son of Abū Saʿd. al-Azraq's own son, ʿAbd Allāh, disappears from sight early, possibly lost in action. In 1250 al-Azraq sent a mission to the queen of Aragon, consisting of a cousin Abū 'l-Ḥasan b. Hudhayl, the *qāʾid* Abū ʿUmar, and as head of the group his confidant Abū 'l-Qāsim b. Hilāl.

Like Játiva, Alcira, or Denia this mountain region was a recognizable unit or zone, loosely a dependency of Denia. It had witnessed the breakup of the Almohad empire and its Valencian waliate under Abū Zayd, the rise of the Murcian hero Ibn Hūd briefly to dominion over most of al-Andalus, the rally of Valencian sheiks around Zayyān of the local Banū Mardanīsh to seize Valencia city, and the ensuing civil war between all three Muslim rulers which precipitated the Christian crusade. The relatively independent blocs of Játiva, Alcira, and Denia tended to drift toward Murcian leadership, to the point where Castile's crusaders in Murcia could claim them as legitimate targets of their own crusade. As Murcia itself fell under Castilian control, Valencia's southern Muslims were isolated, between two rival crusades. Though lesser castle-sheiks haunted these southern mountains, al-Azraq towered above them. He could control the inland roads and threaten the coastal road down Jaume's new kingdom. A wily and charismatic leader, he maintained a salaried army, according to King Jaume; his wheat surpluses alone could finance independence or victory.

Less than three years after our charter, al-Azraq's revolt of 1247 would widen into a small countercrusade in 1248, and after a decade's unrest culminate in the Valencian rebellion of 1257–8. During that rising al-Azraq soon captured over a dozen castles, vanquished a crusader host of three thousand, ambushed and nearly killed Jaume, negotiated several times with Castile and secured tributary protection, and in the final bitter campaign lost sixteen castles to the king in a single week. Brought low by a bribed traitor, al-Azraq still managed to impose a negotiated peace in 1258, and rode into exile, some of his castles still in his family's hands. Two decades later he stormed back into the Valencian kingdom with the Morocco–Granada invasion forces of 1276, and fell as a martyr outside Alcoy in his native mountains. al-Azraq entered the *Cròniques dels reis d'Aragó* of Pere IV as the great 'captain' in Valencia to whom 'all the Saracens gave allegiance' until Jaume's successor 'King Pere killed him and his followers' (in fact Pere was not present nor even king yet). In Valencian folklore al-Azraq lived on as a bogeyman to threaten naughty children, his name transmogrified into 'dragon': 'El Drac will get you!' The citizens of Alcoy annually memorialize his defeat in the celebrated *Moros y Cristianos* mock battle and gala. A more personal memento is the Arabic document now in hand.[2]

THE TEXTS: IMAGES OF SELF

The Castilian interlinear comprises not one but two documents, the first speaking in the name of al-Azraq, the second being Alfonso's reply. In the first, al-Azraq appears as 'Habuadele Yuan Fudayl,' vizier and lord (*sen[y]or*) of Alcalá; the middle component of his name was not a Castilianate affectation 'Juan' as some thought but merely 'Aven' for 'ibn.' The Muslim here proclaims publicly that 'I make myself your vassal, lord Don Alfonso, first son of the king of Aragon.' He gives Prince Alfonso eight castles 'with their villages (*alcarias*) and jurisdictions,' their pasturage, and other unspecified rights. He turns over Pop and Tárbena castles immediately, retaining his family castles of Alcalá and Perpunchent permanently. He keeps the other four for three years only, giving half their revenues to Alfonso now, and all revenues and possession 'free and quit' when the three years end. A final provision licenses the Muslim to acquire more castles in the immediate future as part of the ongoing crusade: 'as many castles as I can win (*ganar*) from now on for three years.' For these also he must give 'half the revenues,' turning them over completely to Alfonso after three years.

Alfonso's counter-document within this Romance text describes him as 'the prince (*infant*), first son of the king of Aragon,' who 'receives you' as his 'cherished and very exalted and honored and faithful vassal.' The prince confers the two main castles on the Muslim's family for ever, 'to give, sell, pledge' or treat in any way. He also gives for three years the revenues of 'two villages (*alcarias*) Ebo and Tollos,' not named in the homage. Finally, Alfonso swears to abide by the agreement 'just as is written above' in the first Romance document, on condition that 'you be my vassal for the castle of Alcalá and for that which I give you.'

Surprisingly, the Arabic text is neither a translation of the Castilian nor the original for it. Though loosely a counterpart, it is a single document and it approaches the agreement in a different spirit. It contains no mention of vassalage, fidelity, personal obligation, or Islamic allegiance (*bay'a*), or obedience. The stance is objective, impersonal. The only concession to a relationship is an introductory phrase noting that this agreement is published as 'a noble decree ordered by the exalted prince' Alfonso and a context implicitly acknowledging that a tributary or clientage situation exists. In technical format it is not an Islamic treaty but rather a decree from the prince to an inferior. Nor is there any emphasis on a lasting arrangement, beyond the Muslim's keeping his own main castles for 'the duration of the reign of the exalted prince' and 'perpetually.' This is a simple 'agreement for three years.' It spells out those details which protect al-Azraq's rights. Even where content coincides with the Romance text, the Arabic presentation is more businesslike, its dominant note clarity. Arabesques are reserved to the exordium, briefly conceding honorifics which carry no obligation. By contrast, contemporary Arabic documents such as Zayyān's letters to Fernando of Castile are often incandescent with the usual honorifics, and rather indirect on business matters.[3]

One of al-Azraq's provisions reveals that he is negotiating from strength, retaining as in a truce the military *status quo*: 'property and retainers may remain' in all his castles until three years are up. After spelling out the loss of Pop and Tárbena 'which he will now hand over,' he retains 'Alcalá castle with its revenues and the revenues of the villages of Perpunchent' (the castle already mentioned must be indirectly included), and for three years the other four castles plus 'the revenues of Ebo and Tollos.' For the four castles, the Arabic version specifies revenue as 'the tenth (*al-'ushr*),' namely the classic Islamic tenth of agricultural produce. A particular novelty in the

Arabic is the agreement by Alfonso to give to 'the *qā'id* Abū Yaḥyā b. Abū Isḥāq, the lord [*ṣāḥib*] of Castell de Castells,' two villages in perpetuity. Since Castell is one of al-Azraq's castles, the provision may afford a glimpse of a Valencian military 'hierarchy': al-Azraq as main ruler and this newcomer (rescued here from anonymity) as subordinate in the Castell region and warden of its castle. On the other hand, the association with this *qā'id* with title of *ṣāḥib* may reveal a coordinate ally, ruler of the neighboring bloc.

Finally, the surrender is converted into an alliance: 'whatever castles (*ḥuṣūn*) the vizier obtains for the lord of Aragon, either by force or by capitulation, the vizier will have half the revenue' for three years, after which 'he will hand them over' to the prince. Here is a startling view of Jaume's mountain campaign at its midpoint: there are more than a few castles outside al-Azraq's immediate lordship which remain unsubdued, and they are significant enough to enter the treaty as a special proviso. Some of these al-Azraq hopes to bring over 'by their friendship' to capitulate; others can only be gained 'by force.' We now know that this item meant something different to Alfonso and to al-Azraq. Since al-Azraq was to revolt before the three years were up, in a well-orchestrated rising which would occupy King Jaume on and off for a decade, he has obviously planned to use these next two years in rallying his neighboring castle wardens and *aljamas* secretly to his cause. On the other hand, Alfonso just as obviously felt he had turned the lord of the mountains around, removing the keystone of the enemy's castle-system there. This explains why King Jaume's mountain crusade seemed to come to an end so swiftly, and why Valencia's region most formidably defended by nature as well as by a measure of the engineering arts seemed so meekly to have surrendered.

Other details may be gleaned from the Arabic. Islamic titles were a shifting screen designedly modest or ambiguous; only context can reveal a given authority's degree of power. I have treated the topic of Valencian Islamic titles elsewhere. Here it will only be necessary to note that al-Azraq's preferred title was 'vizier': 'the most illustrious *wazīr*, the noble, the highest, the most eminent, the most exalted.' Alfonso's text makes him 'vizier and lord of Alcalá,' *alguazil* (Catalan *alguatzir*) expressing the Arabic cognate. Unlike its meaning in the East as a kind of prime minister, the term in Spain at this time was an indiscriminate honorific, attached to no specific office; the vizier could be a bureaucrat, courtier, peace officer, governor, main minister (as at Murcia), or a class of administrators (as at Tortosa). Like the lords of Alcira and Crevillente (each using *ra'īs*) or the dynast of Játiva (as *qā'id*), the 'lord of Alcalá' had chosen a suitably modest equivalent for ruler. Nor did al-Azraq unfurl a vulgarly extended lineage with that title; he merely gave his *kunya* and his father's name, a combination echoing that of his warrior forebear here, Abū 'Abd Allāh b. Hudhayl.

As for the Christian party, 'Dūn Alfunshu' becomes in the Arabic 'the exalted prince (*al-malik*), the heroic, the most fortunate, he whose beneficence is hoped for and sought, the Infante [*alīfant* for *al-ifānt*].' He is the 'son of the exalted king (*al-malik*), the divinely assisted, the lord of Aragon.' King Jaume is thus *ṣāḥib Araghūn*, while both he and Alfonso share *malik*; but the latter term had long ago declined in Spain from meaning 'king' alone to vaguely designating local rulers, governors, or mere functionaries. What is significant is that King Jaume is associated in Alfonso's treaty. The Romance version makes a strong connection of its own: Alfonso supplies 'first son of the king of Aragon' in both his documents, and concludes his validation at the bottom with 'firstborn.' Does this echo his recent rebellion against his father, underlying the reconciliation and military association? Does it distance Jaume's new child Pere, the rival and firstborn of the king's legitimate marriage? Whatever its psychological impact, not too much should be made of its technical import; law and custom favored division of estate among nobiliary sons here, not primogeniture, a condition even more applicable to a congeries of realms. Still, as Jesús Lalinde Abadía notes, the thirteenth century saw an inchoate but irreversible orientation toward primogeniture, and Alfonso's Aragon must have reflected that trend more strongly than mercantile Catalonia. In al-Azraq's 1250 document alluded to above, introducing his own envoys while acknowledging the king's recent envoy Joan de Mur (*di Mūra*, not the editor's Juan de Mora), the Muslim leader wrote 'from the castle of Alcalá' and conceded to Jaume a wider title: 'sultan, king of the Christian lands and king of eastern al-Andalus,' namely eastern Islamic Spain (*malik al-Rūmīya wa-malik sharq al-Andalus*), reflecting the flattery of rebel politics.

THE TEXTS: PEOPLE AND PLACES

Witnesses to the charter reward attention. All are Christian magnates; the Islamic ruler had no need of nobiliary association. Alfonso's proud signum device is prominent, a combination of large circles around crosses framed by triangular offshoots. Five witnesses precede this validation, in doublets across the page. Pero Maza comes first, an Aragonese noble whom Jaume had once left as co-governor of conquered Majorca with another baron. Maza was with Jaume at Minorca's surrender, and more recently during the Játiva and Biar sieges. Though an Aragonese (a thoughtful touch in this post-rebellion moment), he was also Jaume's man. The Catalan Guillem Huc comes next, lord of Serrallonga, whose widow Geralda and son Bernat Huc would still be holding that castle in 1271. Guillem was to serve Jaume notably at the 1266 siege of Murcia. Pere Sans or Pedro Sánchez, whose final name here seems 'Gurren' (Chabás read Guerren), is Pero Sánchez Garín, royal butler for the kingdom of Aragon and lord of Sangurrín, modern Sangorrín north-west of Zaragoza. Starting the final doublet is Gombau 'the knight,' undoubtedly Gombau d'Entença (de Entenza), younger son of the magnate Bernat I lord of Entenza; Gombau had been with Jaume at Valencia city's surrender, and after al-Azraq's later defeat became lord of Torís in Alcalá Valley. In last place comes Ramon de Montpeller (modern Montpellier), a brother of the dispossessed Count Guillem IX, who will be found in the king's entourage in 1248 at Valencia city. The only signature irrecoverable is that of the scribe, which falls into the torn bottom of the manuscript. His validating signum emblem is clear and may afford a clue. Presumably he was from Alfonso's princely chancery, and had administered rather than drafted the Romance charter; Alfonso's documents have disappeared wholesale, while a cursory review of Jaume's parchments for these years does not turn up any duplicate signum for this scribe among the variety available.

The witnesses were a noble crew, in all, representing the sweep of Jaume's realms. They show that Jaume was well represented, and that Alfonso's was no isolated baronial adventure. The king's presence was not required, of course, even for a surrender to crown forces; Jaume was close by in the mountains, as we shall see, and he had sound reasons for sending a delegate. This was an act of confidence in and solidarity with his recently dissident son, as well as a handsome reward in vassalage. al-Azraq himself had Castilian sympathies, in any case, and had probably been in direct contact with this very Alfonso's rebellion in the previous year. Finally, the arrangement reflected a delicate military balance; al-Azraq was a long way from defeat. Jaume could not afford to stay in these mountains much longer, and certainly not for another half-year siege as at Valencia, Játiva, and Biar; pressing crises, as we shall see, were shaping in his wider world. By keeping in the background, Jaume patched up a swift and dazzling end to his crusade.

Like the people in the text, the castles invite analysis and comment. Simple identification poses problems. The Arabic text affixes no place for its drafting or execution, perhaps significantly; the Castilian presents its date line in Latin with the place as *Puteulum*, diminutive for a well (*puteus*). Its Catalan equivalent might be Puzol as a toponym derived from *pou* in the diminutive, or else Pouet. Chabás suggested the spot called 'El Poet,' about 400 paces south of Alcalá, whence water comes for Alcalá's *plaza*. This siting of the ceremony corresponds with other rituals of surrender, as at Valencia city where the crusaders erected a suburban pavilion for the signing.

The eight castles can be translated and located. Alcalá, the Arabic text's al-Qal'a, was al-Azraq's central Vall de Alcalá, with its capital and the Muslim's 'palace' at Alcalá de la Jovada. Castiel, the Arabic Qashtāl, is Castell de Castells (also Castells de Serrella), whose Islamic castle on nearby Penya del Castellet lies a near total ruin. Churolas, the Arabic text's Jurūlash or Jarūlash, is a problem. Chabás conjectured that it was Cairola, now a ghost town not far from some castle ruins in the Vall de Ebo. It is tempting to match it instead with the hamlet of Chirles (Xirles) in the Polop district. A more likely place is Cheroles, however, described by King Jaume both as 'the castle of Seta and Cheroles' and 'the castles of Seta and Cheroles with their districts.'[4] The etymological fit, its location in the Vall de Seta, and its abrupt appearance in Jaume's possession in spring 1258 when the defeated al-Azraq was going into exile, all support the identification. Gallinera, the Arabic text's Ghallinayra, is the Vall de Gallinera with its eight towns, its mighty castle at Benimarsoc, and its supporting castle at Benisilli. Margarita castle, the Arabic Marghalīṭa, is a peak-refuge near the present town of Margarida, close to the great castle of Planes. Borbunchen, Arabic Burbunjān, is Perpunchent near Lorcha in a valley of the Benicadell *sierra*; its castle ruins rear impressively today. Pop, the Arabic text's Būb, comprised a double castle on two peaks of a ridge dominating its Vall de Pop; King Pere in 1285 ordered it destroyed, but it would later become a major center of Morisco revolt. Tarbana, Arabic Ṭarbana, is Tárbena with its castle, today reduced to a tower and ruined walls. The village (*qarya*) of Ebo or Ābu (and Abu) corresponds to the Vall de Ebo. Tollo or Tūlu is the Toyllo listed in the crusaders' *Repartiment* as a hamlet under Seta; this is Tollos, a little zone or district south of Alcalá and east of Castell.

This leaves two places, introduced only in the Arabic text: the village (*qarya*) of Isbālam and the village of Baṭraqūsh, both given to Abū Yaḥyā 'the lord of Castell.' Baṭraqūsh would seem to be Petracos, probably a site near the plain of that name (where the Jalón River also bears the alternate name Petracos), or the gorge of that name in the Seta Valley near Famorca south of Tollos. It may have disappeared with time, like so many hamlets; it cannot be modern Pedreguer. Isbālam poses even more of a challenge. In 1250 Jaume's commission of barons and bishops met *apud Yspalim* to settle the Aragon–Catalonia boundary dispute, a locality which puzzled Miret. That *Hispalis*, from Greek Ἴσπαλις, was Seville; but its Arabic version was *Ishbīliya*. Some village deep in the Valencian mountains may once have echoed the grander *Hispalis*, and had its accusative form Arabized as Isbālam.

Most of these districts cluster in the triangle of massif which pushes the Valencian coast out to sea at Denia; they lie in its base or thickest hinterland in the regions called Marina Alta, Marina Baja, and El Condado. All remained Mudejar and then Morisco centers; all were difficult of access, while some (Ebo, Alcalá, and Laguart for example) had only a single valley entrance to guard. Displayed as a rough map of correlation, they appear in this order:

Perpunchent	Gallinera	Pego		to Denia
Margarida	Alcalá	Ebo	Laguart	→
	Tollos	Castell	Pop	
	Cheroles/Petracos		Tárbena	
			Polop	

The disposition reveals why al-Azraq was conceding Pop and Tárbena immediately, as nearest the coast and more vulnerable, with Jaume's forces in the Vall de Laguart isolating them. Equally revealing are the inland anchor positions of Alcalá and Perpunchent.

A final problem is the castle of Perpunchent. A trial record discussed in chapter 8 concluded: 'we are certain there had been no castle in Perpunchet in former [Islamic] times,' a finding drawn

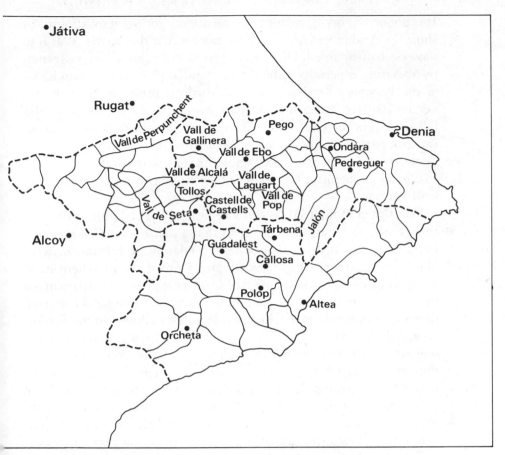

The final campaign: al-Azraq's territory and environs

from elderly Muslims of the area, and a finding upon which that bitter lawsuit was resolved. Islamic 'times' in that legal context meant the situation of a given locality at the moment of surrender. Our Romance text speaking in al-Azraq's name lists Perpunchent as one of eight 'castles' with its *terminus* and villages. Alfonso's portion of that text describes 'two castles, Alcalá and Perpunchent' as given permanently to al-Azraq, the phrase constituting in fact the meat of the prince's letter. The Arabic text lists Perpunchent as a castle (*ḥiṣn*) among the others being kept for three years; but strangely it then gives al-Azraq permanently only the *ḥiṣn* Alcalá with its revenues plus the revenues of the villages (*qurā*) of Perpunchent. If the scribe erred, *qurā* is a slip for *ḥiṣn*. If he deliberately omitted the second castle in this otherwise careful document, what became of it?

255

It is not on the list of castles to be eventually returned to Alfonso. In short the Arabic text neither keeps nor returns that castle. Was it to have been dismantled? Did the context already assume its possession by al-Azraq, especially if the scribe knew beforehand the provisions of the Romance version? Did the Muslims prefer to have the revenues stressed, as more vital than this perhaps refuge-type or else fall-back-type of local fort? Or was Perpunchent considered an integral part, an outpost, of the Alcalá defenses? Taking the Arabic alone, it seems probable (if arguable) that al-Azraq was to hold both castles in perpetuity; following either Romance text, he certainly kept them.

What then of the trial record's negation of an Islamic castle? All three of the al-Azraq texts are clear that a castle (*castielo, ḥiṣn*) stood here. Most Spanish castles, whether Islamic or European, were absurdly small and simple, as chapter 1 noted; Perpunchent must have been among the more negligible, since it does not turn up in the memoirs of Desclot, King Jaume, or Muntaner among the myriad defenses they touch on for the crusade and rebellions. In the *Repartiment*, only a single entry relates to Perpunchent, a group of twenty-one settlers, presumably the beginnings of the 'town' the king's documents mention. al-Azraq must have kept the castle during much of the coming decade of sporadic rebellion; it was in crown hands by at least the late 1250s. Guillem de Plana, a royal functionary, received a salary of 2,377 sous in March 1259 for his past custody of 'the castle.' Exactly a year later, Jaume gave 'the castle and town of Perpunchent' for life to Gil Garcés de Azagra, of Albarracín's ruling family, one of Jaume's main courtiers and crusading barons. Perpunchent became the centerpiece of Gil's personal fortune, so he arranged to have it put up for auction at his death in 1273, to provide his legacies. 'Many buyers' bid on the castle, the king writes, 'with its buildings, palisades (*palaciis* for *paliciis* ?), towers, walls (*muris*), defensive works, outer low-walls (*barbicanis*, not a mere gate defense here), stoneworks (*murallis*),' and with all the district, villages, mills, revenues, and inhabitants. The buyer, Ramon de Riusech, paid 67,000 Valencian sous, only to see the Perpunchent countryside explode in revolt three years later. The Hospitallers acquired it in 1289, and in 1319 the Templar groups which had survived as the order of Montesa. In all this history the castle evolved far from its simpler origins. Unless Azagra had been very busy during his decade's tenure, however, or unless the crown is describing Perpunchent in 1273 by rhetorical fancies, the original may have been militarily stronger than its documentary obscurity suggests.

Probably the *ḥiṣn* here had no fiscal–administrative role, nor even a military function until the outbreak of war. It could well have been a fall-back or reserve position, garrisoned only during rare danger in these out-of-the way mountains, perhaps not related to the scattered hamlets even as a refuge. In that case, our Romance text reflects the crusaders' perception of such contructions as militarily significant 'castles,' and perhaps al-Azraq's ambiguity toward a throwaway minor *ḥiṣn* which was not as important to him as the village revenues of the region which shared its name. Thus the Muslim witnesses in our boundary case persuaded the commissioners that their villages in this wild valley 'stood alone,' the *ḥiṣn* of the central state being 'no castle' to them, despite the terminology of our present document. al-Azraq's Arabic statement definitely posited villages whose revenues were part of the valley and unity called Perpunchent, an informal concept which need not have excluded the castle. The vital point here seems to be that no town or administrative entity centered the villages of this remote and difficult cul-de-sac, the rare administrative connections for these 'villages by themselves' being met *ex distantia* with extrinsic expedients by central authority.[5]

THE CALENDAR SCANDAL: 1244 OR 1245?

To situate the charter's content into its all-important context, the scandal of its contradictory dates must first be confronted and resolved. The Castilian text was 'given on the sixteenth day of April' in the era 1282. The Spanish era, normal dating for documents concerned with Aragon, was thirty-eight years later than the more common Christian era, yielding the equivalent date 1244. The Arabic text is just as clear: 'this was written on the fifteenth of the month of Dhū ['l-]Qaʿda in the year 642.' In Islam's lunar calendar of twelve months, alternating thirty and twenty-nine days, Dhū 'l-Qaʿda is the eleventh month. The Hijra year 642 began on Friday, 9 June 1244, when 160 days of the Christian calendar as reckoned today had elapsed; it ended on the equivalent of Sunday, 29 May 1245. Thus the fifteenth of Dhū 'l-Qaʿda must be translated as 15 April 1245; if the year is assimilated to 1244 by scribal error, leap-year intervenes to make this 14 April 1244. The date as it stands may

257

be translated with even more precision. Since an Islamic day began at sunset on the day before, the equivalence for the Arabic date is from about six o'clock on April 14 to the same time on April 15, or in terms of the working day squarely 15 April 1245. The contradiction between the Christian and Islamic dating of our charter is therefore double: 1244 versus the Arabic 1245, and 14 or better 15 April versus 16 April.

To choose one date over the other at whim is unconscionable. To prefer one while rejecting the other throws doubt on the document's validity. To suspect two unrelated documents is impossible, either from content and month or from the clumsy interlinear form; they both deal with the same castles of the same principals, according to the same time-schedule. To hypothesize a Romance version prepared a year earlier and saved for interlinear Arabic the next year is not only improbable in view of chancery practice but impossible because the contents are predicated upon the moment's military situation. Driven back in desperation upon scribal error, despite the solemnity of this surrender occasion, the obstacle arises that the date is not the usual administrative or convenient filing device but is itself vital to the text's substance, a timer for receiving and surrendering large revenues, as the body of the Arabic document makes clear 'from the present date which is stated at the end of the decree.' To assume that Islamic dates are careless, even if true for some chroniclers or later copyists, is most imprudent in the case of a formal charter and foolish in our case where revenues hang on just when this contract starts running. All doors seem closed. There is one way out, however, which can account for the day and the year, by which there was no error and the dates jibed.

The first question must be: if there was an error, which party was more likely to have made it? The Arabic version deserves more credence for several converging reasons. (1) If both texts really come from the same year, the Arabic is one to two days earlier. The Castilian thus becomes a posterior paraphrase, more likely to have translated the Arabic date than to have stated the current Christian year. This priority is buttressed by the very appearance of the two texts: the Arabic laid out in even unhurried lines, surrounded by the cramped Romance fitted in at topmost and bottom lines. The priority is also confirmed by the context of each version, the Romance being organized as two documents, each therefore shorter than the Arabic and necessarily omitting serious elements. (2) The date was more crucial for the Muslim party. The crusaders' version is essentially a document giving homage plus a document accepting it, with economic concessions added, so that the precise date is less relevant and a matter of less concern. The Arabic version is a no-nonsense business contract, assuming as is likely their collaboration in its drafting, adding important monetary specifics the Castilian text does not bother to include, all hinging on an exact time span. The Arabic expressly states this dependence on chronology as soon as the honorifics are over. Alfonso's first document mentions 'three years' only four times and toward the end of the statement; his second document gives the words twice but reductively as a single thought ('for those three years and after those three years'). The Arabic is built around its date; the Castilian, by its double form as much as by its content, focuses equally strongly on permanent vassalage. (3) Alfonso's date is by numerals, where the year differed from the previous or the coming year by a single small stroke of the pen in the Spanish era: MCCLXXXII. The Spanish era was clumsy anyway; and transposition of the lunar into the solar calendar, when the Islamic year traversed both Christian years 1244 and 1245, may have been a rare challenge for this particular scribe.

Scribal error by either party is a *deus ex machina*, however; the historian can do better. If the actual date was 1245, the two date lines can converge. If the actual happening transpired in 1244 no ingenuity can match the dates. In 1245 Easter Sunday fell precisely on 16 April, the very day of the Romance draft. (In 1244 it had been 3 April.) Assume that the Muslim scribe prepared the Arabic text the day before, as given, leaving space for the crusaders' interlinear text as well as for next day's witnesses and seals. The Arabic date then fits comfortably: 15 April 1245. The crusaders would then have waited overnight, reserving actual surrender and homage to Easter day itself. The pressure to do so would have been irresistible. The last days of Lent, especially Good Friday and the Saturday of the tomb, were no time which a planner would choose for any public ceremony. Heavy liturgical activity, but no Mass at all on the day of the fifteenth, at the end of a long season of fasting, made that day a time of melancholy. King Jaume expressed his low opinion of a bishop who dispensed soldiers in the field from the Lenten fast. Easter Sunday was a major solemnity, a time of joy, and a greater feast liturgically than Christmas. It was the perfect time for the last symbolic act of Jaume's long crusade; aside from a mop-up aided by al-Azraq himself, the war would formally end on the day of Christ's resurrection. Early morning Mass in the field, with its Te Deum and acclamations, would have been followed by the triumph of reconciliation and absorption of Muslims now become vassals. The whole war had ended, return home was imminent, victory was theirs and Christ's. Thus the discrepancy of days becomes natural.

The documents are still a year apart. Can this scenario unify them? Here it is important to remember that the medieval man knew many calendars and was sophisticated in their use. Calendar zones were as much a part of the traveler's or merchant's life then as time zones or foreign currency differences are to us. Alfonso the Learned, operating his Castilian troops along the Valencian border at this time, illustrates the phenomenon. In a prolog to his law code the *Siete partidas*, in a chronological note which seems to go back to his own early drafts, Alfonso dates his authorship by ten different calendars, including the Islamic, Hebraic, and Persian. In his astronomical tables, Alfonso gives no fewer than forty-five separate calculations to bring as many calendar differences into line. Until Jerry Craddock produced his critical edition of Alfonso's note in 1974, garbled copies had made it seem less accurate.[6] The chancellor directing our Castilian text may well have chosen a special calendar device, rare in these parts but for that very reason appropriate to this rare occasion of international importance. What choices faced him? Christian calendars began the year on a variety of days, depending on the region: 1 January (as with the Spanish era), 1 March, 25 March of the 'preceding' year, 25 March of the 'current' year (favored by crown documents in Valencia at this time), 1 September, and 25 December.

A calendar available, ancient in its form and still very popular in neighboring France, began the year on Easter Sunday – *anno a resurrectione*, or *anno a paschate domini*, or *mos gallicum*. By that calendar, the Arabic text would in Christian eyes have been drawn on the last day of Lent and of the year 1244 or era 1282; the Islamic date was thus equivalent to 1244 in one calendar, 1245 in another. The Romance text was drafted on the first day (16 April) of 1245 or era 1283. If one is to adduce scribal error (and I do not), here is another place for it. The two years are only a day apart, the new year is beginning this very day, the scribe is either forgetful (as we all are in writing the new year on its first morning) or else slips when transposing the unfamiliar Easter year and Islamic date into the princely chancery's traditional Spanish era. The error by one day issuing as different years would be petty and understandable. And one day's revenue in the general contract would have been a negligible matter on so joyous an occasion.

But it is not necessary to predicate even so small a margin of error. Alfonso's Christian scribe who had received the Arabic text on the day it was written, 15 April, would have placed the Romance script between its lines that same afternoon or evening so as to have the charter ready for signing on Easter morning. He would seem to be in 15 April 1244 by the Easter calendar but would have had to write down 16 April. Either of two reasons might explain this. Since actual signing would occur tomorrow morning, that was the only proper date for the official charter, whatever the Muslim scribe may already have done to fulfill the Muslims' part of the contract. al-Azraq's participation was finished except for his ceremonial presence; the witnesses would all be crusaders. There is also an alternative explanation simply from calendar technicality. At this period the vespers or vigil counted from Saturday noon as part of Easter Sunday; Alfonso the Learned employs this, for example, in his chronological note of 1256 just discussed. Alfonso's scribe or chancellor, accustomed to projecting himself forward a full year frequently when he dealt with crown documents, which often delayed starting the year until March, by the same reflex projected himself back into 1244 now as soon as he chose the calendar beginning on tomorrow's Easter. He then put down the only day possible: tomorrow's signing date and today's vigil date, *both* correctly 16 April. To be absolutely accurate, he ought to have written 16 April 1283, namely 1245, rather than mixing Saturday's 1244 with Easter Sunday's 1245 into the Spanish era. He may have mixed them deliberately, however, as a celebratory choice incorporating the anticipation involved in Lenten 1244 as well as the joyous night-vigil standing already for Easter day 1245. Custom involving charters from Aragon then forced him into stating this as an era year rather than expressing it openly as *in anno resurrectionis*. If the calendar mechanics did not follow this pattern, the historian must fall back upon scribal error in one of the ways suggested above.

1244 CONTEXT: YEAR OF CRISES

Even if the dates could not be made to coincide, or if the formalities of the two texts did not point to 1245 as the preferred choice in a deadlock, analysis of extrinsic events makes 1244 implausible as the date for Alfonso's activity and 1245 highly likely. Analysis of both years is necessary, in any event, to put the document into its context, thus greatly enlarging its historical meaning. Muslim authors say nothing about our episode, a humiliating but marginal event for them; King Jaume carefully says nothing, lest his public image tarnish. By April 1244, the date on the Castilian text, King Jaume's crusade had just reached a critical point in the mountains which formed Valencia's southern zone and practical limits. Alfonso the Learned, then only the heir of Castile, was pushing his own claims and conquest north out of tributary Murcia into that southern zone; his machinations particularly focused on the keystone Játiva. Jaume had thrown a siege army around Játiva in late 1243 and into 1244, meanwhile carrying on a war of nerves and reprisals against Castilian maneuvers in the neighborhood. Jaume had experienced one fright already in 1241 when Játiva, Alcira, and probably Denia had joined with Islamic Murcia to become briefly part of Hafsid Tunis. The nativist chaos which had succeeded that episode encouraged Castile to force tributary submission on most of Murcia in 1243 and to ambition taking southern Valencia up to and including Játiva. In early 1244, therefore, war with Castile was much more imminent than the fall of sturdy Játiva.

As if that were not enough, Jaume and his eldest son Alfonso were moving rapidly toward civil war. The prince, born in the 1220s, had been legitimated in 1228 when Jaume was having his marriage to his Castilian first wife annulled. Alfonso and his rejected mother had removed to Teruel in Aragon and perhaps for some time to Castile. Jaume's remarriage soon brought a second son, Pere, complicating the problem of succession and inheritance. In May 1243 a third son, Jaume, was born at Montpellier, making the succession question more urgent. In December 1243, at the parliament of Daroca, the king inaugurated Alfonso, now approaching adulthood, as heir to Aragon proper; while the siege of Játiva was going forward during the following month, however, King Jaume disastrously clarified his Daroca action by declaring large border areas to belong to Pere's share, Catalonia. Aragon's cities and nobles were thrown into turmoil; this soon spread over Valencia, as the Aragonese chose sides and took up arms. Civil war threatened. In February 1244 Alfonso placed himself at the head of a coalition rebel army at Calatayud, alongside such notables as the king's uncle Prince Ferran and Prince Pedro of Portugal.

With Castile supporting the rebels as well as maneuvering impressive army units on his Murcian flank, King Jaume agreed to negotiate Valencia's southern border. Absenting himself briefly from the Játiva siege, Jaume labored through stormy meetings with the Castilians to a comprehensive treaty of peace and alliance at nearby Almizra on March 26. Three weeks between the Almizra treaty and our al-Azraq charter allow no time for Jaume to canvass the dissidents in Aragon and Valencia, come to terms with the generalized situation of rebellion, conciliate his son Alfonso, and mount a serious invasion of al-Azraq's formidable domain. Besides, Jaume was locked in the siege of Játiva during that time and until mid-May; with all his resources, he was able to bring that war only to a compromise peace, which left the main castle for two years in Muslim control – more a truce than a victory. The al-Azraq episode does not fit into either Jaume's or Alfonso's schedule and preoccupations in 1244.

After Játiva had been neutralized in May, and with Castile an ally, Jaume doubtless did turn his attention to the Aragonese grievances. He was entering the final stage of his crusade, with glory and estates to offer the malcontents, and with the homage of the mountain castles to promise his son. The rebel Prince Pedro of Portugal was signing an amicable land swap with the king in August 1244; Alfonso entered an agreement with his father on another matter at Foyos in Valencia that September; and Prince Ferran actually fought at the king's side at the siege of Biar in these latter months. All these former rebels will turn up in the 1245 mountain wars. With Jaume in the field, serious solution to the boundary problem itself had to wait until a blue-ribbon commission of 1246, and for such clarifications as Jaume's boundary given to Alfonso along the Cinca River 'from the Alps [Pyrenees] down.' The prince, who led the rebels at Calatayud in 1244, would be at his father's side a year later, associated in a hero's role in the downfall of al-Azraq.

King Jaume drops from sight for over a week as May 1244 turned into June. He may still have been at Játiva, but his last documentary date line 'in the army at Játiva' is 22 May. He may already have moved to the coast, where his crusader admiral Carròs had just received the surrender of Denia on 11 May. Jaume surfaces in the Denia countryside on 6 June at the town of Ondara, and at Valencia city for the first three weeks of August. Both locales are significant and deserve reflection. Ondara stood on the right bank of the Girona

River; upstream at its origins in al-Azraq's headquarters valley of Alcalá, this river bore the very name Alcalá. It crossed the Muslim's valleys of Gallinera, Ebo, and Laguart before coming down on to the plains of Ondara and out to sea. Jaume was positioned therefore on al-Azraq's doorstep, though safely just outside the mountain fastness. Ondara itself was a walled town when Jaume first gave away lands to settlers in 1242 and 1244; it remained three-quarters Morisco until the seventeenth-century expulsion nearly destroyed it. Jaume's actions after the Játiva siege indicate that he was consolidating his recently conquered Denia coastland and planning to enter its mountainous hinterland.

At this point, during an August visit to Valencia city, a startling opportunity diverted him. Two Muslims journeyed there to offer surrender of Biar, 'the best castle of that frontier,' whose possession meant having 'that whole frontier,' according to King Jaume. Biar was the southwest anchor and farthest extreme of his Valencian kingdom. Its Muslims had witnessed the converging forces of Castile and Aragon in their neighborhood, as well as the consequent treaty at nearby Almizra which isolated them as belonging in Jaume's zone of conquest. When Jaume arrived there, however, the town rebuffed him. Without choice, he had to settle into a dogged siege, which was going forward by 5 September 1244 and ended at the beginning of February 1245 when Mūsā al-Murābiṭ gave in. At this point Jaume breaks off his extraordinarily detailed history of the Valencian crusade with a curt sentence: 'when the Muslims saw that I had Játiva and Biar, they surrendered to me all the rest of the kingdom from the Júcar River down to the land of Murcia,' on condition of staying as Mudejars. 'And so I had it all.' There is no hint of an invasion and campaign in the mountains. Not even the name of al-Azraq is mentioned.[7]

1245: THE MOUNTAIN CONTEXT

The interplay of circumstance in 1245 is much more crucial for understanding our document, and will demonstrate in turn how crucial is our document for revising our understanding of the still continuing crusade. This is not merely a matter of background, but of context which provides deeper meaning to a seemingly simple episode. This *annus mirabilis* in Jaume's life has not been closely examined. Historians of the crusade neglect it, as involving mostly anonymous, spontaneous surrenders, little more than administrative gestures after the collapse of real resistance or capacity for resistance. Historians of the realms of Aragon, though aware of French sources which give prominence to Jaume in international affairs this year, tend to follow Miret's rejection of this 'exaggeration.' Revising Miret's dating of the documents, however, Soldevila allows us to reopen the question of Jaume's role in southern France that year. Now the king's movements during each half of 1245 must be reconstructed in essential detail, and the two halves interrelated against the international background. The effect of this larger picture is astonishing.

King Jaume returned from the Biar siege to his headquarters at Valencia in February. Then he made a significant move. Date lines on his letters show him at 'Alaguar' from at least 15 March to 9 May. This Vall de Laguar(t) lay within al-Azraq's rocky domain, deeply past other centers of hostility. The king would not have penetrated there without his crusading host. It is highly unlikely that he would have risked repeating the Biar fiasco by accepting an invitation to receive al-Azraq's voluntary surrender. It is more unlikely that so powerful a leader would have conceded even a deceitful surrender except when confronted by a considerable show of force; the *qā'id* of Játiva had resisted such voluntary surrender because both 'Moors and Christians' would have considered it 'bad' or cowardly, while Christian knights would have despised his 'shame.' al-Azraq was to demonstrate during the next decade that he was more than equal to holding off Jaume's armies.

Laguart Valley held a castle, perhaps today the same as Fleix castle. When Jaume finally did recover it from the rebel al-Azraq over a decade later, he put its care and revenues in the custody of Carròs as bailiff. It proved sufficiently a military obstacle to hinder Jaume's son Pere when putting down the 1276 Mudejar revolt; after victory, Pere ordered 'that you tear down (*diruatis*) that castle, and cause it to be destroyed.' The valley now made a good base camp for Jaume to raid into the surrounding valleys such as Pego, Ebo, and Alcalá. So long a stay in so remote, dangerous, yet relatively less important valley suggests that Jaume was repeating his favorite strategy: enter a region in force, raid and intimidate component elements of its defensive castle-system, grant to lesser centers surrender on generous terms until the more powerful *aljamas* feel isolated, then bluff, negotiate, harry, but avoid major siege if possible, and finally persuade the more stubborn that timely surrender on the same generous terms is preferable to inevitable defeat and exile. If events took this course, with his son Alfonso accepting the main surrender, then Alfonso was obviously operating in tandem with Jaume. Miret i Sans puts Alfonso's half-brother and rival, the five-year-old Prince Pere, also on this campaign, since he seems to sign a charter but with his name in an inappropriately subordinate position; Soldevila notes that his 'P' must be an error for 'F,' Prince Ferran, who was indeed there.

Though the king's desire to conciliate Alfonso and the Aragonese sufficiently explains the prince's role in the surrender, other practical reasons counseled the same maneuver. al-Azraq probably preferred Alfonso as overlord, both as a friend of Castile like himself and as a buffer between him and the king. Even if al-Azraq's own course of action was ultimately a ruse, prudence would have caused him to act as though the short-term settlement might prove permanent. Similarly, the use of Castilian instead of the Latin usual in most surrenders can be explained by the normal routine of the prince's chancery; but it probably reflects as well Alfonso's personal background. Jaume's biographer Tourtoulon characterizes Alfonso as 'completely subject to the influence of Castile.' Miret calls him 'a Castilianized prince who never spoke nor even understood' Catalan. Whether the strongest influence on him was Castilian or Aragonese, Alfonso shared the predilection of his Castilian supporter Alfonso the Learned (both as heir and from 1252 as king of Castile) for Romance in official charters. A decade after our Alfonso's 1244 revolt, Jaume felt it necessary to exact from that son a promise not to support any Castilian attack.[8]

That Jaume did not leave Laguart after al-Azraq's surrender but remained there in the inhospitable mountains for weeks and probably for another month, fits the document's provision about al-Azraq gaining other castles now for himself in the name of the crusade. The royal host was needed as a threatening presence in this phase, though to al-Azraq it was all a charade. While waiting in the valley, Jaume conducted the kind of wrap-up business appropriate to a finished crusade. His surviving four documents of 9 May consist of (1) a long privilege allowing all in Valencia kingdom to sell or alienate their grants at will, despite contrary laws, and assuring them that no further surveys or audits would affect these holdings; (2) a tax exemption for all coming to settle Denia, the coast for this hinterland; (3) extension of Valencia's *Furs* code to the Denia region but also 'in the entire kingdom of Valencia'; and (4) a debt of 600 morabatins in connection with military ransom.

Sometime before he left the valley of Laguart, if we can judge from the time lapse, or possibly at Valencia as he was leaving for his northern realms, Jaume announced solemnly to the pope and the world that his crusade was victoriously over. On that auspicious occasion Jaume communicated his 'fervent desire that a university be established in the very city of Valencia, which will be extremely practical and regenerative, not only for inhabitants of the aforesaid kingdom but also for others.' The model here was the university of Toulouse, founded by Jaume's in-law Ramon VII, in the treaty which ended the Albigensian Crusade in 1229, 'to militate with peaceful doctrine.' Of Jaume's correspondence we have only Innocent IV's two replies from the ecumenical council of Lyons on 10 July, a month after Jaume vacated Valencia. The pope incorporates details of Jaume's plea and enthusiastically grants license for an international papal university. Both of Innocent's letters begin: 'With tremendous joy (*grandi gaudio*) the church exulted when the kingdom of Valencia was torn from the hands of the Saracens.' Writing on other business two weeks later, Innocent lauded Jaume as not only 'beloved of God among the other rulers of the world' but 'acclaimed by the publishing of your great praise among men'; just as Jaume's faith 'had flared forth into brilliant deeds up to the present, may it shine henceforth ever clearer.' To Jaume and his international audience, the Valencian crusade was finally and fully over.[9]

ANNUS MIRABILIS 1245: JAUME'S INTERNATIONAL STAGE

The traditional date for the crusade's completion, Biar's surrender, must thus yield to this final stubborn campaign in Valencia's mountain heart. The last surviving record from the crown, the period placed to a dozen years' fighting here, is this strange document. It becomes stranger still when placed in a broader international context. There is every reason to believe that the end of the crusade was *willed* by Jaume, an illusory victory patched up by the king because he could no longer afford to concentrate his attention in these remote mountains. Seen in this light, his treaty with al-Azraq was really a truce between two phases of a much longer crusade: the stubborn series of campaigns down into 1245, and the campaigns from 1247 to 1258 which Jaume tries to pass off in his memoirs as a later revolt. The king had announced to Christendom that his crusade was victoriously over. On a horizon of disasters, he stood out as an international hero; he could never afterwards admit that he had been made a fool, and that he had left the job half-done. He could never bring himself even to concede a role in the crusade to al-Azraq, except as a traitor in the subsequent revolt. Bitter at his humiliation, he could not mention al-Azraq in his memoirs except with uncharacteristic vindictiveness.

Had Jaume really believed during al-Azraq's surrender that the royal gamble would succeed? Doubtless he had every confidence. Jaume prided himself as a negotiator as well as a warrior. 'Cunning is better than force,' he wrote; and 'he who doesn't give what hurts, doesn't get what he wants.' Again, experience had showed him that such deals worked to his advantage. He had ended the five-month siege of Valencia city by granting a truce for many years and guaranteeing Zayyān security in nearby strongholds. He had ended the six-month siege of Játiva by accepting only the supporting castle, leaving the main *alcázar* in Muslim hands for two more years. To win Bairén, with 'all that valley' and castles, he had left its *qā'id* in the castle for seven more months, satisfied with only the Muslim's promise. Muslims had always kept their word to him in the matter of surrendering castles, Jaume tells us; there was no reason to think al-Azraq would act differently. Reinforcing this approach, and persuading the king to overlook his own weak position at the margin of the Muslim's domain, was the bare fact that Jaume had no time for a long siege. Even on conquered Majorca island, Jaume would have remembered keenly, last-ditch remnants 'in the hills' held out stubbornly 'all winter, into May'; they showed 'such great strength' that the crusaders 'could do no great damage to their persons,' but had to starve them into a negotiated surrender after a campaign lasting over a half-year. The siege of Biar had recently required nearly six months; as experience would later confirm, al-Azraq's tangle of mountain-castles would have demanded much more.[10]

It is time to review the international situation which was forcing the king's hand. At this precise moment he had an opportunity, if he moved fast and devoted close attention, to foil the French invader in southern France and reestablish the autonomy of his father's fiefs there. The Capetian hold on Occitania, validated especially by marriage, had become tenuous. True, attempts to dislodge the French by force had just failed. Viscount Ramon Trencavel had led an invasion out of King Jaume's realms in 1240, regaining Carcassonne and other territories, but was roundly defeated. With Jaume's connivance Count Ramon VII of Toulouse and King Henry III of England then led an international coalition against the French in 1242; this enterprise eventually collapsed, with treaties drawn in January and April 1243. Where arms had failed, however, marriage now promised victory. King Jaume, the count of Toulouse, and Jaume's cousin Count Ramon Berenguer of Provence maneuvered to marry Toulouse to the designated heiress of Provence, Beatriu. A child of such a marriage would void the French treaties, and recreate an independent Occitania.

The count of Toulouse first needed a divorce from Jaume's aunt, and then a dispensation to marry his own niece. As a preliminary, Ramon VII of Toulouse cultivated the new pope Innocent IV, was relieved of all ecclesiastical censures still clinging from the Albigensian wars, and secured his hold over Toulouse as well as winning from Emperor Frederick II the title Marquis of Provence. Indeed the count became arbiter between pope and emperor until Innocent fled to Lyons in 1244. The marriage plan would be formalized there in May 1245, with the pope resisting French and Castilian pressure to block the dispensations. Meanwhile in mid-1244 Innocent had fled Rome and his enemy Emperor Frederick II, and from Genoa had sought asylum with King Jaume. The king suggested Montpellier as suitable. (The English historian Matthew Paris, always malicious toward Innocent, incorrectly has Jaume refuse the pope hospitality.) Delayed by illness, the pope instead took up residence in early December 1244 at nominally imperial Lyons in the Rhone Valley, where he called for an ecumenical council of Christendom's prelates and princes to convene in May 1245. The fate of southern France was on its hidden agenda. The months after the council would suffice for the formalities of divorce-dispensation investigations. As early as September 1244 Jaume wrote from Valencia to congratulate the pope on his escape to southern France, and promised to visit him there soon.

Another problem preoccupying Jaume in early 1245 was his contest with Castile for control of the Valencian church; after losing the ecclesiastical trial in Navarre in 1240, Jaume had appealed to Rome, where Cardinal Sinibaldo de' Fieschi in July 1243 initiated a new trial. Sinibaldo then became the very Innocent IV who fled to Lyons. No details survive of the political settlement which now gave Jaume control of Valencia's ecclesiastical establishment; the Almizra treaty in March 1244 may have cleared the way, but the intrigues at and after the council of Lyons seem the likely locus. These affairs and indeed all his non-Valencian business had languished for twenty months – nearly two years – while Jaume stubbornly concentrated on his distant Valencian wars. The only time he left that war-torn frontier during that stretch of time was for flying visits to Daroca and Barcelona in connection with his son Alfonso's succession crisis. A personalized set of realms like Jaume's, but especially the challenges and opportunities of a world turned upside-down, demanded his personal activity in the north.

A wider world of affairs also called to Jaume that year, affairs pertaining to his obsession with glory. He had a chance to lead a great crusade to the East, and in the event he did take the cross at this time. In Jaume's own field of expertise, crusading, Christendom had gone from fiasco to disaster. The embarrassing crusade of Frederick II and the confused crusade by the count of Champagne and the earl of Cornwall had made a few gains in 1241. But in July 1244 Jerusalem was definitively and for ever snatched from Christendom, while in October the host of the crusader states went down to defeat near Gaza. An overriding concern at the ecumenical council at Lyons in 1245 was to secure the remaining coastal beachheads and to mount a crusade. In December 1244 Louis IX of France, Jaume's arch-rival and threat to his interests, had announced he would help lead that crusade. When Pope Innocent's formal invitation to Jaume to rescue Jerusalem arrived in January 1245, Jaume was finishing the siege of Biar and still had al-Azraq's mountains with which to contend. Similarly the king had to set aside for the moment his January invitation to the council. Jaume was also concerned to have the crusade exempt his client Tunis from attack (such as King Louis' crusade of 1270 would in fact mount); he did not broach this request until after the council, receiving from the pope a strong negative reply in July 1246.

Since the French king meant to recover Jerusalem by attacking Egypt, and very nearly succeeded during this ultimately disastrous Crusade against Damietta, Jaume may already have targeted his own more glamorous crusading goal. Of the 'Five Wounds' of

Christendom which the Lyons council addressed in mid-1245, the loss of Jerusalem was only one. Equally critical was the imminent conquest of Latin Constantinople by an expanding Greek empire of Nicaea. The Latin emperor himself, Baldwin II, dramatized this crisis by his position at the pope's side during Innocent's address opening the council. Some months later, at the beginning of 1246, Jaume announced he was taking the cross and committing his realms to saving Byzantium as the road to Jerusalem. The pope awarded him the Holy Land indulgences and of course international financing. When al-Azraq's revolt intervened, an embarrassed Jaume had to seek papal commutation from these vows.

Another of the Five Wounds demanding the attention of princes at the council was the horrendous invasion by the Mongols, the most serious external threat European Christendom had ever faced. In 1241–2, with Russia already under their yoke, the hordes had ravaged Poland and Hungary (homeland of Jaume's queen), destroyed an international army, and raided both the Adriatic coast and the environs of Vienna. From Lyons in early 1245, as the menace hung poised over central Europe, Pope Innocent dispatched the first of the major Mongol missions to gather intelligence and to open communication. In all such crises, who was 'more worthy' to respond as Christendom's leader, in the words of the troubadour Olivier lo Templier two decades later, than 'you who have conquered from Tortosa to Biar, and Majorca'? Since he was 'in all the world the most valiant in deeds of arms,' the song continued, 'King Yacme with a third of his forces' could set affairs right in the East. Jaume could not run to meet this destiny, of course, until he had neutralized the lordling al-Azraq.

Thus the months from early June 1245, when he left the kingdom of Valencia, to December 1245 were of transcendent importance to the ambitious king. He did not play an open role at the council, as he was to do so strikingly at the second council of Lyons a quarter-century later. He remained within Catalonia while his procurators and proxies worked overtly. For two weeks after leaving Valencia he stayed in the Tarragona district, in contact with the metropolitan of his realms there, who would shortly leave for the council. The counts of Toulouse and Provence were also personally at Lyons. Spanish bishops, including Jaume's crusader bishop of Barcelona, were the most active single group at the council. A letter from Innocent to Jaume reveals the presence also of 'Eximen Pérez your special envoy' there. The likeliest identification is Jimeno Pérez de Tarazona, governor of Valencia city in 1240 and later procurator general of the Valencian kingdom, better known by his Valencian title Arenós. The inseparable companion and military ally of the ex-*walī* of Valencia Abū Zayd, he has already appeared in chapter 9 as a professional Roman lawyer, whose son and daughter married respectively the daughter and son of Abū Zayd. A hero of the crusade from its earliest moment, this knight would have been a striking advertisement to the king's crusader achievements.

We cannot be sure that Jaume did not venture into southern France during the July and August months of the council itself, since he drops from sight then. (His possible appearance on 29 July at Lérida rests on a Mercedarian charter, a genre notoriously untrustworthy.) On 13 September he finally appears signing a decree at Barcelona, organizing that city's administration; but even that stay may have been a flying visit down from Roussillon. Charter date lines do show him in southern France at Perpignan, in the latter part of October. Soldevila argues that he made his headquarters there until nearly June of 1246, and dismisses as a calendar confusion Miret's notice of an apparent return briefly to Valencia in early 1246. These dates, and their lacunae, are important for interpreting other evidence for Jaume's actions in summer and fall 1245. How had the plot to reestablish Occitania progressed?

HIDDEN HISTORY: LOSS OF PROVENCE, DREAM OF BYZANTIUM

The count of Toulouse did win his annulment on 25 September, but by then affairs had taken a disastrous turn. The count of Provence, father of the bride, had just died on 19 August 1245 while returning from the council. The French court blocked the processing of Toulouse's added dispensation, while it maneuvered for a dispensation of its own to marry the heiress Beatriu to the French king's brother, the vaultingly ambitious Charles of Anjou. Jaume had to take direct action. He believed himself to have become now the legal male heir to Provence, and considered Beatriu his ward. According to the French chronicler Guillaume de Nangis, echoed later by Matthew Paris, Jaume led troops to abduct Beatriu at Aix-en-Provence. With Soldevila's destruction of Miret's chronological problems over this episode, it can now be reconstructed in depth.

The materials lie at hand among the neglected papal bulls in Jaume's archives, strangely not consulted by Soldevila or others who touch on the problem. As Jaume was sieging Biar in January 1245, Pope Innocent IV sent a circular from Lyons inviting him to the proposed crusade in the Holy Land. An accompanying letter revealed to the king that 'we plan to travel soon beyond the mountains; and if we pass by your lands, we desire to see you personally' and to offer assistance in Jaume's current difficulties with Barcelona's bishop 'as also in other affairs which involve your highness.' Jaume had little hope of disengaging from his crusade long enough for such a visit, but he immediately responded by sending an embassy under the Provençal Huc de Forcalquier, master of the Hospitallers in Aragon and Catalonia. Innocent's further response in mid-February gratefully acknowledged that 'you had made preparations to receive us and all our household with all reverence and honor,' an act in accord with Jaume's 'extraordinary devotion to the Roman church.' The pope may have had in mind Jaume's agreement in 1239 after Valencia city's fall, to lead his armies for the Guelph cause against the Hohenstaufens in Italy, as well as his current crusading fame.

There is no need to dwell on the progress of the council, on the unexpected death of the count of Toulouse in August, or on the ominous delay in the dispensation needed by the count. We can instead take up directly those papal bulls that afford both confirmation and details of Jaume's rash raid into Provence. On 11 November 1245 Innocent wrote the king how he 'had received with pleasure into our presence recently [our] beloved sons, your notary Guillem de Bell·lloc and the knight Pere de Vilaregut, sent by your highness.' Bell·lloc or Belloch was a university doctor-of-laws and 'citizen of Valencia' currently serving as a subchief of the royal chancery. The pope had 'diligently' examined the contents of the letters these two presented, as well as 'what these envoys desired to propose in your name.' They 'recounted' how Jaume had attempted to force an entrance into Provence 'under arms,' and 'had suffered grievously' when his maneuver was 'blocked' by unnamed 'others entering Provence with an armed corps.' Since the pope favored Jaume above 'the other kings and princes of the world,' he was distressed to see him dishonored by usurpers of his rights. 'Immediately upon hearing' the envoys' complaint, Innocent directed his reforming legate in those parts to see that 'those who invaded that land under arms' leave without delay, 'so that your rights be preserved unbroken.' 'If perchance they scorn obeying the order,' the pope recommended that Jaume override obstacles and employ 'any licit means you can to defend your rights.'

Two days after Jaume's envoys left Lyons with their charter of unqualified support, additional dismaying news reached the pope. Ecclesiastical authorities had excommunicated King Jaume! Probably this was the work of that same archbishop of Lyons who was to preside later at Beatriu's marriage to Charles of Anjou. Innocent reacted swiftly, drafting and executing his countermandate that same day and sending it off to the king. The pope explained how he had only just now heard 'the news of the excommunication.' He 'did not send you this letter through your envoys, who had recently left our presence, because [the news] was not known by us while they were here'; but 'immediately after they left,' Innocent 'took care to send this off to you.' The papal remedy was drastic. Proclaiming his contrary intention 'to honor you as a special son of the Roman church and loyal in everything' and 'as a sign of special favor,' he 'thoroughly revoked' any excommunication 'against your person during a two-year period without our special mandate.' The odd time-limit allowed for completion of Jaume's Occitan plans.

These two documents of 11 and 13 November establish the chronology of Jaume's raid into Provence. Date lines of his other surviving documents place him at Perpignan from 22 through 26 October; by 29 October he had travelled up to Salses, a coastal castle just south of Narbonne. He could easily have been in Montpellier by the last day of October, since he was able in 1258 to hurry the entire distance from Perpignan to Montpellier in less than two days. A fast galley could have carried a raiding party to the Rhone, but Emperor Frederick II had a fleet of twenty galleys standing off the Provençal coast as part of his own son's bid for Beatriu's hand. The overland rush to Aix-en-Provence would not have taken long, perhaps four or five days. The pope's letter of Monday 13 November describes Jaume's force as 'blocked' when it entered Provence or perhaps 'foiled' (*interdictum*). This might mean that his rightful progression was threatened, forcing withdrawal, or that he had reached his target area but prudently withdrew; he may have reached any point between the Provençal border and Aix, and indeed he may slyly have concealed from the pope more active details of aggressive action and bloodshed.

By the time the story reached the contemporary chronicler

Matthew Paris in England, the protagonist was 'a noble' of Provence, poor in lands but 'valiant and powerful in military matters,' who carried Beatriu to a nearby castle, which he then had to defend against both her relatives and her party. A 'tumultuous struggle, bitter and ruinous' ensued until the king of France intervened. The thirteenth-century monk Guillaume de Nangis, in his bilingual (Latin and French) biography of Louis IX describes how the French king traveled to Lyons after the council, out of a 'burning desire to see' Pope Innocent. The king had assembled for this trip 'no small multitude of the soldiery of the kingdom' for proper display. The French text sets the meeting at Cluny, which may represent a delay and diversion of the king's visit later that month. Whatever the chronology that November, King Louis had gone surrounded by a hundred knights, a hundred esquires, a hundred crossbowmen, and a hundred men-at-arms. Thus the French had 'an incredible and glorious multitude of knights' in or near the Rhone Valley just as King Jaume was about to make his move in early November. It is difficult to think that the French had moved so daunting a force toward the imperial territory of the Rhone out of an innocent desire to impress the pope. About to return home, says Nangis, Louis heard that 'the king of Aragon had surrounded Beatriu with a well-equipped army [in the French 'a large host'] and had shamelessly put her under siege': 'armato circumvenerat exercitu, et obsederat impudenter.'

Louis now dispatched a large part of his Lyons army (*partem copiosam*) to free Beatriu by force. 'The affair for which the knights had been assigned was brought to conclusion against the king of Aragon powerfully and swiftly.' Nangis has Louis only now conceive the idea of marrying his brother Charles of Anjou to the Provençal heiress, opening negotiations toward this end, and then sending Charles to the marriage 'with a display [*venustas*] of innumerable soldiers' into Provence. The French historian may be exaggerating Jaume's force, and elevating his action into a considerable siege, to glorify King Louis. Set against the papal documents in Jaume's archives, however, the essential skeleton of the story stands clear. Joined with Matthew's more gossipy account, it would seem that Jaume rushed a raiding force toward Aix-en-Provence, perhaps conscious of King Louis' more elaborate force going into Lyons. By Jaume's account he might seem not to have actually reached Beatriu; by Matthew's he bore her off to a castle; by Guillaume's he besieged her. Jaume's force must have been relatively small, since it was unable to confront the French army and retreated. No further details of this 'seizure' can be gleaned from the poem of Guillaume Guiart, who included the episode in his *Branche des royaux lignages* in 1306. What was Jaume's timetable in this project? Allowing four or five days for Jaume's embassy of protest to reach Lyons and to extract the letter supporting his claims, Jaume's raid would probably have reached Aix by the weekend of Saturday 4 November, presented its claims or executed its minatory maneuvers on the next day or so, and then precipitately have pulled back perhaps on Tuesday as the envoys dashed north.

Time was now running out for Jaume. Toulouse's second dispensation had aborted, and the hapless Toulouse himself was adrift alone in Provence, appealing for diplomatic support. The pro-French faction, which included Beatriu's widowed mother, had possession of the heiress. And Angevin troops had arrived. The obvious final ploy for Jaume was to marry one of his sons to Beatriu, working through his champion the pope (who could not have been enthusiastic over the previously projected marriage of Toulouse, a former foe of papal aims). A scant two months had passed since the armed confrontation, when both factions again moved into action almost simultaneously. On 24 January of the new year Innocent acknowledged the arrival of Jaume's envoy and letter proposing 'marriage between your son' and Beatriu; this son was surely Alfonso rather than the small child Pere, but the king may ambiguously have left his options open. The pope 'rejoiced with high elation at this solution' until, as before, bad news followed. 'Afterwards we understood that the noble Charles, brother of the king of France, went into Provence to espouse the same woman.' Innocent did not think this could have happened 'without that woman's will and consent.' Now he 'feared lest by this action the affair of your son may be prevented, since it would not be easy to oppose Charles in this.' Innocent pleaded with Jaume 'not to show yourself so upset over this, even though it may not be acceptable to you, as to take action rashly in the heat of anger,' or 'to do anything which might (far be it!) cause harm (*dispendium*).' He urged the king to have recourse to 'diligent deliberation,' secure in the knowledge that the pope was 'prepared and ready to accede willingly to your wishes about this,' since he considered Jaume 'the principal defender of the church among the other kings and princes of earth.' A week after this letter left Lyons, Charles of Anjou on 31

January 1246 hurriedly married Beatriu. Charles, 'angered' at the improvised or unsuitably simple nature of the celebration, according to Matthew Paris, 'muttered' during it about the lack of 'pomp' due to 'worldly high birth.'

The blow to Jaume's pride and international reputation was severe, on the very morrow of his announcing the end of his Valencian crusade. He needed to regain momentum as the premier champion of Christendom. Falling back to Valencia, the scene and symbol of his triumphs, he elaborated a project to lead his own crusade to rescue the foundering Latin empire of Constantinople. On 18 March Innocent approved Jaume's plans 'to cross the sea in support of the Empire of Romania [Byzantium],' offering 'the indulgence given to crusaders going to help the Holy Land' as well as interim papal protection for Jaume's kingdom. This enterprise too would abort, as al-Azraq rose from the buried past to contest the king's hold on Valencia in 1247.

In all this hidden history, the gossiping chroniclers were closer to the truth than the modern historians who rejected or selectively followed them. Without having seen these papal bulls, Miret i Sans led a generation into the belief that Jaume could not have been in southern France for much of this time. Soldevila reversed Miret's chronology but remained skeptical about the raid, preferring to think Jaume schemed from the sidelines. The older French historians followed the French chronicler Guillaume de Nangis; but Tourtoulon, and moderns generally, including Soldevila, reject that chronicler's report that Jaume tried to marry a son to Beatriu. As Soldevila argues: why now and not before; why the support for Toulouse then, and not for his own son; and how could he hope to overcome the close family relationship between his son and Beatriu? Historians seem not to have known also of Jaume's Byzantine crusade-project, as they have not known about his title as papal admiral and captain general seen above in chapter 4. Thus Jaume's papal bulls reveal definitively the larger Jaume, the champion of Christendom who could not be patient in the confines of al-Azraq's mountains, the autobiographer who slyly kept these failures from the pages of his memoirs, a Don Quixote of almost-possible dreams. If Jaume's Occitan and Byzantine projects have their essential documentation in these bulls, however, so by context and implication does the final chapter of his Valencian crusade.

The year 1246 was not to be a good one for Jaume. Even as he prepared for his Byzantine spectacular, Jaume, in a fit of anger at his Dominican friend the bishop of Gerona Berenguer de Castellbisbal, ordered the latter's tongue to be cut out. Pope Innocent upbraided Jaume in June: 'our mind is stunned by the enormity of the crime.' John Tolet in England wrote that 'Spain is raging to the extent of cutting out the tongues of bishops.' Jaume's fame, for the Valencian crusade presumably finished during the past year, supported him in these months of excommunication and penance. Matthew Paris explains how the pope and Christian community accepted his repentance, 'because he had so loyally waged war against the Spanish Saracens (*Hispanos Sarracenos*) and gloriously had triumphed.' As for southern France, a decade's unwonted peace now descended between France and the realms of Aragon, from 1245 to 1254; as Jordan notes, 'the importance of this interlude cannot be ignored.' Another crisis would then blow up, the princes Pere and Jaume would lead an invasion of France, and in 1258 the treaty of Corbeil would end for ever the interests of Jaume's dynasty over most of Occitania. From Francia and Occitania the present France would emerge; when circumstances presented an opportunity for intrusion by the realms of Aragon in 1271, King Jaume was to forbid Prince Pere to yield to that temptation. The year of decision had been 1245. Only chance had snatched victory that year from Jaume and his two counts. With such heady international intrigues, a prize so precious, and this culmination of all his previous maneuvers in the wars of southern France promising final success, al-Azraq's mountain hinterland must have seemed a trifling matter.[11]

AL-AZRAQ TRAPPED: JAUME'S MEMOIRS BREAK OFF

What of al-Azraq's own context in early 1245? Everything conspired to encourage a truce with the Christian invaders. After years of turmoil and opportunity, with the political scene kaleidoscopically shifting, Maghribian politics had simplified. Options were few and movement minimal. To his north and east, Játiva had made its separate peace, its lesser citadel now garrisoned by crusaders. Along his Denia coast and lowlands, Jaume had broken this last of Valencia's major regional powers. To the south the Biar–Castalla border castles had collapsed. Wherever he looked, al-Azraq's mountain region was surrounded by crusader conquests. Murcia, farther south, so long the hope and bulwark of al-Andalus in this generation, had panicked before the advance of Castile, Aragon, and especially Granada; by the treaty of Alcaraz in spring 1243 Murcia made itself a client state of Castile, accepted crusader garrisons, and loaned its armies to help subdue dissident local areas.

The other regions of Islamic Spain had been collapsing with dismal regularity before King Fernando's advance – a roll call of cities and castles from 1243 through 1245. Ibn al-Aḥmar was establishing Nasrid Granada, but his realm was still embryonic, its glories in the far future. In late 1244 and early 1245 Granada saw its fringes erode under crusader waves and its bulwark Jaén ever more desperately isolated. By the beginning of April 1245, the very month of al-Azraq's treaty, Castile launched the special raids designed to culminate in the formal siege of Jaén from August 1245. Surrounded by its enemies, Almohad Africa and Castile, Granada could only look forward to the lesser evil it finally chose: to gain time Ibn al-Aḥmar bound himself as the vassal of Fernando and made Granada tributary to Castile, signing away half his rents and sending troops to help the crusaders.

Wider Islam was hardly less desperate. No help could come from Almohad Morocco, locked in war with its Marinid rivals; a great victory for the Almohads near Fez in 1244 merely triggered renewed Marinid advance in 1245. Soundest of all the North African fragments, Hafsid Tunis was the last hope of Spanish Muslims. Besieged Valencia had appealed there for help and had received a token fleet; Zayyān's Murcian realm had made it their anchor; Granada was under its aegis; Seville and Jerez looked to its aid. But the Hafsid ruler had turned instead to rapprochement with Jaume the Conqueror, signing a political–commercial treaty in 1240 or 1241, ratified by Pope Gregory IX in April 1241. In a dance of embassies and negotiations from now until 1246, Tunis evolved into a semi-client and protectorate of Jaume. al-Azraq, like his neighbors Játiva, Murcia, and Granada, could only feign vassalage status and regroup against a day of changed circumstance.[12]

Jaume himself began the tradition of ignoring or downplaying the final year of the crusade. His memoirs pass over the siege of Biar only briefly, because 'it would make too long a report'; and he dismisses all that follows, as we have seen, in a single sentence. Historians naturally follow him in assuming a wave of panicky 'spontaneous surrenders,' in Tourtoulon's phrase, by nameless and unimportant chieftains in a pattern of no consequence. Our document, even in the accessible Castilian, is virtually ignored for understanding the crusade, and anyway would have seemed to apply to 1244. Jaume's own charters say little of Valencia in 1245. From Zurita and Tourtoulon to Soldevila and Ubieto, the royal lead has misled.

Why did Jaume's autobiography brush aside the campaign of that spring in 1245? The answer seems clear. His memoirs are a labor of self-love, focusing narrowly on his military 'deeds' and victories. He carefully omits real failures at arms, such as his abortive invasion of Valencia by a siege of Peñíscola in 1225. By the time he dictated his book, hindsight made it all too obvious that al-Azraq had been cleverer than the king in 1245, that he had played at surrender, and that Jaume had accepted the collapse of this vital region with precipitate overconfidence and without the usual safeguards and garrisons. Worse yet, al-Azraq fooled the king again, this time nearly terminally, during the revolt he subsequently raised. al-Azraq 'came to me' and said he wanted to become a Christian and to marry a relative of Carròs the lord of Denia. Jaume trustingly rode to al-Azraq's castle of Rugat, where his small party was savagely ambushed and the king himself nearly killed. 'No Saracen ever broke faith with me,' declares Jaume, 'except al-Azraq in the affair of Rugat.' Jaume does describe the long, slogging war by which he then mastered these mountains and negotiated al-Azraq into exile. But he so telescopes the action that chronology is obscured and the revolts seem an episode independent of the crusade. The king mentions al-Azraq now for the first time, giving him the prime role throughout that revolt, always speaking of him as doomed to defeat by the valiant Jaume. His chancery documents scorn the Muslim as 'al-Azraq our traitor' and 'al-Azraq our betrayer.' The king's disdain and outrage burst out in his boast: 'I had taken from al-Azraq everything he owned, and I had thrown him out of my country.' This was the campaign Jaume should have mounted, had circumstances permitted, in 1245.

Understanding all this, we are in a position to solve an outstanding literary mystery. The king's autobiography, so influential in the development of Catalan literature, loses its artistic integrity at precisely this point. In form as well as content the post-Biar years represent an enormous gap. The narrative breaks off for the ensuing two decades, in effect, with only a scattering of ill-coordinated data; it picks up the thread of action again after that interval. This inexplicable break has led literary scholars to posit two great stages of composition, the first at Játiva in 1244 (with redactive improvements to 1252), and the second at Barcelona in 1274. Each stage may have had an inner stage as well, respectively around 1230 and 1270. Miquel Coll i Alentorn, in a recent summation of this consensus, notes that the first of the two 'great stages' ends with the fall of Biar and general collapse of the Muslims in chapter 360; what follows is 'a long lacuna of nineteen years (from 1245 to 1264), for which no more appears than a few notices, disorganized and incoherent, about the revolt of al-Azraq.' The king's book mirrors his life at that stage: collapse of all his plans, cover-up before the world, grim coping with al-Azraq behind the façade of normality, insistence that the continuing war was an inconsequential epilog, wild talk of exiling all Valencia's Muslims, and continuance in fact of a crusade which now dare not speak its name. This was no time for self-glorifying memoirs; real life had burst the fantasy asunder and had demoralized the king as editor of his own life. Thus the year 1245, obviously crucial in the history of Mediterranean Spain, also furnishes the clue by which we can finally understand the basic structure of this great work of literature.[13]

TWO CULTURES: THE *DHIMMA* OPPRESSION

Confronting the Arabic and Castilian texts, we confront two kinds of rulers, two mentalities, two cultures. Alfonso is welcoming the Muslim into the Christian 'feudal' world. Whether from expediency alone or a common model of surrender, or friendship and respect between two Castilophiles, he is generous. Most of the Muslim's current holdings and garrisons stay in place for three years, and his family is confirmed in power at his two main territories. Alfonso acts indifferent to prosaic details, summing them swiftly with princely disdain for haggling minutiae. His hailing of al-Azraq as 'beloved, high, honored, and faithful' seems more than honorifics, precisely because the brevity of the text throws the exordium into relief and because the tone and purpose are personal rather than aimed at business. The document is as much King Jaume's as his son's, as is shown by the persons who witness it, the presence of the king nearby at Laguart, and al-Azraq's acknowledgement in the Arabic. That consideration elevates the welcome, and gives its generous terms a more universal frame.

King Jaume was not receiving his first Muslim vassal but one of a long series. In 1236 the Almohad *wālī* of Valencia had done 'homage of the hands' to Jaume, for example, swearing 'to make peace and war for you,' accepting the king as his 'good and legal lord.' Abū Zayd himself had the many Christian castellans of his estates as 'vassals of you, the *sayyid*.' The *qā'id* of Játiva as vassal was 'to protect and defend me and my interests,' to respond to the claims 'a lord makes on his vassals,' and in disputes to accept the arbiter Jaume chose ('one of the great men of Spain by family and by nobility'). Jaume was sensitive to social parity, noting how Minorca island was 'thickly settled with Moors of good family' under its sultan who became the king's 'man and vassal.' In Spanish usage such terms need not be properly feudal, but their context here confirms a formal meaning. And these Muslims bore themselves as aristocrats. Abū Zayd even as a Christian kept his Almohad titles, eagle seal, and the lifestyle of a prince, robed in scarlet, turbaned in silk, with a great retinue. The lord of Játiva 'looked in truth to be a noble,' mounted on 'a splendid horse' with gold-inlaid appurtenances and with 'a richly jewelled sword around his neck,' attended by a retinue of 'four hundred Saracen horsemen.' Revolt after revolt was to pare down these grand figures over the next decades, reducing the Mudejar populace to local and lesser leaders. But for a moment here two nobiliary cultures converged.[14]

Surface illusion in our documents conceals a stubborn reality. al-Azraq's Arabic charter, by tone and content alike, proclaims his understanding of his relationship a tributary alliance, set forth in a business contract. The shorter document done in his name in the Castilian text is no supplement but merely a selective paraphrase incorporating Alfonso's idiosyncratic view. Conscious of this bifurcation of tone and intent, we must look with some mistrust on the same aspects of other crusader 'versions' of documents whose Arabic is long gone, such as King Jaume's treaties with Abū Zayd. Even a strict translation, as with the Romance version of Uxó's charter, may give us some pause.

This chapter's confrontation of principals and texts underlines important theses on Islamic–Christian relations in this book. King Jaume's treatment of his Mudejars was not by intent either intolerant or ungenerous. It was not tolerant in a modern sense either; and it was conditioned both by immediate expediency and by the framework of a war and conquest which reduced the loser to subordinate, marginal existence in a world alien and inimical by very structure. Here is the burden and tragedy of any *dhimma*-model society: not the particulars such as heavy taxes or restrictions or petty humiliations or erosion of privileges or popular hostility, but the very gifts which the conqueror kindly confers, the separate and cherished structure which excludes the victim from the dominant, vital structure. Had all promises been kept, all harassment removed, and the face of friendship shown to Mudejars consistently, the *dhimma* exclusion would still have been an oppression as much as a concession.

If this was true of the status in a static sense, it was more so when considered as a dynamic – the acculturative pressures inherent in experiencing overlords who misperceive each element of one's culture. To drift toward the newcomers meant compromises in language, in unfettered expression of religion under any circumstance, in fighting alien wars, in accepting a changing physical milieu (especially in immigrant-filled cities with their Gothic churches), in adapting one's local authority-patterns, in accepting the Christian king as high court of judicial appeal, and in submitting or coping in countless ways. To retreat more firmly within community bounds was even worse, rendering them inflexible, reactionary, stiffening against growth.

And the institutions or elements making up one's life became distorted as they were accommodated to the alien. Muslim warriors treated too long as vassal knights either take on some color of the alien form or react and fossilize. An *aljama* council, addressed as *capitols* and asked to function in some ways as such, does not become a commune but it subtly alters shape. The very concessions that guaranteed Islamic structures slowly changed those structures, or even made them caricatures. In this sense, kindness kills and the smile is as lethal as the knife. For a society whose religious, socio-cultural, and political forms are so essentially meshed, even acceptance as *dhimmī* (in a society itself meshed with Christianity) was unnerving. Islamic theologians who urged all conquered Muslims to flee to an Islamic land, at peril of their souls, possessed true insight into the dilemma. Mudejarism's *maḥāllat* equivalent in Sicily, after the Normans had conquered that island from the Muslims, seemed intolerable to the poet ʿAbd al-Ḥālim. The Sicily he loved in his youth as 'a garden of immortal felicity' now seemed in his mature years 'a burning gehenna.'

All that having been considered, Valencia's subculture Mudejarism was still the best bargain in a bad situation. It saved many essentials even while distorting them, and set the foundations for community cohesion during two centuries to come. For this first generation particularly, it allowed survival in a mosque-filled milieu unchanged to the careless eye, laws and religion available, juridical officials and farming rounds much the same, language and landscapes and many social habits as before. Privileges still existed; demographic weight mocked the inadequate Christian immigration; and (to judge from Boswell as a *terminus ad quem*) the economic situation of Mudejars was prosperous and their society still diversified. There is no evidence that Valencia's Mudejars were leaving in undue numbers yet, though the expulsions after each rebellion had serious effect. Only at mid-fourteenth century would the normal leakage of population toward Islamic countries suddenly turn into a devastating mass movement. Boswell has explored that later phenomenon, consequent upon 'an abrupt and dramatic decline in their economic stability and well being.'

Our transitional generation under Kings Jaume and Pere had passed a long half-century since the crusaders had broken into central Valencia to take up positions at Puig within sight of the walls of doomed Valencia city. They had passed forty years since the fall of Biar and official ending of the crusade, during which time their youngsters had grown into maturity and new generations had begun. In that time they had seen one cultural world die and an Islamic subculture evolve to replace it. As though warmed by a setting sun, strong still in their memories, their pride and hope attested by serious revolts, this Mudejar generation in this landscape remained vital. Though the Guadalaviar River ran tears, as the poet al-Qarṭājannī wrote (d. 1285), they might still have seen their native Valencia as the 'Paradise' sung by another contemporary poet, the Valencian Ibn Ḥarīq: though 'surrounded by 'famine and war,' 'Valencia is the dwelling of all beauty.'[15]

THE KING'S AUTOBIOGRAPHY:
THE ISLAMIC CONNECTION

My monograph of psychohistory on King Jaume's personality, presented in its essentials as my presidential address in 1975 before the American Catholic Historical Association, took up the neglected but central structural problem of King Jaume's autobiography. Why would a Mediterranean ruler leach out of his memoirs almost everything characteristic of his urban mercantile realms, as sophisticated as any city-state region of Dante's Italy, to present himself relentlessly in the self-image of a warrior Roland? An overlooked key for unlocking this and other recurrent puzzles in his book is the ideology of 'deeds' announced in the king's title for the autobiography, and the military episodes which were reorganized into a summa to sing the old rascal's 'spiritual' epic.

Structural problems still remained. Why was this the only royal autobiography in medieval Europe, for example, and why did the trajectory of narrative stretch literally from womb to tomb? As long as such puzzles haunted the text, the specter of a royal ghostwriter could not be absolutely exorcised; at least one scholar continues to see him on the stairs. I believe that a further frame of reference has been overlooked, and that it can be found in the Islamic influences so strongly reinforced during Jaume's lifelong crusading in the Balearics and especially in Valencia. I proposed this thesis, in a revised version of the psychohistory essay, at Zaragoza in 1976, before the tenth International Congress on the History of the Crown of Aragon, and shall give it wider dissemination here.

In all the topics of the present book, the figure of Jaume is a connecting thread. The course of crusade and settlement is inseparable from his character and direction. His very autobiography is essentially the story of the Balearics and Valencian crusades, with half the space going to Valencia. Since any study of the Valencian experience must start in the autobiography, seeing the enterprise through the eyes of its principal agent, the king's frames of reference are of paramount importance. In the topics of our own book, too, the theme of Islamic–Christian convergence provides another connecting thread; this theme appears boldly in the very structure of Jaume's volume. A twin problem needs to be confronted now: the current counterthesis by Jaume Riera i Sans on authorship, and the autobiographical format itself.

By way of refreshing the memory, it can be said that Jaume left us a personal memoir, a labor of love which can fill two volumes and which took most of his adult life to complete. Done in cooperation with secretaries in his native Catalan, it is a unique treasure: the only autobiography by a medieval king except for an imitation a century later by his descendant Pere the Ceremonious. It bristles with textual difficulties, especially in its inclusion of prosified poems, its imitation of epic themes, and its stages of redaction. Jaume himself had probably promoted the kind of poetry he later worked into his prose text (affecting roughly one-sixth of the chapters), as propagandistic news-releases to the general populace, though he does not seem to have been a genuine patron of troubadours on the scale of his father and grandfather. Archibald Lewis is studying the phenomenon of the king's 'anti-troubadourism.' He suggests that Jaume recoiled from troubadour emphasis on feelings and love – perhaps also identifying their influence with his father's softness, rejection of the infant Jaume, and foolish early death at the battle of Muret.

Literary battles over the autobiography, culminating in the recent works of Riquer and Soldevila, have established its authorship and authenticity beyond cavil, have reassured us as to the general historical accuracy even of the poetical fragments, and have tentatively concluded that the first half was redacted in the Valencian kingdom around 1244 and the second at Barcelona in 1274, the whole project probably originating as a record of the Majorca campaign. These stages were nuanced above in chapter 10, where the inexplicable break of two decades with its 'incoherent' jumble of notes became the key for finally understanding the autobiography's basic structure. Miquel Coll i Alentorn has recently summed the process of composition as 'an intense intervention of the monarch, directing his assistants, orienting them, indicating to them sources of information, revising the task and completing it when necessary with records and personal observations.' The memoirs are self-serving like many autobiographies, of course, and have been polished and structured over many years of the king's career. But 'the marvelous pages' of these 'personal memoirs,' Martí de Riquer sums up, are 'without any reserve' the king's own, with his collaborating secretaries much less intrusive than was once thought; the king's book permits us therefore 'to approach closely' his thought patterns, intentions, and intimate feelings.[1]

The perennial problem of identifying the king's redactor has just been reopened by Jaume Riera i Sans. The quality and quantity of ecclesiastical and especially biblical trappings in this *Llibre dels feyts* persuade him that the redactor 'has to have been a very cultivated and educated churchman,' probably the king's chancellor and bishop of Huesca, Jaume Sarroca. Manuel de Montoliu and others have also favored Sarroca; Lluís Nicolau d'Olwer confined his influence to the second part, while Miquel Coll i Alentorn allows him only remote oversight even there. Riquer represents a current consensus in believing that there were multiple collaborators in the lengthy project. Riera puts himself 'in open opposition' to Riquer's application of 'author' and 'absolute paternity' to King Jaume, from whom 'the Catalan text directly emanates.' He argues to the contrary that 'it is an ecclesiastic who loans his pen to the king and makes him speak in the first person.' The dismal 'level of religious culture' found in contemporary Catalan chroniclers, contrasted with the learning displayed in several biblical tags by Jaume's memoirs, furnish the proof. (Clumsy 'anomalies' even in such tags indicate that the writer is disguising his style to seem a lay learning.) Riera's argument is serious, closely argued, and in the end unpersuasive. The ecclesiastical redactor, admitted by all, has obviously stuck a few biblical raisins into the royal pudding. The king doubtless expected no less and applauded these borrowed bits. It is crucial to remember, however, that a redactor is not an author.

Decisive arguments against substantive, rather than stylistic, intervention by the redactor include the following. (1) Such a figure moved in a sophisticated university atmosphere and in the post-Lateran IV generation; Sarroca himself was an expert in jurisprudence from Bologna University, when that training took a theological rather than a narrowly legal approach. But the spirituality and basic theology of the king's *Llibre*, however costumed in clerical erudition, is primitive and unclerical, and at times almost a baptized paganism. (2) The author presents his subject as pious; but Jaume emerges a poor figure of a Christian even by the standard of his own age, while boastful of his Christian bravery and service to the church. If the redactor as author slyly meant to present the king as a sinner, on the other hand, he equally strayed from the clerical path – neither making Jaume really penitent nor counterbalancing sins against pieties, but enthusiastically adapting and promoting the warrior-king's bizarre view of Christian spirituality. In neither hypothesis could a cleric representing the ecclesiastical culture of the mid-thirteenth-century

Mediterranean world have proposed the substance or the viewpoint of the *Llibre dels feyts*.

(3) A cultivated cleric of that time would hardly have created so unlikely a genre as a royal autobiography (a surprising form for the king himself, who alone might carry it off). A university graduate would not have chosen Catalan over Latin for so major a work, or have produced only this single masterwork of imagination and remained otherwise silent save for technical legal writings, or have omitted all but the king's military glories – saying nothing of Jaume's creative role in the legal renaissance, for example, his relations with the Catalan and Valencian communes, his interaction with the mendicants, and his endowing a network of language schools to convert Moors and Jews. In short, the specific piety of the *Llibre dels feyts* is the strongest argument against a clerical or bourgeois intervention except at a formal and secretarial level. Turn all these arguments around, however, and they buttress the king's claim to authorship at every level but the most formal.

This is a lay-knight's book, religiously naive, militaristic in focus, centered on the life of camp and weaponry and honor, dovetailing exactly with the mentality in much of the king's independent documentation, and bearing the stamp of his education by the Templars in their monastery–barracks. A cleric, a university lawyer, or a burgess as redactor(s) could only reflect but not conceive or share religion and life in that perspective. The narrow focus and intent also help explain the royal author's carelessness about historical sequence and exact chronology, which is leading Antonio Ubieto to question the integrity of our manuscript. It is not necessary to postulate revisions and interpolations during the sixty-seven years intervening between Jaume's death and our present manuscript copy, nor to insist unduly on the king's manipulation of the facts so as to favor his own views: where an historian would be at fault, the royal moralist or prophet is only reserving his energies for larger issues.[2]

Though the king's autobiographical format was unique, it did not arise in an ambience uncongenial or without precedents. Non-royal autobiography was a familiar enough genre, while both autobiography and biography centering on the crusades was becoming popular. This neglected connection deserves attention from literary scholars. Riquer suspects an influence 'in the tradition of the *Confessions* of St Augustine.' Far more important, and totally neglected, is the connection between Jaume's book and the autobiography–biography genre among Islamic rulers. This is not at all the psychological connection Américo Castro intuited, by which Muslims were so passionately and introspectively personal that radical 'autobiographical expressionism' came to mark Spanish character generally;[3] that tells us nothing of Jaume's memoirs, unique in their very existence, whatever stream of self-regard may have marked his contemporaries in other ways in these realms. The connection between Jaume's autobiography and its Islamic-ruler counterpart, on the other hand, is direct. (For a very different Islamic effect on the king's memoirs, the devastating destruction of their artistic integrity caused by al-Azraq's demoralizing countercrusade, see pp. 278–81 above.)

Franz Rosenthal, in his massive *History of Muslim historiography*, has summed our knowledge of the role of biography, especially biography of rulers, in medieval Islam. Islamic historical writing dwarfed that of Byzantium and medieval Europe 'in sheer bulk.' Biography was prominent in historical production by Muslims from the very beginning 'and eventually achieved a dominating position in it,' so that for many Muslims 'history becomes almost synonymous with biography.' Preoccupation with biography was rooted in the Islamic religious experience; it thus became 'a necessary subject for theologians,' and a practical community service on the part of historians. Moreover, 'the most common monograph treatments of contemporary

287

history were those undertaken upon orders of the ruling sovereign who wished to see his deeds . . . or the one or other outstanding event of his reign immortalized in writing.' Rulers often kept diary notes for this purpose, and their official biographies were autobiographical in purpose and preparation; they commissioned, co-planned, and oversaw to the extent that the dividing line between a ruler's biography and his memoirs 'is often not clearly definable.'

The relevance of the Islamic model to Jaume's book becomes even clearer when we realize that these rulers' autobiographies–biographies had as their general feature the display of ethical qualities and behavior, frequently by means of anecdotes and episodes. Rosenthal realized that this ubiquitous historical activity 'cannot have remained concealed to medieval Western scholars who had contact with the Arabs,' and that men like William of Tyre or Jacques de Vitry knew Arabic historical work. Yet there was no apparent influence from Arabic forms or contact upon medieval European historiography (or indeed until the seventeenth century, when Islamic historiography helped shape a more universalist and modern approach). The one exception was Christian Spain, where the political situation in the thirteenth century 'stimulated a certain interest.' Rosenthal does not pursue this last aside. But King Jaume did pride himself on his knowledge of Muslim ways, could adapt himself on occasion to the rhetorical conventions and etiquette. of Muslim foes, sat as a kind of sultan for legal appeals from decisions of any *qāḍī* for the Muslim segments of his people, and was on intimate terms with a literary dynast like Abū Zayd (Valencia's last ruler, eventually a Christian) or like Yaḥyā b. 'Īsā of Játiva.

In his *Llibre dels feyts* we shall see the same controlling theological frame, the same dominant ethical purpose, the same linear narrative from birth to death (an inclusiveness disquieting to a number of modern commentators on Jaume's book), the same concentration on wars and victory, the same anecdotal approach, the same selection of some central deed (here the Majorcan–Valencian conquest), the same thirst for fame, the same revelation of the human self, the same use of subauthors or redactors, and (if Soldevila's conclusions are accepted) the same preliminary keeping of notes toward eventual composition. It would be a mistake to insist upon imitation or even direct influence, or to search comparatively for close parallels of structure and composition, or to ignore European independent springs. But it is foolish not to acknowledge some measure of Islamic influence upon Jaume's work (as in other contexts we now discern so clearly, for example, for Dante and Aquinas). The Islamic model affords an explanation particularly for the king's intent and general format. In view of what we have come to learn about the constant, osmotic interchange between Europe and Islam in Spain, scholars should devote attention to this convergence in the *Llibre dels feyts*.[4]

SURRENDER DOCUMENTS

In transcribing and presenting the constitutions below, the following sigla are employed: °[] for holes, requiring editorial conjecture or reconstruction from helpful fragments; \/ for inserts above a line; . . . for irrecoverable material; and ⟨ ⟩ for deteriorated, partially conjectural or reconstructed text. Punctuation, capitalization, and paragraphing are introduced; soft *ti*, usually *ci* in the original, is thus standardized as *ci*; *j* is rendered *i*, but *u* and *v* are distinguished; in general the Madrid archival *Normas* for historical, as against literary, transcription are followed, with modifications. For Romance, modern accents have not been supplied. Deletions by scribes, as well as minor orthographical adjustments, are not indicated. Double rates ('1273 or 1274') reflect the ambiguity in translating the Florentine incarnational calendar between January 1 and March 24. Paraphrase translations, marginalia, and ample textual notes to guarantee 'respect' for the minutiae of the Jacobine originals are provided in my forthcoming *Diplomatarium*.

1

ACA, Jaume I, Reg. Canc. 38, fol. 3r,v

Játiva
27 June 1276

Noverint universi quod nos infans Petrus etc. conced º[imus] vobis, ⟨to⟩ti aliame Sarracenorum de Eslida, quod remaneatis in domibus et hereditatibus et possessionibus quas habere consuevistis in Eslida, et populetis vos et omnis posteritas vestra in dicto loco per secula cunº[cta], recipientes vos et omnia º[bona] vestra in nostra commanda et nostro guidatico speciali.

Et teneatis legem vestram; et faciatis oraciones vestras in meschitis vestris; et possitis docere filios vestros, de vestro alchorram et aliis libris vestris. Et possitis facere instrumenta vestra matrimonialia, vendicionum, et omnium aliorum contractuum in posse vestri alcaidi et alcaldi. Et alaminus sit de aliama vestra, et eligatur ad cognicionem Sarracenorum vestrorum; remittentes vobis omnem demandam, quam vobis possemus facere quia fuistis in guerra contra nos.

Et non teneamini solvere nobis vel nostris aliquid, racione census et loguerii ville vestre ⟨u⟩sque in hunc diem. Et omnes Sarraceni qui sunt extra Eslidam possint libere et sub nostro guidatico reverti ⟨*sic*⟩ apud Eslidam, et habere ibi possessiones eorum secundum quod habere consuevistis. Et vos et vestri teneamini dare nobis et nostris decimam panis, olei, et omnium aliorum fructuum – exceptis [*deleted*: fructibus] ficubus et uvis que sunt in letonariis [cf. *Catalan* 'lledoner'] et aliis arboribus et ortaliciis que fiant ad opus comedendi; de illa tamen ortalicia que vendetur, similiter teneamini dare decimam.

Preterea teneamini dare nobis et nostris quolibet anno quadringentos bisancios (videlicet pro quolibet bisancio III solidos et dimidium regalium Valencie). De quibus solvatis nobis quolibet anno CCᵒˢ bisancios in mense Augusti, et alios ducentos bisancios in mense Octubris. Et vobis dantibus nobis dictos CCCCᵒʳ bisancios et decimam superius nominatam, non teneamini nobis dare vobis vel vestris [=vos vel vestri] aliud censum, servicium, vel º[p]eitam nec aliquam aliam exaccionem: nisi in dicto castro corruerint muri, vel si contigerit aliquid operari in dicto muro, teneamini iuvare alcaidum dicti castri in dicto opere.

Preterea apportetis qualibet die ad opus dicti castri duas cargas de lignam et aquam [*sic*] ad habundanciam dicti castri. Et alcaidi dicti castri non petant vobis ova, gallinas, nec aliqua alia servicia seu aldeas [?], in festis pascarum nec in nupciis vestris. Et possitis deco[que]re panem vestram in furnis vestris, sicut consuetum erat tempore Sarracenorum; et quod aliquis non possit vos compellere ad balneandum nisi secundum quod vobis placuerit.

Et si aliquis vestrum vellet transferre se in alium locum, causa habitandi, possit hoc facere sine aliqua contradiccione, et vendere hereditatem quam habuit in Eslida aliis Sarracenis. Et habeatis [*fol. 3v*] preterea alcharream de Guairaga sicut consuevistis habere. Et hereditates meschitarum sint de meschitis, sicut consueverunt esse tempore Sarracenorum. Et possit unus vestrum hereditare alium secundum

289

legem vestram. Preterea concedimus vobis quod alcharie de Beata et de Lauret et de Ayn et de Behyu si°[n]t de cetero ad consuetudinem de Eslida.[1]

Datum Exative, v kalendas Iulii, anno domini MCCLXX sexto.

2

ACA, Jaume II, Reg. Canc. 196, fols. 164v–165

Alfandech, 26 September; or
Valencia city, October 1277 ?
And Valencia city
1 April 1298

Noverint universi quod nos Iacobus etc., viso quodam privilegio litteris arabicis scripto, sigillo pendenti illustrissimi domini regis Petri inclite recordacionis patris nostri sigillato, in quo privilegio (de arabico in latinum ad mandatum nostrum fideliter transcripto) continetur qualiter idem dominus rex Petrus pater noster concessit ac remisit Sarracenis vallis de Alfandech omne malum et dampnum quod per eos tempore guerre extiterat perpetratum.

Et quod inhabitarent ac tenerent hereditates et possessiones suas, prout inter eos divise fuerunt ac eciam consignate. Et quod aliquis [*fol. 165*] ex ipsis Sarracenis non posset vendere nec alienare hereditates seu possessiones suas alicui, nisi solummodo Sarracenis.

Et quod remanerent et starent in lege et çunna sua, et possent docere filios suos in libris suis in meçquita eorum, et tenere çabaçalanum. Et quod hereditamentum quod consuevit esse meçquite: quod esset et perstaret ad eandem meçquitam, prout consueverat temporibus retroactis. Et quod unus Sarracenus posset alii Sarraceno hereditates suas dimittere, prout consuetum erat fieri temporibus retroactis. Et possent facere helimosinam et oracionem suam, prout tempore Sarracenorum erat fieri consuetum.

Et quod solverent l'almageram et alios reditus prout erat fieri consuetum. Et possent eligere et ordinare de seipsis alcaldi et alaminum, qui iudicaret inter ipsos secundum çun[n]am et libros eorum. Et quod possent emere sal prout consuetum est fieri temporibus retroactis. Et quod quilibet Sarracenus qui affugisset \ad terram/ guerre, vel extra regnum \nostrum/, posset redire ad predictam vallem de Alfandech, et populare ac remanere ibidem salve et secure, ita quod aliquis non presumeret pro redempcione captivitatis sue aliquid petere ab eodem.

Et quod possent portare arma per totam terram et iurisdiccionem ipsius domini regis. Et quod aliquis ex eis non caperetur seu impediretur calonia seu crimine alterius, sed quisque impeteretur proprio crimine seu culpa. Et quod possent pascere ganata sua grossa et minuta in terminis dicte vallis de Alfandec, prout erat fieri consuetum. Et quod omnes Sarraceni predicti tam masculi quam femine remanerent sub fide dei et ipsius domini regis, absque aliqua fraude, salvi et securi cum omnibus bonis suis; et quod contra predicta nullus auderet venire. Et quod possent eligere de seipsis alcadi et alaminum, iuxta voluntatem et consilium eorundem, prout hec in predicto privilegio lacius sunt contenta.

Idcirco ad humilem supplicacionem nobis per partem dictorum Sarracenorum de Alfandech factam, gratis et ex certa sciencia per nos et nostros predictum privilegium et omnia et singula in eodem contenta laudamus, concedimus, approbamus, ac eciam confirmamus, sicut melius dici et intelligi potest ad bonum et sanum ac sincerum intellectum Sarracenorum predictorum et suorum, prout in dicto privilegio sunt contenta et prout eo hactenus cessi sunt. Mandantes procuratori vel eius locum tenenti, iusticiis, baiulis, et universis aliis officialibus nostris presentibus et futuris quod predictam concessionem et confirmacionem nostram firmam habeant et observent; et faciant inviolabiliter obs[*fol. 165v*]ervari; et non contraveniant nec aliquem contravenire permittant aliqua racione.

Datum Valencie, kalendas Aprilis, anno domini MCCXC octavo.

Egidius de Iacca

Signum + Iacobi dei gracia regis Aragonum etc.

Testes sunt: Iacobus de Xerica   Iaçpertus de Castronovo

Bernardus Guillelmi de   Petrus Martini de Luna   Artaldus de Luna
Entença

Fuit clausum per Egidium de Iacca

3

ACA, Pere III, Reg. Canc. 44, fol. 149v–150

Valencia
18 July 1279

Dominus rex concessit Sarracenos de Quart, et de speciali gracia remittit eis omnia maleficia per ipsos commissa in guerra transacta que fuit in regno Valencie.

Ita quod possint stare salve et secure in hospiciis eorum; et tenere et colere hereditates suas, scilicet quilibet eorum unam iovatam, dum ipsam coluerint; et dividere hereditates suas prout consueverint.

Concedit eciam eis quod utantur çuna eorum; et quod possint [habere] libros legis sue; et orare ac tenere eorum mohe [=*mu'adhdhin, English muezzin?*] in meçquitis eorum; et docere filios suos in scolis; et quod alter alteri possit legare et dimittere bona sua secundum çunam et legem eorum; et quod habeant alaminum et cadium Sarracenorum, prout ipsi voluerint.

Tunc quam nunc sit alaminus Caçim Alponti [Qāsim al-Būntī], dum sufficiens fuerit et legalis; qui alaminus cum consilio senum possit iudicare inter ipsos. Nemo enim possit iudicare causas civiles [*deleted*: vel criminales], que inter vos ventilate fuerint, preter dictos cadius et alaminus [*sic*] tantum. Nullus ipsorum possit vendere vel impignorare hereditatem nisi suo simili Sarraceno.

Concessit eciam eis quod possint ire per totam dominacionem eiusdem salve et secure, et uti mercimoniis suis, ipsis solventibus pedagia et alia iura prout consueverunt et continetur in carta quam super hoc habent a domino Iacobo etc. Et alter ipsorum pro altero non capiatur, racione alicuius calonie.

Preterea quod dent [*fol. 150*] et solvant terciam partem fructuum et expletarum suarum. Et quod colant vineas bene. Et donent pro lignis quolibet anno CL solidos regalium. Et quod solvant in omnibus exaccionibus quibus solvere consueverint a tribus annis etc. Et quod dividant aquam ut consueverunt.

Concedit eciam eis quod si aliquis Sarracenus vel Sarracena de terra regis affugerit ad loca Sarracenorum, et de ipsis partibus noviter voluerit ad populandum apud Quart, sit ibi forrus et liber. Mandantes universis officialibus etc. quod predicta observent.

Datum Valencie, XVII kalendas Augusti, anno predicto [MCCLXXIX]. Samuel alfaquimus.

4

ACA, Pere III, Reg. Canc. 44, fol. 149

Valencia
20 July 1279

Nos Petrus etc. remittimus et indulgemus universis Sarracenis de Seta omnia maleficia et dampna que intulerunt in terra nostra tempore terre [= guerre] preterite, constituentes eos qui nunc ibi sunt et ex nunc ad populandum ibi venerint sub nostra proteccione et custodia cum omnibus bonis et rebus eorum, voluntes eos in propriis domibus et hereditatibus permanere.

Concedimus eis insuper quod possint adorare et legere in mezquitis eorum et muethden [*mu'adhdhin*; *see doc. 3*] tenere secundum morem legis eorum, et filios suos docere libros legis sue.

Item volumus et concedimus quod quilibet Sarraceni qui apud Setam venire voluerint ad populandum, salvi veniant et securi.

Et si aliqui Sarraceni vel Sarracene, qui affugerint de terra Christianorum ad partes extraneas Sarracenorum ubi sint forri, possint ibi venire ad populandum salve et secure si voluerint. \Mandantes officialibus etc./

Datum [Valencie], xiii kalendas Augusti, anno predicto [MCCLXXIX]. Petrus de Sancto Clemente.

5

ACA, Pere III, Reg. Canc. 44, fol. 160

Valencia
14 November 1279

Nos Petrus etc. concedimus Sarracenis Moncanet [*sic*]: quod sint salvi et securi in persona et rebus suis sub fide dei et nostra, scilicet in locis sive terminis de Çagra et de Salum [?] et de Pop et de Callosa et de Algar et de Godalest et de Confrides et de Castell et de Gallinera et de Alcala et de Benamaneçil et de Ebu. Promittimus eciam eis ad habitandum ravale de Denia.

Promittimus eciam eis quod remaneant in locis predictis; et possint hereditare bona sua ad invicem per açunam eorum et consuetudinem; et quod non sit iudex inter eos nisi alcadi et alami eorum; et quod possint legere libros et açunam eorum, et faciant oraciones in mesquitis suis cum suo sabassala, secundum quod consueverunt; et quod nullus Sarracenus capiatur pro debitis alterius, nisi fuerit in eis principalis debitor vel fideiussor (hoc excepto quod pro debitis vel iniuriis quibus nobis tenentur, capiantur unus pro alio); et quod nullus Sarracenus capiatur per testimonium Christiani, nisi per testimonium Christiani et Sarraceni, secundum privilegium quod habent a domino Iacobo etc. Mandantes etc.

Datum Valencie, xviii kalendas Decembris [anno domini MCCLXXIX]. Petrus Marches.

Facta fuit carta quod esset divisor de predictis Abrahim Abinçumadii.

VALENCIAN JEWS: A MINI-CARTULARY

For sigla and editorial procedures see the introductory paragraph of appendix 2.

1

ACA, Jaume I, Reg. Canc. 10, fol. 53

Lérida
29 October 1257

Nos Iacobus etc. recognoscimus et confitemur debere vobis, Iahudano de Cavalleria baiulo Cesarauguste, tria milia solidorum iaccensium, in quibus nos vobis instituimus debitores pro Palazino de Focibus, cui debebamus tria milia solidorum racione custodie et expensarum quas fecit in castro de Alponte, et ipse eos denarios vobis debebat.

Que III milia solidorum assignamus vobis et vestris habenda et recipienda in primis collectis quas facietis pro nobis, et in reditibus baiulie Cesarauguste, quam pro nobis tenetis.

Datum Ilerde, IIII kalendas Novembris, anno domini MCCL septimo.

2

ACA, Jaume I, Reg. Canc. 10, fol. 55

Játiva
5 May 1258

Per nos et nostros ven °[d] imus vobis Petro de Barchinona habitatori Algezi°[re] et vestris in perpetuum quasdam domos franchas et liberas, quas Mechadanus quon°[dam] Iudeus Valencie habebat in Aliagira, sicut affrontant ex una parte cum domibus domini Rostayn, et de duabus partibus in via publ°[ica], et ex alia parte in d°[o]mibus que fuerunt den [=de En] Cibrian.

Iam dicta°[s] itaque domos cum solis et suprapositis, introitibus, exitibus, affronta°[cionibus], et suis pertinenciis universis a celo in abissum, vendimus vobis et vestris ad omnes voluntates vestras et vestrorum cuicumque volueritis perp°[etuo] faciendas, exceptis militibus atque sanctis.

Pro hac vendicione recepimus a vobis CC solidos regalium Valencie, de quibus bene paccati sumus ad voluntat°[e]m nostram; promittentes vobis quod faciem°[us] vos et vestros dictas domos habere et tenere et in pace pacifice possidere contra omnes personas.

Datum Xative, III nonas Madii, anno domini MCCL octavo.

3

ACA, Jaume I, Reg. Canc. 10, fol. 66 *bis*, r,v¹

Cocentaina
(26 May) 1258

Per °[n]os et nostros vendimus et de presenti tradimus tibi, Cete uxori quondam Mubari°[ch] Machadani Iudei Valencie, et tuis in per°[petuum] domos, ortos, vineas, campos, et omnes alias hereditates ac possessiones quas predictus Mubarich Machadanus habebat in Mezlata, et in Raffalsoternos: videlicet unam vineam que est in Mezlata, et confrontat ex °[un]a parte cum vinea Iohannis Luppi, et ex alia parte cum honore Garcie de Podio alcaidi de Mezlata, et ex alia in carraria, et ex °[ali]a parte in campo °[ia]mdicti Magadani; et quendam campum qui confrontatur ex una parte cum vinea Michaelis Enegeç, et ex alia in vinea dicti Garcie de Podio, et ex alia in campo dicti Iohannis Luppi, et ex alia in carraria, et ex alia parte in campo Michaelis de Alcheçar.

Item unum campum qui est in Raffalsoternos et fuit Eximini Romei, in quo sunt domus; et confrontatur ex duabus partibus in honore Tivicini, et ex alia in carraria de Quart in campo Dominici de Alffambra, et ex alia parte in carraria. Et alium campum qui fuit dicti Eximini Romei, et confrontatur ex una parte in carraria, et ex alia in domibus Iohannis Claver, et ex altera in campo Petri de Campa quondam et Michaelis Petri de Sancta Maria, et ex alia [parte] in honore iamdicti Tevicini. Et alium campum qui fuit Petri Guarnerii; et confrontatur ex una parte cum honore Petri de Planis, et ex alia cum hereditate Guillelmi de Lertç, et ex alia cum honore Assencii de Turolio, et ex alia in figerali Petri de Orta et est unum brassal in medio.

Et alium campum qui fuit den [= de En] Marco; et confrontatur ex una parte in honore Iohannis Claverii, et ex alia in honore Tevº[ic]ini et in brassal, et ex alia parte in honore Guillelmi de Lerç et honore Michaelis Petri de Sancta Maria. Et quandam vineaº[m] cum quodam mayolio; et confrontatur in honore Iohannis Claverii ante dicti ex una parte et Martorelli Picaperes, et ex alia in vinea Nicholai et est unum brassal in medio, et ex alia in vineis Arnaldi Bertrandi et Petri Olerii et Guillelmi de Lerç, et ex alia in mayolio Dominici Catalani. Que omnia nobis confiscata fuerunt racione mortis Avingam⟨er⟩ Sarraceni, quem ipse maritus tuus fecit ocº[cidi]: ex qua causa nos exercentes iusticiam fecimus ipsum suspendi.

Sicuti igitur iam dicta omnia predictis includuntur affrontacionibº[us] et terminantur, et sicut predictus Mubarich maritus tuus ipsa melius habebat et possidebat, et sicut nos eciam eadem melius habemus et habere debemus: vendimus tibi et tuis in perpetuum tamquam plus offerenti, facta legitima subastacione, cum suis affrontacionibus, introitibus, exitibus, aquis, arboribus fructif⟨er⟩is et infructiferis, melioramentis factis et faciendis, et cum suis iuribus et pertinenciis omnibus a celo in ab⟨iss⟩um integre, sine aliquo nostro nostrorumque retentu, et precio videlicet quattuor milium CC solidorum regaº[lium] Valencie. Et si quid predicta [= de predictis] que tibi vendimus plus valent vel valebunt precio ante dicto, totum illud quod plus vaº[let] vel valebunt [= valebit] damus tibi et tuis ad faciendum inde tua propria voluntate; renunciantes scienter om⟨ni⟩ º[iuri], foro, et consuetudini, scriptis et non scriptis, quibus contra predicta vel eorum aliquid nos vel nostri modo aliquo ⟨venire⟩ possemus.

Et extrahentes predicta omnia et singula de iure nostro, dominio, et potestate, eadem in ⟨ius⟩, [*fol. 66 bis v*] dominium, et potestatem tuam transº[feri]mus et tuorum, inducentes te et tuos de presenti in eorum corporalem possessionem cum hoc publico instrumento perpetuo v⟨ali⟩turo, ad habendum, tenendum, possidendum, vendendum, alienandum, impignorandum, et ad omnes tuas º[tuorumque] voluntates cui et quibus volueritis libere perpetuo faciendas, exceptis sanctis º[c]lericis, militibus, et personis religiosis. Promittimus eciam tibi quod predicta omnia et singula faciemus te et tuos habere et tenere in perpetuum, integrº[e et] in pace, contra omnes personaº[s]; et tenebimur inde tibi et tuis de firma et legali eviccione.

Est autem sciendum quod, cum post suspendium Mubarich Machadani predicti nos fecissemus bona ipsius omnia eº[m]parari, tu supplicasti nobis quod solvemus tibi ius tuum quod, tam racione dotis tue quam racione donacionis quam iam dictus maritus tuus tibi fec[er]at in bonis eius, habebas. Et nos fecimus discuti et videri quod ius tu habebas in º[i]psº[i]s. Et invenimus quod secundum ius et foros Iudeorum, et secundum instrumenta que iamdictus maritus tuus tibi fecerat, habebas terciam partem in bonis predictis que tibi vendimus, racione donacionis quam ipse tibi fecerat. Et ex alia parte habebas, super eisdem, CCL morabatinos racione tue dotis. Quod totum fuit extimatum ascendere et valere tria milia quingentos [XXX]III solidos et IIII denarios regalium.

Quare volumus et concedimus tibi quod hec tria milia quingenti XXXIII solidi et IIII denarii cedant in solucionem iuris tui predicti, et tu ea reº[tin]eas de precio vendicionis iam dicte. Residuos autem quingentos LXVI solidos et VIII denarios, et ex °[a]lia parte CC solidos regalium, quos nobis donas pro domibus et fructibus hereditatis predicte de Rahal °[s]o°[t]ernos istius anni presentis, confitemur nos habuisse et recepisse a te et inde esse bene paccatos ad voluntatem nostram, renunciantes omni excepcioni non numerate pecunie atque doli.

Datum Cocentanie, vii °[kalendas] Iunii, anno domini MCCL octavo.

4

ACA, Jaume I, Reg. Canc. 11, fol. 190

Játiva

11 January 1261 (not 1260)

°[Nos concedimus] vobis toti aliame Iudeorum Xative quod nullus Iudeus vestrum possit se excusare, racione franchitatis °[a] nobis sibi conc⟨esse [?]⟩ quin teneatur simul vobiscum facere vicinaticum; nec possit se desistere de vestris catanis, neque de vestris alarmis sicut ⟨in aliama [?]⟩ Iudeorum Valencie.

Volumus tamen quod illi, qui franchi ex concessione nostra sunt, per dictum tempus franchitatis non tenean°[tur] p°[ei]tare in aliquibus peitis per tempus ipsarum franchitatum. Transacto vero tempore ipsarum franchitatum, peitent et peitare tenean°[tur] simul vobiscum in omnibus peitis. Mandantes etc.

Datum Xative, iii idus Ianuarii, anno domini MCCLX.

5[2]

ACA, Jaume I, Reg. Canc. 11, fols. 199v–200

Valencia city

9 April 1261

Per nos et nostros consulte et ex certa sciencia laudamus, concedimus, et confirmamus vobis Vivas [sic] filio de Iucefo Abenvivas et Faquimo filio de Iucefo Abencunayna Iudeis civitatis Valencie, et vestris in perpetuum vendicionem quam Martinus Sancii de Loriz et Maria Diaz uxor eius vobis fecerunt, pro precio duorum milium septingentorum solidorum regalium Valencie, de omnibus domibus, ortis, vineis, et tota hereditate quam habebat et habere debebat in Malilla et suis terminis, que omnia sunt in terretorio civitatis Valencie; ita quod predictas omnes domos, ortos, vineas, et hereditatem predictam habeatis vos et vestri in perpetuum, teneatis, possideatis, et expletetis, cum omnibus melioramentis ibi factis et faciendis, et cum introitibus, exitibus, et affrontacionibus, et suis pertinenciis universis a celo in abissum, ad omnes voluntates vestras et vestrorum inde libere perpetuo faciendas, exceptis militibus, sanctis, et personis religiosis, prout melius et plenius [in] instrumento publico vendicionis in[de] vobis et vestris a predicto Martino Sancii et uxore eius Maria facto continetur.

Promittentes bona fide per nos et nostros quod contra predicta vel eorum aliqua non veniemus, nec aliquem veniere [sic] permittemus, unquam aliquo tempore aliquo modo vel aliqua racione; immo faciemus vos et vestros, et quem vel quos volueritis, omnia et singula supradicta habere et tenere et pacifice possidere et percipere in perpetuum contra omnes personas, dum tamen vos faciatis querelantibus de vobis super premissis secundum forum et [fol. 200] °[c]onsuetudinem Valencie °[iust]icie complementum. Mandantes baiulis, iusticiis, et universis aliis officialibus et sub°[di]tis nostris, presentibus °[et futur]is, quod predicta omnia et °[s]ingula observent, et faci°[a]nt ab omnibus inviolabiliter observari.

Datum Valencie, v idus Aprilis, anno domini MCCLX primo.

6

ACA, Jaume I, Reg. Canc. 14, fol. 14

Zaragoza
1 March 1263 (not 1262)

Assignamus vobis, Egidio Eximini baiulo regni Valencie a rivo Xucari citra, omnes reditus et exitus portatici nostri Turolii, et omnes reditus et exitus Iudeorum Turolii, ad faciendum expensas in cequia Aliasire necessarias.

Concedentes vobis quod omnes predictos reditus et exitus possitis obligare et impignorare ad opus predictarum expensarum; promittentes vobis quod faciemus vos dictos reditus et exitus tenere et percipere in pace, vel ipsos cui ipsos reditus obligaveritis, vobis redden⟨tibus⟩ nobis compotum de eisdem expensis.

Datum Cesarauguste, kalendas Marcii, anno domini MCCLX secundo.

7

ACA, Jaume I, Reg. Canc. 14, fol. 19r,v³

Lérida
8 May 1263

Nos Iacobus etc. vendimus et tradimus vobis, Samueli genero Çaleme de Darocha, a proximo preterito festo pasce resurreccionis domini usque ad IIII annos primos venturos et continue completos, salinas nostras de Archos; et quod teneatis caldiras in quibus decoquitur sal ipsarum salinarum, et domos, et terium, sicut iam consuevistis tenere; ita videlicet quod quolibet anno detis et solvatis nobis duodecim mille solidos, sic quod in presenti anno detis et solvatis Petro de Berbegal archipresbiteri Daroce octo mille solidos et eodem archipresbiteri mille solidos pro custodia castri de Çancharies, et septingentos solidos custodie vecamenti salis predictarum salinarum. Residuos vero duo mille CCC solidos recipiatis in solucionem debitorum que nos debemus Çaleme de Darocha socero vestro.

In sequentibus vero annis, faciatis soluciones de septem mille solidis quolibet anno, ubi nos vobis mandaverimus; et residuos quinque mille solidos recipiatis quitios in solucionem debitorum que dicto Çaleme socero vestro debemus. Vos vero faciatis soluciones de denariis de quibus nobis tenemini respondere, tam de presenti anno quam sequentibus, per tres terminos uniuscuiusque anni, iis denariis.

Et sic vobis solvente [=solventibus] dictos denarios prout superius est expressum, habeatis [et] teneatis dictas salinas, et reditus et exitus earundem recipiatis, per totum spacium dictorum IIII annorum; promittentes vobis quod in dictis salinis aliquid non tangemus vel accipiemus, nec tangi vel accipi faciemus seu permittemus, per totum spacium supra dictum. Immo faciemus vos et vestros dictas salinas habere et tenere, et reditus earundem percipere, pacifice et quiete.

Nos autem faciemus vobis tenere vecamentum salis predicti sic quod non sint ausi [fol. 19v] in Turoli°[o] nec in aliis locis [aut] villis uti, vel eius aldeis uti [sic], de alio sale nisi de salinis predictis, prout in i°[n]str⟨uccione⟩ quam tenet ille qui est custos dictarum salinarum plenius continetur, sic quod illi qui emerint sal de dictis salinis teneantur dare XV denarios iaccenses pro qualibet fanecha, sive cruda fuerit sive decocta.

Nos autem faciemus in dictis salinis vos, et homines vestros, et res vestras consistere salve pariter et secure. Mandantes concilio de Archos quod vos et homines vestros et res vestras manuteneant et defendant, ita quod nullus sit ausus pignorare vel capere bestias, nec aliquas res vestras, in aliquo loco, aliquo modo, vel aliqua racione nisi principales fuerint debitores vel fideiussores pro aliquo constituti.

Datum Ilerde, VII idus Madii, anno domini MCCLX tercio.

8

ACA, Jaume I, Reg. Canc. 12, fol. 92v

Lérida
29 June 1263

Iacobus dei gracia rex Aragonum, Maioricarum, et Valencie, comes Barchinone et Urgelli, et dominus Montispessulani fidelibus suis baiulo et iusticie Xative presentibus et futuris, salutem et graciam. Sciatis quod filii Iohannis de Guarigues, et filii Haron[4] quondam alfaquim nostri, super facto illius hereditatis que fuit dicti Haron quam dedimus dicto Iohanni de Garigues, fuerunt apud Ylerdim coram nostri presencia constituti; et quilibet eorum ostenderunt nobis omnia privilegia et iura sua.

Quibus visis et intellectis, dictam hereditatem adiudicavimus dictis filiis Iohannis de Garigues. Quare vobis firmiter et districte dicimus et mandamus quatenus in dicta hereditate dictis filiis Iohannis de Garigues, et quibus ipsi eam vendiderint, racione predictorum filiorum dicti Haron de cetero nullum impedimentum faciatis nec fieri ab aliquo permittatis. Et deinceps omne instrumentum filiorum dicti Haron annullamus, quod non possit hostendi contra dictam hereditatem predictorum filiorum Iohannis de Garigues penitus ac eis sanius.

Datum Ilerde, III kalendas Iulii, anno domini MCCLX tercio.

9

ACA, Jaume I, Reg. Canc. 12, fol. 93v

Barcelona
8 July 1263

Recognoscimus vobis Samueli et Issacho, filiis de Aron Iudeo quondam alfaquimo nostro, quod comparuistis multocies coram nobis, supplicantes ut redderemus vobis quandam hereditatem quam dederamus predicto patri vestro apud Xativam, quam hereditatem nos postea dederamus Iohanni de Garriga, unde constet nobis nos fecisse donacionem de dicta hereditate predicto patri vestro.

Nolentes facere vobis aliquam iniuriam, promittimus et convenimus vobis predictis Samueli et Issacho filiis quondam de Aron quod, hinc usque ad proximum festum venturum natalis domini, in emendam sive restitucionem dicte hereditatis, dabimus vobis hereditatem apud Xativam tria milia solidorum regalium valentem. Quod nisi fecerimus incontinenti, promittimus vobis dare racione dicte hereditatis tria milia solidorum predicte monete ad voluntatem vestram.

Datum Barchinone, VIII idus Iulii, anno domini MCCLX tercio.

10

ACA, Jaume I, Reg. Canc. 12, fol. 103v

Barcelona
20 August 1263

Per nos et nostros damus et concedimus vobis, fideli nostro Iahudano de Cavalleria baiulo nostro in Cesaraugusta, et vestris in perpetuum illam placiam terre nostram que est in orta Valencie. Et affrontat ex duabus partibus cum orto vestro quem emistis a filiis Bertrandi de Valars quondam, et ex alia parte in via publica, et ex alia in quadam carraria per quam itur ad hereditatem quondam Arnaldi de Fonte et ad regale sive ortum nostrum et ad quendam alium ortum vestrum quem emistis a Sancio de Valle.

Quam placiam sive terram habeatis vos et vestri in perpetuum, per hereditatem propriam, francham, et liberam cum omnibus melioramentis et hedificiis que ibi feceritis, et cum introitibus et exitibus, affrontacionibus et suis pertinenciis universis a celo in abissum, ad omnes voluntates vestras et vestrorum inde libere perpetuo faciendas, exceptis militibus, clericis sanctis, et personis religiosis.

Datum Barchinone, xiii kalendas Septembris, anno domini mcclx tercio.

11

ACA, Jaume I, Reg. Canc. 12, fol. 106v

Barcelona
29 August 1263

Fidelibus suis baiulo et iusticie Valencie, salutem et graciam. Mandamus vobis firmiter quatenus non permittatis aliquem vel aliquos intrare domos nec regalia fidelis nostri Iahudani de Cavalleria baiuli Cesarauguste, nec in eisdem [h]ospitari, nisi processerit de voluntate predicti Iahudani de Cavalleria.

Et si aliquis ibi intrare voluerit vel hospitari, ab illo vel illis penam habeatis quam forus Valencie dictaverit et requiret. Et hoc non mutetis aliqua racione; alias sciatis quod nobis plurimum displiceret.

Datum Barchinone, iv kalendas Septembris, anno domini mcclx tercio.

12

ACA, Jaume I, Reg. Canc. 12, fol. 106v

Barcelona
29 August 1263

Concedimus vobis universis et singulis Iudeis Muriveteris quod de illis quingentis solidis, quos nobis datis et dare tenemini quolibet anno in festo natalis domini pro tributo, non detis nec solvatis nobis nisi CCC solidos quolibet anno in dicto festo dum nostre placuerit voluntati.

Mandantes baiulo nostro Muriveteris quod a vobis predictos CCC solidos exigat et habeat, quolibet anno in festo natalis domini, et non amplius dum nostre placuerit voluntati ut est dictum.

Datum Barchinone, iiii kalendas Septembris, anno domini mcclx tercio.

13

ACA, Jaume I, Reg. Canc. 13, fol. 167

Egea
29 March 1264

⟨Per⟩ nos et nostros laudamus, concedimus, et confirmamus vobis Mosse filio Bahiel alfaquimi nostri quondam, et vestris in perpetuum, illam partem hereditatis vobis pertinenᵒ[t]em ex particione facta inter Salamonem alfaquimum nostrum et vos ac fratres vestros; videlicet quasdam domos et vineas in Muroveteri et terminis suis, et alcharream in Albacet cum suis pertinenciis, et vineas in termino Muriveteris in loco vocato Raval et in Conillera, et domos in Valencia que fuerunt Anxe [or Anye] Sarraceni, et hereditatem quam habetis in Algezira (videlicet campos quos habetis in Barralbeso [sic], et ortum quem ⟨hab⟩etis in Alcanicia, et molendinum in termino Algezire in loco vocato Alfaz, et domos in Algezira) secundum quod in carta particionis facta inter dictum Salamonem et vos et fratres vestros plenius continetur.

Ita quod predicta omnia habeatis, teneatis, et possideatis ad faciendum inde vestras proprias voluntates, sicut in dicta carta particionis continetur, exceptis sanctis clericis et personis religiosis.

Datum Exee, IIII kalendas Aprilis, anno domini MCCLX quarto.

14

ACA, Jaume I, Reg. Canc. 13, fol. 170v

Calatayud
10 May 1264

Per nos et nostros laudamus, concedimus, et confirmamus vobis, Salamoni filio Bahielis quondam alfaquimi nostri, partem illam hereditatis vobis pertinentem ex particione facta inter vos et fratres vestros et Salamonem alfaquimum nostrum: videlicet quandam vineam in Cesaraugusta in loco vocato Raval, et hereditatem in termino Muriveteris in loco vocato Cunilera et in Gausa, et unum campum in termino Algezire in loco vocato Alcanicia, prout in carta particionis melius et plenius continetur.

Ita quod predicta omnia habeatis, teneatis, possideatis, et expletetis vos et vestri ad faciendum inde vestras proprias voluntates cui et quibus volueritis, exceptis militibus, sanctis clericis, et personis religiosis.

Datum in Calataiubo, VI idus Madii, anno domini MCCLX quarto.

15⁵

ACA, Jaume I, Reg. Canc. 17, fol. 40

Valencia city
19 July 1269

Nos infans Petrus etc. concedimus vobis, universis Iudeis Gandie tam presen°[t]ibus quam futur°[is, concessionem a patre nostro datam: uti e]is libertatibus ⟨quas⟩ homines Gandie habent et utuntur super lezda et pedatico, per ea videlicet loca in quibus ⟨eis⟩°[dem hominibus] ⟨Gandie predicta⟩ libertas concessa est per dictum dominum regem patrem nostrum.

Mandantes ba°[iu]lis, iusticiis, al°[ca]i°[dis et universi]⟨s hominibus⟩ locorum regni Valencie quod vobis sicut hominibus Gandie predictam libertatem teneant teneant [sic] °[et quod contra concessio]nem ipsam vos vel res vestras in aliquo non molestent.

Datum Valencie, XIIII kalendas Augusti, anno domini MCCLXIX.

16

ACA, Jaume I, Reg. Canc. 37, fol. 7

Tarazona
11 June 1270

Nos infans Petrus etc. absolvimus, remittimus, et perpetuo remittimus [sic] vobis, Salamoni filio Boniude de Turre et tuis, perpetuo omnem peticio⟨nem⟩, questionem, et demandam realem et personalem, et omnem penam civilem et criminalem quam contra te vel bona tua possemus proponere vel movere racione vulneris illati Salamoni Vitali, Iudeo Burriane, de quo tu fuisti inculpatus. Ita scilicet quod racione dicti vulneris non possimus nos nec nostri, nec autem aliquis tenens locum nostrum vel officialis noster, de cetero te vel tuos aut aliqua bona tua petere, dem°[an]dare, aut in causam trahere seu in aliquo convenire; sed sitis inde tu et tui, cum omnibus bonis et rebus tuis mobilibus et inmobilibus habitis et habendis, liberi et perpetuo absoluti, sicut melius dici potest et intelligi ad tuum tuorumque salvamentum et bonum intellectum, te tamen faciente predicto Salamoni super hoc de querela quam a te habeat iusticie complementum.

Pro hiis autem difinicionem et absolucionem, concedimus nos a te habuisse CC solidos iaccenses, in quibus renunciamus excepcioni non numerate pecunie et non recepte.

Datum Tirasone, tercio idus Iunii, anno domini millesimo CCLXX.

17

ACA, Jaume I, Reg. Canc. 37, fol. 35v

Lérida
6 February 1272 (not 1271)

Noverint universi quod nos infans Petrus etc. enfranquimus te, Samuel Za Reyal Iudeum nostrum habitatorem Burriane, quod a die scilicet quo incepisti tenere domicilium in Burriana usque ad IIII annos completos continue venientes, ab omni questia, peyta, et communi seu qualibet alia exaccione, que nobis vel alicui, nostro nomine, dare nullatenus ten[e]aris; sed per totum dictum tempus IIII annorum sis francus ab omnibus supra dictis et singulis, prout a nobis plenius hoc concessum est Iudeis nostris populatoribus Burriane.

Mandantes firmiter baiulis, et aliis officialibus predictis domini regis et nostris, quod hanc franquitatem nostram observent et faciant observari et non contraveniant vel contravenire permittant, si de nostri confidunt gracia vel amore.

Datum Ilerde, VIII idus Februarii, anno domini MCCLXX primo.

18

ACA, Jaume I, Reg. Canc. 21, fol. 46v

Montpellier
6 July 1272

Per nos et nostros damus et concedimus tibi, Petro Ballisterio, diebus omnibus vite tue ortum illum qui fuit Mayrii Iudei quondam, et qui est intus aliafariam Xative – et qui affrontat ex una parte cum pinna castri maioris Xative, et ex alia in via que vadit ad dictum castrum, et ex alia in iuderia Xative.

Predictum vero ortum damus tibi sub hac forma: quod ipsum habeas et teneas diebus omnibus vite tue prout domos nostras dicte aliafarie tenere et possidere debes. Mandantes etc.

Datum in Montepessulano, II nonas Iulii, anno domini MCCLXX secundo.

19[6]

ACA, Jaume I, Reg. Canc. 23, fol. 19v

(March ?) 1274 or 1275
[In Catalan]

Item comta En Salamo de la Cavalleria de les rendes de Morvedre, de IIII meses menys VII dies que les te°[nc]h, e de X meses XXIII dies que les tenc, dals part entro que les pres En Ramon Ricart, e de les rendes d·Almonezir, e de les rendes de Segorb, e de les rendes d·Uxo, del temps que les tench. Comta \de/ les rendes d·Almonezir intro [sic] el primer dia de Giner que passat es.

Et [sic] egualades reebudes ab dates, deu li tornar lo seynnor rey – VII mils DIII sous de reals. E deu comtar de les rendes d·Almonezir de Giner ença.

20

ACA, Jaume I, Reg. Canc. 19, fol. 156

Barcelona

9 August 1274

Noverint universi quod cum denunciatum fuisset nobis Iacobo dei gracia etc. contra te Vives, Iudeum baiulum de Alfandec de Marinnen filium Iuceffi Aben Vives, quod tu vel alius racione tui accipiebatis singulis annis a Sarracenis de Alfandech alquenam ipsorum Sarracenorum ad racionem duorum solidorum [per] arovam, que valebat ut dicebatur de quattuor ad sex solidos; et quod tu mutuabas vel faciebas mutuari eisdem Sarracenis ad usuras magnas, ultra cotum nostrum, denarios et aliam pecuniam; et quod de vicio sodomitico culpabilis eras; et alia eciam plena capitula contra te denunciata nobis fuerunt, et oblata in scriptis per Azachum Barbuti scilicet, et per Zalemam Barbuti, Abrahimum Samariani, et Abrahimum Gerundini Iudeos, et per Abdella Dahui Sarracenum de Alfandech – nosque, super vicio sodomitico predicto, testes recipi fecerimus et non invenerimus probatum contra te vicium ante dictum, et super inquirendis aliis contra te denunciatis et propo [s]itis procedere non velimus – idcirco per nos et nostros absolvimus te dictum Vives et omnia bona tua ab omni peticione et demanda ac pena civilibus et criminalibus, si quas contra te habebamus et imponere poteramus racione criminis sodomitici supra dicti vel racione alterius cuiuslibet criminis, culpe, maleficii, seu delicti pro quibus contra te usque in presentem diem, quo presens scribitur carta, possemus agere civiliter vel criminaliter quoquomodo.

Et absolvimus eciam, difinimus, ac remittimus tibi (ac universis et singulis illis qui pro te tenerentur [*sic*] dictam baiuliam de Alfandech, et qui de dicta alqueria emerunt vel mutua fecerunt dictis Sarracenis, dum tu ipsam baiuliam tenuisti) omnem peticionem et demandam ac penam civiles et criminales quas contra te vel ipsos aut bona tua vel eorum habebamus vel habere sive movere, imponere, seu infligere poteramus, racione empcionis predicte alquerie vel lucri per te vel ipsos facti in ipsa alqueria, aut in aliis rebus cum Sarracenis predictis, au[t] racione dictarum usurarum vel quorumlibet que contra te vel ipsos denunciata vel proposita fuerint, ut superius continetur.

Ita videlicet quod, pro predictis vel eorum aliquo, non possimus nos seu nostri facere vel movere tibi \seu/ tuis peticionem aliquam seu demandam, nec aliquam penam civilem seu criminalem in personas vel res tuas vel eorum imponere seu infligere ullo modo; sed sitis tu et tui et ipsi ac sui, cum omnibus bonis vestris presentibus et futuris, liberi et immunes ac penitus perpetuo absoluti ab omnibus et singulis supra dictis et aliis contra te vel ipsos denunciatis et propositis, ut dictum est, ac si hic essent comprehensa omnia et singula capitula contra te proposita de quibus te absolvimus ut est dictum, et sicut melius et utilius dici potest et intelligi ad tuum et ipsorum bonum et sanum ac sincerum intellectum. Mandantes etc.

Et si forte karissimus filius noster infans Petrus faceret tibi dicto [P][7] Vives aliquam peticionem seu demandam (de tempore per quod dictam baiuliam tenuisti pro dicto filio nostro, de quo cartam vel albaranum habes, vel racione iniuriarum per te vel locum tuum tenentes factarum Sarracenis predictis, ⟨seu⟩ racione alicuius pene sive calonie predictorum de quibus te absolvimus) nos in istis ponemus ante, et te inde indempnem servabimus cum omnibus bonis tuis.

Sed si ipse filius noster demandam tibi fecerit, occasione dicte baiulie racione compoti aut minus compoti, ex hoc respondere tenearis eidem; et nos ex hoc te non teneamur indempnem servare. Mandamus itaque firmiter etc.

Datum Barchinone, v idus Augusti, anno domini MCCLXX quarto.

21

ACA, Jaume I, Reg. Canc. 19, fol. 172

Barcelona
6 September 1274

Guidamus et assecuramus vos Azachum Barbut, Çalemam Barbut, et Abraham Samaria, et Abraham de Gerunda, Iudeos Valencie et omnia bona vestra ubique habita et habenda; ita quod Vives filius Iuceffi Abenvives, Iudeus Valencie, vel aliquis alius Iudeus de sua parentela ⟨non possit vos accusare⟩ vel aliquem vestrum de aliquibus criminibus; nec ad ipsorum accusacionem vel denunciacionem possit fieri inquisicio ⟨contra vos, nisi primo obligaverint se ad talionem⟩.[8]

Sed si de debitis vel aliis quibuslibet factis civilibus querimoniam proponerint contra ⟨vos, tenearis eis⟩ respondere et facere inde ius. Mandantes etc.

Datum Barchinone, VIII idus Septembris, anno domini MCCLXX quarto.

22[9]

ACA, Jaume I, Reg. Canc. 20, fol. 228v

Lérida
24 March 1275 (not 1274)

Per nos et nostros damus et concedimus vobis Ermengaudo de Selgua et vestris in perpetuum, in emendam undecim iovatarum terre quas vobis et Matheo fratri vestro quondam dederamus in termino de Algeroz de Algezira, cum carta nostra quam vos nobis reddidistis, illas VIII iovatas terre quas David Almascaran Iudeus habebat ex donacione nostra in cequia de Algezira. Quas quidem nos ei emparavimus, eo quia dictus David ivit ad populandum apud Oriolam et in dicta hereditate non facit residenciam personalem; ita scilicet quod dictas VIII iovatas terre, non obstante dicta donacione dicti Davidis, habeatis vos et vestri in perpetuum, teneatis, possideatis, et expletetis ad dandum, vendendum, impignorandum, alienandum, et ad omnes vestras vestrorumque voluntates cui et quibus volueritis inde libere faciendas, exceptis sanctis clericis et personis religiosis.

Retinemus tamen quod vos faciatis in Algezira residenciam personalem, et quod dictas VIII iovatas terre non possitis vendere hinc ad X annos primos venturos.

Datum Ilerde, IX kalendas Aprilis, anno domini MCCLXX quarto.

23

ACA, Jaume I, Reg. Canc. 20, fol. 242

Lérida
17 April 1275

Quod nos Iacobus dei gracia etc. Per nos et nostros concedimus et indulgemus vobis, aliame Iudeorum Valencie presentibus et futuris in perpetuum, quod non teneamini respondere de aliquo in posse iusticie Valencie; nec iusticia Valencie capiat vel captum seu captos detineat aliquem vel aliquos Iudeos sive Iudeas aliqua racione; sed baiulus Valencie, presens scilicet vel futuri, cognoscat de querimoniis omnibus que de vobis seu de quolibet vestrum habebuntur qualibet racione, et capiat illos Iudeos sive Iudeas qui capiendi fuerint quacumque racione, et captos detineant in capcione sive carcere nostro Valencie.

Concedentes eciam et indulgentes vobis quod nos vel nostri aut aliqui nostri officiales non possimus Iudeos vel Iudeas, qui vel que apud Valenciam venient populatum, inquietare vel demandare aliquo modo, nec contra eos inquirere racione alicuius criminis seu maleficii vel debiti – si quod ipsi, antequam in Valencia se mutent, fecerint seu commiserint quoquo modo extra terram nostram; et quod omnes illi Iudei qui fugierunt de terra nostra racione cuiuslibet criminis de quo fuerint inculpati, in quo sentencia lata non fuerit vel quod per testes sufficientes probare non possit, possint tornare et stare salve et secure, ita quod ipsa racione in tormentis non ponantur, ipsis tamen facientibus querelantibus de ipsis iusticie complementum, et dantibus fideiussores idoneos quod stent iuri super ipsis.

Concedimus eciam et damus vobis et vestris quod aliquis Sarracenus seu Sarracena alicuius Iudei seu Iudee habitatorum Valencie vel aliorum locorum regni eiusdem non pignorentur vel emparentur eisdem Iudeis, racione debiti seu peite aut alterius cuiuslibet exaccionis sive demande regalis, dummodo alia bona inveniantur dominis ipsorum Sarracenorum que eis valeant pignorari; nec obstet in hiis forus Valencie aliquis faciens in contrarium quoquo modo. Mandantes etc.

Datum Ilerde, xv kalendas Madii, anno domini MCCLXX quinto.

24

ACA, Jaume I, Reg. Canc. 20, fol. 252r,v

Lérida
6 May 1275

Quod cum Matheus de Monte Regali miles et Dulcia uxor eius et Guarnerius de Monte Regali frater dicti Mathei vendiderint vobis, Astrugo Iacobo Xixo Iudeo nostro, furnum, balnea, cellarium, et molendina sua sita in civitate Valencie et terminis suis, pro precio triginta milium solidorum regalium Valencie cum carta prout in ea continetur: idcirco nos Iacobus etc. ad instanciam et supplicacionem dicti Mathei et uxoris sue et fratris eius predictorum, per nos et nostros instituimus nos vobis dicto Astrugo Iacobo Xixo Iudeo nostro et vestris in perpetuum fidanciam salvitatis et eviccionis predicte vendicionis furni, balneorum, cellarii, et molendinorum predictorum, que ipsi Matheus et Dulcia uxor sua et Guarnerius frater dicti Mathei predicti vendiderint vobis et vestris ut dictum est et in carta ipsius vendicionis plenius continetur.

Ita videlicet ut nos et nostri teneamur salvare et defendere, vobis dicto Astrugo Iacob et vestris in perpetuum, omnia et singula vobis et vestris a dicto Matheo et uxore sua et Guarnerio fratre dicti Mathei vendita, ut est dictum. Et teneamur eciam inde vobis et vestris perpetuo de eviccione et legitima [*fol. 252v*] guarencia contra omnes personas, secundum forum Valencie in iudicio et extra iudicium ubique, sicut ipsi de eviccione et guarencia predictorum se vobis obligarunt in dicta carta et [= ut] in ea melius continetur, et sicut melius etc.

Volentes eciam quod procurator noster regni Valencie et baiulus Valencie presens scilicet et futuri teneantur, nomine et loco nostri, salvare et defendere vobis et vestris predicta omnia et singula, et de eviccione et guarencia ipsorum, dum nos vel nostri successores in regno Valencie non fuerimus personaliter constituti, sicut nos si presentes essemus facere deberemus, quandocumque et quocienscumque vobis vel vestris inde fuerint requisiti, non expectato nostro alio mandamento. Et predicta omnia firma habeant et observent etc.

Datum Ilerde, ii nonas Madii, anno domini MCCLXX quinto.

25[10]

ACA, Jaume I, Reg. Canc. 20, fol. 331v

Valencia city

15 March 1276 (not 1275)

Per nos et nostros laudamus, concedimus, et confirmamus tibi, Vitali de ⟨Favars⟩, et tuis in perpetuum stabilimentum illud, quod Iacobus de Linars baiulus noster Candie fecit tibi et tuis, de quodam molendino construendo et hedificando in termino Candie cum carta publica scripta per Bertrandum scriptorem puᵒ[b]licum Candie, prout in ea plenius continetur; ita videlicet quod tu et tui possitis facere et construhere, ac constructum [h]abeatis ibi in dicto loco in perpetuum, dictum molendinum ad censum in dicta carta contentum, et ad dandum, vendendum, impignorandum, ac alienandum et ad omnes tuas et tuorum voluntates inde cuilibet faciendas exceptis militibus et sanctis, et salvis nobis et nostris dicto censu in dicta carta contento et alio pleno iure et dominio nostro, prout in eadem carta a dicto Iacobo de Linars tibi facta plenius continetur.

Concedimus eciam tibi et tuis quod, ad opus et usus dicti molendini, possitis semper accipere aquam ei necessariam de rivo vocato de Villa Longa, a molendino scilicet Ashaachi Barbut Iudei quondam infra; et nullus hoc tibi et tuis prohibeat, nisi iusta racione et necesitate rigandi terram suam vel alia iusta causa illud valeant prohibere. Mandantes firmiter baiulo, iusticie, et iuratis Candie presentibus et futuris quod predicta firma habeant et observant et non contraveniant, nec aliquem contravenire permittant aliqua racione.

Datum Valencie, idus Marcii, anno domini MCCLXX quinto, presentibus Bernardo Guillelmi de Entença, Petro Ferrandi, Atho de Focibus, Ferrarino de Liçana, Raimundo de Moncada.

THE AL-AZRAQ TREATY

CASTILIAN TEXT

The transcript respects text and orthography, introduces paragraphs and punctuation, regularizes capitalization, separates a few words from their prepositions (with apostrophe where appropriate), omits the accent over y, renders the ampersand (twice replaced by the scribe in the text as *et*) always as *et*, and indicates line endings by slashes to allow correlation with the Arabic. For other sigla see p. 288. The text has only a few obvious abbreviations; it distinguishes *u* and *v*, but does not always form them distinctively. Points isolate castle names, and dashes separate each word and number-group in the date.

ACA, Jaume I, perg. 947

El Poet, at Alcalá

16 April 1244

Conoscuda cosa sea a quantos son et seran: como yo Habuadele Yuan Fudayl, alguazil et senor d'Alcala, me fago vuestro vassallo de vos senor / don Alfonsso primero fijo del rey d'Aragon, et do vos ocho castielos – el uno dizen Pop, et el otro Tarbana, et Margarita, Churolas, Castiel, / Alcala, Galinera, et Borbunchen.

Estos castielos sobredichos vos do con sus alcarias, et con terminos, et con pastos, et q [=con] quanto les perteneçe. Et /d'estos avandichos castielos do a vos senor don Alfonsso dos castielos luego, Pop et Tarbana; et retengo pora mi Alcala et Borbunchen, por eredat pora mi et pora mios fijos et pora mio linage et por fer de los toda mi voluntade. Et los otros quatro castielos – Margarita, Churolas, /Castiel, et Galinera – estos tengo yo por tres annos, en tal convenencia que ayades vos senor don Alfonsso la meetad de la renda, et yo la otra / meetat; et complidos estos tres annos, que vos de los castielos forros et quitos sin tota mala pleytesia, con todos sos terminos et con todos sos de- / rechos assi como de suso dicho es.

Et demas fago esta convenencia conbusco sennor: que de quantos castielos yo pueda ganar d'aqui adelant fasta / los tres annos que vos de la meetat de la renda; et los tres annos complidos, que vos de los castielos que ganare con los otros quatro, assi como de / suso dicho es.

Et yo don Alfonsso por la gracia de dios infant, primero fijo del rey d'Aragon, recibo a vos Abuabdele Yuan Fudayl alguazil et se- /nor d'Alcala por mio amado et mucho alto et muy onrrado et mio fiel vassallo. Et otorgo et do vos dos castielos, Alcala et Borbunchen, por eredamien- / to a vos et a todo vuestro linage por dar, vender, enpenar, et por fer de los toda vuestra voluntat.

Et do vos las rendas de dos alcarias de Hebo et de / Tollo por estos tres annos et depues de los tres annos que me lexedes estas dos alcarias con los otros castielos.

Demas juro et convengo et otorgo, que / tenga todas estas convenencias assi como °[de] s[uso s]cripto es, pero assi °[que] del castielo d'Alcala et de lo que vos do que seades mio vassallo.

Data carta / apud Puteulum, die Aprilis, era MCCLXXXII⁰./

Testes huius rei:	dompnus Guillelmus Hugo	dompnus Gonbaldus miles
dompnus Petrus Maça	dompnus Petrus Sancii Gurren	dompnus Raymundi de Montepessulano

Sig + num Alfonssi infantis, illustris regis Aragonum primogeniti.

Ego . . . mandato ipsius hanc cartam scripsi; et hoc sig + num meum apposui loco, die et era prefixis.

ARABIC TEXT

I shall present the Arabic original in a joint article with my colleague Paul Chevedden, who prepared the translation below as well as a transcription, translation, and extensive morphological–syntactic and other stylistic analysis to come. Professor James Monroe of the University of California at Berkeley contributed valuable suggestions. Marginal numbers below indicate successive lines of Arabic text. As in previous documents, intrusions in square brackets clarify the content. The document itself is discussed at length in chapter 10.

ACA, same charter, interlinear

Same place
15 April 1245

1) In the name of God, the Compassionate, the Merciful. May God bless our Lord Muḥammad and his family.

2) This is a noble decree, ordered by the Exalted Prince [al-malik], the Heroic, the Most Fortunate, [he whose beneficence is] hoped for [and] sought, the Infante Don Alfonso, son of the Exalted King, the Divinely Assisted, the Lord of Aragon,

3) [conferred] upon the Most Illustrious Wazīr, the Noble, the Highest, the Most Eminent, the Most Exalted Abū ʿAbd Allāh b. Hudhayl, may God honor him. [Wherefore] the abovementioned Exalted Prince makes an agreement with him for three [years]

4) from the present date, which is stated at the end of the decree, that his [the Wazīr's] property and retainer[s] may remain in his castles, and that the abovementioned Wazīr will give to

5) the abovementioned Exalted Prince two castles, namely Pop and Tárbena, which he will now hand over to him. The rest of the castles will remain in the possession of the abovementioned Wazīr, namely Castell, Cheroles,

6) Margarida, Alcalá, Perpunchent, and Gallinera, until the end of three years. But the abovementioned Wazīr will hand them over to the abovementioned Prince

7) when the three years have expired, except for the castle of Alcalá with its revenues and the revenues of the villages of Perpunchent, which will remain henceforth in the perpetual possession of the abovementioned Wazīr

8) and his descendant for the duration of the reign of the Exalted Prince. [Furthermore], the Exalted Prince will give to the abovementioned Wazīr the revenues of Ebo and Tollos for the duration of the three years. When

9) he [the Wazīr] hands over to him [the Prince] the abovementioned castles, namely Margarida, Castell, Cheroles, and Gallinera, he [the Wazīr] will [also] hand over to him [the Prince] Ebo and Tollos. The Exalted Prince [also agrees] to give to the qāʾ[ʾid]

10) Abū Yaḥyā b. Abū [I]shāq, the Lord of Castell, the village[s] of Ispalim [?] and Petracos to be his perpetually for the reign of the Prince, [both] for himself and his descendant.

11) [It is further agreed] that the Wazīr will give to the Exalted Prince from the four castles, which he will hand over to him [after] these three years [i.e., Margarida, Castell, Cheroles, and Gallinera], half the tithe [al-ʿushr]; and whatever

12) castles the Wazīr obtains [for] the Lord of Aragon, either by force or by capitulation [literally: either by power or by their friendship], the Wazīr will have half of the revenue [from these castles] for the duration of the three years. But when

13) the three years expire, he [the Wazīr] will hand them [i.e., the castles which he has obtained] over to him [the Prince] along with the four [other] castles [i.e., Margarida, Castell, Cheroles, and Gallinera]. Written on the fifteenth of the month of Dh-u [ʾl-] Qaʿda in the year 642 [15 April 1245].

Notes

I MUSLIM—CHRISTIAN CONFLICT AND CONTACT

1 See bibliography.
2 Fletcher, *León*, 8–9. Cantarino, *Monjes y musulmanes*. Pastor de Togneri, *Del islam al cristianismo*, e.g. 9–17, 129–34. Glick, *Islamic and Christian Spain*, and *Irrigation*. Castro, *Spaniards*, posthumous *Essays*. Sánchez-Albornoz, *Spain*. Epalza, 'Ibn Sidah,' 171n., Epalza and Llobregat, '¿Mozárabes en tierras valencianas?' and below, pp. 178–9. Bramon, *Contra moros*, ch. 2. Monroe, *Shuʿūbiyya*, 5–8; *Poetry* 12–15.
3 *Congresso Liguria–Catalogna*, e.g. 70ff., 81ff., 576ff. Bonnassie, *Catalogne*. Lewis, *Society*.
4 Recent work on the thirteenth-century Islamic littoral includes Huici's magisterial *Valencia musulmana*, and the works by Barceló Torres, Bazzana, Boswell, Bramon, Epalza, Guichard, Molina López, Poveda Sánchez, Tapia Garrido, Urvoy, Vilar, the Balearic monographs by Rosselló Bordoy, and works in the proceedings of the *II Coloquio hispano–tunecino*, in the bibliography.
5 *Naval power*, ch. 7.
6 *Muslim communities*, 400.
7 Joan Fuster, intro. to Burns, *Jaume I*; Guichard, 'Sofra,' 64–5.
8 Burns, *Islam*, 9–10, 48 (quotes).
9 Boswell, *Muslim communities*, 88. Cardaillac, *Morisques*, 153.
10 Burns, 'Mudéjares: metodología,' 456–7; *Colonialism*, 11, 27–8; 'Transition,' 89, 93. Boswell, *Muslim communities*, 232, 242, despite fiscal ruination on 235ff. Roca Traver, 'Vida mudéjar,' 139.
11 Ibn Khaldūn, *Muqaddimah*, I, ch. 2, sec. 23.
12 Burns, 'Christian feudal order,' 105–6; 'Royaume chrétien'; *Islam*, 164, 167, 169, 170, 311–12.
13 Guichard, 'Société rurale,' 51.
14 *Muqaddimah*, I, 273, 335; II, 305.
15 *Ibid.*, I, 315–16, 380–2, 470; II, 116–17. Alfonso, *Primera crónica*, II, ch. 1037. Ibn Jubayr, *Voyages*, II, 277. al-Maqqarī, *Dynasties*, I, 101–2. For the 'feudal lords' of ninth-century Tunisia, defying central power from the fortresses they 'owned,' see Talbi, 'Economy in Ifrīqiya,' 212, 217. Bresc, 'Mudéjars et la Sicile,' 55–6. Ahmad, *Islamic Sicily*, 36.
16 Torres Delgado, *Reino nazarí*, 75, 85. Barceló, 'Abū Zayd,' 107. Muntaner, *Crònica*, ch. 9. *Crónica de San Juan de la Peña*, ch. 36.
17 *Llibre dels feyts*, chs. 242, 307–9. Guichard, ''Seigneur musulman,' 283–334. Burns, *Islam*, chs. 13–14 (lords); *Colonialism*, 234.

18 Bazzana and Guichard articles in bibliography. Lévi-Provençal, *L'Espagne musulmane*, ch. 2, pt 1.

19 Guitart, *Castillos de Aragón*, I, 27; II, 13, 81–2.

20 ACA, reg. 46, fol. 37 (11 April 1280): 'Dilecto suo Çapate alcaydo de Biar, salutem et dileccionem; mandamus vobis quatenus compellatis ipsos populatores de Biar qui deputati sunt ad residendum in albachara castri de Biar per Iacobum de Linares procuratorem hereditatum dicti castri quod transferant incontinenti et teneant eorum domicilia in eodem albachara; datum Algezire, idus Aprilis anno domini MCCLXXX.' Reg. 44, fol. 169v (13 February [1279] 1280): 'Baiulo et iusticie Corbarie; mandamus vobis quatenus non compellatis nec compelli permittatis Peretum de Sobirats ad construhendum domicilium, et residenciam faciendum, intus castrum de Corbaria, quum nos concedimus ei de gracia quod dictum domicilium suum construat et residenciam faciat sicut alii faciant extra murum dicti castri; datum Valencie, idus Februarii.' At the end of the year another order gave to Pero López de Zorito 'açoloquiam castri nostri de Corbaria, ita quod eandem açoloquiam condirectam teneas, et in ea maneas et hospicium tuum teneas dum nobis placuerit' (reg. 48, fol. 193 (8 December 1280)). Reg. 50, fol. 120v (14 July 1281): 'edificaverint domos in albacario castri de Corbaria'; 'destruatis et diruatis omnes alquerias et domos.' The Bocairente document is in ch. 9, n. 7.

21 Antonio Aragó, 'Tenentiae castrorum,' 566.

22 *Llibre dels feyts*, chs. 113–14, 128, 130–1, 153, 164–9, 187, 194–203. Desclot, *Crònica, c.* 49. Jiménez da Rada, *De rebus Hispaniae*, bk VI, ch. 5.

23 Talbi, 'Economy in Ifrīqiya,' 212, 213, 217, 219, 224. Udovitch, 'Land tenure,' 17. Ashtor, 'Industry,' 99, 119. Hansen, 'Ottoman Egypt,' 473. Nowshirvani, 'Iran agriculture,' 473. Keddie, 'Change in the Middle East,' 776, 779. Chalmeta, 'Concesiones territoriales,' 86; 'Féodalité,' 99. Bosch, 'al-Andalus', 189. Burns, *Islam*, 50, 233, 278 (Poliak), 372. Arié, *L'Espagne des Naṣrides*, 227 ('vassaux'). Lapidus, *Muslim cities*, 64, 260, index ('corvées').

24 *Islam*, 22.

25 *Muslim communities*, 41–2.

26 *Islamic and Christian Spain*, 151. Arié, *L'Espagne des Naṣrides*, 351–2.

27 *Islam*, 102–3; *Colonialism*, 110. Glick, *Islamic and Christian Spain*, 151. Tarradell, *País valencià*, I, 147–55. Guichard, 'Sofra,' 64, 70. Chalmeta, review in *Hispania*, XXXVII, 439–42.

28 *Islam*, chs. 6 and 7 and bibliography for the surrender charters; pp. 225, 407 (Maryam). Arié, *L'Espagne des Naṣrides*, 220. Boswell, *Muslim communities*, 219, 232–6. Ibn Khaldūn, *Muqaddimah*, II, 279. Talbi, 'Economy in Ifrīqiya,' 214–19, 221–3, 231, 237. Udovitch, 'Land tenure,' 18. Keddie, 'Change in the Middle East', 766.

29 Guichard, 'Société rurale,' 41–52. Boswell, *Muslim communities*, 336–8. Rubiera, 'Falsos antropónimos.'

30 Poveda, 'Toponimia de Mayūrqa,' 75–101. *Llibre dels feyts*, ch. 318. Arié, *L'Espagne des Naṣrides*, 226 (Granada).

31 Glick, *Irrigation*, esp. ch. 10.

2 SURRENDER CONSTITUTIONS

1 Morony, 'Iraq communities,' 113–35; 'Conquerors and conquered,' 73–87. Goitein, *Mediterranean society*, II, 404. Innocent IV, *Les registres*, I, 424, no. 2838. Cohen, *Friars and Jews*, ch. 10. *Partidas, part.* 7, *tits.* 24–5. Epalza, 'Mozárabes,' 'Morisques.'

2   Font Rius, *Cartas de población*, I, ix, xxii; II, 785–6, and 'Ascó y Ribera.' Burns, *Islam*, 156. Muldoon, *Popes, lawyers, infidels*, ch. 1, and pp. 15–22, 30ff., 50–2. Epalza, 'Morisques, Mudéjares.'

3   Burns, *Islam*, 119–21, 257n. (lawsuit). Chabás, 'Moros de Eslida,' 262–3. *Col. dip.*, I, 241 (charter).

4   ACA, reg. 10, fol. 82 (1 July 1258) waives mismanagement claims 'de Eslida, de Beyo, de Ayn.' Reg. 11, fol. 266v (2 July 1258?): 'item in Eslida DC morabatinos . . . et debet tenere Gaucerandus de [Montecatheno] castrum de Eslida, et eius fructus recipere de paschale transacto ad duos annos cum suis expensis.' Reg. 10, fol. 131 (23 February [1259] 1260): 'quod reciperet compotum a Galserando de Montechatheno de reditibus castri [et ville] de Eslida et . . . traderet castrum et villam de Eslida Guillelmo de Angularia.' Pere III, reg. 38, fol. 3r,v (27 September 1276) below in appendix 2, doc. 1. On Teresa and Jérica see p. 208 below.

5   Soldevila, *Pere*, part 2, I, 23, 31; appendix 1, docs. 50 (29 December 1276), 52 (13 January [1276] 1277); appendix 2, Pere's itinerary. ACA, Pere III, reg. 39, fol. 184 (9 April 1277) has the first post-revolt castellan: 'noverint universi quod nos Petrus dei gracia rex Aragonum tradimus et commendamus vobis Raimundo Calvera militi de domo nostra, dum nobis placuerit, custodiam et retinenciam castri de Eslida; volentes et concedentes vobis quod, dum dictum castrum pro nobis tenueritis et nobis placuerit, habeatis et recipiatis pro custodia et retinencia dicti castri quolibet anno tria milia solidorum regalium.'

6   ACA, 'Liber patrimonii regii Valentiae,' a finding-aid codex of 1590, has Anfòs IV in 1416 record a privilege of Martí I (20 July 1409) that incorporates an order by Pere IV (12 March 1365) listing the castle and its Sierra de Eslida jurisdiction as then including Eslida, Ahín, Veo, Sueras, Fanzara, Lenxe, Vilalbuig, Lauret (Lloret), and Alid. Anfòs adds (his spellings): Almexerta, Benisahada, Ampadars, Selim, Alfeig, Eslida Valley, Almexera (different from the first above), Ahín Valley, Beniculeymen castle, Cauden near Suera, and Alcudia near Fanzara. Pere III Reg. 44, fol. 164v (12 December 1279) to 'comiti Dionisio' in 1244 'Bebo et Ayn,' later exchanged at the plea of 'comitisse Ungarie et filiorum vestrorum Amoris et Gabrielis'; reg. 22, fols. 107–8 (25 September 1278): 'solvatis nobis D solidos, racione cartarum quas habuistis de scribania nostra.'

7   ACA, Pere IV, reg. 1205, fols. 45–6: 'la qual fou feta e dada en lo castell Sarrana a XII dies de Març en l'any . . . del nostre regne XXX,' addressed to 'vosaltres moros del castell e vall d'Eslida qui per malvars consells enganars contra nos e la nostra corona vos erets rebellats e alçats e donats al rey de Castiella nostre publich enemich.' The first request is: 'demanen los moros de la Serra d'Eslida que lo senyor rey los conferin la carta feta per lo rey En Pere de bona memoria als moros d'Eslida.' Others include: 'item demanen que no sey tenguts de pujar aygua al castell'; 'item demanen que puxen cantar la çala'; 'item demanen que sien franchs de delme e de primicia.' Boswell, *Muslim communities*, 362–5, 392.

8   Piles Ros, *Bayle de Valencia*, docs. 90, 352; see docs. 99, 103, 126, 211, 229, 256, 290, 335, 357, 367, 392, 419, 517.

9   Burns, *Colonialism*, 162–73; 'Socioeconomic structure,' 254–9. Guichard, 'Problème de structures,' 703–4; 'Sofra,' 64–71. Boswell, *Muslim communities*, 167–9.

10 Toledo Girau, *Alfandech*; *Aguas*; *Monasterio de Valldigna*. Gascón, *Valldigna*; *Tabernes*. Muntaner, *Crònica*, ch. 9. Desclot, *Crònica*, ch. 49. *Llibre dels feyts*, ch. 313 (not the 'Alfandec' of ch. 253). *Repartiment*[1], under dates and beneficiaries of 1238 and 1249.

11 Soldevila, *Pere*, part 2, I, 14, 112, and appendix, docs. 12, 15, 27, 101. Burns, *Crusader kingdom*, I, 61, 82. Note 6 above on fees.

12 ACA, Jaume II, reg. 196, fols. 164v–165v (simply October or else 26 September 1277, and 1 April 1298), below in appendix 2, doc. 2. Cf. Toledo Girau's loose Castilian version, *Alfandech*, 71–2.

13 'Alfondeguilla y Castro,' 126–37, charter. Guichard notes a charter for Buñol in 1254 in ACA, reg. 282, fols. 46v–47v ('Sofra,' 65).

3 CHRISTIAN–MUSLIM CONFRONTATION

1 Harden, 'Element,' 63, 73–4, 77–9. Metlitzki, *Araby in England*, 177–86. Waltz ('Missions,' 170–86) repudiates Cutler's concept of pre-thirteenth-century missions to Muslims ('Conversion,' 57–71, 155–64). For background to the intellectual and mission confrontation, see works cited in the bibliography by Alverny (1965); N. Daniel; Kritzeck; Malvezzi; Monneret de Villard; Muldoon; Southern; Sweetman; Vernet.

2 Chenu, *Thomas d'Aquin*, intro.

3 Massignon, 'Ibn Sab'in,' 674–5.

4 Torres Fontes, *Reconquista de Murcia*, 73–4. *Itinerari*, 263 (1 October 1257).

5 Mansilla, *Documentación pontificia*, 44, doc. 27 (15 October 1088). Dunlop, 'Mission to Muslim Spain,' 259–310. Cutler, 'Monk of France,' 249–69.

6 Kritzeck, *Peter*, 20, 64, 116. Alverny, 'Traductions du Coran,' 69–131. Rubió y Lluch, *Cultura catalana*, I, docs. 323, 334, 361 (Catalan translations). Fita, 'Noticias,' 456 (1192). Mansilla, *Documentación pontificia*, 149, doc. 124 (17 November 1184), and his *Iglesia y curia*, 75 (the scribal Marrachios may stand not for Morocco but Marrakesh, to balance Seville).

7 Kritzeck, *Peter*, 161. Bernard, *De consideratione*, I, 1, 3 (*Opera*, III, 433); Baron, *Jews*, IV, 300. Cutler, 'Missions to Muslims,' 337–9; 'Innocent III,' 92ff. Vitry, *Lettres*, 83, 87–9, 94, 97, 137, 152.

8 Bacon, *Opus maius*, part 7, sec. 4, 787ff.; part 3, sec. 14, 112. Bacon's *Opus tertium* of 1267 targets: 'philosophi infideles, Arabes, Hebraei, et Graeci, qui habitant inter Christianos, ut in Hispania et in Aegypto et in partibus Orientis' (295). Dubois, *Recovery*, 115–16, 123–4, 150–1. *Scriptores praedicatorum*, I, 265 (Tripoli).

9 Daniel, 'Apocalyptic conversion,' 129–30, 138, 143–4.

10 Altaner, *Dominikanermissionen*, 108.

11 Penyafort report in Coll, 'Escuelas,' XVII, appendix 2, 138 (not 1246, but 1256 or 1258). Dufourcq, *L'Espagne catalane*, 98, 120, 188, 205, 248, 251, 260–70, 285. Ibn Khaldūn also records the conversions of the Almohad exiles. On Innocent IV's attempt to convert the Almohad al-Murtaḍā in 1246 through the Aragonese friar Lope Fernando de Ayn, see Tisserant and Wiet, 'Murtaḍâ,' 49.

12 Dufourcq, *L'Espagne catalane*, 270: similar episode in Ibn Khaldūn, *Berbères*, II, 403.

13 Muntaner, *Crònica*, chs. 44, 52. Zurita confuses him with the brother of the king of Tunis, and dates the episode 1281 (*Anales de Aragón*, lib. IV, ch. 13); Ibn Khaldūn notes that Muslims denounced him to Tunis as irreligious.

14 Ibn Khaldūn, *Berbères*, II, 439–40. Dufourcq, *L'Espagne catalane*, 413, 488–94.

15 *Llibre dels feyts*, ch. 375 (al-Azraq).

16 *Bullarium Sancti Iacobi*, 166, Innocent IV (24 September 1245): 'Zeit Aazon rex Zale illustris.'

17 Muntaner, *Crònica*, chs. 52, 85. Throop, *Criticism of the crusade*, 134–5 (conversion prophecies).

18 *Crónica de San Juan de la Peña*, ch. 35.

19 *Documentos*, I, 350 (12 March [1242] 1243), quote. Coll, 'Escuelas,' XVII, 138 (Penyafort). 'Ordinatio ecclesiae', fol. 145.

20 'Journey from Islam'; 'Riots,' ACA, Pere III, reg. 39, fol. 210v (26 June 1277) adds three converts who helped sixty settlers sack Alcira's Moorish quarter.

21 Daniel, *Franciscan concept of mission*, ch. 5, for Spain pp. 41–5; ch. 6 on ideology. Burns, *Crusader kingdom*, I, 198–207; II, 467–9. Cohen, *Friars and Jews*, chs. 2, 3, 9.

22 Colbert, *Córdoba martyrs*; Cutler, 'Spanish martyrs'; Waltz, 'Martyr movement.'

23 Amorós Payá, 'Perusa y Saxoferrato.' Ibn 'Idhārī, *al-Bayān*, I, 321.

24 *Cortes de Aragón, Valencia, Cataluña*, I, 123. Watt, 'Philosophy under the Almohads,' 106.

25 *De rationibus fidei*, chs. 1, 2.

26 Massignon, 'Ibn Sab'īn,' 660. Burns, 'Riots,' 380–1.

27 Lull, *Opera latina*, II, 404–5, IV, 103; *Doctrina* (with commentary) in Sugranyes, *Lulle*, 92; *Blanquerna*, chs. 43, 86; and texts in Peers, *Lull*, 67, 93. Cohen, *Friars and Jews*, ch. 8, his convert-or-banish approach to Jews.

28 Lull, *Blanquerna*, chs. 55, 75, 84, 88, 93–5; cf. chs. 50, 61, 76, 87, 88. Hillgarth, *Lull*, 28, 41, 48. Garcías, *Miramar*.

29 Müller, *Konzil von Vienne*, 696. Tritton, *Muslim education*, 144–5.

30 Bacon, *Opus tertium*, 88, 303–4.

31 Altaner, *Dominikanermissionen*, ch. 5. Coll, 'Escuelas,' XVII, 136–8 (pope).

32 *Raymundiana*, 31–2, notes on 60–1, by executor. Gerard de Frachet's 1254 'Vitae,' 3 (colleague). Pere Marsili's 1312 'Vita,' 13–14. Cohen, *Friars and Jews*, 163–9.

33 Humbert de Romans, in *Litterae magistrorum*, 19, doc. 5. Cf. Coll, Berthier, Cortabarría. Marsili, 'Vita,' 12 (*philosophus*).

34 Marsili, 'Vita,' 12. Dating the move from Murcia 1279–80, Coll posits a short-lived *arabicum* at Barcelona between the Tunis loss and the Murcia creation, but this conjecture owes something to his refusal to credit a Murcian school until 1266.

35 *Acta capitulorum*, 612 (1250). Burns, *Crusader kingdom*, I, 204–5; II, 470. Coll's conjecture that a language school functioned at Valencia from 1258 to 1266 is allied to his dubious theory on the origins of the Murcian school ('Escuelas,' XVII, 133).

36 *Litterae magistrorum*, 40, doc. 8b.

37 *Acta capitulorum*, 626 (1250). Coll, 'Escuelas,' XVIII, 62; XVII, 135.

38 Burns, *Crusader kingdom*, I, 204, 209; II, 470, 473.

39 Coll, 'Escuelas,' XVIII, 77 (provincial *acta*).

40 Martínez Ferrando, *Jaime II*, doc. 57 (13 August 1308).

41 Eimeric, 'Vita,' 32. Fernández y González, *Mudéjares*, doc. 35 (8 December 1254).

42 Dufeil, 'L'Orient à Paris,' 48–9, concludes these must have been Near Eastern Christians of varied rites, but contemporary preoccupation with conversion suggests other hypotheses. *Corpus iuris canonici*, under *Clementinae*, *lib.* V, *tit.* I, *c.* 1.

43 Asín, 'Averroísmo de Aquino,' esp. 320–3. Getino, *Summa y Pugio*, sums up Asín's position (5–8), refutes it by chronology (8–19), poses and answers minute objections, then broadens the discussion. Asín's ghost lingered in the further corners of academe until decisively laid to rest by Llovera, in his 'Discurso inaugural de la sección de teología en el congreso de la Asociación para el progreso de las ciencias,' at Barcelona, 1929. Llovera supplemented

Getino's chronological approach; he gained wide circulation by allowing long quotations and paraphrases from his speech (never published in full) to appear in the popular manual by Tomás and Joaquín Carreras y Artau, *Historia de filosofía española* (1939), 163–6.

44 Casciaro, *El diálogo de Tomás con musulmanes y judíos*, 44. Marc more generally assigns the work as beginning between November 1269 and March 1270, ending between mid-December 1272 and mid-February 1273 (*Contra gentiles*, I, intro.). Murphy sums up Marc's external and internal evidence, in the light of the previous controversy, in 'Date and purpose of the *Contra gentiles*,' 405ff. Weisheipl, *Thomas*, 130–2, 360; and the opposition of Huerga, " 'Summa' y 'Pugio,' " 533–57.

45 '*Contra gentiles* à Paris,' 223ff.

46 Marsili, 'Vita,' 12. Coll, 'Escuelas,' XVII, 130 (names); XVIII, 79–80 (1312 provincial *acta*). *Repartimiento de Murcia*, viii-ix.

47 Burns, *Crusader kingdom*, I, 206. Eimeric, 'Vita,' 32 (quote).

48 On Puigventós see Diago, *Predicadores*, 47–8; Escolano, *Décadas de Valencia*, II, ch. 1 (misdating his death as 1320); Sorió, *De viris illustribus*, 48. On Martí see esp. Robles, *Escritores dominicos*, 68–77, with seven bibliographies and over two hundred parallels between the *Pugio* and *Contra gentiles*; see also Collell, *Escritores dominicos*, 171–3. Cohen, *Friars and Jews*, ch. 6; and *Llibre dels feyts*, ch. 490.

49 Coll, 'Escuelas,' XVII, 123. The Arabic–Latin lexicon or word list attributed to Martí, *Vocabulista in arabico* – later debated and given other attributions – was probably done by Martí in Valencia, glossed by contemporaries elsewhere, and preserved in an amplified, late-thirteenth-century copy made at Majorca (Sanchis Guarner, *Parlars romànics de València*, 135–40).

50 Ibn Rashīq, text in 'Una polémica en Murcia,' 67–72, from al-Wansharīshī (d. 1508). The episode dates from after the tributary conquest in 1243 and before his father's death in 1263. Ibn Rashīq was still living in 1275–6; if his beardless adolescence situates the episode around 1250, my attribution of an early date for Murcia's school gains strength; in any case, this disposes of Coll's date of 1266.

51 Ibn Khaldūn, *Muqaddimah*, III, 117–18. Dufourcq, *L'Espagne catalane*, 580–2, 585–6. Urvoy, 'Langue arabe et les missionaires,' esp. 420–5; her *Ulémas andalous*, ch. 3, and 202–7; and her 'Mouvements religieux,' 224–5, 251–2, 281, 289, 291–3. Cardaillac, *Morisques*, 348. On the Valencian preaching program see Burns, 'Journey from Islam,' 345–6, 352–3.

4 PIRACY: ISLAMIC–CHRISTIAN INTERFACE

1 *Mediterranean world*, II, 867. On contraband and smuggling see Burns, 'Renegades,' 341ff.

2 Kedar, *Genoese and Venetian*, 23–4, 29–31, 178.

3 See bibliography. Later Catalonia and the Mediterranean are better served; see for example Putzulu (1959), Ferrer i Mallol (1968), Airaldi (1974), Hinojosa (1975), Fonseca, Balletto, and Martignone (all 1978), Bresc and Guiral (1980), and on sixteenth-century Valencia García Martínez (1980), Martínez Ortiz (1982), and Mollat (1975, 1980).

4 Aunós, *Derecho catalán*, 166–7. García Sanz, *Marina catalana*, 121, 123, 130. *Libro del consulado*, tit. 12, six chapters. Del Treppo, *Els mercaders catalans*, 20. Salavert, 'Expansión mediterránea,' 380–1. Schaube, *Handelsgeschichte*, no. 7. Paris, *Chronica*, III, 384 ('piratis et vispilionibus referta, mercatoribus et peregrinis . . . inimicissima'), 505. For Jaumes's title 'almiray i capitani general de l'esgleya

de Roma' see the letter from the sultan of Nasrid Granada (23 July 1272), edited by Torres Delgado, 'Mediterráneo nazarí,' 235.

5 *Mediterranean society*, I, 330.

6 Dufourcq, *L'Espagne catalane*, 83.

7 *Llibre dels feyts*, ch. 92.

8 Capmany, *Memorias*, II, part 1, 33, doc. 16; cf. 66, doc. 43; Jaume here extended a Barcelona privilege of 1118 (I, 117–18). Dufourcq, 'Vers l'Afrique,' 19–24.

9 Gazulla, *Jaime*, docs. 34 (Ampurias count), 37 (Tripó), 40 (Cancull), and 62 (Marget). González Hurtebise, 'Documents inédits,' 1224 (Grony): 'facere omne malum quod facere poteritis ullo modo.' Vincke, 'Königtum und Sklaverei,' appendix, doc. 3 (July 1264) (archbishop).

10 Gazulla, *Jaime*, 64 (Cartagena; first license). ACA, reg. 19, fol. 95 (25 January 1274): 'noveritis nos concessisse Romeo de Castelleto militi almirallo et magistro Bonifacio capitaneo navis et galee armatarum Dertuse et sociis eorundem quod, ubicumque in portu et extra portum invenerint Iudeos vel Sarracenos aut res aliquas terre regis Tirmicii [*sic*], possint eos et eas capere et sibi licite retinere'; 'valeat autem concessio predicta in isto viatico, donec reversi fuerint de eodem.' *Ibid.*, separate charter: 'et est sciendum quod dictus Romeus de Castelleto nec aliqui de dicta armatura non debent capere vel impedire aliquem vel aliquos Iudeos qui de terra regis Trimicii ad terram nostram domini regis Aragonum causa populandi voluerint transmutare.' Fols. 95v–96 (24 January 1274): 'quidem Sarracenus senex' and others. Fol. 100v (3 February 1274): 'nullus de nostri gracia confidens, cursarius scilicet vel alius, audeat aliquam navem vel lignum in dicto portu ... invadere, capere, detinere, oscorcollare, forciare, pignorare, offendere vel gravare.'

11 *Itinerari*, docs. on 263, 270, and Miret i Sans, 'Represàlies a Catalunya,' 289–304, 385–417, including Pelós. Burns, *Islam*, 288. Dufourcq, 'Vers l'Afrique,' docs. of 1273–4. ACA, reg. 48, fol. 83v (15 July 1280), Abingalel; reg. 61, fol. 118v (4 May 1283), Macià, Ribalta; reg. 57, fol. 189 (29 August 1285); I shall publish these separately.

12 *Aureum opus*, Jaume I, doc. 32 (19 June 1250); Pere I (III of Catalonia), doc. 15 (1 December 1283). *Itinerari*, 493 (5 February 1274), on Manuel. *Col. dip.*, I, doc. 382 (19 June 1250); doc. 262 (24 September 1243). ACA, Pere III, reg. 61, fol. 126 (6 June 1283): 'conduxerat iam ante inhibicionem ... maiorem partem hominum necessariorum ad dictum armamentum ac ... logerii ipsarum.'

13 Dufourcq ed., 'Guerre Sarracenorum,' docs., 57, 80, 116, 119, 177, 193, 218, 238, 245, 304.

14 *Col. dip.*, III, doc. 1410 (7 September 1272). ACA, Bulas pontificias, Inn. IV, leg. 12, no. 64 (1 June 1251), Pandolfo, and reg. 38, fol. 106 (11 December 1276), which I shall publish soon. Reg. 41, fol. 54v (6 April 1279): 'Franciscum de Grimaldo et quosdam complices suos habitatores Nice cum quodam lembo armato ... cepisse violenter et rapuisse quoddam lignum Badocii civis Barchinone honeratum tritico et quandam barcham Boni Amici de Palafrugello honeratam genero'; 'caricari fecerant apud Narbonam causa portandi ipsum in Provincia.'

15 ACA, reg. 20, fols. 324v–325 (28 February [1275] 1276): 'Nos Iacobus dei gracia etc. intelleximus per te Petrum Moragues cursarium Valencie quod, cum tu intravisses in cursum ad partes Spanie contra Sarracenos cum uno ligno armato, et quidem homo nomine Alquer (qui totum in ipso cursu seu viatico ibat ad solidatam pro remerio in ipso ligno) victualia furaretur, tu ea racione abscidisti sibi auriculam cum cultello in viatico ante dicto. Idcirco, cum cuilibet domino ligni armati sit licitum homines ipsius ligni dum in cursu suo

fuerit pro maleficio (si quidem fecerit) corrigere et punire: per nos et nostros, si ita est quod racione predicta abscidisti auriculam dicto Alquer ut superius continetur, absolvimus et diffinimus te ab abs[c]isione auricule ante dicte, et ab omni peticione et demanda quam tibi possemus facere racione predicta, et ab omni eciam pena civili et criminali quam contra personam vel res tuas possemus infligere eadem racione.'

16 ACA, reg. 41, fol. 133v (21 July 1259); 'quod Garsias Sancii de Sancta Cruce morans in Requena abstulit iniuste ipsi Petro centum et decem et octo penas cirogrillorum, quas idem Petrus emerat in Castella et pro ipsis solverat iura que dare debebat. Que quidem Garsias, licet ab illustri rege Castelle mandatum recepit licatorie super restitucione dictarum penarum et procurator regni Valencie eidem Garsie scripsit similiter super eo, restituere noluit dicto Petro penas iam dictas.'

17 ACA, Pere III, reg. 43, fol. 8 (23 July 1284): 'scribaniam armate nostre Valencie, ita quod quando contingat nos facere armatam in Valencia, sitis scriptor tabule ipsius armate et utamini officio scriptoris in ipsa tabula.' Fol. 18 (8 August 1284) shows the financing of this or a companion fleet by the usual bonds (*albarana*): 'Petro Jordani quod veniat apud Tirasonam cum omnibus denariis quos debet tornare domino regi de armada anni preteriti et presentis, et de reditibus Emposte, et cum omnibus albaranis ipsarum armatarum et reditibus Emposte.' Crown appointments as ship secretary could bear time limits, as in a 1264 document to 'tibi Petro Eximini de Spellunca hinc ad quinque annos proxime completos scribaniam galee nostre quam apud Valenciam fieri facimus et armari, ita scilicet quod tu in dicta galea vadas et sis scriptor ipsius galee . . . mandantes firmiter comiti galee predicte quod te et non aliquem alium in scriptorem in scriptorem [*sic*] recipiat et habeat' (*ibid.*, reg. 13, fol. 158v, March 29).

18 *Furs*, preface. Boswell, *Muslim communities*, 174, 178, 234–5 (incl. draft, jails), though his *palomers* seem 'steersmen' (cf. Valencian nautical *paloma*). For *llenys* as scouts see Muntaner, *Crònica*, chs. 82, 135; as messengers, chs. 98, 105, 113, 130; of eighty oars, ch. 253; 'better oared,' ch. 83; with crossbowmen, ch. 130; of Catalan merchants, ch. 284; and on Valencia chs. 36 (seamen) and 31, 44, 92, 276–7. *Llibre dels feyts*, ch. 305 (*Montpellier*). For Alfonso see below, n. 22. See also Dotson, 'Galley design,' 20, 30; Robson, 'Catalan fleet'; La Mantia, *Codice*, docs. 25, 222, 226, 241. ACA, reg. 46, fol. 204v (14 June 1284): 'possitis armare ibidem quodam [*sic*] lignum de LXXX remis.'

19 Doc. in n. 15. *Itinerari*, 567.

20 Burns, *Islam*, 42–3. Torres Delgado, *Reino nazarí* and 'Mediterráneo nazarí,' has the earliest Arabic document on Granadan piracy, a 1272 seizure of a commercial ship of Jaume's people at Almería. For fourteenth-century materials see Arié, *L'Espagne des Naṣrides*, 272–6; Alarcón and Garcīa de Linares, *Documentos árabes*, docs. 5, 60–7, 129–31.

21 Soldevila, *Pere*, part 2, I, appendix, doc. 59 (10 March [1276] 1277), summons. Burns, *Islam*, 334. ACA, reg. 23, fols, 54v–55 (16 June 1276): 'ut mittant galeas apud Deniam in subsidium.'

22 *Fori*, rub. 137, *no.* 2; *rub.* 119, *no.* 14; cf. *rub.* 68, *no.* 38; *rub.* 128, *nos.* 2, 6. Luttrell, 'Galley oarsmen,' esp. 92–6. *Partidas, part.* 2, *tit.* 28, *ley* 6, II, 321; *part.* 2, *tit.* 24, *leyes* 4, 6, 9; *part.* 5, *tit.* 9, *ley* 13; *part.* 7, *tit.* 14, *ley* 18; cf. *part.* 5, *tit.* 9, *ley* 13, and *part.* 7, *tit.* 14, *ley* 18.

23 ACA, reg. 19, fol. 117 (27 March [1272] 1273); 'aliqui ex illis quos conducetis seu ad logerium ibunt vobiscum'; 'aliquod maleficium seu delictum dum in armamento fuerint ante dicto'; 'facere iusticiam debitam, prout fuerit facien-

dum secundum quod almiralli . . . facere consueverunt.' *Col. dip.*, III, doc. 1201 (6 February [1264] 1265). Reg. 40, fol. 95 (19 April 1278): 'tam in terra quam in mari iusticiam universis et singulis deputantis vel deputandis ad predictas armatas tam civiliter quam criminaliter faciendo, mandantes universis comitibus, nautis, marinariis et omnibus aliis hominibus predictarum armatarum quod vobis ut almirato nostro obediant.' ACA, Pere III, reg. 40, fol. 57v (13 January 1278), two documents on Pisà, which I shall publish soon.

5 KING JAUME'S JEWS: PROBLEM AND METHODOLOGY

1   See bibliography. Even for periods after Jaume I, there is little beyond the Piles Ros articles on the fifteenth century, Doñate Sebastiá's article and chapter, the Magdalena Nom de Déu articles and monographs which concentrate rather on the later centuries (samples in bibliography), Bernabéu López, Marcó i Dachs, and Hinojosa Montalvo (1979). My doctoral student, Leila Berner, currently finishing a thesis on the Barcelona Jews under King Jaume, has in hand a long-range project to transcribe all his documents on the Jews.

2   *Bayle de Valencia*, 48–50.

3   See bibliography. Local histories for Valencia usually ignore the Jews of Jaume's era or make passing mention.

4   Romano, 'Análisis de Régné,' 247ff.; his own articles, while concerned with King Pere and the realms in general, cast light on figures and movements of Jaume's Valencia; see especially his 'Funcionarios judíos.'

5   *Morella*, III, 556–9. Other misreadings include 'ut Iudei alii esse nostre' for 'alii terre nostre,' and 'in' for a crucial 'et.' The original is in ACA, reg. 12, fol. 143, from Zaragoza on 10 February [1263] 1264. The charter in *Col. dip.*, I, doc. 424 (8 May 1252), refers only to privileges for Majorcan Jews, delivered at Morella. *Repartiment*,[1] nos. 935, 3419, 3680.

6   ACA, reg. 14, fol. 60v (13 July 1264): expenses 'ad opus galaiarum quas fieri facimus in Valencia' assigned partly from the rents 'in iudaria Valencie nova.' (Martínez Ferrando, *Catálogo*, I, no. 561, misses this reference to the Jews.)

7   Burns, *Colonialism*, 270–91, 'Role of the Jews,' and 291–322, 'Christian financiers and collectors,' with some 150 manuscripts quoted.

8   Romano, 'Funcionarios judíos,' 8–9. Shneidman, *Aragonese–Catalan empire*, II, 485.

9   ACA, reg. 10, fol. 62v (29 April 1258): 'diffinimus tibi Ioanni Sancii, alumpno Ade de Paterna, et tuis in perpetuum . . . omnem accionem, racione Avingamerro, Sarraceni nostri, quem olim nequiter occidistis.' For Adam's family, career, and names see Burns, *Colonialism*, 292–9. Soldevila, *Pere*, part 1, I, 121. Torres Fontes, *Reconquista de Murcia*, 103. ACA, Pere III, reg. 44, fol. 149 (October 1279): 'intencio sit nostra et propositum homines nostros tam Christianos quam Iudeos quam Sarracenos in iusticia conservare.' Reg. 42, 148v (8 October 1279): 'conantur ipsos Iudeos ad fidem catolicam reducere minis, violenciis, et nonullis opprobriis, propter quod per populares locorum nostrorum, non predicacionis intencione ad ipsas sinagogas euntes sed potius ad illusionem et scandala, dicti Iudei possent offendi graviter et occidi . . . plurimum turbaremur: quia predicti Iudei sunt potius munitis induccionibus et racionabilibus suasionibusque aspiratibus attrahendi, cum nemo ad fidem nostram cogatur invitus.'

10 Garbell, 'Pronunciation of Hebrew,' 647ff., with attention to Catalan and Arabic deformations; Kaganoff, *Jewish names*, 12ff., 64, 98. Roca Traver provides an overlay map of Valencia city's Jewish quarter in 'Vida mudéjar,' 20;

Bramon has a color overlay in 'Judío,' *GERV*, VI, 88. Dufourcq, *Histoire économique*, 171–2. Baer, *Jews*, I, 193–5.

11   ACA, reg. 23, fol. 19v (March (?) [1274] 1275), below in appendix 3, doc. 19. *Itinerari*, 348, 352, 390, 473, 485–6, 506 (Ricard), and 423, 537 (Cascall: 'per batallam a caval in posse nostri [regis]'). *Col. dip.*, III, doc. 1408 (31 August 1273). Vendrell Gallostra, 'La familia Caballería,' 115–54, with our period largely from catalogs. On Judá and Salamó or Salomó in Valencia see Burns, *Colonialism*, 274–5.

6 PORTRAIT GALLERY: JEWS OF CRUSADER VALENCIA

1   ACA, reg. 10. fol. 53 (29 October 1257), below in appendix 3, doc. 1. Reg. 12, fol. 103v (20 August 1263) and fol. 106v (29 August 1263), below in appendix 3, docs. 10, 11.

2   ACA, reg. 10, fol. 55 (5 May 1258), and fol. 66 *bis*, r,v (26 May 1258), below in appendix 3, docs. 2, 3. *Col. dip.* II, doc. 744 (3 May 1258), omitted in the Martínez Ferrando catalog.

3   Of four uses in doc. 3, 'Mubarich' is clear. 'Mach[a]danus' with a stroke through the ascenders occurs three times and 'Magadanus' once (variously declined). Huici's transcription of reg. 9, fol. 29v, gives 'Mequadanus' but the manuscript itself reads 'Meq[a]danus' with a rolling or curved stroke over the *q*. Martínez Ferrando's 'Mubanch' cannot be a misprint since it occurs again in the index (*Catálogo*, I, nos. 116, 128).

4   Goitein, *Mediterranean society*, II, 68–77, 316. Neuman, *Jews in Spain*, II, ch. 3.

5   Burns, *Islam*, 411 (*qāḍī*), 314–15 (al-Tīfāshī, wife Mascarosa, son Sa'd).

6   ACA, reg. 19, fol. 156 (9 August 1274), below in appendix 3, doc. 20. On Ben Vives see Burns, *Colonialism*, 277–81. Though Kaganoff believes the name Vives 'is found among neither Jews nor gentiles' in medieval Spain (*Jewish names*, 57), Catalan Christians and Jews alike used it. Goitein, *Mediterranean society*, II, 237 (Salāmah).

7   Gual, *Vocabulario*, docs. 3 (24 September 1243), 6 (10 March 1250), 7 (1 September 1251), 12 and 13 (1271); cf. docs. 2 (19 August 1243), 14 (30 June 1271), and 25 (April 1298).

8   ACA, reg. 21, fol. 6 (30 July 1271): 'mandamus vobis firmiter quatenus Gentono Barbuti argentario . . . pro operatorio quod tenet a nobis in Valencia ad certum censum prout in carta quam inde [h]abet a nobis continetur, et faciendi [*sic*] ius suis querelantibus, non emparetis nec claudatis.' See also below in appendix 3, doc. 21 (6 September 1274); doc. 20's 'Abrahimus Samariani' becomes 'Abraham Samaria' here, while 'Abrahimus Gerundini' (fully written out, with a tail of the initial letter making an elaborate but otiose overstroke) becomes 'Abraham de Gerundi.'

9   ACA, reg. 20, fol. 331v (15 March [1275] 1276), below in appendix 3, doc. 25.

10   ACA, reg. 15, fol. 95v (25 or 26 April 1268): 'pro se et familia sua . . . et erat plenius in carta predicta quod uxor sua posset induere vestes de omni panno excepto presseto rubeo, non obstante statuto Iudeorum facto vel faciendo'; the surname is *aveczunana* with an overstroke from *v* to the last letter. Gual, *Vocabulario*, 399. *Llibre dels feyts*, ch. 310 (Bairén).

11   ACA, reg. 11, fol. 199v (9 April 1261), below in appendix 3, doc. 5.

12   ACA, reg. 14, fol. 120 (29 May 1271): 'in toto augmento quod tu et pater tuus fecistis nobis . . . castrorum de Godalesto et de Confrides et de Penaguila et de Castello.' Reg. 16, fol. 257v (2 April 1271): 'Davidi Almascaran Iudeo Valencie

unum banchum . . . ante archam rotli [cf Catalan *rotlle*] sinagoge Valencie.'
On David see Burns, *Colonialism*, 287-8.

13 ACA, reg. 20, fol. 228v (24 March [1274] 1275), below in appendix 3, doc. 22.
The earlier forfeiture is *ibid.*, reg. 19, fol. 84v (8 December 1273): 'Simoni de
Sancto Felicio scriptori nostro ad opus unius filii tui'; 'Abraham Almascarani
Iudeum et David filium eius'; 'in hereditate Abrahe et Davidis supra dicti'; 'et
quattuor iovatas terre in illis sex que remanent ad dandum de hereditate que
assignata fuerat Abrahe Almascorani [*sic*] et Davidi predictis, que sunt inventi
absentes.' On Orihuela's Jews see Vilar, *Orihuela*, II, 215-51; III, 55-8.

14 ACA, reg. 20, fol. 252r,v (6 May 1275), below in appendix 3, doc. 24 On Astruc
see Burns, *Colonialism*, 285-6. Bofarull, 'Jaime I y los judíos,' doc. 59 (27 April
1266): 'in herem molsenuch [=*malshinut*].' Catalan *vet* means prohibition or
veto, and in medieval times also meant excommunication; this may be one of
the bans of varying severity in the Jewish community, rather than something
related to the *Bet Din* (the *aljama* court). A *taqqānā* or agreed statute of a Jewish
community in Spain could be used to coerce conformity; the Hebrew word also
entered Catalan as *tacany(a)* for pejoratives such as conspiracy or deceit.
Mordecai's first name seems to relate to Arabic Mus'ad (modern German–
Jewish Muskat has a different origin as spice dealer).

15 ACA, reg. 14, fol. 19r,v (8 May 1263), below in appendix 3, doc. 7. Fol. 41 (14
September 1263) to 'Çaleme de Daroca Iudeo Montissonis' and issued at
Monzón; his bailiate was 'de reditibus et exitibus nostris iudarie Ilerde, et de
exitibus erbe et domus olei de almacera Ilerde, et correture lini et lane Ilerde.'
Related documentation is in Burns, *Colonialism*, 289-90. ACA, Reg. 14, fol. 14
(1 March [1262] 1263), below in appendix 3, doc. 6. The early salt industry of
Valencia is a topic almost wholly neglected; but see Betí, 'Sal de Peñíscola,'
129-32, and Gual, 'Mapa de la sal hispánica,' 483-97.

16 ACA, reg. 12, fol. 92v (29 June 1263), and fol. 93v (8 July 1263), below in
appendix 3, docs. 8, 9. Burns, *Islam*, 22, 253-4, with reference to the confusion
of Neuman, Soldevila, Tourtoulon and others on this point, the comments of
Neuvonen and Steiger, and see Romano, 'Judíos escribanos y trujamanes,'
71-105.

17 ACA, reg. 37, fol. 7 (11 June 1270), below in appendix 3, doc. 16. The Martínez
Ferrando catalog indexes Salomó as Ben Juda, though its entry copies the
manuscript correctly as Bonjuda; the puzzling name is akin to other Catalan
Jewish names like Bonsenyor and (Christian) Bons(h)oms. Vidal appears
briefly in Soldevila, *Pere*, part 2, I, doc. 32, with text on p. 16; a common
Catalan Christian name, it was popular among Jews as 'translation' or equivalent to Hebrew Hayyim.

18 ACA, reg. 13, fol. 167 (29 March 1264) on Moisès, and fol. 170v (10 May 1264)
on Salomó, below in appendix 3, docs. 13, 14. Burns, *Colonialism*, 275-6. There
is a L'Alfàs in neighboring Gandía; but a negligibly small place now lost could
sustain some other transliteration such as Els Alfacs (and Els Alfaixs: both
toponyms meaning sandbank in a river delta). Martínez Ferrando separately
lists 'Mosse Alconstanti' in his index, unaware that our brothers and Baḥya
belonged to that family. Is the repetition of Raval in doc. 13 as a location for
vineyard(s) a scribal error, or is this place distinct from the vineyard at
Zaragoza's Rabal in doc. 14? Aside from the generic *rafal*, or compound-name
places like Rafalaceit, there seems to be no other Arraval or Raval except a
section of the city itself bearing that name in King Jaume's day (see Chabret,
Sagunto, II, 403, 405).

19 ACA, reg. 12, fol. 106v (29 August 1263), below in appendix 3, doc. 12. The

1275 document is in reg. 23, fol. 8v (23 July): 'tributum istius anni Iudeorum regni Valencie . . .: Iudei Valencie, V milia solidorum; Iudei Muriveteris, Onde, Burriane, et Segorbii, II milia solidorum; Iudei Algezire, CCCC solidos'; since the 1272 collection lumped Onda–Burriana–Segorbe as worth 1,000, with Murviedro 1,000, the 1275 complex of all four as worth 2,000 should be similarly divided. See also reg. 16, fol. 176 (30 June 1279): 'carta franquitatis hominibus Xative sub forma communi spacio trium annorum racione duodecim milium solidorum, que dederunt domino regi in auxilium transitus ultramaris.' No corresponding note survives for Játiva's Jews, but the pattern is clear; and since the previous year's lump sum included that year's taxes as well, the spread for both Christian and Jewish taxes here must cover four full years.

20 ACA, reg. 19, fol. 169v (5 September 1274): 'vobis aliame Iudeorum in Xativa presenti et future quod singulis annis de cetero donetis et dare teneamini nobis et nostris sexcentos solidos regalium Valencie pro tributo.' Reg. 11, fol. 190 (11 January [1260] 1261), below in appendix 3, doc. 4. Reg. 10, fol. 81 (2 July 1258): 'cum nos concessimus tibi Mosse Avengayet Iudeo Xative quod esses franchus et immunis ab omni peita seu tributa et a quolibet alio servicio regali usque ad V annos completos, secundum quod in carta quam inde a nobis habes plenius continetur: volentes tibi facere graciam specialem, concedimus tibi dicto Mosse quod transactis dictis V annis sis franchus et immunis per duos annos continue subsequentes,' according to details of the previous exemption. The catalog also mistakes this as a single exemption.

21 ACA, reg. 37, fol. 35v (6 February [1271] 1272), below in appendix 3, doc. 17. Reg. 11, fol. 190 (11 January [1260] 1261), appendix 3, doc. 4.

22 ACA, reg. 19, fol. 108 (25 March [1273] 1274): 'fecerimus graciam franquitatis quinque annorum omnibus Iudeis qui apud Xativam venire voluerint ad populandum'; the 4 July 1268 charter follows, and afterwards the episode of 'Açach Abenianah Iudeo Toleti qui racione dicte franquitatis venisti apud Xativam populare.' The 'lost' document is not noticed by the Martínez Ferrando catalog (I, no. 1165) nor directly by Régné (no. 582). Reg. 19, fol. 101v (17 February [1273] 1274): 'ultra illos scilicet quinque annos per quos Iudeos ibi populandis concessimus'; 'si . . . mutabit se vel suum domicilium in alium locum, teneatur solvere partem suam in peitis.' Reg. 16, fol. 159 (23 April 1269): 'possitis ponere in herem et in nidui gamur, et inhibere eis sepulturam cimiterii vestri et omnem ordinem legis vestre.' The second punishment here is the Hebrew *niddui* for excommunication, and *gamur* for absolute or final or complete.

23 ACA, reg. 21, fol. 46v (6 July 1272), below in appendix 3, doc. 18. Reg. 17, fol. 114v (12 March [1267] 1268): 'vendicionem quam Mayr quondam baiulus noster ipsius loci' of Gandía; cf. Martínez Ferrando, *Catálogo*, I, no. 751. Reg. 16, fol. 198v (1 July 1270): 'comparavit coram nobis . . . Mayrius Iudeus apud Valenciam,' with the standard slight punctuation to differentiate *y* from *ii*, which Martínez Ferrando mistook as supplying an *n* following a *ti* (*Catálogo*, I, no. 986); he is not a 'judío de Valencia,' nor does he belong in the index with the already decreased landowner of Játiva. Our appended document has an ambiguous squiggle over the *ii* of *Mayrii*; it is too large and misplaced to dot a *y*, and the wrong shape and position to indicate *n* or a contraction; it could be a malformed *er*, but seems rather to be a sloppy punctuation for the *ii*: the double slash often resembles an *n* or *z* over that double letter, and this shepherd's crook seems merely the second slash with ligature. The standard Catalan form of the name is Maïr (variants Mayr, Mahir), for the Hebrew name Meir ('light').

24 ACA, reg. 20, fol. 338 (21 April 1276): 'per preces et instanciam nuncii, quem rex Tunicii nobis modo misit, absolvimus . . . tibi Raimundo de Volpelleros.' Fol. 340 (21 April 1276): 'ad instanciam nuncii . . . Guillelmo de Arceriis in vita tua baiuliam molendinorum.' Dufourcq, *L'Espagne catalane*, 126–7, 195–7, on Tunisian *entente*. Reg. 19, fol. 13 (20 April 1276): 'ad preces nuncii regis Tunicii qui ad nos modo venit . . . stabilimus tibi Abrafimo Avingabello Iudeo Valencie . . . operatorium nostrum situm in intrata iudarie Valencie in loco vocato La Soch.' Régné has 'Lasoé.'

25 ACA, reg. 17, fol. 40 (19 July 1269), below in appendix 3, doc. 15; cf. Martínez Ferrando, *Catálogo*, I, no. 930. *Col. dip.*, I, doc. 328 (15 June 1247).

26 ACA, reg. 20, fol. 242 (17 April 1275), below in appendix 3, doc. 23.

<h3 style="text-align:center">7 THE LANGUAGE BARRIER</h3>

1 Bramon, 'Tres llengües,' 17–47, and *Contra moros*, 144–54. Barceló, 'La llengua àrab,' 123–49. Fuster and Guichard below in n. 9, Sanchis Guarner in n. 7, and Epalza in n. 5 as well as in ch. 1, n.2.

2 Martí, *Vocabulista in arabico* (see ch. 3 above, n. 49). Ribera Tarragó, 'Ayala.' Colin ('al-Andalus', *EI²* I, 501–3) allows for possible language differentiations on a large scale among Valencian rural Moors. Harvey, 'Arabic dialect of Valencia'; Corriente, *Bundle*, preface. Cf. Pérès, 'L'arabe dialectal,' 290, 298.

3 Lévi-Provençal, *L'Espagne musulmane* (1950–3), revised as *España musulmana*, IV, xix, 47–8, and V, 96, 103–4, with opinions of Terrasse, Ribera, and the editor García Gómez. Gimeńez Soler, *Corona de Aragón*, 293–4. See also Imamuddin, *Muslim Spain*, 134–5, 187–8; and on the earlier period but by implication applicable to the later, Watt and Cachia, *Islamic Spain*, 56. Chejne, *Muslim Spain*, 184–5, 375–7. Burckhardt, *Moorish culture*, 81. Corriente, *Bundle*, 6–7. Pastor de Togneri, *Del islam al cristianismo*, 38.

4 *Orígenes del español*, 418–32.

5 Ibn Khaldūn, *Muqaddimah*, III, 352; he contrasts the Berbers, who had a mere gloss of Arabic speakers over a Berber-speaking population, with Spain (Granada) where Arabic played a greater role and non-Arabic speakers were more recent immigrants (367); Spaniards displayed interior differences of dialect (351–3). On the linguistic borderline between the Tortosa and Valencia dioceses (which falls deeply within the Valencian kingdom, coincides with the older frontier between Islamic Tortosa and Valencia, and probably reveals pre-Arabic dialect divergences), see Burns, *Crusader kingdom*, I, 43. For Glick–Bulliet see above, p. 4. Epalza, 'Ibn Sidah', 163–6, and above, pp. 4–5.

6 Carreras, 'Lenguaje valenciano,' 570–85, esp. 583. Sanchis Guarner, *Llengua dels valencians*, 134–5 (Primitiu). Simó Santonja, *¿Valenciano o catalán?* Ubieto, *Orígenes de Valencia*, I, 190–1; he returns to the subject elsewhere, as in his recent *Idioma romance y los valencianos*.

7 Sanchis Guarner, *Historia lingüística de Valencia*, 135–6, 144, 147; and his *Aproximació*, I, 91–101, 128–35.

8 *Col. dip.*, I, doc. 106 (19 March 1232 or 1233), in *Itinerari*, 101). Burns, *Crusader kingdom*, I, ch. 15.

9 Chabás, 'Viaje literario,' 190. Ribera, *Disertaciones*, II, 352–7. Lacarra, 'Reconquista y repoblación,' 69. Bayerri, *Tortosa*, VI, 423–7, citing Ribera, Sánchez-Albornoz, and others. Fuster, *Poetes, moriscos, i capellans*, 95–113. Guichard, *al-Andalus*, 23–9, 33, 271–2, 393–402. Epalza, above in n. 5.

10 *Llibre dels feyts*, chs. 78, 436, 437, 439, on Murcia; 119 (Minorca), 321, 416. Chabás, *Distribución*, 3–6 (1244).

11 BUV, codex 145: Bulas, reales órdenes y concordias sobre diezmos, doc. 21 (29 May 1242): 'carta scripta erat latinis diccionibus, interlineata litteris arabicis vel sarracenicis, idem quod ipse dicciones latine significantibus in effectu; series vero dicti privilegii quantum ad dicciones latinas sequitur sub hac forma.' Fernández y González, *Mudejares*, docs. 15, 23, 47, 53. Alfandech above in ch. 2. *Col. dip.*, I, doc. 151 (28 May 1236). Majorca's *Repartiment* is in both Latin and partial Arabic versions; the Arabic may be the lost original of 1232 or a contemporary copy, the Latin and Catalan versions of 1267 reflecting either a translation or a Latin original. Carmen Barceló has shown that Uxó's Romance charter is a 1368 translation from the lost Arabic; see Ubieto, *Orígenes de Valencia*, I, 192–3, and contrast Castro, *Spaniards*, 254. For al-Azraq, see ch. 10. ACA, reg. 11, fol. 199 (9 April 1261): 'vobis Domenico March[esii] . . . prout in instrumento sarracenico.' Burns, *Islam*, 333 (Finestrat), 267 (Alcira). *Homenaje a Codera*, 28–33 (Chivert).

12 ACA, Pere III, reg. 41, fol. 97 (27 March 1279): 'tradidimus Samueli alfaquimo quandam litteram assecuramenti Sarracenorum de Carbonera que erat sarracenica.' Reg. 44, fol. 142v (22 June 1279): 'tradidimus Samueli alfaquimo quandam cartam pergamini sarracenicam . . . de Godalest [Guadalest].' Reg. 48, fol. 6v (29 April 1280): 'quandam litteram sarracenicam que ut Samuel alfaquimus dixit.' *Llibre dels feyts*, ch. 414. Grayzel, *Church and Jews*, doc. 45 (4 November 1220). Romano, 'Abenmenassé,' 255 (13 February 1284).

13 *Llibre dels feyts*, chs. 79, 182, 189, 411, and p. 278 (verse). Roca Traver, 'Vida mudéjar,' 177n. (1282). Sanchis Guarner, *Aproximació*, I, 100–1.

14 *Llibre dels feyts*, ch. 367. ACA, Pere III, reg. 46, fol. 221v (9 July 1284): 'fuit scriptum in arabico universis Sarracenis domini regis regni Valencie.' Muntaner, *Crònica*, ch. 85 (Pere). Bofarull ed., *Rentas*, 115 (1317). For a 'littera sarracenica' of 1280 by Játiva Muslims paying taxes, see Burns, *Colonialism*, 223n.

15 *Llibre dels feyts*, chs. 60, 85. Muntaner, *Crònica*, ch. 247; Soldevila's edition prefers 'ani ben i soltan.' *Crónica latina de los reyes*, 114; ending in 1236, its author may be Bishop Domingo of Palencia or Bishop Juan of Burgos.

16 Sáenz de Aguirre ed., *Collectio conciliorum Hispaniae*, V, 286. Boswell, *Muslim communities*, 384–5.

17 All quotes in Fuster (above, n. 9). Cardaillac, *Morisques*, 64, 153. Labarta, 'Libros,' 72, 'Documentos,' 110–17.

18 *Examination of three faiths*, 77.

19 *Muqaddimah*, I, esp. ch. 2, sections 22–3, and ch. 3, sec. 5.

8 BOUNDING THE MOORISH FRONTIER

1 See Prescott, *Boundaries and frontiers*, ch. 6, on internal administrative–historical bounds, and Sawyer ed., *Medieval settlement*, esp. parts 1, 2. Vila, *Divisió territorial de Catalunya*, esp. 37–48.

2 Efforts to establish a modern Valencian comarcal map include Sanchis Guarner, *Nomenclàtor geogràfic*, and his historical survey 'Límits i demarcacions històriques del regne de València'; Beüt i Belenguer, *Geografia de València*, 104, and his *Comarques valencianes*. Jaén i Urban, *Qüestions territorials*, chs. 2, 6 (zones); see also Sancho Comins, 'Comarcas castellonenses' for past and new approaches, and Juan i Fenollar, *Qüestió comarcal*, to decentralize and vitalize by comarcalization.

3 See above, p. 66.

4 Pastor, *Castellón de Rugat*, 148–58. Traver Tomás, *Antigüedades de Castellón*, esp.

35–44. *Itinerari*, 216. Cf. Andreu Valls, 'Términos de Miravet, Albalat y Cabanes,' north of Castellón. Fontavella, *Gandía*, 309ff. ACA, Pere III, reg. 46, fol. 72 (31 March 1282), Palma: 'ad loca de quibus questio est, personaliter accedentes interrogato consilio Christianorum et Sarracenorum.'

5 *Fori, rub.* l, nos. 3, 4. Piles Ibars, *Cullera*, chs. 11–14, with documentary appendices. Chabás, *Denia*, II, ch. 1, esp. 22ff. An example of sheepwalk boundaries, non-Valencian, is a range Jaume described for the Knights Templar, bounded (*terminatum*) by his Gerona bailiff (*Col. dip.*, I, doc. 291; 23 October 1245).

6 Walter, *Memoriale*, I, 407.

7 Escolano, *Décadas de Valencia*, II, *lib.* 8, ch. 31; Burns, *Colonialism*, 258–61 (docs.). 'Abd el-Karīm ed., *España musulmana*, 98, 126–9, 160, 199, 213, 281. al-Idrīsī, *Geografía*, 74, 101–6, 161–3, 185–6. For al-Ḥimyarī, al-Waṭwāṭ, the Cid, and registers see Burns, *Islam*, 54, 58–9.

8 *Col. dip.*, I, doc. 238 (1 January [1241] 1242). *Fori, rub.* 1, no. 1. Jaume II (attribution by Chabás) is in *Furs*, I, *lib.* I, *rub.* 1. Valencia's southern boundary is in the Almizra treaty, *Col. dip.*, I, doc. 269 (26 March 1244). See also Ubieto, 'Frontera entre Aragón–Valencia,' 95ff.; Palacios Martín, 'Frontera de Aragón con Castilla,' including Valencia, 475ff.

9 ACA, reg. 19, fol. 24 (23 June 1273): 'vobis universis et singulis hominibus de Casteyll Havib . . . quod sitis de termino regni Valencie, et quod . . . teneamini uti secundum forum Valencie et non secundum forum Aragonie vel Turolii.' Reg. 16, fol. 212 (17 [?] September 1270): 'ad dividendum terminum de Cireso de quo est contencio inter vos ex una parte et homines de Castro Habib ex altera.'

10 *Fori, lib.* I, *rub.* I, no. 2. *Col. dip.*, I, doc. 361 (2 August 1249), Alcira. Sarthou Carreres, *Játiva*, I, 91–3.

11 Burns, *Crusader kingdom*, I, 45, 83, 89. Gual has mapped Valencian post-crusade settlements according to the custom-law each imported ('Territorialidad,' 272, 280), while Ubieto has linguistic, seignorial and other maps (*Orígenes de Valencia*, I, esp. maps 5–7).

12 *Col. dip.*, I, doc. 120 (22 November 1233), Benifassà. Miralles, *Salsadella*, esp. 19, 62–3 (Cuevas). Another *tinença* still known popularly by that name is Alcalatén (Alcora, Chodos, Lucena del Cid, and Useras), given by Jaume I to Jimeno de Urrea.

13 *Col. dip.*, I, doc. 139 (11 May 1235), Burriana; doc. 142 (23 December 1235), Cervera; doc. 264 (29 November 1242), Montornés; doc. 374 (29 April 1250), Onteniente; II, doc. 989 (26 February 1274), Garx or Garg. *Itinerari*, 115 (1 January 1235). For non-Valencian examples of bounding a settlement directly in the town constitution, see Font Rius, *Cartas de población*, I, doc. 242 (1222), Ulldecona; doc. 275 (1238), Vallcanera; doc. 276 (1239), Alcanar; doc. 283 (1244) Valle de Batea.

14 *Col. dip.*, I, doc. 383 (August 1250), Uxó; doc. 323 (5 May 1247), Foyos; II, doc. 441 (21 July 1245), Onda. ACA, reg. 11, fol. 166 (29 August 1259): 'termini siquidem castri et alcherie de Becorb affrontant cum terminis de Palaz quod est de regno Castelle et cum terminis de Cortes et de Millar que sunt de regno Valencie et cum serra de Çaiden [?] que est de regno Valencie et cum terminis de Putri [?] et prout dividuntur termini de Castella et de regno nostro Valencie; termini similiter alcherie de Benatriz affrontant cum rivo de Guadalaviar.'

15 ACA, *ibid.*, fol. 238 (18 January [1260] 1261): 'vobis Petro Enneci, procuratori karissimi filii nostri infantis Sancii, et vestris in perpetuum quod alqueria vestra de Benizanon, que est in termino de Liria, habeat omnes terminos et

aquas quos et quas tempore Sarracenorum habebat.' Fol. 238v (22 January [1260] 1261): 'sciatis quod dedimus terminos alquerie de Benizano que est dilecti nostri Petri Enneci . . . illos scilicet quos habebat tempore Sarracenorum; quare mandamus vobis quatenus, visis presentibus, recipiatis testimonium Sarracenorum nostrorum ravalli de Liria qui in facto ipsorum terminorum sciunt super ipsis terminis, et testimonium Halaf vicini de Ribaroya et de alfaqui Alayelli, ponentes ipsum Petrum . . . prout per testimonium dictorum Sarracenorum inveneritis.' Glick, *Irrigation*, 236–9.

16   *Col. dip.*, I, doc. 1048 (21 January [1243] 1244): 'a quibusdam minus sane intelligentibus.' *Ibid.*, II, doc. 460 (13 May 1247): 'causam predictorum terminorum ac limitum . . . iudex . . . personaliter insimul cum eis ivit videre terminos seu limites . . . recepto utriusque partis multorum proborum virorum secundum formam a iure traditam recipiendorum testium testimonio'; 'ubi precipi fieri, me presente, magnum limitem de lapidibus.' Any number of boundary pacings, arbitrations, quarrels, and trials can be found in upland Aragon proper at this time; for sample cases see Canellas ed., *Concejo*, I, doc. 95 (1259), a parish; 68 (26 May 1242), two towns; 102 (2 April 1263), and 104 (6 April 1263), two other towns; 91 (24 February 1259); 103 (2 April 1263); 126 (1 February 1269); 136 (11 July 1269).

17   ACA, reg. 11, fol. 241 (13 April 1261): 'in presencia iudicis, iusticie, iuratorum, et tocius concilii Turolii, et ipsis videntibus et volentibus et non in aliquo contradicentibus, divisimus et assignavimus pro terminis castri et ville de Exerica terminos subtus scriptos, videlicet ex parte podii seu castellario quod dicitur Toro, sicut aque decurrunt de monte Algarau versus villarre balistarii, et de dicto villari usque ad cabeçum rasum . . . et est certum quod ipsi fuerunt protestati.'

18   Fullana, *Concentaina*, 62–6 (doc.); the Latin request for a commission is in ACA, reg. 15, fol. 134 (28 January [1268] 1269), and differs from the published version by a half-dozen grammatical and spelling errors. 'Violence' might then ensue, as when the lord of Montornés destroyed the legal markers: 'mollones sive signa posita . . . manu armata,' angering the king (ACA, Pere III, reg. 41, fol. 58 (14 April 1279)).

19   ACA, reg. 16, fol. 210v–211 (2 September 1270): 'Bernardus Ispanus procurator universitatis hominum de Liria asserit et proponit'; Blasco 'dicebat quia [=quod] dicta universitas turbabat sibi possessionem . . . tamquam terminum Lirie'; 'fuit citatus semel, secundo, et eciam tercio perhemtorie, et nichilhominus'; 'extiterit et remissus contumax, predictas nostras citaciones contempnendo, et ius (si quod sibi competebat) in predictis non prosequendo.'

20   ACA, reg. 16, fol. 210v (2 September 1270), a separate document: 'dilecto suo Blascho Eximini de Arenoso, salutem et dileccionem: mandamus vobis quatenus, visis litteris istis, ante nostram presenciam compareatis per vos vel vestrum sufficienter procuratorem, paratus respondere et facere ius hominibus de Liria, super facto peticionis quam vobis faciunt ipsi de Orset, de Perdixinos, et de Rafal Abinhazmon; et hoc aliquatenus non mutetis, alias sciatis quod procedemus contra vos prout de iure fuerit procedendum.' Pere III, reg. 42, fol. 157 (20 October 1279):Berenguer Espanyol and Arnaut Vinader 'pro universitate de Liria comparuerunt coram nobis, et supplicarunt quod faceremus mandari exequcioni quandam sentenciam . . . adiudicando dicte universitati Alcublas de la Pedrosa pro termino de Liria.' *Ibid.*, fol. 199v (2 January [1279] 1280): 'dilectus frater noster Iacobus, filius dompne Taresie, dixit nobis quod volebat vobiscum componere super facto termini de Alcubles et quorundam aliorum locorum de quibus est contencio inter vos et ipsum.'

21   The career of de Azagra can be followed summarily in the king's documents: *Itinerari*, 38, 56, 116, 196, 214, 216–17, 242, 270, 299, 410, 437, 485, 487. Gil Ximèn (Jiménez) of Teruel makes his last public appearance, at the king's palace in Valencia, on 17 July 1273 (441). On Perpunchent see pp. 254–7.

22   ACA, reg. 15, fol. 82 (27 February [1267] 1268): 'sobre las alquereas de Gayanas e de Fontizeles, que el dito don Gil Garces dezia que devian seer de termino de Perpunxen, e el dito don Gil Exemeniz dezia que las ditas alcherias nunquam foron de termino de Perpunxen, que siempre foron alquereas pro si mismas'; 'que recebiesse homne testimonias de moros ancianos ... que avia estado en tiempo de moros que assi que se seguis'; 'recebieron las testimonias de los mas veyllos e mas ancianos moros de las vezindades darrador bien de LXX e de LXXX e de XC annos'; 'nos somos ciertos que en tiempo de moros no avia castiello en Perpunxen antigament'; 'don Rodrigo rector de la eglesia de Concentayna.' 'No castle in Perpunchent' must mean in relation to these villages of Perpunchent Valley: for this argument and for the Muslims' castle there, see below, pp. 254–7. Reg. 16, fol. 228 (12 January [1270] 1271): 'per nos et nostros laudamus, concedimus et confirmamus tibi Petro Eximini donacionem, quam tibi dedit Egidius Eximini pater tuus, de alcheriis de Gayanas et de Fonteçiellas cum carta ut in ea continetur, ita scilicet quod tu et quem volueris loco tui habeatis et possideatis dictas alcherias, secundum quod eas dicto Egidio Eximini dedimus et in carta nostra predicta quam inde ei fecimus melius et plenius continetur; mandantes firmiter baiulis, iusticiis, alcaidis et universis aliis etc. quod predicta omnia firma habeant etc.' Reg. 21, fol. 118 (30 March 1273): 'quod possitis vendere castrum de Perpuxen at alios omnes honores quos Egidius Garces quondam habebat in regno Valencie,' to satisfy his debts and legacies. Reg. 19, fol. 28v–29v (12 June 1273): 'multi em[p]tores ad illud emendum obtulerint.'

23   Betí, *Ros[s]ell: pleito*, with fifty pages of documents.

24   *Llibre dels feyts*, ch. 36 (county). *Col. dip.*, I, doc. 138 (11 May 1235), agreement; doc. 368 (16 February 1250). Blasco's bounding of Castell de Cabres is in *BSCC*, LVI (1981), 547–9. Betí, *Morella*, 96–100, docs. 12, 16. *Col. dip.*, I, doc. 330 (28 July 1247). See also the Teruel–Arenós suit in Caruana, 'Pleito: Albentosa.' A further stage of the Cantavieja lawsuit is in ACA, Pere III, reg. 40, fol. 50v (23 December 1277): a team of two assessors 'dividendi terminos.'

25   'Asignación: Borriol–Onda,' 88–9 (1282). Piles Ibars, *Cullera*, 204 ff., 218, 229.

26   ACA, reg. 19, fol. 105r,v (20 February [1273] 1274): 'quod cum ad reges et principes spectet populacionibus quas faciunt certos terminos assignare ... damus ... populatoribus populacionibus [=populacionis] Ville Regalis, quam in termino Burriane statuimus facienda[m], terminos certos: scilicet a cequia maiori Burriane sursum versus dictam populacionem, et exinde sicut affrontat cum termino de Nuules, et exinde usque al [*sic*] antiguor vocatum Misquitiella quod est versus Bechim, et exinde ad malonem cohopertum cabecii in quo scinditur petra, et usque in rivum de Millars.' Traver García transcribed another original at the ARV, in his *Villarreal* (33–6), apparently with omissions and alterations. See also Ferrer Navarro, 'Villarreal,' 412. I am uneasy about my 'malonem petra,' since both previous transcriptions read 'mollonem' and it may well be a variant of Catalan *molló*; *cabeç* does not seem to be a village but a natural feature.

27   ACA, reg. 11, fol. 192 (24 January [1260] 1261): 'alqueriam de B°[enic]olet ... in valle de Albaida in termino castri de Vilella, cum rafalis.' Reg. 12, fols. 68v–69 (6 September 1262): 'alqueriam cum suis rafalis in termino de Saxona que vocatur Algorfes,' the *cum rafalis* formula being repeated four times. Reg.

37, fol. 61v (11 February [1272] 1273): 'locum vocatum Arnales que est in termino de Ador alcheria de Palma.' Reg. 11, fol. 228r,v (7 October 1260): 'in alcheriis que dicuntur de Vilella et raal Alcortoix'; fol. 225v (26 August 1260): 'turrim illam que est in alcharia que dicitur Guxllen in termino de Onteniente'; fol. 161 (1 April [not 8] 1260): 'illud casale molendinorum quod est iuxta alqueriam de Riola et de termino ipsius alquerie, que alqueria est de termino Corbarie.' Other *raals* or *rafals* designated also as *alquerias* in the *Repartiment*[1] include nos. 190, 370, 1962, 2256, 2393, 2487, 2890, 2952. Guichard, 'Problème de structures,' 709–12; and 'Tours de défense,' 75–82, 103–5. Coromines, *Diccionari*, I, 168–9, 226–7, analyzes *aldea* and *alqueria* in the Catalan context, where the latter meant a village less often than 'a farm (*mas*) large or small or a small circle of houses under a common landlord.'

28 Burns, *Islam*, 55.

29 ACA, reg. 15, fol. 135r,v (29 January [1268] 1269): 'inter Baldovinum de Baldovino medicum vicinum Xative ex una parte et Guaresches de Gerunda et quosdam alios vicinos Xative ex altera'; properties 'intus Podium Grossum vinearum Xative sive ultra rivum vocatum de Albayda et infra caminum de Barchitano pertinebant ad ipsum Baldovinum et sunt de termino alquerie de Chiu'; 'non sunt in termino dicte alquerie nec dicta alqueria tempore Sarracenorum terminos habebat certos'; 'sentenciando dicimus et mandamus quod dicta alqueria de Chiu debet et habeat solummodo pro termino tantum quantum Sarraceni dicte alquerie de Chiu laborare consueverunt et laborabant in circuitu dicte alquerie tempore quo nos Xativam adquisivimus a Sarracenis.' The principle is expressed: 'habito consilio richorum hominum et militum ac eciam aliorum, cum iam in simili casu in regno Valencie fuerit indicatum quod aliqua alcheria regni Valencie non habet terminos certos, nisi illos terminos tantum quos Sarraceni eiusdem alquerie laborare consueverint, redeundo inde eadem die de sua laboracione ad ipsam alqueriam, sentenciendo dicimus et mandamus: quod dicta alqueria de Chiu debet et habeat solummodo pro termino . . .' Cf. copy of 1308 AHN, ords. milits., perg. real 124.

30 ACA, Pere III, reg. 39, fol. 188 (17 April 1277): 'Baldovinus de Baldovino vicinus Exative defunctus constituit in tutorem filiis et bonis suis in testamento suo dictum Eximinum Sapata, et cum ipse sit miles et sit occupatus negociis nostris . . . removimus a dicta tutela dictum Eximinum Sabata.' *Col. dip.*, I, doc. 230 (31 October 1241).

31 *Repartiment*[1], nos. 212, 1314, 1384, 1724, 3658, 3898 (Baldoví), 2261–5, 2828 (Guarescas). *Col. dip.*, I, doc. 334 (24 March 1248).

32 ACA, reg. 21, fol. 19 (7 April 1272): 'laudamus, concedimus, et confirmamus vobis Eximino Petri de Oris militi et vestris in perpetuum: terminos quos Sancius Eximini prior Sancte Christine assignavit auctoritate et mandato nostro alquerie vestre, vocate Alfofara et site in termino de Bocayren in regno Valencie, cum carta publica scripta per Dominicum de Cepiello scriptorem publicum Cocentanie, prout in ea plenius continetur; ita quod vos, et vestri successores qui post vos dictam alqueriam habuerint, habeatis ipsos terminos assignatos a dicto priore in carta predicta, prout in ea continetur.' On Orís, see below, ch. 9, n. 7, with text. Pere III, reg. 42, fol. 243 (3 April 1280): 'universis Sarracenis tam senibus quam aliis existentibus in Muntesa, Engera, Xella, Quesa et aliis locis convicini'; 'in controversia . . . super terminis castrorum de Navarres et de Bolbait fuerint electi arbitri per ipsas partes'; 'mandamus vobis quatenus quandocumque per ipsos arbitros fueritis requisiti, perhibeatis in huiusmodi testimonium veritati, alias damus licenciam ipsis arbitris quod ad hoc prout faciendum fuerit vos compellant.'

33 ACA, reg. 16, fol. 208v (18 May 1270): 'in causa que vertebatur inter Petrum Noves nomine et voce Orie Petri uxoris sue, et procuratorem ipsius agentem ex una parte, et Arnaldum Scriba procuratorem Sancii Roiz de Corella et Petri Roiz manumissorem testamenti Roderici Diez ex altera, sub examine magistri Sancii prioris Sancte Cristine auditoris predicte cause a domino rege eis concesso'; 'quod quidem castrum dividit terminos suos cum terminis de Xerica et de Segorb et de Villa Malepha et Dalmonecir, et ipsi [termini] tenent Mathet et Pavyas, alquerias termini dicti castri de Gayvel, et dicta Oria Petri sit heres dicti patris sui ab intestato in dicto castro cum terminis suis'; 'proponit quod dictus Rodericus Diez et antecessores sui tenuerunt et possiderunt dictas alquerias . . . nedum per tres annos immo per XXX et sic tuti sunt prescripcione'; 'tandem nos Iacobus dei gracia . . . visis et auditis peticionibus . . . [quoniam] constitit nobis per legitimos testes quod dicte alquerie petite site sunt infra terminum sive territorium castri de Gayvel et sint de termino castri de Gayvel . . . eidem Petro Noves nomine dicte Orie Petri uxoris sue adiudicamus.'

34 *Itinerari*, docs. on 115, 118, 122, 130-1 (Roda), and 441, 444, 448 (Noves). Burns, *Crusader kingdom*, I, 33, 35, 145, 164, 169, 381, 386, 387 ('non consuevit firmare propria manu'), 449 (Díez); 270, 487 (Escrivà).

35 ACA, reg. 28, fol. 46v (17 March [1272] 1273): 'reddistis quandam cartam donacionis °[quam domi]nus rex pater noster fecit Eximino Petri Dumite de alcheria de Mateto, et cartam eciam quam idem Eximinus Petri fecit F[erra]ndo D°[i]ez de vendicione ipsius alcherie de Mateto; item, reddistis nobis quoddam albaranum in quo dictus dominus °[rex] confitetur °[debere] Roderico Diez ducentos morabatinos, racione unius equi quem emit ab eo; que omnia instrumenta recuperavimus a vobis, racione filie Roderici Diez.' *Itinerari*, 78, 104 (*maiordomus*).

36 ACA, reg. 35, fol. 27 (30 April 1273): 'ex parte nostra et Sancie Ferrandis pupille, filie quondam Rod[e]rici Diez, que est sub tutela et posse nostro, recognoscimus et confitemur vobis Abrahim Abin Afia quod dedistis et solvistis, racione Aaron Abin Afia fratris vestri procuratoris [nobis et] d°[ict]e Sancie Ferrandis . . . VIII milia XLV solidos et VI denarios regalium Valencie.' Pere had been the daughter's guardian at least since the opening of 1271, when he speaks of receiving the revenues of Benaguacil castle 'racione tutele °[San]cie Ferrandiz filie Roderici Diez quondam,' in fol. 27 (31 January 1270). Reg. 21, fol. 137v (23 March [1272] 1273): 'dilectis suis Sancio Roderici de Corella et Petro Roderici de Corella, manumissoribus testamenti Roderici Dies quondam . . . noveritis nos vidisse venerabilem episcopum barchinonensem . . . noviter conquerentem de vobis super castro de Almonezir et valle eiusdem, que ad se de iure asserit pertinere.'

9 REAL ESTATE AND LITERARY ECHO

1 ACA, reg. 14, fol. 124r,v (3 December 1271): 'fuit ostensa quedam carta scripta per manum Petri scribani Eximini Petri de Arenoso, prout per ipsam apparebat et sigillo pendenti eiusdem Eximini Petri sigillatam, cuius tenor talis talis [*sic*] est.' For the 1273 document see n. 12.

2 Loaysa, *Crónica* (Morel Fatio, García, Ubieto edns). Soldevila in *Llibre dels feyts*, 151, 353. *Itinerari*, 200 (13 October 1249), 'Bigneres.'

3 *Llibre dels feyts*, ch. 414.

4 ACA, reg. 21, fol. 40v (2 June 1272): 'concedimus et confirmamus vobis Raimundo de Populeto procuratorio nomine Jaufridi de Loaysa et eidem

Jaufrido et suis in perpetuum plateam intrate porte vocatam de Roteros, et turres eciam et vallum ad barbacanam que sunt versus monasterium Sancte Eulalie'; 'balneorum sitorum iuxta [*not* intra] moreriam Valencie cum domibus et corralis suis.' The baths of the Moorish quarter itself were near the walls *inside* that suburb; they come into view only in 1338, perhaps dating back to our time (Burns, 'Baths and Caravanserais,' 457). *Repartiment*[1], nos. 235, 1793, 1795, 2293.

5 *Repartimiento de Murcia*, pp. 49, 221–3, 235, 243, 248, 251, including Don Joffre, García Jofre, Arnaldin, Alexander, Çer Andrea, 'el fijo de Ser Andrea,' Bertholomeo and Jacomin 'de Don Joffre.' See too Torres Fontes, *Documentos de Murcia*, II, docs. 86 (1285), 91 (1285), 107 (1295), 149 (1307), and 170 (1305), and IV, doc. 13 (1290). *Repartimiento de Sevilla*, II, 333–4 (September, October, 1258), 340–1 (February, August, 1263), 49, 175, 263, 236, and 351; cf. I, 319–20. Gonzálvez, 'Loaysa.'

6 Loaysa, *Crónica*, opening paragraphs. *Itinerari*, 185 (26 November 1246). Ballesteros, *Alfonso X*, 54 (correspondence). ACA, Pere III, reg. 22, fol. 81 (15 March [1277] 1278) calls 'Garcia Joffre' to war 'cum equis et armis' as a Valencian vassal.

7 ACA, reg. 19, fol. 107v (22 February [1273] 1274): 'dominus rex dedit ad feudum Eximino Petri de Oriç castrum de Bocayren, ita quod possit dictum castrum operari et ibi facere domos quascumque voluerit ad opus mansionis sue, et in quibus dominus rex et sui possint hospitari quocienscumque in dicto loco venerit.' Reg. 10, fol. 83v (2 July 1258): 'quod de precio quod habeatis de possessionibus extra regnum Valencie, emeretis possessiones in regno eodem.' Reg. 20, fol. 337v (9 April 1276): crown assignment to him on the Bocairente revenues to repay grain purchases, e.g. 'pro duodecim kaficiis tritici, ad viginti et quattuor solidos pro kaficio.' Reg. 22, fol. 47r,v (6 July 1276): 'inter nos et vos de retinencia castrorum de Orchita et de Serra et de Mola et de Carmoxen, temporis per quod ipsa castra tenuistis pro dompna Berengaria Alfonsi quondam,' the king's mistress. Sanchis y Sivera, *Nomenclátor*, 151. Fullana, *Concentaina*, 52, 483. *Itinerari*, 210 (1251), 312 (1261), 452 (1271), referring to *Llibre dels feyts*, ch. 380; but cf. Soldevila's note on that man as an Arenoso in his edition of the *Llibre*, p. 343. *Col. dip.*, I, doc. 388 (14 January [1250] 1251), Sella. On Ximèn see above, pp. 212, 221–2.

8 Charter of 1265 within 1271 document above, n. 1: 'presentibus Ser Andree avunculo suo et Egidio Sancii alcaido de Bah[n]eras et de Serrella, quibus locum suum dedi[t] super divisione predicta.' The *Itinerari* has Gil Sanç d'Alagó buy farmland at Almizra in 1258, and a Gil Sanç appears in 1263 (274–5, 336–7).

9 Charter of 1265 within 1271 document in n. 1: 'fecimus venire coram nobis Hametum Aben Amar Alpetrosi alaminum de Bahnerras, Maomat Amnahilban aluminum de Biar, Cayt Abin Tarama et Abdala Abderegit, Sarracenos quondam de Bocayren qui sciebant bene terminos de Bocayren, de Bayneras, et de Serraella; quibus omnibus Sarracenis predictis constitutis in nostra presencia, in illo loco super quo dicta contencio °[erat], mandavimus eis quod in fide et legalitate ipsorum dividerent et assignarent terminos de °[Bocayren], de Bayneres, et de Serrella secundum quod solebant esse tempore quo villa de Bocayren erat °[proprium] de Sarracenis'; 'ad[=ab] fonte Abirada qui dicitur Margabeneni usque ad fontem de Abenyça, et °[usque] ad hereditatem Alexach, et usque ad hereditatem de Halleycen, et usque ad hereditatem °[de] Çalim Alaxach, et usque ad rivum qui discurrit ex parte de Loriga, et usque ad heredita°[tem] de Abnalhararb, et usque ad hereditatem de Ibraym Alaxach,

et usque ad hereditatem de Alarico et Gavice in sursum, et usque ad hereditatem de Iuçef Almoxat, et usque ad montem ad locum ubi est terra alba, et inde sursum usque ad Serellam prope Bayneras'; 'et omnia que sunt de dictis locis et hereditatibus . . . sunt et debent esse de terminis de Bayneras et de Serrella.' The *terra alba* may mean a kind of whiting-clay (Catalan *albà* for *albar*) or even relate to light sandy soil (Catalan *terra alberenca*), but it is also a technical term in Spanish Arabic for an area left fallow; the Arabic meaning of 'good' may not be relevant here.

10 *Itinerari*, 449 (1271), 456 (1271), 458 (1272), 460 and 463 (1272), 482 and 483 (1273). *Llibre dels feyts*, ch. 157, with note (p. 268). Charter of 1265 within 1271 doc. in n. 1: 'quod annuaverat, per Christianos et Sarracenos anticos, illos esse terminos locorum predictorum.'

11 ACA, reg. 9, fol. 49 (17 November 1257): 'tibi Petro Didaci °[filio] quon°[dam] Roderici Muynnos.' Reg. 14, fol. 139 (11 February [1271] 1272): 'racione scilicet Margarite filie Andree de Podio Viridi quam vobis tradi facimus in uxorem, et quas dicte Margarite damus de speciali gracia in suo casamento.' *Itinerari*, 428 (July 1269), 495 (March 1274).

12 ACA, reg. 19, fol. 77 (2 December 1273): 'confirmamus particionem seu terminacionem terminorum castrorum de Serrella et de Bayneres'; 'mandantes firmiter quod predicta particio seu terminacio terminorum dictorum castrorum plenam habeat perpetuo firmitatem.' Pere III, reg. 40, fol. 149 (25 August 1278): 'racione castri de Serrella quod a Sarracenis recuperavimus.'

10 AL-AZRAQ AND THE FRENCH CONNECTION

1 Burns, *Islam*, 422-32 and notes, with *Colonialism*, 351-6, for chroniclers and other applicable sources. Soldevila, *Pere*, part 2, I, appendix, doc. 58 (Arabic). *Col. dip.*, I, doc. 151 (28 May 1236), Abū Zayd signature. Alarcón and García de Linares, *Documentos*, docs. 115 (1277), 155 (1287), 145 (1292), 156 (1295), but especially 154 (1250). For other authors named, see bibliography, and Burns, *Islam*. Burns and Chevedden, 'al-Azraq's treaty' (authorship).

2 Burns, *Islam*, 323-32, 356-7, incl. chronicles. Chabás, 'Documentos,' 204-5, and 'Alazrach,' 280-2. Momblanch, 'Jaime,' 220-2. Alarcón, *Documentos*, no. 154 (1250).

3 Texts below in appendix 4. Zayyān letters in Molina, 'Zayyān en Murcia,' 177-82.

4 ACA, reg. 10, fol. 103 (15 June 1258): 'in termino de Cherolles in loco vocato Tollo inter Serellam et Font Avaram.' Fol. 103v (22 May 1258): 'in castris de Seta et de Cherolis et eorum terminis.' Fol. 108v (4 April 1259): 'alcaido de Çeta et de Cheroles.' Reg. 16, fol. 211 (6 September 1270): 'castrum de Seta et de Cherollis cum omnibus alcareis, terminis.'

5 *Itinerari*, 205 (*Hispalis*). Above, p. 323n. (trial). *Col. dip.*, II, doc. 875 (18 March 1260), Azagra grant. ACA, reg. 19, fol. 28v (12 June 1273): 'multi emptores,' 'cum domibus, palaciis . . .' Reg. 10, fol. 106 (14 March 1259). AHN, Ords. milits., Montesa, perg. 129: 'castrum et villam de Perpunxen cum alqueriis et terminis' to Riusech (6 July 1273). On Perpunchent see above, pp. 210-12.

6 'La nota cronológica,' 363-90.

7 Zurita, *Anales de Aragón, lib.* I, ch. 41 (Daroca, Calatayud, rebellion). *Llibre dels feyts*, chs. 358-60 (king's quotes). Molina, 'Zayyān en Murcia,' 166 (Hafsid Tunis). *Itinerari*, docs. of 1243 through 1246; on Jaume's son Alfonso see 78 (1229), 98 (1232), 111 (1234, Teruel), 153 (1241, not editor's 1242), 186 (1246), 203 and 205 (1250), 218 (1251), 230-2 (1253), 239-43 (1254), 245

(1255), 260 (1257), 271 (1258), 285 (1259), 297 and 309 (1260, death), 328 (1262). Soldevila, *Pere*, part 1, I, 31 (Alps). Chabás and his editor Figueras, *Denia*, I, 186–7n., II, 17–19n., on the traditional and Conde date 11 May, and Ubieto, *Orígenes de Valencia*, 160. See also Sagarra, 'Alfonso: documentos,' 286, 288; Mestre Palacio, 'Ondara,' 420–5.

8 *Llibre dels feyts*, ch. 336 (*qā'id*). *Itinerari*, 177 (Prince Pere). ACA, reg. 46. fol. 105v (18 September 1283): 'ipsum castrum incontinenti diruatis et dirui faciatis.' Tourtoulon, *Jaime*, II, 75.

9 ASV, Innocent IV, reg. 21, fol. 213v, two docs. (10 July 1245): 'grandi gaudio exultavit ecclesia . . . non solum regno predicto sed aliis etiam vicinis nimis erit utile . . . distributionibus cotidianis dumtaxat exceptis.' The Laguart documents are quoted in *Itinerari*, 171–2; cf. below, p. 278, al-Azraq. ACA, Bulas pontificias, Innocent IV, leg. 8, no. 13 (23 July, 1245): 'et apud homines magne laudis preconia commendabilis . . . et in terris singularis commendationis excellentia nomen grande.'

10 *Llibre dels feyts*, chs. 43 (cunning), 113–14 (Majorca), 244 (hurts), 310, 314, 356 (Muslim word).

11 ACA, Bulas pontificias, Innocent IV. (I shall publish in full as an article all pertinent items of 1245–6; selections follow.) Leg. 7, no. 3 (25 January 1245): 'si terre tue appropinquaverimus, desideramus personaliter te videre.' No. 6 (15 February 1245): Forcalquier: 'paraveras ad recipiendum nos totamque nostram comitativam.' Leg. 8, no. 17 (11 November 1245): 'quia vero, sicut idem nuntii referebant, grave nec immerito magnificentia regalis pertulerat quod – aliis in Provinciam armata manu intrantibus – tibi in ipsam cum armis intrares fuerat interdictum'; 'ut illis, qui terram ipsam intraverunt armati . . . quod de ipsa recedere non postponant, ut iura tua valeant illesa servari'; 'nobis placet quod, inhibitione aliqua non obstante, labores quibus licitis modis poteris pro tuis iuribus defendendis.' No. 13 (23 July 1245): 'Ensiminus Petri tuus specialis nuntius ad concilium.' No. 18 (13 November 1245): 'excommunicationis nuntiationem tibi et contra te factam esse nuperrime intellecto . . . ipsam penitus revocamus'; 'nuntios tuos qui nuper a nostra presentia recesserunt.' No. 19 (24 January 1246): 'de contrahendo matrimonio inter natum tuum et nobilem mulierem . . . Provincie . . . multa fuimus exultatione gavisi, sed postmodum intelleximus quod nobilis vir Karolus . . . in Provinciam ad eandem mulierem desponsandam accedit'; 'non tamen ostendas ex hoc adeo te turbatum ut inconsulte in iracundie calore procedas'; 'inter alios orbis reges et principes tanquam precipuum defensorem ecclesie specialem, parati sumus et prompti tuis votis super hiis . . . annuere.' No. 20 (18 March 1246): 'çelo vivifice crucis accensus transfretare proponas in succursum imperii Romanie.' Benoit, *Actes de Provence*, I xxxv-vi. Paris, *Chronica*, IV, 404, 485, 505, 545–6, 578. Nangis, 'Gesta Ludovici,' 352–3, and his *Vie*, 355–6. Soldevila, *Catalunya*, 298–300; *Pere*, part 1, I, 86 (hope). Jordan, *Louis IX*, 32 ('importance'). Berger, *Louis et Innocent*, ch. 4. Riquer, *Trovadores*, III, 1475 (Olivier). Linehan, *Spanish church*, 160–2, 193. Engels, 'Jaime I y la política internacional,' 224–9.

12 Arié, *L'Espagne des Naṣrides*, 58–60. Dufourcq, *L'Espagne catalane*, 96–9, 248–55.

13 *Llibre dels feyts*, quotes from chs. 356–61, 375–7. Tourtoulon, *Jaime*, II, 81. Zurita, *Anales de Aragón, lib.* III, ch. 47. ACA, reg. canc. 10, fol. 67 (27 February 1258): 'Aladrachum traditorem nostrum'; again on fol. 78 (March 18); and on fol. 67 (February 27): 'Aladrach proditorem nostrum.' *GEC*, IX, 250–1 (Coll).

14 Burns, *Islam*, chs. 12–14 (contemporary quotes).

15 Ahmad, *Islamic Sicily*, 68. Boswell, *Muslim communities*, 236–42. Burns, *Islam*, 3,8 (poets).

APPENDIX 1

1 Burns, 'Portrait,' 6, and full bibliography in notes. Riquer magisterially reviews the textual problems (*Literatura catalana*, I, 394–5, 402); but the introduction to Soldevila's edition has much to add, especially in his refutation of Josep de Villarroya, recovery of verse segments, and explanation of Jaume's authorship in these verses. Both men should be read on the relation between the present Catalan text and the Latin version by Pere Marsili. Probably our earliest (or Poblet) Romance text of 1343 is much the same as the missing original, with our Latin version a translation of a similar previous Romance text. To the charge that Jaume was uneducated or illiterate (most strongly adduced by Giménez Soler), see the very different but supplementary responses of Tona i Nadalmai, *Minyonia*, 202–5, and Soldevila, *Grans reis*, 35–7. See too Riquer, 'Mundo cultural,' 296–305; López Elum, 'Juglares de Jaime I,' 257–8; Coll, *GEC*, IX, 250–1 (quote); and the recent defense of Jaume's authorship of the *Saviesa*, by Sola Solé, *Llibre de doctrina*, 12–17.

2 Riera, 'Redactor,' 575–89. Riquer, 'El prosista Jaime,' 11. Montoliu, 'Redacció,' 25ff. Ubieto, *Orígenes de Valencia*, I, 75–6.

3 *Spaniards*, 311; his *Structure*, 303–9.

4 Rosenthal, *Muslim historiography*, 100, 102–4, 173–4, 196 (quotations).

APPENDIX 2

1 Ayn and Behyu are Ahín and Veo. Beate may be a scribal miscopy for nearby Betxí, today Bechí, just west of Alcudia de Veo; the *Rationes decimarum Hispaniae*, collecting crusade tithe, exempted Bechí for three years running, 'quia locus a Sarracenis fuit destructus' (I, 176). Lauret must represent Lloret; places like Lauri and Liriet are too far away to be meant.

APPENDIX 3

1 This stray folio was intruded into register 10, as compatible from the date and style of its documents. The missing date is conjecturally reconstructed from remaining fragments, with kalends more probably than ides; the king's itinerary tends to support this date. Martínez Ferrando, *Catálogo*, I, no. 128, has it briefly as a mere sale, with both names erroneously transcribed.

2 The son's name or office in the manuscript is *ffaqmo* with overstroke; on the Jewish *alfaquim*, see chapter 6. His father's name has *Cu* or *Tu*, ending with *ayna*, linked by either an elaborate *n* or malformed *y*; thus Cunaina or Cuyaina is possible. Martínez Ferrando's 'Aben Tuinayna' is impossible, Régné's 'Abentuyayna' improbable. The combination 'Aczmel Avenczunana' in a separate document indicates *sh* as introducing the surname, rather than *s* or *z*, yielding Shunana.

3 The standard Roman foliation here is 19r,v but with an Arabic 18 at the top plus 18 *bis* at the bottom (later folios delete this Arabic series of numbers). The confusion arose from binding-in an alien folio (present 18, with 66 at the bottom), between the original folios 17 and 18.

4 Throughout the manuscript the name is Haro with stroke over *o*, probably meant as indeclinable though possibly for genitive Haronis. Document 9 below clearly has dative *alfaquimo* and undeclined Aron; note Joan's surname as plural here (singular Garriga).

5 Despite damp damage and holes, the full document can be recaptured under

quartz lamp or reconstructed from fragments as clues. Context, formulas, and spacing suggest that the long phrase supplied is a reasonable approximation of the original.

6 The March dates for collection of surrounding items suggests that month as the earliest for this series of notations; this would make the year ambiguous, at least up to March 25, and thus it is not possible to assign a place (assuming the king was present where this note was made, which is not certain) except in a general way. Thus 1 March 1274 found Jaume between (or at either) Valencia and Ulldecona, while 1275 on that day puts him at Lérida. If the document does fall within the dubious weeks of March, then 1275 should probably be preferred to 1274. Martínez Ferrando, *Catálogo*, I, no. 1699, dates this merely '1274' as 'notes about crown rents,' and contains no reference to the Jewish connection. Not in Régné, 'Catalogue.'

7 The manuscript's large *P*, here in brackets, seems a scribal repetition of the previous P[etrus] by error. After *mandantes* there is a deleted date, probably including an original earlier document now lost, to which the subsequent sentences were later added. This suppressed date line is: 'Datum Barchinone, III nonas Augusti, anno domini MCCLXXIIII [August 3].'

8 The *lex talionis* which existed then not only in Jewish law but in Catalan codes like Barcelona's *Usatges* and (in a modified, indirect way) Tortosa's *Costums*, made the accuser liable to an equivalent penalty for charges he could not sustain.

9 Martínez Ferrando does not mention David, mistakes the 11 jovates as a grant being given, and supplies the different name Ermengol; he retains the manuscript's Selgua, and as Setlgua in the index (*Catálogo*, I, no. 1791). Ermengod became castellan of Bairén in 1276.

10 If the name Llinars or Llinàs does not derive from the toponym in Catalonia, the Castilian surname Llinares, early established in Valencia, may be its origin. 'Favars' is clear only under the quartz lamp. The entry in Martínez Ferrando, *Catálogo*, I, no. 1955, has no reference to Isaac. Not in Régné, 'Catalogue.'

Bibliography of published works cited

For archives and manuscript depositories, as well as abbreviations, see the list
p. xi–xii.

'Abd al-Karīm, Gamal, ed. *La España musulmana en la obra de Yāqūt (s. XII–XIII)*.
Granada 1974.
*Acta capitulorum provincialium ordinis fratrum praedicatorum, première province de Provence,
province romaine, province d'Espagne (1239–1302)*, ed. Célestin Douais. Toulouse
1894.
Ahmad, Aziz. *A history of Islamic Sicily*. Edinburgh 1975.
Airaldi, Gabriella. 'Pirateria e rappresaglia in fonti savonesi dei secoli XIII e XIV,'
Clio, X (1974), 67–88.
Alarcón y Santón, M. A., and Ramón García de Linares, eds. *Los documentos árabes
diplomáticos del archivo de la corona de Aragón*. Madrid 1940.
Alfonso X, the Learned. *Espéculo*, in Vol. I of his *Opúsculos legales*, 2 vols. (Madrid
1836).
  Primera crónica general de España, ed. Ramón Menéndez Pidal *et alii*, 2 vols. Madrid
1955.
  Las siete partidas, ed. Real academia de la historia, 3 vols. Madrid [1807] 1972.
Altaner, Berthold. *Die Dominikanermissionen des 13. Jahrhunderts*. Habelschwerdt 1924.
Alverny, Marie Thérèse d'. 'La connaissance de l'islam en occident du IXe au
milieu du XIIe siècle,' *L'Occidente e l'islam nell'alto medioevo* (Spoleto 1965),
577–603, 791–803.
  'Deux traductions latines du Coran au moyen âge,' *Archives d'histoire doctrinale et
littéraire du moyen âge*, XVI (1947–8), 69–131.
Amorós Payá, León. 'Los santos mártires franciscanos B. Juan de Perusa y B. Pedro
de Saxoferrato en la historia de Teruel,' *Teruel*, XV (1956), 5–142.
Andreu Valls, Guillermo. 'Los antiguos términos de Miravet, Albalat y Cabanes,'
BSSC, LI (1975), 213–43.
Aquinas, Thomas. *Liber de veritate catholicae fidei contra errores infidelium, qui dicitur
Contra gentiles*, ed. Pierre Marc *et alii*, 3 vols. Tours 1961–7.
  De rationibus fidei contra Saracenos, Graecos et Armenos, ed. R. A. Verardo, in *Opuscula
theologica* (Rome 1954), no. 13.
Aragó Cabañas, A. M. "Las 'tenentiae castrorum' del reino de Valencia," *I Congreso
de historia del país valenciano (q.v.)* II, 567–77.
Arié, Rachel. *L'Espagne musulmane au temps des Naṣrides (1232–1492)*. Paris 1973.
Asamblea de cronistas oficiales de Valencia [*Crónica de*]. Valencia. VII (1970); IX (1974).
Ashtor, Eliyahu. 'Levantine sugar industry in the late Middle Ages,' *Islamic Middle
East* (q.v.), 91–132.

'Asignación de lindes entre los castillos de Borriol y Onda' (Colección de cartas pueblas, no. 71), *BSCC*, XXIII (1947), 88–9.

Asín y Palacios, Miguel. 'El averroísmo teológico de Santo Tomás de Aquino,' *Homenaje a Codera* (*q.v.*), 271–331.

Aunós Pérez, Antonio. *El derecho catalán en el siglo XIII*. Barcelona 1925.

Aureum opus regalium priuilegiorum ciuitatis et regni Valentie, ed. Lluís de Alanyà. Valencia [1515] 1972.

Bacon, Roger. *Opera quaedam hactenus inedita*, ed. J. S. Brewer (includes *Opus tertium*; *Opus minus*; *Compendium studii*), 2 vols. London 1858–96.

Opus maius. ed. J. H. Bridges, 3 vols. Oxford 1897–1900.

Transl., R. B. Burke, 2 vols. New York [1928] 1962.

Baer, Yitzhak. *A history of the Jews in Christian Spain*, 2 vols. Philadelphia 1961–6.

ed. *Die Juden in christlichen Spanien: Urkunden und Regesten*, 2 vols. Farnborough, Hants. [1929–36] 1970.

Ballesteros Beretta, Antonio. *Alfonso X el Sabio*. Barcelona 1963.

Balletto, Laura. *Mercanti, pirati e corsari nei mari della Corsica (sec. XIII)*. Genoa 1978.

Barceló Torres, M. del C. 'L'Alfondeguilla y Castro: la situación de los mudéjares castellonenses en el siglo XIII,' *BSCC*, LVI (1980), 126–37.

'La llengua àrab al país valencià (segles VIII al XVI),' *Arguments* (Valencia), IV (1979), 123–49.

'El sayyid Abū Zayd: príncipe musulmán, señor cristiano,' *Awrāq*, III (1980), 101–9.

Baron, S. W. *Social and religious history of the Jews*, 2nd edn rev. 18 vols. New York 1952–80.

Bayerri y Bertoméu, Enrique. *Historia de Tortosa y su comarca*, 8 vols. Tortosa 1933–60.

Bazzana, André. 'Eléments d'archéologie musulmane dans al-Andalus: caractères spécifiques de l'architecture militaire arabe de la région valencienne,' *al-Qanṭara*, I (1980), 339–63.

'Problèmes d'architecture militaire au Levant espagnol: le château d'Alcalá de Chivert,' *Etudes de castellologie médiévale* (Caen 1977), 21–46.

and Pierre Guichard. 'Recherches sur les habitats musulmans du Levant espagnol,' *Colloquio internazionale di archeologia medievale*, 2 vols. (Palermo 1976), I, 59–100.

See also Guichard.

Benoit, Fernand, ed. *Recueil des actes des comtes de Provence appartenant à la maison de Barcelone (1196–1245)*, 2 vols. Paris 1925.

Berger, Elie. *Saint Louis et Innocent IV*. Paris 1893.

Bernabeu López, Rafael. 'Judíos de la Castilla valenciana,' *IX Asamblea de cronistas* (*q.v.*), 379–85.

Bernard of Clairvaux. *De consideratione, ad Eugenium papam*, in *Opera*, ed. Jean Leclercq *et alii* (Rome 1957–68), III.

Berthier, André. 'Les écoles des langues orientales fondées au XIIIe siècle par les dominicaines en Espagne et en Afrique,' *Revue africaine*, LXXIII (1932), 84–102.

'Un maître orientaliste du XIIIe siècle: Raymond Martin O. P.,' *Archivum fratrum praedicatorum*, VI (1936), 267–311.

Betí Bonfill, Manuel. 'La gabela de sal de Peñíscola,' *BSCC*, I (1920), 129–32.

Morella y el Maestrazgo en la edad media. Castellón de la Plana 1972.

Rossell: pleito que por su dominio sostuvieron en el siglo XIII. Castellón de la Plana 1920.

Beüt i Belenguer, Emili. *Les comarques valencianes*. Valencia 1970.

Geografia elemental del regne de València. Valencia 1971.

Bofarull i Sans, Francesc de. 'Jaime I y los judíos,' *I Congrés* (*q.v.*), 818–943.

Los judíos en el territorio de Barcelona (*siglos X al XIII*), *reinado de Jaime I, 1213–1276*. Barcelona 1910.

Bofarull i de Sartorio, Manuel de, ed. *Rentas de la antigua corona de Aragón*, in *Colección de documentos inéditos del Archivo general de la corona de Aragón*, ed. Prosper de Bofarull i Mascaró *et alii*, 41 vols. (Barcelona 1847–1910), XXXIX.

Bonnassie, Pierre. *La Catalogne du milieu du Xe à la fin du XIe siècle, croissance et mutations d'une société*, 2 vols. Paris 1976.

Bosch Vilá, Jacinto. 'El siglo XI en al-Andalus,' *Jornadas de cultura árabe e islámica* (Madrid 1981), 183–95.

Boswell, John. *The royal treasure: Muslim communities under the crown of Aragon in the fourteenth century*. New Haven 1977.

Bramon, Dolors. *Contra moros i jueus: formació i estratègia d'unes discriminacions al país valencià*. Valencia 1981.

'Judío,' *Gran enciclopedia valenciana* (*q.v.*), VI (1972), 88–91.

'Una llengua, dues llengües, tres llengües,' *Raons d'identitat del país valencià ('pels i senyals')*, ed. Pere Sisè (Valencia 1977), 17–47.

Braudel, Fernand. *The Mediterranean and the Mediterranean world in the age of Philip II*, 2 vols. New York 1975.

Bresc, Henri. 'Course et piraterie en Sicile (1250–1450),' *AEM*, X (1980), 751–65. See also *I Congreso internacional de historia mediterránea*.

'Mudéjars des pays de la couronne d'Aragon et Sarrasins de la Sicile normande,' *X Congrés* (*q.v.*), III, 51–60.

Bullarium equestris ordinis militae Sancti Iacobi de Spatha, ed. José López Agurleta and Antonio Aguado de Córdoba. Madrid 1719.

Burckhardt, Titus. *Moorish culture in Spain*. London 1972.

Burns SJ, Robert I. 'Baths and caravanserais in crusader Valencia,' *Speculum*, XLVI (1971), 443–58.

The crusader kingdom of Valencia: reconstruction on a thirteenth-century frontier, 2 vols. Cambridge, Mass., 1967.

Diplomatarium regni Valentiae, 5 vols. Princeton, in press.

Islam under the crusaders: colonial survival in the thirteenth-century kingdom of Valencia. Princeton 1973.

Jaume I els valencians del segle XIII. Valencia 1981.

'Journey from Islam: incipient cultural transition in the conquered kingdom of Valencia (1240–1280),' *Speculum*, XXXV (1960), 337–56.

Medieval colonialism: postcrusade exploitation of Islamic Valencia. Princeton 1976.

Moors and crusaders in Mediterranean Spain: collected studies. London 1978.

'Mudejar history today: new directions,' *Viator*, VIII (1977), 127–43.

'Los mudéjares de Valencia: temas y metodología,' *I Simposio internacional de mudéjarismo* (Madrid 1981), 453–97.

'The Muslim in the Christian feudal order: the kingdom of Valencia,' *Studies in medieval culture*, V (1976), 105–26.

'Renegades, adventurers, and sharp businessmen: the thirteenth-century Spaniard in the cause of Islam,' *CHR*, LVII (1972), 341–66.

'Le royaume chrétien de Valence et ses vassaux musulmans (1240–1280),' *Annales: économies, sociétés, civilisations*, XXVIII (1973), 199–225.

'Social riots on the Christian–Moslem frontier: thirteenth-century Valencia,' *AHR*, LXVI (1960–1), 378–400.

'Socioeconomic structure and continuity: medieval Spanish Islam in the tax records of crusader Valencia,' *Islamic Middle East* (*q.v.*), 251–81.

'Spanish Islam in transition: acculturative survival and its price in the Christian

333

kingdom of Valencia,' *Islam and cultural change in the middle ages*, ed. Speros Vryonis, Jr. (Wiesbaden 1975), 87–105.

'The Spiritual life of James the Conqueror, king of Arago-Catalonia, 1208–1276: portrait and self-portrait,' *CHR*, LXII (1976), 1–35, revised and expanded in *X Congrés* (*q.v.*), II, 323–57.

and Paul Chevedden. 'al-Azraq's surrender treaty with Jaime I and Prince Alfonso: Arabic text and Valencian context.' In press.

Cabanes Pecourt. See *Crónica latina*; Huici; *Libre*.

Canellas López, Angel, ed. *Colección diplomática del concejo de Zaragoza*, 2 vols. Zaragoza 1972–5.

Cantarino, Vicente. *Entre monjes y musulmanes: el conflicto que fue España*. Madrid 1978.

Capmany y de Monpalau, Antonio. *Memorias históricas sobre la marina, comercio y artes de la antigua ciudad de Barcelona*, 3 vols. Barcelona [1779–92] 1962–3.

Cardaillac, Louis. *Morisques et chrétiens: un affrontement polémique*. Paris 1977.

Carreras y Artau, Tomás and Joaquín. *Historia de la filosofía española*. Madrid 1939.

Carreras i Candi, Francesc. 'El lenguaje valenciano,' *Geografía general del reino de Valencia*, 5 vols. (Barcelona 1918–22), I, 550–85.

Caruana y Gómez de Barreda, Jaime. 'El pleito por Albentosa, una villa que pudo ser valenciana,' *I Congreso de historia del país valenciano* (*q.v.*), II, 495–9.

Casciaro, José María. *El diálogo teológico de Santo Tomás con musulmanes y judíos*. Madrid 1969.

Castro, Américo. *An idea of history: selected essays*. Columbus, Ohio, 1977.

La realidad histórica de España. Mexico City 1954.

The structure of Spanish history. Princeton 1954. Revised as *The Spaniards: an introduction to their history*. Berkeley 1971.

Cavanilles, Antonio. *Observaciones sobre la historia natural, geografía, agricultura, población y frutos del reyno de Valencia*, 2 vols. Valencia 1795–7.

Chabás y Lloréns, Roque. *Distribución de las aguas en 1244 y donaciones del término de Gandía por D. Jaime I*. Valencia 1898.

'Documentos,' *El archivo*, I (1886–7), 204–5.

'Don Jaime el Conquistador y Alazrach,' *El archivo*, IV (1890), 280–2.

Historia de la ciudad de Denia, ed. Francisco Figueras Pacheco, 2 vols. Alicante [1874–6] 1972.

'Viaje literario al Archivo general de la corona de Aragon,' *El archivo*, I (1886–7), 187–90.

'Zahen y los moros de Uxó y Eslida,' *El archivo*, I (1886–7), 262–3.

Chabret, Antonio. *Sagunto: su historia y sus monumentos*, 2 vols. Barcelona 1888–9.

Chalmeta Gendrón, Pedro. 'Concesiones territoriales en al-Andalus,' *Cuadernos de historia*, V (1975), 1–90.

"El 'Kitāb fi ādāb al-ḥisba' de al-Saqaṭī" *al-Andalus*, XXXII (1967), 125–62, 359–98; XXXIII (1968), 193–5, 367–434.

'Le problème de la féodalité hors de l'Europe chrétienne: le cas de l'Espagne musulmane,' *II Coloquio hispano–tunecino* (*q.v.*), 91–115.

Chejne, Anwar. *Muslim Spain: its history and culture*. Minneapolis 1974.

Chenu, M.D. "Les 'gentils' au XIIIe siècle," in his *Introduction à l'étude de Saint Thomas d'Aquin*. Paris 1950.

Chevallier, Dominique. 'The western presence in the Arab Middle East,' *Islamic Middle East* (*q.v.*), 751–60.

Chivert charter, in *Homenaje a Codera* (*q.v.*), 28–33; and in *BSCC*, XXIV (1948), 226–30.

Cohen, Jeremy. *The friars and the Jews: the evolution of medieval anti-Judaism*. Ithaca, N.Y., 1982.

Colbert, E. P. *The martyrs of Córdoba (850–859): a study of the sources.* Washington, D.C., 1962.

Coll, J. M. 'Escuelas de lenguas orientales en los siglos XIII–XIV,' *Analecta sacra tarraconensia,* XVII (1944), 115–38; XVIII (1945), 59–90; XIX (1946), 217–40.

Collell Costa, Albert. *Escritores dominicos del principado de Cataluña.* Barcelona 1965.

II Coloquio hispano–tunecino de estudios históricos. Madrid 1973.

Congrés d'història de la corona d'Aragó. I (1913); IV (1959–70), 2 vols.; X (1979ff.), 3 vols. to date.

I Congreso de historia del país valenciano, 4 vols. Valencia 1973–80.

II Congreso internacional de estudios sobre las culturas del Mediterráneo occidental. Barcelona 1978.

I Congreso internacional de historia mediterránea. Palma 1973 (= *AEM,* X (1980)).

I Congresso storico Liguria–Catalogna. Bordighera 1974.

Coromines, Joan. *Diccionari etimològic i complementari de la llengua catalana,* 2 vols. to date. Barcelona 1980ff.

Corpus iuris canonici, ed. Emil Friedberg and E. L. Richter. 2 vols. Leipzig 1879–81.

Corriente, Federico. *A grammatical sketch of the Spanish Arabic dialect bundle.* Madrid 1977.

Cortabarría Beitia, Angel. 'L'etude des langues au moyen âge chez les dominicains,' *Mélanges de l'institut dominicain d'études orientales du Caire,* X (1970), 189–248.

Cortes de los antiguos reinos de Aragón y de Valencia y principado de Cataluña, 27 vols. Madrid 1896–1922.

Craddock, J. R. "La nota cronológica inserta en el prólogo de las 'Siete partidas'," *al-Andalus,* XXXIX (1974), 363–90.

Crónica latina de los reyes de Castilla, ed. M. D. Cabanes Pecourt. Valencia 1964.

Crónica de San Juan de la Peña. Latin and aragonese versions, ed. Tomás Ximénez de Embún, as *Historia de la corona de Aragón.* Zaragoza 1876.
  Catalan version, ed. A. J. Soberanas Lleo, as *Crònica general de Pere III el Ceremoniós.* Barcelona 1961.

Cutler, Allan. 'The first crusade and the idea of conversion,' *MW,* LVIII (1968), 57–71, 155–64.
  'Innocent III and the distinctive clothing of Jews and Muslims,' *Studies in medieval culture,* III (1970), 92–116.
  'The ninth-century Spanish martyrs' movement and the origins of western missions to the Muslims,' *MW,* LV (1965), 321–39.
  "Who was the 'Monk of France' and when did he write?," *al-Andalus,* XVIII (1963), 249–69.

Daniel, E. R. 'Apocalyptic conversion: the Joachite alternative to the crusades,' *Traditio,* XXV (1969), 127–54.
  The Franciscan concept of mission in the high Middle Ages. Lexington, Kentucky, 1975.

Daniel, Norman. *Islam and the West: the making of an image.* Edinburgh 1962.

Del Treppo, Mario. *I mercanti catalani e l'espansione della corona d'Aragona nel secolo XV.* Naples 1973. Also as *Els mercaders catalans.* Barcelona 1976.

Desclot, Bernat. *Crònica,* in Soldevila, *Cròniques (q.v.),* 403–664.

Diago, Francisco. *Historia de la provincia de Aragón de la orden de predicadores.* Barcelona 1599.

Doñate Sebastiá, J. M. *Datos para la historia de Villarreal,* 4 vols. Villarreal 1972–7.
  'Las juderías de la Plana,' *I Congreso de historia del país valenciano (q.v.),* II, 811–20; also in *Datos,* IV, 23–38.

Dotson, John E. 'Merchant and naval influences on galley design at Venice and

Genoa in the fourteenth century,' *New aspects of naval history*, ed. C. L. Symonds (Annapolis 1981), 20–32.

Dubois, Pierre. *The recovery of the Holy Land*. New York 1956.

Dufeil, N. M. 'Traces d'Orient à Paris au XIII siècle,' *RHCM*, II (1967), 48–9.

Dufourcq, Charles-Emmanuel. "Catalogue chronologique et analytique du registre 1389 de la chancellerie de la couronne d'Aragon, intitulé 'Guerre Sarracenorum 1367–1386' (1360–1386)," *Miscelánea de textos medievales*, II (1974), 65–166.

L'Espagne catalane et le Maghrib aux XIIIe et XIVe siècles. Paris 1966.

'Vers la Mediterranée orientale et l'Afrique,' *X Congrés* (*q.v.*), I, 5–90.

and Jean Gautier-Dalché. 'Histoire de l'Espagne au moyen âge' (bibliographies: titles vary), *Revue historique*, CCXLV (1971), 127–68, 443–82; CCXLVIII (1972), 367–402; cont. in *Moyen âge*, LXXIX (1973), 73–122, 285–319.

and Jean Gautier-Dalché. *Histoire économique et sociale de l'Espagne chrétienne au moyen âge*. Paris 1977.

Dunlop, D. M. 'A Christian mission to Muslim Spain in the eleventh century,' *al-Andalus*, XVII (1952), 259–310.

Eimeric, Nicolau (moot attribution). 'Vita antiqua,' *Raymundiana* (*q.v.*), no. 11.

Engels, Odilo. 'El rey Jaime I de Aragón, y la política internacional del siglo XIII,' *X Congrés* (*q.v.*), 213–40.

Epalza, Míkel de. 'Les Morisques vus à partir des communautés Mudéjares précédents' (in press).

'Notas sobre el lingüista Ibn Sidah y la historia de Denia y su región en el siglo XI,' *Revista de instituto de estudios alicantinos*, no. 33 (1981), 161–72.

and Enrique Llobregat. '¿Hubo mozárabes en tierras valencianas? Proceso de islamización del Levante de la Península (Sharq al-Andalus),' *Revista del Instituto de Estudios Alicantinos*, 36 (1982), 7–31.

Escolano, Gaspar. *Décadas de la historia de la insigne y coronada ciudad y reino de Valencia*, ed. J. B. Perales, 3 vols. Valencia [1610–11] 1878–80.

Eslida charter, in Huici, *Colección* (*q.v.*), I, 351–2 (1242).

Favreau, M. L. 'Die italienische Levante-Piraterie und die Sicherheit der Seewege im XII. und XIII. Jahrhundert,' *Vierteljahrschrift für Sozial-und Wirtschaftsgeschichte* [Wiesbaden], LXV (1978), 461–510.

Fernández y González, Francisco. *Estado social y político de los mudéjares de Castilla*, Madrid 1866.

Ferrer i Mallol, M. T. 'Els corsaris castellans i la campanya de Pero Niño al Mediterrani (1404),' *AEM*, V (1968), 265–338.

Ferrer Navarro, Ramón. 'Una fundación de Jaime I: Villarreal,' *EEMCA*, X (1975), 403–37.

Fita, Fidel, ed. 'Noticias,' *Boletín de la real academia de historia*, XI (1887), 454–8.

Fletcher, R. A. *The episcopate in the kingdom of León in the twelfth century*. Oxford 1978.

Fonseca, Luis Adão da. *Navegación y corso en el Mediterráneo occidental: los portugueses a mediados del siglo XV*. Pamplona 1978.

Font Rius, José. 'La carta de seguridad de Ramón Berenguer IV a las morerías de Ascó y Ribera del Ebro (siglo XII),' *Homenaje a Lacarra* (*q.v.*), I, 261–81.

ed. *Cartas de población y franquicia de Cataluña*, 2 vols. as tome one to date. Madrid 1969ff.

et alii, eds. *La reconquista española y la repoblación del país*. Zaragoza 1951.

Fontavella González, Vicente. *La huerta de Gandía*. Zaragoza 1952.

Fori antiqui Valentiae, ed. Manuel Dualde Serrano. Madrid 1967. See also *Furs*.

Fullana Mira, Luis. *Historia de la villa y condado de Concentaina*. Valencia [1920] 1975.

Furs de València, ed. Germán Colón and Arcadio García Sanz, 3 vols. to date. Barcelona 1970ff.

Fuster, Joan. *Poetes, moriscos, i capellans*. Valencia 1962.

Garbell, Irene. 'The pronunciation of Hebrew in medieval Spain,' *Homenaje a Millás-Vallicrosa (q.v.)*, I, 647–96.

García Martínez, Sebastián. *Bandolerismo, piratería, y control de moriscos en Valencia durante el reinado de Felipe II*. Valencia 1977. Amplified as *Bandolers, corsaris, i moriscos*. Valencia 1980.

García Sanz, Arcadio. *Història de la marina catalana*. Barcelona 1977.

Garcías Palou, Sebastián. *El Miramar de Ramón Llull*. Palma de Mallorca 1977.

Gascón Pelegrí, Vicente. *Historia de Tabernes de Valldigna*. Valencia 1981.

Repertorio bibliográfico de Valldigna y pueblos de la comarca. Valencia 1968.

Gazulla, Faustino. *Jaime I de Aragón y los estados musulmanes*. Barcelona 1919.

Gerard de Frachet. 'Vitae fratrum ordinum praedicatorum,' *Raymundiana (q. v.)*, no. 1.

Getino, Luis [Alonso]. *La Summa contra gentiles y el Pugio fidei*. Vergara 1905.

Giménez Soler, Andrés. *La edad media en la corona de Aragón*. Barcelona 1944.

Glick, Thomas. *Irrigation and society in medieval Valencia*. Cambridge, Mass., 1970.

Islamic and Christian Spain in the early middle ages. Princeton 1979.

Goitein, S. D. *A Mediterranean society: the Jewish communities of the Arab world as portrayed in the documents of the Cairo Geniza*, 3 vols. to date. Berkeley 1967ff.

González Hurtebise, Eduart, ed. 'Recull de documents inèdits del rey En Jaume I,' *I Congrés (q.v.)*, 1181–1253.

Gonzálvez, Ramón. 'El arcediano de Loaysa y las parroquias urbanas de Toledo en 1300,' *I Congreso internacional de estudios mozárabes*. Toledo 1978.

Gorce, M. M. 'La lutte *Contra gentiles* à Paris au XIIIe siècle,' *Mélanges Mandonnet, études d'histoire littéraire et doctrinale du moyen âge*, 2 vols. (Paris 1930), I, 223–43.

Gran enciclopèdia catalana, 15 vols. Barcelona 1969–80.

Gran enciclopedia de la región valenciana, 12 vols. Valencia 1973–7.

Grau Monserrat, Manuel. 'La judería de Morella,' *Sefarad*, XXII (1962), 69–81; XXIV (1964), 286–321.

Grayzel, Solomon. *The church and the Jews in the XIIIth century*. New York 1966.

Gual Camarena, Miguel. 'Contribución al estudio de la territorialidad de los fueros de Valencia,' *EEMCA*, III (1947–8), 262–89.

'Para una mapa de la sal hispánica en la edad media,' *Homenaje a Jaime Vicens Vives*, ed. Juan Maluquer de Motes, 2 vols. (Barcelona 1965–7), I, 483–97.

Vocabulario del comercio medieval, colección de aranceles aduaneros de la corona de Aragón (siglos XIII y XIV). Tarragona 1968.

Guerrero Lovillo, José. *Las Cantigas: estudio arqueológico de sus miniaturas*. Madrid 1949.

Guichard, Pierre. *al-Andalus: estructura antropológica de una sociedad islámica en occidente*. Barcelona 1976.

"Le problème de l'existence de structures de type 'féodal,'" *Structures féodales et féodalisme dans l'occident méditerranéen (Xe–XIIIe siècles)* (Rome 1980), 699–725.

'Le problème de la sofra dans le royaume de Valence au XIIIe siècle,' *Awrāq*, II (1979), 64–71.

"Un seigneur musulman dans l'Espagne chrétienne: le 'ra'is' de Crevillente," *MCV*, IX (1973), 283–334.

'La société rurale valencienne à l'époque musulmane,' *Estudis d'història agrària*, III (1979), 41–52.

and André Bazzana. 'Les tours de défense de la huerta de Valence au XIIIe siècle,' *MCV*, XIV (1978), 73–106.

See also Bazzana.

337

Guiral, Jacqueline. 'Course et piraterie à Valence de 1410 à 1430,' *AEM*, X (1980), 759–65. See also *Congreso internacional de historia mediterránea*.

'Les gens de mer à Valencia, fin XVe, début XVIe,' *I Colloque sur le pays valencien a l'époque moderne* (Pau 1980), 35–41.

Guitart Aparicio, Cristóbal. *Castillos de Aragón*, 2 vols. Zaragoza 1976.

Hansen, Bent. 'An economic model for Ottoman Egypt,' *Islamic Middle East (q.v.)*, 473–520.

Harden, A. R. 'The element of love in the *chansons de geste*,' *Annuale mediaevale*, V (1964) 63–79.

Harvey, L. P. 'The Arabic dialect of Valencia in 1595,' *al-Andalus*, XXXVI (1971), 81–115.

Hillgarth, Jocelyn. *Ramon Lull and Lullism in fourteenth-century France*. Oxford 1971.

The Spanish kingdoms, 1250–1516, 2 vols. Oxford 1976–8.

Hinojosa Montalvo, José. 'Actividades comerciales de los judíos en Valencia (1391–1492),' *Saitabi*, XXIX (1979), 21–42.

'Piratas y corsarios en la Valencia de principios del siglo XV (1400–1409),' *Jerónimo Zurita*, V (1975), 93–116.

Homenaje a Don José María Lacarra de Miguel, 2 vols. Zaragoza 1977.

ed. Eduardo Saavedra *et alii*. Zaragoza 1904.

Homenaje a Don José María Lacarra de Miguel, 2 vols. Zaragoza 1977.

Homenaje a Millás-Vallicrosa, 2 vols. Barcelona 1954–6.

Huerga, Álvaro. "Hipótesis sobre la génesis de la 'Summa contra gentiles' y del 'Pugio fidei,'" *Angelicum*, LI (1947), 533–57.

Huici Miranda, Ambrosio. *Historia musulmana de Valencia y su región*, 3 vols. Valencia 1970.

ed. *Colección diplomática de Jaime I, el Conquistador*, 3 vols. Valencia 1916–22.

and M. D. Cabanes Pecourt, eds. *Documentos de Jaime I de Aragón*, 3 vols. to date. Valencia 1976ff.

Ibn 'Idhārī (Aḥmad b. Muḥammad b. 'Idhārī, Abū 'l-'Abbās, al-Marrākushī). *al-Bayān al-mugrib fi-ijtiṣār ajbār muluk al-Andalus wa al-Magrib*, tr. Ambrosio Huici, 2 vols. Tetuan 1953–4.

Ibn Jubayr. *Voyages*, ed. Maurice Gaudefroy-Demombynes. 4 vols. Paris 1949–65.

Ibn Kammūna. *Examination of the three faiths: a thirteenth-century essay in the comparative study of religion*, ed. Moshe Perlman. Berkeley 1971.

Ibn Khaldūn. *Histoire des Berbères et des dynasties musulmanes de l'Afrique septentrionale*, ed. Paul Casanova and Henri Pérès, tr. William MacGuckin, baron de Slane, 4 vols. Paris 1925–56.

The Muqaddimah: an introduction to history, tr. Franz Rosenthal, 3 vols. Princeton 1967.

Ibn Rashīq (al-Ḥusayn b. 'Atīq b. al-Ḥusayn b. Rashīq al-Taglibī al-Mursī). 'Una polémica religiosa en Murcia en tiempos de Alfonso el Sabio,' ed. Fernando de La Granja, *al-Andalus*, XXXI (1966), 47–72.

al-Idrīsī. *Geografía de España*. Valencia 1974.

Imamuddin, S. M. *Some aspects of the socio-economic and cultural history of Muslim Spain, 711–1492 A.D.* Leiden 1965.

Innocent IV, Pope. *Les registres*, ed. Elie Berger, 4 vols. Paris 1884–1921.

The Islamic Middle East, 700–1900: studies in economic and social history, ed. A. L. Udovitch. Princeton 1981.

Jackson, Gabriel. *The making of medieval Spain*. London 1972.

Jaén i Urban, Gaspar. *Qüestions territorials al país valencià*. Sagunto 1979.

Jaime I y su época. Alternative title for *X Congrés (q.v.)*.

Jaume I. *Llibre dels feyts del rei en Jaume*, in Soldevila, *Cròniques* (*q.v.*), 1–402.
See also Sola (moot attribution to Jaume).

Jiménez de Rada, Rodrigo. *De rebus Hispaniae*, in his *Opera*, 1 vol. to date. Valencia [1793] 1968.

Jordan, William. *Louis IX and the challenge of the crusade: a study in rulership*. Princeton 1979.

Juan i Fenollar, R. *La qüestió comarcal*. Valencia 1981.

Kaganoff, B. C. *A dictionary of Jewish names and their history*. New York 1977.

Kedar, B. Z. *Merchants in crisis: Genoese and Venetian men of affairs and the fourteenth-century depression*. New Haven 1976.

Keddie, N. R. 'Socioeconomic change in the Middle East since 1800,' *Islamic Middle East* (*q.v.*), 761–84.

Kritzeck, James. *Peter the Venerable and Islam*. Princeton 1964.

Labarta, Ana. 'Cinco documentos árabes de los moriscos valencianos,' *Awrāq*, III (1980), 110–17.

'Los libros de los moriscos valencianos,' *Awrāq*, II (1979), 72–80.

Lacarra y de Miguel, José. 'La reconquista y repoblación del valle del Ebro,' in Font y Rius, *Reconquista* (*q.v.*), 39–83.

La Granja, Fernando de. See Ibn Rashīq.

La Mantia, Giuseppe. *Codice diplomatico dei re aragonesi di Sicilia*. Palermo 1917.

Lapidus, I. M. *Muslim cities in the later middle ages*. Cambridge 1967.

Lévi-Provençal, Evariste. *Histoire de l'Espagne musulmane*, 3 vols. Paris [1950–3] 1967. Rev. in transl. by Emilio García Gómez, *España musulmana*, 2 vols., in Ramón Menéndez Pidal *et alii*, eds., *Historia de España*, 12 vols. to date (Madrid 1957ff.), IV, V.

Lewis, Archibald. *The development of southern French and Catalan society, 718–1050*. Austin, Texas, 1965.

Naval power and trade in the Mediterranean, A.D. 500–1100. Princeton 1951.

Libre del repartiment del regne de València, ed. M. D. Cabanes Pecourt and Ramón Ferrer Navarro, 3 vols. to date. Zaragoza 1979ff. See also *Llibre del repartiment de València*.

Libro del consulado de mar, ed. Antonio Capmany y de Monpalau, rev. J. M. Font y Rius and A. A. de Saavedra. Barcelona 1965. See also *Llíbre del consolat de mar*.

Linehan, Peter. *The Spanish church and the papacy in the thirteenth century*. Cambridge, 1971.

Litterae encyclicae magistrorum ordinis praedicatorum ab anno 1233 usque ad annum 1376, ed. B. M. Reichert. Rome 1900.

Llíbre del consolat de mar, ed. Germà Colon. 2 vols. Barcelona 1981–2. See also *Libro del consulado de mar*.

Llibre dels feyts. See Jaume.

Llibre del repartiment de València, ed. Antoni Ferrando i Francés *et alii*, 4 vols. Valencia 1978. See also *Libre del repartiment del regne de València*.

Llull. See Lull.

Loaysa, Jofre de (Jofré de Loaísa). *Crónica de los reyes de Castilla*, ed. Agustín Ubieto. Valencia 1971.

ed. Antonio García Martínez. Murcia 1961.

ed. Alfred Morel Fatio, as 'Chronique des rois de Castille (1248–1305),' *Bibliothèque de l'école des chartes*, LIX (1898), 325–78.

Lomax, Derek. *The reconquest of Spain*. London 1978.

López Elum, Pedro. 'Contribución al estudio de los juglares en la época de Jaime I,' *Ligarzas*, IV (1972), 245–58.

Lull [Llull], Ramon. *Blanquerna*, in *Obres essencials*, 2 vols. (Barcelona 1957), I, 111–307.

    Opera latina, ed. Friedrich Stegmüller *et alii*, 5 vols. Palma de Mallorca 1959–67.

Luttrell, Anthony. 'Late-medieval galley oarsmen,' *Le genti del mare mediterraneo*, ed. Rosalba Ragosta, 2 vols. (Naples 1982), I, 87–101.

MacKay, Angus. *Spain in the middle ages: from frontier to empire, 1000–1500*. London 1977.

Magdalena Nom de Déu, José. *La aljama hebrea de Castellón de la Plana en la baja edad media*. Castellón de la Plana 1978.

    La aljama de judíos de Burriana (siglos XIII-XV). Villarreal 1978.

    'Calonies de los judíos valencianos en 1381,' *BSCC*, LIV (1978), 156–66.

    'Notas sobre los conversos castellonenses en 1391,' *BSCC*, LIII (1977), 161–70.

    'Población, propiedades e impuestos de los judíos de Castellón de la Plana durante la baja edad media,' *Sefarad*, XXXIV (1974), 273–8.

Malvezzi, Aldobrandino. *L'Islamismo e la cultura europea*. Florence 1956.

Mansilla Reoyo, Demetrio. *Iglesia castellano-leonesa y curia romana en los tiempos del rey San Fernando*. Madrid 1945.

    ed. *La documentación pontificia hasta Inocencio III, 965–1216*. Rome 1955.

al-Maqqarī (Aḥmad b. Muḥammad al-Maqqarī). *The history of the Mohammedan dynasties in Spain*, tr. Pascual de Gayangos, 2 vols. London [1840–3] 1964.

Marcó i Dachs, Lluís. *Els jueus i nosaltres*. Barcelona 1977.

Marsili, Pere. 'Vita Sancti Raymundi de Pennaforti (1312),' *Raymundiana (q.v.)*, no. 8.

Martí, Ramon. *Pugio fidei adversus Mauros et Judaeos*. Farnborough, Hants., [1687] 1967.

    Vocabulista in arabico, ed. Celestino Schiaparelli. Florence 1871.

Martignone, Franco. 'Fatti de pirateria nel Mediterraneo occidentale nel secolo XV,' *II Congreso del Mediterráneo (q.v.)*, 297–307.

Martínez Ferrando, Jesús E. *Catálogo de los documentos del antiguo reino de Valencia*, 2 vols. Madrid 1934.

    Jaime II de Aragón, su vida familiar, 2 vols. Barcelona 1948.

Martínez Ortiz, José. 'Gentes de Teruel en una expedición marítima contra piratas,' *BSCC*, LVIII (1982), 79–91.

Massignon, Louis. 'Ibn Sab'īn et la 'conspiration ḥallāgienne' en Andalousie, et en orient aux XIIIe siècle,' in *Etudes d'orientalisme dediées à la mémoire de Lévi-Provençal*, ed. Emilio García Gómez *et alii*, 2 vols. (Paris 1962), II, 660–81.

Menéndez Pidal, Ramón. *Orígenes del español*. 3rd edn. rev. Madrid 1950.

Mestre Palacio, Joaquín. 'Rectificación en la ruta que siguió El Cid desde Elche a Valenciá (el"Ondia" de la *Gesta R.C.* no corresponde a "Ondara" sino a la "Ombria" del Pop),' *I Congreso de historia del país valenciano (q.v.)*, II, 420–5.

Metlitzki, Dorothy. *The matter of Araby in medieval England*. New Haven 1977.

Miralles Sales, José. *La villa de Salsadella*. Castellón de la Plana 1974.

Miret i Sans, Joaquim, ed. *Itinerari de Jaume I 'el Conqueridor.'* Barcelona 1918.

    'Les represàlies a Catalunya durant l'edat mitjana,' *Revista jurídica de Catalunya*, XXXI (1925), 289–304, 385–417.

Molina López, Emilio. "Azīz b. Jaṭṭāb, destacada personalidad política, científica y literaria murciana del siglo XIII,' *Miscelánea medieval murciana*, IV (1978), 63–86.

    Ceyt Abu Ceyt: novedades y rectificaciones. Almería 1977.

    'El gobierno de Zayyān b. Mardaniš en Murcia (1239–1241),' *Miscelánea medieval murciana*, VII (1981), 157–82.

'El Levante y Almería en el marco de la política interior del emir murciano Ibn Hūd al-Mutawakkil (1236–1238),' *Awrāq*, II (1979), 55–63.

Mollat, Michel. 'Essai d'orientation pour l'étude de la guerre de course et de la piraterie (XIIIe–XVe siècles),' *AEM*, X (1980), 743–9. See also *I Congreso internacional de historia mediterránea.*

ed. *Course et piraterie* [XV Colloque international d'histoire maritime, 1975], 2 vols. Paris, in typescript.

Momblanch y Gonzálbez, F. de P. 'El rey D. Jaime y las guerras de Alazrach,' *VII Asamblea de cronistas* (*q.v.*), 213–73.

Monneret de Villard, Ugo. *Lo studio dell'Islām in Europa nel XII e nel XIII secolo.* Vatican City 1944.

Monroe, J. T. *Hispano-Arabic poetry.* Berkeley 1974.

The Shu'ūbiyya in al-Andalus. Berkeley 1970.

Montoliu, Manuel de. 'Sobre la redacció de crònica d'En Jaume I,' *Estudis romànics,* II (1917), 25–72.

Morony, Michael G. 'The conquerors and the conquered: Iran,' *Studies in the first century of Islamic society,* ed. G. H. A. Juynboll (Carbondale, Ill., 1982), 73–87.

'Religious communities in late Sasanian and early Muslim Iraq,' *Journal of the economic and social history of the orient,* XVIII (1975), 113–35.

Muldoon, James. *Popes, lawyers and infidels: the church and the non-Christian world, 1250–1550.* Philadelphia 1979.

Müller, Ewald. *Das Konzil von Vienne, 1311–1312, seine Quellen und seine Geschichte.* Münster 1934.

Muntaner, Ramon. *Crònica,* in Soldevila, *Cròniques* (*q.v.*), 665–1000.

Murphy, Thomas. 'The date and purpose of the *Contra gentiles,*' *Heythrop journal,* X (1969), 405–15.

Nangis, Guillaume de. 'Gesta Sancti Ludovici regis Franciae,' and (facing pages) 'Vie de Saint Louis,' *Receuil des historiens des Gaules et de la France,* ed. Martin Bouquet, *et alii,* 24 vols. (Paris 1737–1904; repr. Farnborough, Hants, 1968), XX, 309–465.

Neuman, Abraham. *The Jews in Spain: their social, political, and cultural life during the middle ages,* 2 vols. Philadelphia 1942.

Nowshirvani, V. F. 'The beginnings of commercialized agriculture in Iran,' *Islamic Middle East* (*q.v.*), 547–91.

O'Callaghan, Joseph. *A history of medieval Spain.* Ithaca, N.Y., 1975.

'Ordinatio ecclesiae valentinae,' in Sanchis y Sivera, *Diócesis* (*q.v.*), II, 192–412.

Ortí Miralles, Francisco. *Historia de Morella,* 3 vols. Benimodo, Valencia, 1958.

Palacios Martín, Bonifacio. 'La frontera de Aragón con Castilla en la época de Jaime I,' *X Congrés* (*q.v.*), II, part 2, 475–95.

Paris, Matthew. *Chronica majora,* ed. H. R. Luard (Rolls series), 7 vols. London 1872–83.

Pastor Alberola, Enrique. *Castellón de Rugat (estudio histórico–geográfico).* Castellón de Rugat 1973.

Pastor de Togneri, Reyna. *Del islam al cristianismo en las fronteras de dos formaciones económico-sociales: Toledo, siglos X-XIII.* Barcelona. 1975.

Peers, E. A. *Ramon Lull, a biography.* New York 1929.

Pérès, Henri. 'L'arabe dialectal en Espagne musulmane aux Xe et XIe siècles de notre ère,' *Mélanges offerts à William Marçais* (Paris 1950), 289–300.

Piles Ibars, Andrés. *Historia de Cullera,* 2nd edn. Cullera 1972.

Piles Ros, Leopoldo. *Estudio documental sobre el bayle general de Valencia, su autoridad y jurisdicción.* Valencia 1970.

'La judería de Alcira (notas para su estudio),' *Sefarad,* XX (1960), 363–76.

'La judería de Burriana: apuntes para su estudio,' *Sefarad*, XII (1952), 105–24.

'Los judíos en la Valencia del siglo XV: el pago de deudas,' *Sefarad*, VII (1947), 151–6.

Poveda Sánchez, Angel. 'Introducción al estudio de la toponimia árabe–musulmana de Mayūrqa,' *Awrāq*, III (1980), 75–101.

Prescott, J. R. V. *Boundaries and frontiers.* Totowa, N. J., 1978.

Putzulu, Evandro. 'Pirati e corsari nei mari della Sardegna durante la prima metà del secolo XV,' *IV Congrés (q.v.)*, I, 155–172.

Ramos y Loscertales, J. M. *El cautiverio en la corona de Aragón durante los siglos XIII, XIV y XV.* Zaragoza 1915.

Rationes decimarum Hispaniae (1279–1280), ed. José Ruis Serra, 2 vols. Barcelona 1946–7.

Raymundiana seu documenta quae pertinent ad S. Raymundi de Pennaforti vitam et scriptam, ed. Franciscus de Balme *et alii*. Rome 1891–1901.

Régné, Jean. 'Catalogue des actes de Jaime Ier, Pedro III, et Alfonso III, rois d'Aragon, concernant les juifs,' *REJ*, LX (1910), 161–201; LXI (1911), 1–43; LXII (1911), 38–73. Also as *History of the Jews in Aragon: regesta and documents, 1213–1327*, ed. Yom Tov Assis and Adam Gruzman. Jerusalem 1978.

Repartimiento de Murcia, ed. Juan Torres Fontes. Murcia 1960.

Repartimiento de Sevilla, ed. Julio González. 2 vols. Madrid 1951.

Ribera Tarragó, Julián. 'La doctrina cristiana en lengua arábiga, de Martín de Ayala,' in his *Disertaciones y opúsculos*, 2 vols. (Madrid 1928), II, 330–5.

Riera i Sans, Jaume. "La personalitat eclesiàstica del redactor del 'Llibre dels feyts,'" *X Congrés (q.v.)*, III, 575–89.

Riquer, Martí de. *Historia de la literatura catalana*, 4 vols. Barcelona 1964.

'El mundo cultural en la corona de Aragón con Jaime I,' *X Congrés (q.v.)*, I, 293–312.

'El prosista Jaime el Conquistador,' *Conmemoración de la fiesta nacional del libro español* (booklet). Madrid 1977.

Los trovadores, 3 vols. Barcelona 1975.

Robles, Laureano. *Escritores domínicos de la corona de Aragón, siglos XIII–XV.* Salamanca 1972.

Robson, J. A. 'The Catalan fleet and Moorish sea-power (1337–1344),' *English Historical Review*, 74 (1959), 386–408.

Roca Traver, F. A. 'Un siglo de vida mudéjar en la Valencia medieval (1238–1338),' *EEMCA*, V (1952), 115–208.

Romano, David. 'Análisis de los repertorios documentales de Jacobs y Régné,' *Sefarad*, XIV (1954), 247–64.

'Los funcionarios judíos de Pedro el Grande de Aragón,' *BRABLB*, XXVIII (1969–70), 5–41.

'Los hermanos Abenmenassé al servicio de Pedro el Grande de Aragón,' *Homenaje a Millás-Vallicrosa (q.v.)*, II, 243–92.

'Judíos escribanos y trujamanes de árabe en la corona de Aragón (reinados de Jaime I a Jaime II),' *Sefarad*, XXXVIII (1978), 71–105.

Rosenthal, Franz. *A history of Muslim historiography*, 2nd edn rev. Leiden 1968.

Rosselló Bordoy, Guillem. *L'islam a les illes balears.* Palma de Mallorca 1968.

Mallorca musulmana (estudis d'arqueologia). Palma de Mallorca 1973.

Rubiera Mata, J. M. 'Falsos antropónimos bereberes en la toponimia arábigo-valenciana.' In press.

Rubió y Lluch, Antoni, ed. *Documents per l'història de la cultura catalana mig-eval*, 2 vols. Barcelona 1908–21.

BIBLIOGRAPHY

Sáenz de Aguirre, José. *Collectio maxima conciliorum Hispaniae et novi orbis*, 6 vols. Rome 1753–5.

Sagarra, Ferran de. 'Noticias y documentos inéditos referentes al infante Don Alfonso, primogénito de Don Jaime y de Doña Leonor de Castilla,' *BRABLB*, IX (1921), 285–301.

Salavert, Vicente. 'Nuevamente sobre la expansión mediterránea de la corona de Aragón,' *II Congreso del Mediterráneo* (*q.v.*), 359–88.

Sánchez-Albornoz, Claudio. *España, un enigma histórico*, 5th edn, 2 vols. Madrid 1973. Tr. as *Spain: a historical enigma*, 2 vols. Madrid 1975.

Sanchis Guarner, Manuel. *Aproximació a la història de la llengua catalana: creixença i esplendor*, 2 vols. Barcelona 1980–1.

Contribució al nomenclàtor geogràfic del país valencià. Barcelona 1966.

Introducción a la historia lingüística de Valencia. Valencia 1950.

'Límits i demarcacions històriques del regne de València,' *Obra completa*, 1 vol. to date (Valencia 1976), I, 87–123.

La llengua dels valencians. Valencia 1972.

Els parlars romànics de València i Mallorca anteriors a la reconquista, 2nd edn rev. Valencia 1961.

Sanchis y Sivera, José. *La diócesis valentina*, 2 vols. Valencia 1920–1.

Nomenclátor geográfico–eclesiástico de los pueblos de la diócesis de Valencia. Valencia 1922.

Sancho Comins, José. 'Las comarcas castellonenses,' *BSCC*, LVII (1981), 157–91.

Sarthou Carreres, Carlos. *Datos para la historia de Játiva*, 2nd edn, 8 fasc. to date. Valencia 1976ff.

Sawyer, P. H., ed. *Medieval settlement*. London 1976.

Schacht, Joseph. 'Droit byzantin et droit musulman,' *Convegno di scienze morali, storiche e filologiche* (Rome 1957), 197–218.

Schaube, Adolf. *Handelsgeschichte der romanischen Völker des Mittelmeergebiets bis zum Ende der Kreuzzüge*. Berlin 1906.

Scriptores ordinis praedicatorum, ed. Jacques Quétif and Jacques Echard. 2 vols. Paris 1719–21.

Shneidman, Jerome Lee. *The rise of the Aragonese–Catalan empire, 1200–1350*, 2 vols. New York 1970.

Siete partidas. See Alfonso X.

Simó Santonja, Vicente. *¿Valenciano o catalán?* Valencia 1975.

Singerman, Robert. *The Jews in Spain and Portugal: a bibliography*. New York 1975.

Sivan, Emmanuel. *L'islam et la croisade*. Paris 1968.

Sola Solé, J. M., ed. *Llibre de doctrina*. Barcelona 1977.

Soldevila, Ferran. *Els grans reis del segle XIII: Jaume I, Pere el Gran*. Barcelona 1955.

Història de Catalunya. Barcelona 1963.

Pere el Gran, 2 parts in 4 vols. Barcelona 1950–62.

ed. *Les quatre grans cròniques: Jaume I, Bernat Desclot, Ramon Muntaner, Pere III*. Barcelona 1971.

Sorió, Baltasar. *De viris illustribus provinciae Aragoniae ordinis praedicatorum*, ed. J. M. de Garganta Fabrega. Valencia 1950.

Southern, R. W. *Western views of Islam in the middle ages*. Cambridge, Mass., 1962.

Sugranyes de Franch, Ramón. *Raymond Lulle, docteur des missions, avec un choix de textes*. Schöneck–Beckenried 1954.

Sweetman, J. W. *Islam and Christian theology: a study of the interpretation of theological ideas in the two religions*, 2 vols. London 1954–67.

Talbi, Mohamed. 'Law and economy in Ifrīqiya (Tunisia) in the third Islamic century: agriculture and the role of slaves in the economy,' *Islamic Middle East* (*q.v*), 209–50.

Tapia Garrido, J. A. *Almería musulmana (711–1482)*, 2 vols. Almería 1976–8.

Tarradell, Miquel *et alii*. *Història del país valencià*. 3 vols. to date. Barcelona, 1965ff.

Throop, P. A. *Criticism of the crusade: a study of public opinion and crusade propaganda.* Amsterdam 1940.

Tisserant, Eugène, and Gaston Wiet. 'Une lettre de l'Almohade Murṭadâ au pape Innocent IV,' *Hespéris*, VI (1926), 27–53.

Toledo Girau, Josep. *Las aguas de riego en la historia de Valldigna*. Castellón de la Plana 1958.

    El castell i la vall d'Alfandech de Marinyèn. Castellón de la Plana 1936.

    El monasterio de Valldigna. Valencia 1944.

Tona i Nadalmai, A. *Minyonia del bon rey Jaume: el conqueridor, la dona i la llegenda*. Barcelona 1973.

Torres Delgado, Cristóbal. *El antiguo reino nazarí de Granada (1232–1340)*. Granada 1974.

    'El Mediterráneo nazarí: diplomacia y piratería (siglos XIII–XIV)', *AEM*, X (1980), 227–35.

Torres Fontes, Juan, ed. *Colección de documentos para la historia del reino de Murcia*, 7 vols. to date. Murcia 1963ff.

    'Los judíos murcianos en el siglo XIII,' *Murgetana*, XVIII (1962), 5–20.

    La reconquista de Murcia en 1266 por Jaime I de Aragón. Murcia 1967.

Tourtoulon, Charles de. *Etudes sur la maison de Barcelone: Jacme Ier le Conquérant*, 2 vols. Montpellier 1863–7. Revised in translation by Teodoro Llorente, *Don Jaime I el Conquistador*, 2 vols. Valencia 1874.

Traver García, Benito. *Historia de Villarreal*. Villarreal 1909.

Traver Tomás, Vicente. *Antigüedades de Castellón de la Plana*. Castellón de la Plana 1958.

Tritton, A. S. *Materials on Muslim education in the middle ages*. London 1957.

Ubieto Arteta, Antonio. *Los almorávides, el idioma romance y los valencianos* (Temas valencianos no. 29, pamphlet). Valencia 1978.

    'La creación de la frontera entre Aragón–Valencia y el espíritu fronterizo,' *Homenaje a Lacarra (q.v.)*, II, 95–114.

    Orígenes del reino de Valencia: cuestiones cronológicas sobre su reconquista, 3rd edn, 2 vols. Valencia 1977–9.

Udovitch, A. L. 'Technology, land tenure, and rural society,' *Islamic Middle East (q.v.)*, 11–26.

Urvoy, Dominique. 'Une étude sociologique des mouvements religieux dans l'Espagne musulmane de la chute du califat au milieu du XIIIe siècle,' *MCV*, VIII (1972), 223–93.

    Le monde des ulémas andalous du V/XIe au VII/XIIIe siècle: étude sociologique. Geneva 1978.

    'Les musulmans et l'usage de la langue arabe par les missionnaires chrétiens au moyen âge,' *Traditio*, XXXV (1978), 416–26.

Vendrell Gallostra, Francisca. 'Aportaciones documentales para el estudio de la familia Caballería,' *Sefarad*, III (1943), 115–54.

Vernet, Juan. 'El conocimiento del islam por la cristiandad del occidente a través de los cantares de gesta,' *BRABLB*, XXXI (1965–6), 351–4.

Vila, Pau. *La divisió territorial de Catalunya*. Barcelona 1977.

Vilar, J. B. *Historia de la ciudad de Orihuela*, 3 vols. to date. Orihuela 1976ff.

Vincke, Johannes. 'Königtum und Sklaverei im aragonischen Staatenbund während des 14. Jahrhunderts,' *Gesammelte Aufsätze zur Kulturgeschichte Spaniens*, XXV (1970), 19–112.

Vitry, Jacques de. *Lettres de Jacques de Vitry (1160/1170–1240), évêque de Saint-Jean d'Acre*, ed. R. B. C. Huygens. Leiden 1960.

Walter of Coventry. *Memoriale*, ed. William Stubbs, 2 vols. London 1872–73.

Waltz, James. "Historical perspectives on 'early missions' to Muslims: a response to Allan Cutler," *MW*, LXI (1971), 170–86.

  'The significance of the voluntary martyr movement of ninth-century Cordoba,' *MW*, LX (1970), 143–59, 226–36.

Watt, W. Montgomery. 'Philosophy and theology under the Almohads,' *I Congreso de estudios árabes e islámicos* (Madrid 1964), 101–7.

  and Pierre Cachia. *A history of Islamic Spain*. Garden City, N.Y., 1967.

Weisheipl, O. P., James. *Friar Thomas d'Aquino: his life, thought, and work*. Garden City, N.Y., 1974.

Zurita, Jerónimo. *Anales de la corona de Aragón*, ed. Angel Canellas López, 8 vols. to date. Zaragoza 1967ff.

Index of proper names

Principal references are in italic